Advertising: Planning and Implementation

ADVERTISING

Planning and Implementation

Sangeeta Sharma
Associate Professor
Department of Languages
Birla Institute of Technology and Science
Pilani

Raghuvir Singh
Director
JK Padampat Singhania
Institute of Management and Technology
Gurgaon

PHI Learning Private Limited
Delhi-110092
2013

₹ 350.00

ADVERTISING: PLANNING AND IMPLEMENTATION
Sangeeta Sharma and Raghuvir Singh

ISBN-978-81-203-2973-7

The export rights of this book are vested solely with the publisher.

Seventh Printing ... ... **August, 2013**

Published by Asoke K. Ghosh, PHI Learning Private Limited, Rimjhim House, 111, Patparganj Industrial Estate, Delhi-110092 and Printed by Rajkamal Electric Press, Plot No. 2, Phase IV, HSIDC, Kundli-131028, Sonepat, Haryana.

Contents

Part Two ADVERTISING RESEARCH AND STRATEGY

Part Three CREATIVITY AND ADVERTISING

Preface

Advertising has today become one of the most important aspects of all the businesses and to imagine the life sans it is almost impossible. Advertising was quite ingenuous a few decades back, as the technology was not complicated. With limited media choices, advertising did not face much competition. However, the simplicity in advertising did not continue for long.

In the recent past, there was growth of innumerable broadcast and TV channels. The national dailies and magazines also grew multifold. It was the time for the advertisers to search for the right medium to reach the customers. Apart from the traditional medium, many other media options, which were never heard before, are now available. The production technology can now provide special effects to the advertisements. The web advertising, an interactive media, is a prime example of technological advancements. Today, the advertising has become an indispensable marketing tool of the corporate world. It has undergone a sea change and is still moving towards unpredictability. The practitioner cannot really predict the future of advertising.

Though there are several international books on Advertising, they lack Indian context and case studies. Also, the few Indian books available on the subject do not provide a wide coverage. In this book, we have conceptualized the theory in the form of objective-specific course book, keeping in view the students' needs and the challenging nature of the subject of Advertising.

The book is divided into five main sections—Advertising Basics, Advertising Research and Strategy, Creativity and Advertising, Advertising Media and Integrated Marketing Communications. In all, there are fifteen chapters in the book, which cover all the important aspects and key issues of advertising. We have taken ample care in including all the aspects of advertising so that the students, teachers and practitioners can find one composite source of reference and learning.

Part one of the book on Advertising Basics deals with fundamentals of advertising and relationship of advertising with the society as well as its effects on the society. This part also reviews important marketing concepts, which have relevance to advertising. Part two on Advertising Research and Strategy elaborately deals with various concepts of consumer behaviour and their impact on advertising. Advertising research and account planning are also discussed in this part along with the working of advertising and advertising planning. Part three on Creativity and Advertising discusses in detail how ad designers make creative advertisement with the help of the copywriters and ad designers. The layout of advertisements is discussed with the schematic representation. Part four on Advertising Media deals with the various media, mainly print, electronic and outdoor, including the Web. The strategy in developing the advertisements for various media along with their advantages and disadvantages is elaborated clearly. Part five on Integrated Marketing Communications discusses integrated marketing communication tools and advertising in multicultural environment. This part has been specifically included to help the readers keep abreast with the current trends in the advertising world.

This book is the outcome of the concerted efforts of many friends, students and colleagues. Though writing on advertising was fun, it required perseverance and patience. We are glad that finally we could make it. We would like to extend the deep sense of gratitude to Prof. L.K. Maheshwari, Vice Chancellor, BITS Pilani, for being the constant source of inspiration. Thanks are due to Prof. S. Venkateswaran, Advisor and Professor Emeritus, BITS Pilani, for his encouraging remarks at every stage. We also extend our heartfelt thanks to Prof. A.K. Sarkar, Dean, Instructional Division and Faculty Division – I, BITS Pilani for his unflinching support.

We would like to record the efforts made by our students—Nazim-ur-Rahman, Sai Muppur, Aparajith Ramnath, Aditya Satija, Anita Reddy, Bharat Pasupulati, T Sandeep Thomas Mathew, I Sindhura, Sowmya Ghanti, Spandana Reddy and Sarla in searching the apposite advertisements for this book.

At home front, Dr. Sangeeta Sharma says thanks is very measly word to show her gratitude for her husband, Suresh, who monitored her regularly to find the progress of the chapters. She accepts that the completion of the manuscript was possible only because of his support. Her two sons, Amrit and Anuj, were very supportive during the book-writing period when they had to sacrifice their time with her. They never complained. She fondly thanks Ms. Usha Manjunath, a friend and colleague, for her constant encouragement and support throughout this period.

Similarly, Dr. Raghuvir Singh gives immense thanks to his wife, Anju, for showing great admiration and patience during the time the book was being written. She has been very supportive and inspiring and has always reminded him for timely completion of this work. His two sons, Ashish and Abhinav, and daughter, Babita, were very supportive and shared keen interest in progress of the book. All of them have willingly sacrificed their comforts, fun and good time, otherwise they would have had with him during all this time.

Sangeeta Sharma
Raghuvir Singh

Part One

Advertising Basics

CHAPTER 1

Advertising: Introduction

LEARNING OBJECTIVES

After reading this chapter, you will be able to:

- Examine the growing importance of advertising.
- Learn the definition of advertising, focusing on the sights-and-sounds approach.
- Unravel the history of advertising.
- Know and classify the various media of advertising.
- Understand the AIDAS Technique.

CHANGING SCENARIO

CASE STUDY: LALITAJI

First launched in 1959 by Hindustan Lever Limited (HLL), *Surf* quickly became synonymous with detergent powders and remained at the top as the largest-selling detergent powder in the country until *Nirma* came. The late 1970s found HLL reeling under the stiff onslaught of Karsanbhai Patel's low-priced *Nirma*. To respond to *Nirma*, Lintas' legendary Alyque Padamsee came up with the memorable advertising campaign for *Surf*, featuring a middle-class housewife played by Kavita Chaudhary. Overnight, people on the street could identify *Lalitaji*, the practical, sensible, challenging, no-nonsense housewife who lectures us on the difference between *'sasti cheez aur asli cheez'* (cheap thing and the real thing). She was everybody's mother, wife, daughter-in-law or neighbour. More importantly, the Indian middle-class housewife, HLL's main customer segment, wanted to actually be the strong-willed, level-headed character that *Lalitaji* portrayed.

Soon, in an ironic twist, the character that became a celebrity because of brand advertising became larger than the brand itself. By the late 1980s, *Nirma* had got itself a similar *Deepikaji* who bettered a wily grocer and stressed if the same quality could be had for a lesser price, *"Koi yeh kyon le, Woh na le?"* (why would one buy this, and not that?)

Lalitaji makes a convincing statement and the brand becomes a success overnight.

The detergent wars were just beginning with Proctor and Gamble opening a new front with *Ariel* in the premium segment. All of a sudden, the rules of the game changed. There was an entirely new segment with customers who were ready to pay the price for better quality.

"In a sense, the character created for *Surf*, *Lalitaji* also explored the serial idea. Every one loves characters and continuing story lines", says Alyque Padamsee.

HLL launched *Surf Ultra* with *Laitaji's* household, an urban nuclear family where she was put in the modern role of a quintessential housewife who was looked upon by everyone around her as a guardian angel, a problem solver who smartly reassured them *"Daag! Dhoondhte Rehjaoge!"* (Stains! Keep searching for them!)

Unfortunately, with the social structure of India changing, the middle class housewife was no longer the same *Lalitaji* and *Surf Ultra* flopped with Proctor and Gamble capturing a major part of the market share. *'Lalitaji* type' had become a euphemism for the irritating, aggressive know-it-all shopper with whom many could still identify, but probably not as favourably as they did in the 1980s.

In the mid-1990s, HLL was back with *Surf Excel*. More importantly, instead of *Lalitaji*, the protagonist was now a working woman—a lawyer, a journalist, a businesswoman—facing the challenges of everyday life. What was retained was her spotless white garb. When it suffered those inevitable stains, she was calmly reassured by those who looked at her shopping bag—*Surf Excel hai na!* (*Surf Excel* is there!) *Lalitaji* was gone but the brand clicked with the segment yet again!

Yet another *Surf Excel* campaign reflected the changing role of the Indian woman. It showed a yuppie couple entertaining a group of friends when the husband stains his sleeve. Not wanting to disturb his significant other, he reads the instructions on the detergent pack and takes care of the stain himself. She walks in and says knowingly, *"Daag gaya Na!"* (Stains did go!)

So, are the days of *Lalitaji* finally over?

"We are migrating *Surf* to *Surf Excel*, as *Surf* has become generic and many people today refer to any detergent as *Surf*. Besides, we feel that this brand has the chance of attracting new users under the *Excel* name," says Sanjay Dube, Head, Market and Consumer Development, Hindustan Lever Limited.

The jury's still out, but HLL must hope that all those consumers who swear by *Lalitaji* will soon be chanting, *"Surf Excel hai na!"*

ADVERTISING WORLD

Advertising is all over the places, on TV and radio, in newspapers and magazines, on billboards and even plastered across the sides of the buses. It is persistent and persuasive, but it would be simplistic to believe that the power advertising has over us is just about how we spend our money. If an advertisement can really persuade us to buy a product, surely it can be just as effective in persuading us to think in a certain way.

The global market has expanded manifold in the last few decades. Innumerable products are being launched almost every day. The companies are engaged in cut-throat competition to highlight their products. Herein enters the glamorous field of advertising. The more innovative the advertising, the better is the market. Advertising is actually brand building through effective communication and is essentially a service industry. It is a medium which helps to reach more people to communicate brand effectiveness.

Advertising serves three purposes: to recruit new customers, to increase use of goods or services among existing customers, and to help potential customers choose among competing brands. This basic principle holds true for all kinds of products and markets. These three purposes can be merged into a single purpose: market share, or to convince the customer to choose one brand over another and retain him for life. So it basically deals with capturing human feelings and emotions, which makes it one of the most challenging jobs. Advertisers use various means to achieve this. Creativity leads the list, and the idea has to be unique.

Advertising has a great influence on our daily lives whether we are aware or oblivious of it. Billboards, newspapers, television and magazines—all convey messages to the public about various products, companies, travel opportunities, etc. One cannot escape the constant invasion of such advertisements and as a result, ads have become a global phenomenon which we take part in by being both consumers and observers. Ads have become an easily accessible persuasion tactic all over the world. As a result of commercials and other advertisements, companies have been able to reach a wider range of potential buyers. Globalization of advertising has significantly increased consumerism and has allowed certain companies the exposure needed to boost sales.

IMPORTANCE OF ADVERTISING

We are exposed to hundreds of ads every day and even if someone claims that they do not have any effect on him, it is not true. Either consciously or subconsciously, advertisements have a tremendous effect on our lifestyle.

Volkswagen was in red by the end of the Second World War. However, within 10 years after that, its cars were one of the best-selling in the world. The reason was obviously advertising. One such creative ad of Volkswagen (New Beetle) shown below is an exampler of one of the million cases where advertising played a crucial role in reviving the brand or creating a permanent image for a brand. 'Marlboro Man' campaign is considered to be one of the most popular campaigns of the 20th century. It was started in 1955 and even today smokers associate the cowboy image with it.

Volkswagen: Think different.

These are only the direct effects of advertising on brands and the customers.

Advertising can not only change the buying decision, but also has the power to change the mindset and attitude of people. It has been observed that advertising is the reflection of the culture of a nation. In fact, advertising and culture both affect each other. Advertising industry also supports media industry. Media survives on advertising as they go hand-in-hand.

If a good ad says, "This drink has been rated for mature audiences only", then all it needs is a credible medium to reach the customer. In no time, people will start associating ABSOLUT with maturity. In fact, just that happened after this brand campaigned with that baseline. ABSOLUT was a huge success in America.

Advertising can also be used as an effective tool for a social cause. A literacy ad campaign says, "It just takes 10 paisa and one special person to spread literacy. You." Just how long is it going to take if we were to persuade people in person to take up the cause of spreading literacy? Advertising can be instrumental in bringing a commendable change in society by generating awareness among the population about the social causes.

A recent advertisement of *Surf Excel* claims that by using this detergent you can save two buckets of water. Water is a scarce commodity and the conscious use of it can make a difference. Added to this, a prize-winning *Bisleri* advertisement takes up the issue of safety.

Absolute Vodka: Credibility in advertising compaigns.

Advertisements also serve to spread information about the new technology and innovations and keep us up to date as to what is happening in the scientific world. The role of advertising in today's world is not just spreading brand awareness. It also shows us where we stand in the world today.

TATA Salt: Encouraging proactive literacy compaigns.

Bisleri: Play safe.

ADVERTISING DEFINED

The most standard definition of advertising is as follows: "**Advertising** is the non-personal communication of information usually paid for and usually persuasive in nature about products, services or ideas by identified sponsors through the various media." (Bovee 1992, 7). Let us dissect the definition and explain the key terms used in this definition.

Non-Personal

Let us first understand what non-personal is. There are two basic ways to sell anything: personally and non-personally. Personal selling requires the seller and the buyer to be together. There are advantages and disadvantages to this. The first advantage is that the seller has time to discuss in detail everything about the product. The buyer has time to ask questions, get answers and examine evidence for or against purchase.

The second advantage of personal selling is that the seller can see the person to whom he/she is selling the product. He/She can see how the sales message is getting across. If the customer yawns or looks away, he/she is obviously bored, and so the seller can change his approach. He/ She can also see if the customer is hooked, see what features or benefits grab the customer's attention, and emphasize them to close the sale. Finally, the seller can easily locate potential buyers. If you enter a store, you probably have an interest in something that the store sells. Street vendors and door-to-door sellers can simply shout at possibilities. From there on they fit their message to the individual customer, taking all the time a customer is willing to give them.

There are also disadvantages of personal selling. It is quite expensive because it is labour-intensive and deals with only one buyer at a time. Just imagine, even when one tries to sell chewing gum or chocolates, it would cost a large sum of money. In addition, personal selling is time-consuming. Selling a stereo or a car can take days, and major computer and airplane sales can take years by this procedure. In this fast moving world, no one has time to wait.

Nonetheless, although personal selling results in more rejections than sales, and can be nerve-racking and frustrating for the salesperson. Contrarily, when the salesperson is good it is more directed and successful than advertising.

From the above statement, it appears that personal selling is better than advertising, which is non-personal. This is true. Advertising has none of the advantages of personal selling: there is very little time to present the sales message, there is no way to know who the customer is or how he is responding to the message, and the message cannot be changed in mid-course to suit the customer's reactions.

So let us find out the reason for the replacement of personal selling by advertising. Its advantages replace the disadvantages of personal selling, and can emulate some of the advantages. Let's look at the latter.

Advertising is ubiquitous. It is part of us since the time immemorial. Unlike personal selling, the sales message and its presentation do not have to be created on the spot with the customer watching. It can be created in as many ways as the writer can conceive, be rewritten, tested, modified, injected with every trick and appeal known to affect consumers.

Second, although advertisers may not see the individual customer, nor be able to modify the sales message according to that individual's reactions at the time, they do have research about customers. The research can identify potential customers, find what message elements might influence them, and figure out how best to get that message to them. Although the research is meaningless when applied to any particular individual, it is effective when applied to large groups of customers.

Third, and perhaps of most importantly, advertising can be far cheaper per potential customer than personal selling. Unlike personal selling, which deals with one customer at a time, advertising deals with hundreds, thousands and millions of customers at a time, thus reducing the cost per customer. In fact, advertising cost is determined in part using a formula. It is not determined as cost per potential customer, but as cost per thousand potential customers.

Thus, advertising is a good idea as a sales tool. For small ticket items, such as chewing gum and chocolates, advertising is cost-effective to do the entire selling job. For large ticket items, such as cars and computers, advertising can do a large part of the selling job, and personal selling is used to complete and close the sale.

Therefore, even through advertising is non-personal, it is certainly effective.

Communication

Communication is a means by which one person can pass information, ideas or feelings to another through speech or pictures. Thus, communication uses all of the senses: smell, touch, taste, sound and sight. However, of the five, only two are useful in advertising–sound and sight. The advertisement of Phoenix Mill in the 1940s, communicated through just a picture., Sound and sight are the most effective and easily used channels of communication available to advertising. For these reasons, virtually all advertising relies on them.

Sound

Sound is extremely useful for advertising. It can be used in a variety of media, from radio and television to the new technology of binding micro-sound chips in magazines to present 20-second sales messages. It is also capable of presenting words and "theatre of the mind".

Words, the means by which humans communicate their ideas and feelings, are presented by sound, by speaking aloud. Through the use of words it is possible to deliver logical arguments, discuss pros and cons, and evoke emotions.

Through the use of sound it is possible to create what is called "the theatre of the mind". This means that sound can conjure in the listener's mind images and actions that don't necessarily exist. For example, if you want to create the imagination of a party, you only need to use the sound effects of people talking and laughing, the tinkle of glasses and ice, and perhaps music in the backdrop. Even easier, tape record a party and play it back. To evoke images of a soft spring day, the sounds of a breeze rustling leaves, the chirrup of insects, the soft call of birds is sufficient. The listener's mind will take those sounds, combine them, make sense of them and create an image suited to their individual taste. For example, a beer commercial may play the sounds of a bar in the background, and the listeners may imagine themselves in their own favourite bar and perhaps ordering that brand of beer.

Thus, sound in the form of words and effects is quite useful to an advertiser in affecting a listener. This impact is observed in the advertisements of Onida *KY* series.

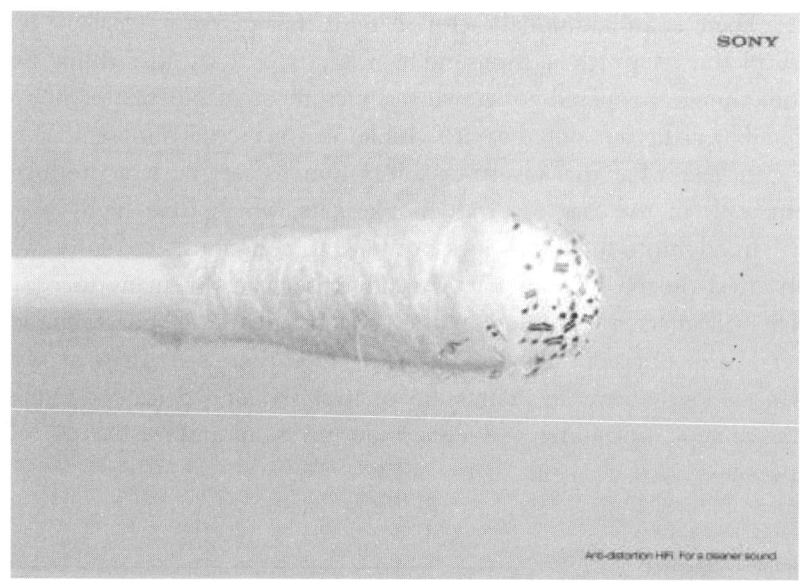

Sony: Effect of sound used at best.

Sight

Sight is arguably the most useful of the communication channels available to an advertiser. Through sight it is possible to use both words and images effectively.

You need not only speak words to convey meaning. They can be printed as well. Although it is difficult to put in written words the emotional impact that is possible in spoken words, with their inflections and subtle sound cues, nevertheless written words are unsurpassed for getting across and explaining complex ideas.

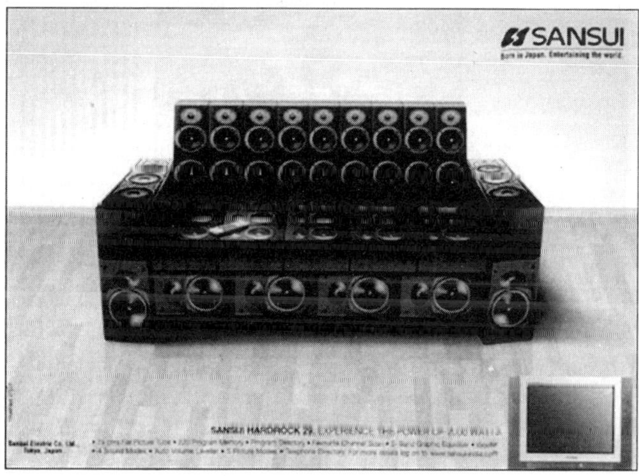

Sansui: The big picture.

There is an additional factor in sight that makes it excellent for advertising. The old cliché, "A picture is worth a thousand words", is correct. Just think how long it takes to describe something as opposed to showing a picture of it. No matter how many words are used, some details will be left out that are visible at a glance. Thus, sight can quickly and concisely show a customer what the advertiser wants him to see, be it a product or its benefits. This is true especially in the case of products like cars, which have high value addition factors.

In addition, the mind does not have to consciously recognize what the eye sees for it to have an effect on the subconscious. An advertiser can put many inconspicuous details into a picture that will affect a customer on the subconscious level. For example, a drop of water on a rose petal may not consciously register ("I see there's a drop of water on this rose"), but will unconsciously leave an impression of freshness and delicacy. A small child looking upward into the camera, unsmiling and eyes wide, gives an impression of sadness and vulnerability, not shortness.

Skoda RS: Automobile ads tend to depend a lot on the visual aspect.

The five forms of human communication can be used to send any message to potential customers. However, not all five are equal. Smell, touch and taste are of little use, but sound and sight are of great value and effectiveness.

Information

Information is defined as knowledge, facts or news. However, you should bear in mind that one person's information is another person's scam, particularly when advertisers talk about their products.

Information comes in many forms. It can be complete or incomplete. It can be biased or deceptive. Complete information is telling someone everything there is to know about something: what it is, what it looks like, how it works, what are its benefits and drawbacks, etc. However, to provide complete information about anything is time consuming and difficult. For example, to tell all about a car would require its appearance, manufacture and manufacturer, what percentage of parts are made in which countries, cost of upkeep, mileage (city and highway), cost (basic and with any and all combination of options), sales and excise taxes per state, preparation costs, insurance costs per state and locale, ride characteristics (noise by decibels, interior and exterior, ergs required for steering and braking, relative comfort of seats, length of reach required to use controls, degrees of lean when cornering), acceleration, braking distance at many different speeds, etc. All of this would require a documentary, not a commercial. Complete information is, therefore, impossible to provide in an ad.

Thus, for advertising, information of necessity must be incomplete, not discussing everything there is to know about the subject. In advertising, what appears is everything that the writer thinks the customer needs to know about the product in order to make a decision about it. That information is generally about how the product can benefit the customer (see the Tata Indigo ad giving a few technical details of the car).

Tata Indigo: An ad communicating information about the product.

Sometimes the consumer is provided not with information that he wants, but only with the information which the seller wants him to have. Sellers, for instance, are not inclined to advertise negative aspects of their products even though those aspects may be of primary concern to the consumer, particularly if they involve considerations of health or safety.

Bias means being partial towards something, feeling that something is better or worse than other things. Biased information about a product is that which emphasizes what is good and ignores what is bad about it. In advertising this is not only normal, but also necessary. Of course, an advertiser is biased towards his own product and against the competitors': selling his product is the way he makes his money, and his competitors' sales reduces that income. Thus, any advertising will use words and images that show how good his product is over his competitors'. This is biased information, but recognized and accepted by industry, regulators and consumers–it is called **puffery**, the legitimate exaggeration of advertising claims to overcome natural consumer skepticism.

Paid For

If an ad is created and placed in the media, the costs of creation and time or space in the media must be paid for. This is a major area in which advertising departs from public relations (PR).

PR seeks to place information about companies and/or products in the media without having to pay for the time or space. PR creates news releases and sends them to news media in the hopes that they will be run. Often PR departments produce events that will be covered by news media and thus receive space or time. However, there is no guarantee that the media will run any of the PR material.

Advertising doesn't have that problem. If time or space is bought in the media, the ads (as long as they follow the guidelines set down for good taste, legal products and services, etc.) will appear. The drawback is that ads are clearly designed to extol the virtues of products and companies, and any ad perceived by consumers is at least partly puffery. PR pieces are usually not so perceived.

Nike: Powerful ad message.

Persuasive

"Persuasive" stands to reason as part of the definition of advertising. The basic purpose of advertising is to identify and differentiate one product from another in order to persuade the consumer to buy that product in preference to another.

Products, Services or Ideas

Products, services or ideas are the things that advertisers want consumers to buy (in the case of ideas, buy means accept or agree with as well as lay out hard, cold cash). However, there is more to products or services than simply items for purchase. Henceforth, products will mean products, services and ideas unless otherwise noted.)

A product is not merely its function. It is actually a bundle of values, and what that product means to the consumer. That bundle may contain the product's function, but also the social, psychological and economic values that are important to the consumer.

For example, if the function of a car (i.e. transportation) is all that is important, then manufacturers would need only to build motorized boxes on wheels, and consumers would be happy with them. However, such is obviously not the case; the number of models and types of cars is huge, and if consumers didn't demand the variety it wouldn't exist. Consumers must find factors other than mere transportation, even if not more important.

Perhaps the value is social. The type of car a person drives is often indicative of that person's social status. A Maruti shows a lower status than a Mercedes Benz. A sports car shows that a person is (or wishes to be perceived as) more socially active and fun loving than a person in a sedan or station wagon. The type of car can even indicate which social group a person wants to be considered a part of; in the 1980s, Volvos and BMWs were the car for yuppies.

The value is economic too. Some cars may be cheaper to run, give better mileage, carry more people or cargo, and cause less damage to the environment.

The above four values–functional, social, psychological and economic–can stand alone. However, for most consumers, the values are bundled together in varying proportions. How closely a product approximates an individual's proportion of values will often determine whether they will buy that product or not.

Companies, through research, try to determine what values consumers want in their products, and then advertise to show how their product satisfies the customers' bundle of values better than the competitors' products. To do this, the company must differentiate their product from competitors'. There are three basic differentiations: perceptible, imperceptible and induced.

Perceptible

Perceptible differences are those that make one product obviously different from others of the same kind. The difference may be in colour, size, shape, brand name or in some other way. In any case, the consumer can easily see that this car or couch or camera is different from other cars or couches or cameras. Perceptible differences allow a person to make an instant identification of one product as opposed to another.

Imperceptible

Imperceptible differences are those that exist between one product and others, but are not obvious. For example, there are imperceptible but profound differences among CP/M, MS-DOS, Apple and Macintosh computers. You can't simply look at a computer and tell which one it is; machines can and usually do look alike. Yet, buying either of them precludes the use of software designed for the other.

The same is applied to Beta and VHS format VCRs. Although both are designed to do the same thing, there are differences between them that are imperceptible on the surface but preclude using the same tapes in both. Besides using cassettes of different sizes, the machines use totally different ways of recording and playing back tapes. while Beta records and plays back diagonally across the tape, while VHS records vertically. Such a difference may seem small, but it means that anything recorded on Beta cannot be played back on VHS, and vice versa. Also, Beta's system used more tape per instant and thus, had an advantage in the amount of information per inch of tape, meaning a better sound and picture but less available time. However, VHS overcomes its deficit by improved electronics and better processing of what information it gets per inch of tape. In addition, VHS (read RCA) managed to corner the market on rental tapes of movies (a major use of VCRs) and virtually killed off Beta (read Sony). All the differences between Beta and VHS are imperceptible, but also crucial.

POLO: An ad with a difference.

Induced

For many products, there is no actual substantive difference between one and another. For many brands of cigarettes, beer, cleansers and soaps, rice, over-the-counter health products, etc. ad nauseam, there is essentially no difference between one brand and another. These products are called **parity products**.

For these products, the only way to differentiate one from another is to induce that difference and persuade people that there actually is some difference, and it is important to them. These differences are created through advertising, not through any inherent difference in the products, and that creation often uses appeal. For example, the POLO ad. Does the mint with a hole make any difference to the inherent nature or quality of mint?

The Marlboro Man: An advertising legend.

Another approach is to project an image on a parity product. Marlboro is rugged male, Virginia Slims is independent female, Benson & Hedges is intellectual, Camel is cool and sophisticated. That there is no real difference between one brand of cigarette and another is beside the point. The point is, if you want the image you must use the product. This image approach is so successful that a macho man wouldn't be caught dead (no pun intended) smoking Virginia Slims or Benson & Hedges—he'd feel like a sissy wimp (or rather, that is what he thinks his friends would think he was).

Parity products have the greatest difficulty differentiating one from another. They must rely on creating a trivial or even non-existent difference in the bundle of values their target audience might find important to their purchase decision. However, if and once that difference is firmly established in the target audience's perception, a company can often rely on habit, brand loyalty and/or cognitive dissonance to get repeat business.

Identified Sponsors

Identified sponsors mean whoever is putting out the ad tell the audience who they are. There are two reasons for this: first, it's a legal requirement, and second, it makes good sense.

Legally, a sponsor must identify himself as the sponsor of an ad. This prevents the audience from getting a misleading idea about the ad or its contents. For example, many ads that appear in newspapers look like news articles: same typeface, appearance, use of columns, etc. If the ad is not identified as such, the audience could perceive it as news about a product, rather than an attempt to persuade the audience to buy it. Case in point: what looks like a news article discusses a weight-loss plan. In a journalistic style it talks about the safety, efficacy, and reasonable price of the product. A reasonable person might perceive the ad as an article written by a reporter who had investigated weight-loss programmes and decided to objectively discuss this particular one. Such a perception is misleading and illegal. Since it is an ad, somewhere on it there must appear the word "advertisement" to ensure that the audience do not think it is an objective reporting of news.

It makes good sense for a sponsor to identify itself in the ad. If it doesn't, it is possible for the audience to believe the ad is for a competitor's product, thus wasting all its time, creativity and money that went into making and placing the ad.

Various Media

The various media are the non-personal channels of communication that people have invented and used, and continue to use. These include newspapers, magazines, radio, television, billboards, transit cards, sandwich boards, skywriting, posters, floating hoardings, balloons, anything that aids communicating ideas in a non-personal way from one person or group to another person or group. They do not include people talking to each other: talking is personal and advertising is non-personal; moreover, there is no way to use people talking to each other for advertising—word-of-mouth is not an advertising medium, since one can't control what is said. (The best one could do is to start a rumour, which will undoubtedly distort the message in the telling and is more the province of the PR department.)

HISTORY OF ADVERTISING

Advertising has been around for thousands of years. One way of looking at the cave paintings of Lascaux, which are about 16,000 years old, is as advertising. They could be selling to the spirits of animals the idea of showing up for the hunt.

Nonetheless, advertising recognizable as 'advertising' has been around for millennia. Daniel Mannix, in his book on the Roman games, *Those About to Die,* quotes an ad found on a tombstone:

> "Weather permitting, 30 pairs of gladiators, furnished by A. Clodius Flaccus, together with substitutes in case any get killed too quickly, will fight May 1st, 2nd and 3rd at the Circus Maximus. The fights will be followed by a big wild beast hunt. The famous gladiator Paris will fight. Hurrah for Paris! Hurrah for the generous Flaccus, who is running for Duumvirate!"
>
> (Below this is an ad for the copywriter: "Marcus wrote this sign by the light of the moon. If you hire Marcus, he'll work day and night to do a good job.") (Mannix, 28)

For the first few thousand years, people used advertising to promote two things: locations and services. The above is an example of the first. So were the signs outside taverns and inns. Handbills and posters were also a popular form of advertising. They were passed out promoting such events as plays, or recruiting for the military.

Indian advertising started with hawkers calling out their wares right from the days when cities and markets first began. From shopfront signage and street side sellers to press ads and then the first trademarks, advertising grew rapidly in India. Concrete advertising history begins with classified advertising. Ads appeared for the first time in print in Hickey's *Bengal Gazette,* India's first newspaper (weekly).

Studios marked the beginning of advertising created in India (as opposed to imported from England). Studios set up for bold type, ornate fonts, more fancy, larger ads. Newspaper studios trained the first generation of visualisers and illustrators with major advertisers being retailers like Spencer's, Army and Navy, and Whiteaway and Laidlaw.

The early marketing promotions were retailers' catalogues. Ads appeared in newspapers in the form of lists of the latest merchandise from England.

Let us look at some of the important years in the history of advertising.

Advertising through the ages

1704	The first newspaper advertisement, an announcement seeking a buyer for an Oyster Bay, Long Island estate, is published in the *Boston News Letter*.
1742	Benjamin Franklin's *General Magazine* prints the first American magazine ads.
1843	Volney Palmer opens the first advertising agency in Philadelphia.
1867	New York agency Carlton & Smith begin buying the right to place advertising in religious magazines.
1877	James Walter Thompson buys Carlton & Smith from William J. Carlton, paying $500 for the business and $800 for the office furniture. He renames it after himself and moves into general magazine advertising. Later, he invents the position of account executive. Today, J. Walter Thompson Co. is one of the leading ad agencies in the world.
1882	Procter and Gamble Co. begins advertising *Ivory* soap with an unprecedented budget of $11,000.
1883	**India:** *Horlicks* becomes the first 'malted milk' to be patented on 5th June 1883 (No. 278967).
1893	Asa Briggs Chandler registers Coca-Cola as a trademark.
1898	N.W. Ayer helps National Biscuit Co. launch the first prepackaged biscuit, *Uneeda*, with the slogan "Lest you forget, we say it yet, Uneeda Biscuit." Eventually, the company launches the first million-dollar advertising campaign for Uneeda.
1899	J. Walter Thompson Co. is the first agency to open an office in the UK.
1905	**India:** B. Dattaram & Co. claims to be the oldest existing Indian agency in Girgaum in Bombay.
1906	W.K. Kellogg places his first ad for *Corn Flakes* in six Midwestern newspapers. By 1915, he is as spending one million dollars on national advertising.
1911	For the first time in its history, P&G pays an outside agency, J. Walter Thompson Co., to launch *Crisco*, its new vegetable shortening. Woodbury Soap breaks its "The skin you love to touch" campaign in the *Ladies' Home Journal*. This was the first time sex appeal was used in advertising.
1912	**India:** ITC (then Imperial Tobacco Co. Ltd.) launches *Gold Flake*.
1920	KDKA, Pittsburgh, becomes the first radio station in the US, and is the first to broadcast the results of the 1920 Presidential election.

1922 AT&T's station WEAF in New York offers 10 minutes of radio time to anyone who would pay $100. The Queensboro Corp., a Long Island real estate firm, buys the first commercials in advertising history: 15 spots at $50 a piece. Following the ads extolling Hawthorne Court, a new tenant-owned apartment complex in Jackson Heights' sales total thousands of dollars.

1923 National Carbon Co.'s *Eveready Hour* is the first regular series of broadcast entertainment and music to be sponsored by an advertiser.

1924 Goodrich Tires sponsors the first hour-long show over a network of nine radio stations.

1928 Lintas (Lever International Advertising Services) is formed as a house agency for Unilever in England, Holland and Germany.

1929 American Tobacco Co. spends $12.3 million to advertise *Lucky Strike*, the most any company has ever spent on single product advertising.
India: Walter Thompson Co. Pr. Ltd. formed.

India: The foreign owned ad agencies step in:

- Gujarat Advertising and Indian Advertising set up.
- Expatriate agencies emerge, for example, Alliance Advertising and Tata Publicity.
- L.A. Stronach's merges into today's Norvicson Advertising
- D.J. Keymer gives rise to Ogilvy and Mather and Clarion.

1934 **India:** Venkatrao Sista opens Sista Advertising and Publicity Services as the first full service Indian agency.

1935 Leo Burnett leaves Erwin Wasey to start his own agency in Chicago.

1936 *Life* publishes its first edition. Later, became the first magazine to carry $100 million annually in advertising.
India: Indian Broadcasting Company becomes All India Radio (AIR).

1939 **India:** Lever's advertising department launches *Dalda*—the first major example of a brand and a marketing campaign specifically developed for India.

1941 With 7,500 TV sets in New York City, NBC's WNBT begins telecasting July 1. The first TV spots, featuring a Bulova watch that ticks for 60 seconds, air as open and close time signals for the day's schedule.

	India: *Lux* signs Leela Chitnis as the first Indian film actress to endorse the product and Hindustan Thompson Associates (HTA), the current incarnation of J. Walter Thompson Co., coins the balanced nourishment concept to make Horlicks more relevant to India.
1947	J. Walter Thompson Co. becomes the first agency to surpass $100 million in billings.
1948	Hewitt, Ogilvy, Benson & Mather is launched.
1951	**India:** Vicks *VapoRub*, a rub for colds, causes ripples with its entry in the balm market.
1955	The *Marlboro* Man campaign debuts.
1957	It turned out to be one of the great marketing disasters of automotive history. Ford Motor Co. introduces the *Edsel*. **India:** Vividh Bharati kicks off.
1960	Doyle Dane Bernbach introduces the creative team approach of combining a copywriter with an art director to create its "Think small" campaign for Volkswagen.
1962	David Ogilvy publishes *Confessions of an Advertising Man*. **India:** Indian television's first soap opera—*Teesra Rasta* enthralls viewers.
1963	The Pepsi generation kicks off the cola wars. **India:** Wills filter tipped cigarettes launched and positioned as made for each other, filter and tobacco match.
1964	Ogilvy, Benson & Mather merges with London-based parent company, Mather & Crowther, to form Ogilvy & Mather. After the US surgeon general determines that smoking is "hazardous to your health", *The New Yorker* and other magazines ban cigarette ads.
1966	Following a string of account losses, Rosser Reeves, Ted Bates' first creative chief and promoter of advertising that offers a "unique selling proposition", resigns at the age of 55.
1967	Wells Rich Greene (WRG) is established. Mary Wells is the first woman to head a major agency. **India:** First commercial appears on Vividh Bharati.
1970	Saatchi & Saatchi is established in London.
1971	**India:** Benson's change in name to Ogilvy, Benson & Mather.
1972	**India:** Western Outdoor Advertising Pvt. Ltd. (WOAPL) introduces first closed circuit TV (CCT) in the country at the racecourse in Mumbai.
1976	**India:** Commercial television is initiated.

1978	**India:** First television commercial is launched seen.
1979	**India:** Ogilvy, Benson & Mather's name changes to Ogilvy & Mather.
1980	**India:** Mudra Communications Ltd. set up. **India:** King-sized Virginia filter cigarette enters market as the brand name of 'Charms'
1981	MTV debuts with frenetic video images that change the nature of commercials.
1982	**India:** The biggest milestone in television was the Asiad 1982 when television turned to colour transmission. **India**: Bombay Dyeing becomes the first colour TV ad.
1983	**India**: *Maggi* noodles is launched to become an overnight success. **India:** Manohar Shyam Joshi's *Hum Log* makes commercial television come alive. **India**: Mudra communication sponsors the first commercial telecast of a major sporting event with the India-West Indies series.
1984	**India**: Vicco sponsors telecast of *Yeh Jo Hai Zindagi!*
1985	**India:** Mudra communications makes India's first telefilm, *Janam.* **India:** 915 new brands of products and services appearing on the Indian market.
1986	Saatchi & Saatchi buys Ted Bates Worldwide, becoming the world's largest agency holding company. **India:** Sananda is born on July 31. The Bengali magazine stupefies India by selling 75,000 copies within three hours of appearing on the news-stands. **India:** Mudra Communications creates India's first folk-history TV serial *Buniyaad.* Shown on DD, it becomes the first of the mega soaps. **India:** Price quality positioning of Nirma detergent cakes boost sales
1990	A new medium, Internet is born. **India:** Brand Equity of *The Economic Times* is born.
1991	**India:** First India-targeted satellite channel, Zee TV starts broadcast followed by Star TV.
1992	**India:** Spectrum, publisher of A&M, constitutes its own award known as 'A&M Awards'.
1993	The Internet becomes a reality as five million users worldwide get online.
1995	As its share price plunges 30 per cent, Maurice and Charles Saatchi leave the agency they founded in 1970.
1996	**India:** The Sun TV becomes the first regional TV channel to go live 24 hours a day on all days of the week.

1999	Internet advertising breaks the two billion dollar mark and heads toward three billion dollars as the industry, under prodding from Proctor and Gamble, moves to standardize all facets of the industry.
2003	TV show with built-in advertising is planned.

CASE STUDY: THE LIRIL GIRL

The one icon who has held her stead for an astonishing 30 years is the *Liril* girl. Shrinking attention spans and shifting trends notwithstanding, she continues to epitomise exuberant freshness. The ubiquitous waterfall has morphed into a glacier. The signature tune *Laa la la la laa* has been tweaked to *Uff yu maa*. Why, it's not even the customary lime-green anymore. Variants like Icy Cool and Orange Fresh have brought in new hues. But the effervescence of the Liril girls—from Karen Lunell to the current nymph, Dipika Padukone—is comfortingly familiar.

It was in 1975 that Hindustan Lever Limited added a twist of lime to soapsuds, and created *Liril*, the first ever "lime freshness soap". Research, meanwhile, had thrown up a startling insight that the only time the Indian housewife got to herself was when she closed her bathroom door. That's when she daydreamed about escaping a humdrum life.

"The creative rendition of that insight was a girl bathing in a waterfall", says Alyque Padamsee, ad pundit and creator of the *Liril* girl phenomenon. But then came the tricky part—getting the right waterfall and the right girl! "Some couldn't keep their eyes open under the waterfall. Others didn't exude the right energy. Yet others had qualms about donning a bikini." Then entered Karen Lunell. With permission from her employers, Air India, the crew flew to Kodaikanal. That's where they had found a waterfall, which was perfect in every way.

When the ad was released, the audience was bowled over. The blithe water sprite, the dancing waterfall, the catchy refrain—everything was new and thrilling. The *Liril* girl became the metaphor for freshness and at a deeper level, for freedom from the mundane. It struck a winning chord with the Indian woman and *Liril* zoomed to the top of the premium soap segment.

Karen's romp in icy waterfalls continued for close to 10 years. Says Kailash, "With each film, we experimented with new techniques like flash cuts and slow motion. But we never took her away from the waterfall".

Anjali Jathar was still in college when she was signed on for *Liril*. She was thrilled, but nothing prepared her for the 'waterfall' ordeal. She enjoyed every moment of the filming, including the time in Nepal when she almost drowned. "My raft had capsized and one of the overzealous Nepalese assistants in an attempt to rescue me, ended up pulling me into the rapid.

He probably didn't know I was an excellent swimmer. In the end, I had to kick him and swim to safety", she laughs.

An unrivalled market leader in the 1970s and 1980s, *Liril* was facing a testing time in the 1990s. The woes began with a stagnant market and aggressive competition from a slew of me-too brands. Besides, the girl-in-waterfall routine had become predictable. To infuse variety, *Liril* introduced a shower gel, *Liril Active Gel*.

Out went the waterfall and in came a car wash, and a new *Liril* girl—Pooja Batra. The film had the leggy Miss India pull into a deserted car wash, looking worse for wear. Then, the *Liril* gel gives her an idea and she jumps and dances in the burst of water, ending up as fresh as a daisy.

While this was a marked departure from the previous *Liril* imagery as well as the jingle, it wasn't curtains for the waterfall yet.

The waterfall gushed once more in the next film and under it danced the dimpled, exuberant Preity Zinta. Preity had shot to fame as the impish collegian in the Perk film. With *Liril*, she got a chance to display her bubbly charm as well. It was a rockstar in the jungle theme. So she drummed on plants, blew on reeds, swung on vines and generally let her hair down.

Unlike the previous *Liril* girls, however, Preity didn't turn blue in the icy waterfall. The film was shot on a set where a waterfall was created complete with exotic jungle plants and acrylic stones, because she couldn't swim!

In 1999, *Liril* turned blue for the first time with *Liril Rainfresh*, a blue variant of *Liril Lime*. The film with Hrishita Bhatt dancing in the rain set several precedents. The waterfall was done away with, the *Liril* girl was brought to the city and there was a supporting cast as well.

In mid-2001, the *Liril* girl was spotted on the sands of Rajasthan, taunting a bevy of *matki*-bearing women to throw water on her. This was a fairly radical departure from the blithe, playful *Liril* girls of yore. Says R Balki, Executive Creative Director, Lowe Advertising, "The brand is all about freshness. So how could we use the same metaphors and the same imagery year after year? We wanted to show a little aggression, a little teasing." Tara Sharma, fresh from the London School of Economics, fit the role of the contemporary *Liril* girl. Despite the scorching sand and suffocating heat, Tara went through the routine cheerfully. That was until she heard the location for the next *Liril* shoot—the glaciers in Iceland! Tara laughs, "I didn't have to act at all. Shooting at minus 4 degrees, the shiver was totally natural".

Dipka Padukone in the Liril ad.

After this, Liril launched a new orange variant—*Liril Orange Fresh* with the zesty fragrance of orange. It also marked the debut of the new *Liril* girl—Dipika Padukone.

Spotted on a *Limca* hoarding in Chennai, 18-year-old Dipika exuded the joie de vivre that the agency Lowe was looking for. In the film Dipika capers in the desert with a bunch of village kids. As she leaps and splashes, you're suddenly struck by the absence of a water source. And then dawns realisation, that the Liril girl is the source of water!

Liril orange fresh.

"What we wanted to convey is that the *Liril* girl is so fresh, that she is the source of freshness, which she spreads to all around", explains Balki.

The latest advertisement of *Liril* (*La-ira-ila*) has taken the audience by storm as its bilt appeal to the masses and the freshness coruscated by the models leave an indelible impact on them.

Thirty years is a long time for any brand icon. So is the mystique of the *Liril* girl waning? There are two schools of thought. One, led by her creator, Alyque Padamsee who emphatically states, "Bring back the waterfall and Karen." And the contemporary view that sees the *Liril* girl evolving with time. But one fact is inescapable. The *Liril* girl is one of the most enchanting and enduring fantasies spun by Indian advertising. It will be a long while before her charisma fades.

CLASSIFICATION OF ADVERTISEMENTS

Advertisements have numerous objectives, sometimes other than just selling products. First, let's have a look at the basic outline of the development of an effective advertising campaign. The classification of advertisements is directly related to the advertising plan. By developing an effective advertising plan, the likelihood of a positive return on your advertising investment is increased, regardless of the amount spent. Following are the questions, answers to which the advertiser is supposed to know before designing an ad.

- What do I want my advertising to accomplish?
- Whom should my advertising speak to?
- What should my advertising say?
- Where should I place my advertising?

There are different classifications possible depending on which of the above questions we have in mind while doing the same. We will have look at each of them.

What do I want my advertising to accomplish?

The first step in developing an advertising plan is to specify our advertising goals. One should be as precise as to why he is advertising and what is to be achieved. Everyone wants advertising to increase business, but for the advertising plan to work it requires the advertiser to be more precise. What is important is the prioritization of goals. Advertising works best when it is developed to meet one specific goal at a time.

Whom should my advertising speak to?

Once the advertising goals are determined, the next step is to select the target audience for our message. Advertising that tries to reach everyone rarely succeeds. Successful advertising is written with a specific customer in mind. Target consumers should be described in each of the following:

1. Demographics such as gender, age, income, location of residence or business, etc.
2. Behaviours such as current awareness of your business; the products, services or vendors they currently use, loyalty to you or your competitor's business, etc.
3. Needs or desires such as what benefits consumers look for, the basis on which they will decide whether to use your product or service, and how your business can fulfill those needs, etc.

What should my advertising say?

Once the target audience is decided and what they are looking for in terms of the product or service is offered, it is time to decide what the advertisement will say. Advertisement should always be written to communicate a message that will be seen as important by your target customer. Your advertisement should clearly and convincingly "speak" to your target audience, explaining the important benefits your that product or service offers.

In deciding how to discuss the major benefits of a product or service in the advertisement, four elements AIDA should be kept in mind, that is, to attract Attention, hold Interest, arouse Desire and motivate Action.

Where should I place my advertising?

Apart from the usual newspapers, magazines, TV, transit, today we also have Internet to advertise on.

Now, each question discussed above gives a different classification of ads, as shown in Table 1.1.

Purpose

Product or non-product

The answer to the first question gives rise to the fourth column. The reasons for advertising are numerous. It's not selling a product always. A company might advertise to build its reputation. A product is a good or service for which customers will exchange something of value. The purpose of *product advertising* is to sell the advertiser's goods or services. Services are intangible products. They include financial, legal, medical and other recreational services.

Non-product advertising constitutes institutional or corporate advertising in which the advertiser is trying to polish its image or influence public opinion about an issue. Here the aim is not to sell something, but just to let the public know that such an organization exists.

TABLE 1.1 Classification of Advertisements

Target Audience	Geographic Area	Media Used	Purpose
Consumer	International	Print	Product or non-product
Business	National	Newspaper	Commercial or non-commercial
Industrial	Regional	Magazine	Primary demand or selective demand
Trade	Local	Electronic	Direct action or Indirect action
Professional		Radio	
Agricultural		Television	
		Out-of-Home	
		Outdoor	
		Transit	
		Direct mail	
		Directories	
		Other media	

Commercial or non-commercial

Commercial versus non-commercial advertising is easy to understand. If the idea is to make a profit, it is commercial. Otherwise, it is non-commercial. Most of the ads we see are commercial.

Primary-demand and selective-demand advertising

The famous De Beers ads belong to the first category. These ads stimulate the need for a particular category and the aim is not to sell one brand. 'Diamonds Forever' was used to arouse the need for diamonds and not to sell the brand of De Beers. Associations that represent many manufacturers usually do this type of advertising. Once the need for a particular category is established, selective-demand advertising comes into picture. These ads concentrate on a particular brand of a product and try to promote it. De Beers, after it made diamond jewellery popular, went on for selective demand advertisements.

Direct-action and indirect-action advertising

Sometimes advertisements are designed to get the audience to respond immediately. These types of ads are called *direct-action* ads. Typically, these ads carry a toll-free number and sales-promotion incentives. *Indirect-action advertising* is done primarily to build awareness of the product.

Media Used

Now comes the answer to the second question. How to tell? In other words, which media to use? Popular forms of advertising include newspaper, magazine, radio, television, outdoor and transit. Television is considered to be the best medium for huge audiences across geographic regions. Today, we also have Internet but its reach is very small compared to television.

Geographic Area

Today, ads are aimed at the whole world. With the inception of the concept of 'global presence', no advertiser would waste money on reaching a small audience unless, of course, he is interested in being only a local player. In a way, the second and third question is interrelated. Usually media is decided based on the geographic coverage. Accordingly, we have international advertising, national advertising, regional advertising and local advertising. Retailers do local advertising in their areas and its scope is very narrow.

Target Audience

This is the most important criterion as there wouldn't be a more foolish thing to do than advertising to the wrong person. 'Target audience' is the word used in the industry for a specified audience or demographic group for which an advertising message is designed. The most common advertising in this category is *consumer advertising*. It is aimed at consumers of the products and the message is very simple. The idea is to make them buy goods and services. *Business advertising* aims at business institutions, non-profit organizations and government agencies. Photocopiers belong to this category. Sometimes media is common to both consumer and business advertising.

Industrial advertising targets people who buy or use the materials and services needed to conduct business or to manufacture other products, for example, Earthmoving equipment. *Trade advertising* targets intermediaries in the supply chain such as wholesalers and retailers. The objective is effective distribution of goods in the supply chain. *Professional advertising* aims at professional practitioners such as lawyers, accountants, doctors, dentists and engineers. This category of advertising may be used to persuade professionals to buy a particular product useful in their work. Recent ads about software, which would help doctors in efficient diagnosis, are an example of this category.

ADVERTISING FUNCTIONS

Advertising is one tool that can help a company to achieve goals. It is not the end, but a means to reach the end. The functions of advertising depend on the following advertising objectives:

- To make the product distinct from other competitors'. *Maggie* Noodles advertising banks on the taste and quality, which discriminates it from the other noodles.
- To communicate information. When *Maggie* Noodles advertises, it limpidly informs how it is to be cooked. The procedure of cooking is narrated step by step.
- To goad the users. The *Maggie* advertisement claims to be both healthy and tasty. By offering extra in the same amount and telling several recipes for making it, the ad pushes customers to buy the product.
- To expand the distribution. The *Maggie* initially started with production of noodles. Later, it expanded in soups and ketchup to go for wider distribution. It also made the packaging handy to expand the market.
- To encourage brand preference and loyalty. By offering a slogan of 'easy to cook and easy to eat', Maggie Noodles gave good reasons to consumers to stick to the brand. Now it has given one more offer of providing atta noodles, as Indians have penchant for the food items made of wheat flour.
- To reduce the sales cost. Different strategies for advertising were tried to achieve more sale, which would automatically reduce the cost. *Maggie* Noodles sold in small packet is an attempt to penetrate into the lower strata of society.

NGOs and other non-profit organizations use advertising for many other reasons than to sell the product. They build their image through advertising or do well to the society by taking up social issues. Adverstising functions are discussed in detail in Chapter 2.

ADVERTISING PYRAMID

The basic aim of an advertising campaign is to draw attention of the viewers or prospective customers. The whole gamut of a creative team is involved in designing an advertisement. Let us see what the advertising pyramid is and then discuss the elements involved. See Figure 1.1.

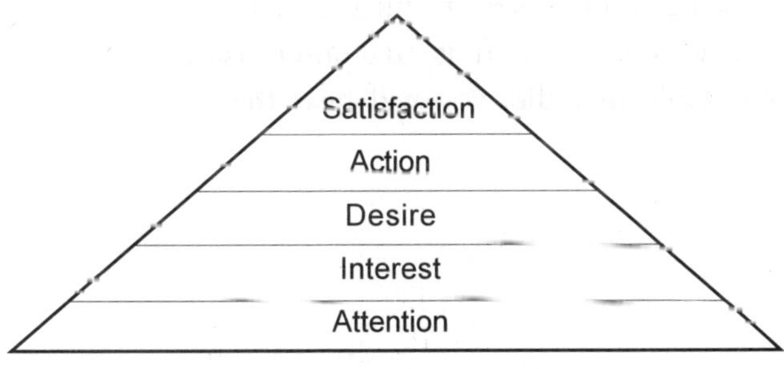

Fig. 1.1 The pyramid.

The five basic element of this pyramid are: attention, interest, desire, action, and satisfaction.

Attention

The first objective of advertising is to capture attention of the reader. This job is easy as even shouting or clapping can draw attention. For print advertisement, this task is done by the headline, as it is the first element of the advertisement to catch attention. Therefore, the copywriter usually makes the headline very catchy by using bigger fonts. The other techniques are to use short punch lines in conversational language. If abstruse language is used then the purpose will be defeated, and the reader will not read further.

'Behind every great adventure lies a great spirit', The headline for Tucson, the four wheeler is quite appealing as the reader's curiosity is raised. The second way by which attention can be caught is by using an appealing picture. Titan has been very successful by giving a picture of Aamir Khan in its advertising. Once attention is caught, the next task is to retain it by creating interest in the reader.

Interest

The advertisement's next objective is to create interest in the readers about the product. After giving a good headline, their interest is retained by further giving elaborations about the key features of the product. This is usually incorporated in the body copy. The copywriter either does it explicitly or implies them. There is less scope of exaggeration in this part, as this is more factual. But certainly, how the information is presented is important.

The copywriter stimulates interest by narrating a dramatic situation, citing a story or may be sprinkling humour. The illustrators use cartoons and pictures to generate interest. In radio, the sound effects and catchy dialogues in nasal voice may retain interest.

Desire

In this step, the advertisement creates a situation for the prospective customer to enjoy benefits of the product vicariously. The writer creates a situation that it is felt by the reader that he/she misses on something if he/she does not use the product. In print advertisement, copywriters fuel up visualization by using phrases like 'think yourself to be the most successful person', or 'imagine'. In television, the strategy used is that after using the product, the user is shown delighted and contented, while in radio, you will hear the announcer saying, "you at your best with your suiting".

The desire lays down the possibility and captivates the consumer's mind. This part is handled delicately as the writer may sometime offend the reader. Certainly, it is one of the difficult parts to write and that is why some of the copywriters omit it.

Action

The purpose of this step is to motivate people to do something. No advertisement is successful if it cannot induce any action. Several phrase like 'offer closes by 30th Jan.', ' 'buy now', 'limited stock', 'buy two, get one free' are used to motivate consumers to buy the product. This is not a difficult step because if the copy is clear then surely the reader will act. Action demanded may be explicit like 'call on us to book, the stock is limited' or implicit 'fly the friendly sky'. Sometimes the sachet of the product is attached along with the advertisement as an action inducing device.

Satisfaction

The tip of the pyramid is satisfaction. After the product is bought, the buyer should have a feel of satisfaction. He should not feel he has not got returns of his money. This parameter helps to make the customer brand loyal in the long run.

ADVERTISING TYCOONS IN INDIA

India, like any other country, has its own legends in the creative area of advertising. The Indian advertising industry has innumerable people with tremendous potential, who have contributed in different capacities to become part of world-class creative coterie. These people have not only made Indian brands popular in their own country, but have paved the way beyond their boundaries through their creative genius. The citation of this creative lot is just the representation of a larger gamut of creatives. Certainly they have those traits in them, which mark their identity as remarkably different.

In a very short stint of 23 years, **A.G. Krishnamurthy** had metamorphosed his agency from Rs 35 lakh company to a Rs 7 billion corporation. He had been contributing to his agency as the copywriter, art director as well as creative director. This is a combination of rare potential found in one entity. He had received four coveted awards—in 1995, he was named as the A&M advertising person of the year in 1997, he was inducted into the hall of fame, Ad Club, Kolkata, in 1998, he was nominated as one of the 25 key figures in the international ad industry, and in the same year he was awarded in India the Premnarayen Award by Advertising Agencies Association of India (AAAI).

A.G. Krishnamurthy

He is a man of great knowledge and skills and had been promulgating the knowledge to the variegated audience for over 45 years in the area of advertising design and communication. **Brendan Pereira** had been Brand Manager at Beecham's International, London. He had also been the creative director in Aiyars Advertising in Mumbai, which is one of the first industry to be elected to the board in that capacity. He was one of the founder of Chaitra Advertising. His contribution is multifarious in the advertising production. His book *Changing Faces*, published in 1999, has added a feather in his cap.

Brendan Pereira

Elsie Nanji began her career two decades back in O&M, and then had her experience in Lintas, Enterprise and Ambience. She has many awards to her credit, including the prestigious International Award at London and the Art Director of the Year award in India for three consecutive years. Her selection as first jury member at the Asia Pacific Adfest in Chiangmai, Thailand, in 1997, is worth mentioning.

Elsie Nanji

He is ranked at the top by *The Economic Times* as the most influential man in Indian advertising. Under his aegis O&M India has won a dozen Lions. In 2004, **Piyush Pandey** became the first Asian to be the President of the Cannes jury. He is exceptional in the area of advertising as he has 500 Indian advertising awards to his credit. Under his leadership, O&M has been named India's most creative agency nine times in the last 10 years.

Piyush Pandey

With the background of Commercial Art Diploma from J.J. Institute, **Gopi Kukde** paved his way in leading ad agencies like Chaitra, Clarion and Everest. He co-founded Advertising Avenues. His creative brilliance is reflected in the campaigns of *Asian Paints, Glaxo, Stanrose fabrics*, and *Hawkins* pressure cooker, just to name a few. He has produced and directed a number of ad films for Advertising Avenues on various brands. He too has won several CAG and Ad Club awards as a laudable sign for his creative talent.

Gopi Kukde

Ivan Arthur

Ivan Arthur has his most of the stint at Hindustan Thompson. He has been the brain behind many award-winning advertisements. Some of those advertisements are–*Air India, Sunsilk, Clinic, Hamdard, Bombay Dyeing, Handyplast, Readers Digest, Haryana Breweries,* and *Phillips.*

He was appositely chosen to be part of the CAG Hall of fame, and has been part of the international task force that designed and launched J. Walter Thompson's Total Branding Protocol that is now being used internationally.

Ivan, being a faculty member of myriad JWT international programme, has addressed different national and international advertising groups. This includes the Phillipine Advertising Congress held in Subic Bay, the Advista Advertising Congress held in Cairo and other advertising clubs in India.

He has authored two books *Once More Upon a Time* and the *Official Souvenir of Pope John Paul II's Visit to India.*

Naved Akhtar

Naved Akhtar began his career 14 years back and since then has worked in Clarion, McCann, Trikaya and Mudra Communications. He has won the Art Director of the Year Award thrice. He has got accolades for his campaigns for *Nescafe, Milkmaid, DCM Toyta, Gillett, Dunlop, Vimal, Rasna, Polo, Bata, Samsung, Yvest St. Laurent, Mitsubishi Lancer* and *Otis.*

Alyque Padamsee

In the field of Advertising, **Alyque Padamsee** has held the coveted post of Chief Executive of Lintas India, which is now one of the leading ad agencies of the country. He even went on to become the Regional Coordinator of Lintas South Asia. Known as the communications guru of India, Padmsee has built brands like *Liril, MRF, Timex, Monte Carlo, Kitply,* etc. and the sensational *Kamasutra* campaign. His most memorable character remains *Lalitaji* (*Surf*) who became a household name.

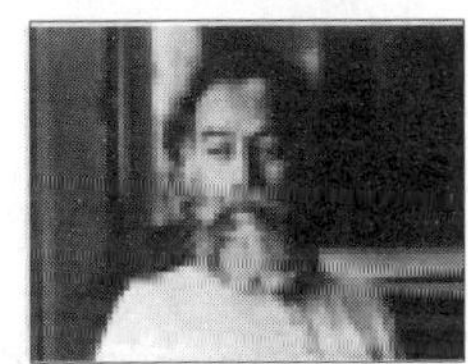
Subrata Bhowmic

Subrata Bhowmic has his name as one of India's leading graphic designers. He has over 34 years of experience in creating workable and cost-saving design solutions, which have won him more than 50 prestigious awards. This also includes 18 President's National Awards. He has experience in fields like textiles, photography, environment, graphics, book design and advertising. In advertising, he has credit of building brands such as *Cali-Cloth, Vimal, Dhara, Remanika, Deepam* and *Handloom House.* Of course, these brands are cherished and loved across by a large section of people.

Sunil Mahadik

Sunil Mahadik is a product of J.J. School, and currently holds the position of managing director and creative head of The Flagship that won the A&M Emerging Agency of the Year Award in 1996. He has won some of the most prestigious awards. In 1992, he got Bombay Ad Club's Advertising Campaign of the Year Award for *Mother's recipe pickles*. In the same year he also bagged the Art Director of the Year Award from the Communication Arts Guild (CAG). In 1996 and 1997, A&M Art director of the year was bestowed on him. Mahadik was the finalist at the International Advertising Awards, New York.

Sunil Sen

Sunil Sen is currently leading superannuated life since 1988, after having a good 33 years innings in Shilpi Advertising as Art Director. He was involved in various media like print, filmmaking, corporate exercises and book designing for different publishing houses.

An internationally reputed designer, Sen has earned several awards from both national and international organizations. In 15 years, he has won 20 National Awards in designing and printing. Commerce have honoured him, he is a recipient of International Clio Awards for various brands, and has also been honoured by the American Institute of Graphic Arts and Tokyo Chambers of commerce. His Centaur Hotel advertising won him the first prize in the Asian Advertising Congress held in Sydney, Australia, in 1977. He also received accolades for Indian typography in the Artypo exhibition.

SUMMARY

Advertising started aeons back in a very unsophisticated form when its objective was to inform. With the passage of time it has become very complicated and sophisticated. With globalization, companies have engaged in cut-throat competition hence, resultantly the importance of advertising has grown manifolds. Every product has its own way to create niche in the market. Today an individual is exposed to innumerable advertisements, and his decisions are predominantly governed by them.

Advertising is non-personal communication of information usually paid for and persuasive in nature about product, services or ideas by identified sponsors through various media. Sound and sight are two important key features in advertising through which the advertisers grab attention.

Tracing the history of advertising, it can be even seen at the cave paintings of Lascaux, which are about 16,000 years old. Earlier, advertising was used to promote two things: locations and services. Today the competition has become tough as all media are fully explored to place advertisements for the maximum reach. Internet advertising is gaining more importance than ever before.

The classification of advertisement is based on four parameters, that is, by target audience, geographic area, the media used and by purpose. An advertising campaign is designed keeping in mind the AIDAS technique, which means attention focusing on consumers' interest, desire, action and satisfaction. If an advertisement satisfies these components, it can be successful.

QUESTIONS

1. How is advertising important in today's scenario? What if it is completely obliterated from society?
2. Identify the three main purposes of advertising.
3. Write down name of minimum 20 places where you have seen something being advertised.
4. Define advertising. Justify Norman Douglas' statement, "You can tell the ideals of a nation by its advertising".
5. Examine the advantages and disadvantages of personal selling vis-à-vis advertising.
6. Separate the following brands according to their advertisements being primarily sound-dependent or sight-dependent:
   Amul, Colgate, Johnsons & Johnson's Baby Powder, Radio Mirchi, Close-Up, Mastercard, Allianz, Hutch, Airtel, Johnny Walker and Intel.
7. Identify five product categories that can be classified for having induced differentiation. Using them, explain the role induced differentiation plays in advertising.
8. Why should sponsors identify themselves in an advertisement?
9. Examine the following advertisements in view of the AIDAS technique.

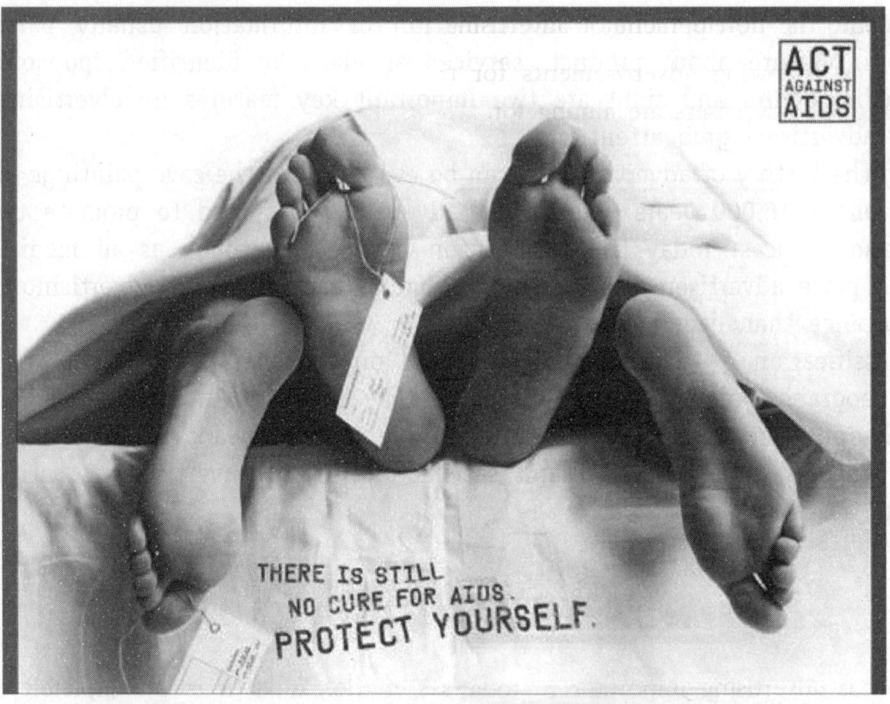
ACT AGAINST AIDS
THERE IS STILL
NO CURE FOR AIDS.
PROTECT YOURSELF.

BAJAJ
Inspiring Confidence
BAJAJ
AVENGER DTS-i
Feel like God
Feel empowered with the 180 cc DTS-i* engine, 16.5 bhp
Feel supreme with ExhausTEC* Technology
Feel immortal with a 5-year warranty*
Feel above all with just Rs. 60,000**

10. Compare the development of advertising in India and abroad in the 20th century.
11. Use the following advertisements for the two Coca-Cola products to compare the market the advertisers are aiming for.

12. Whom do you consider as the man in the advertising world? What characteristics in that individual have made him so significant in this arena?

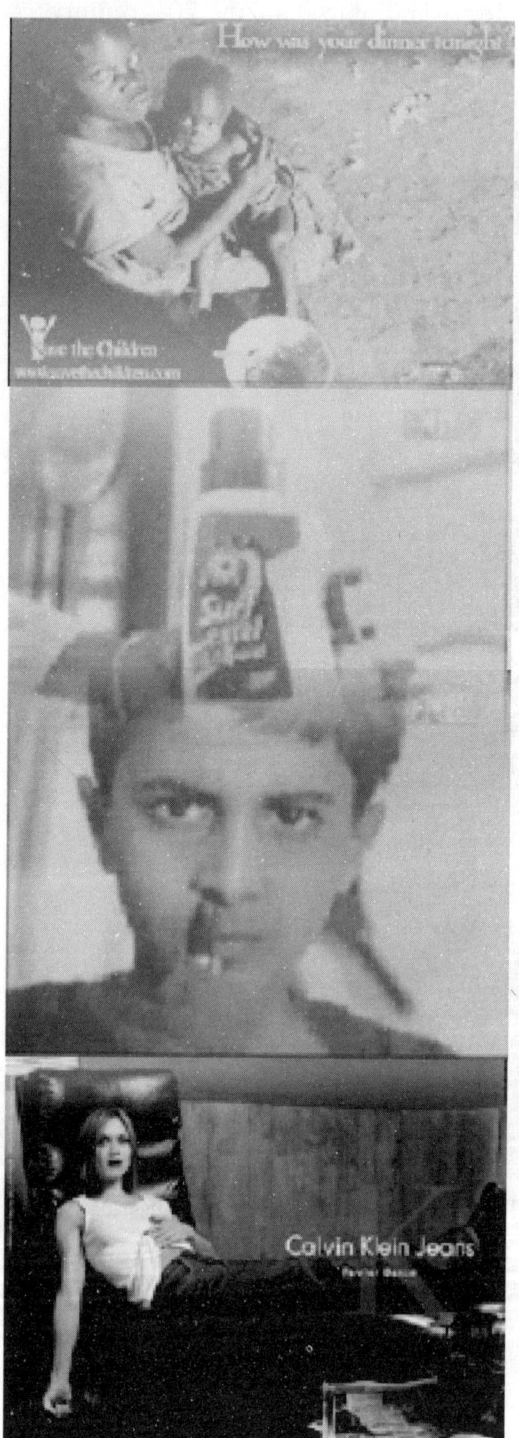

CHAPTER 2

Advertising and Society

LEARNING OBJECTIVES

After reading this chapter, you will be able to:

- Understand the impact of ads on society.
- Study the impact of ads on children and women.
- Learn the ethics in advertising in terms of practices like puffery, surrogate advertising and shock advertising.
- Know the regulatory bodies in advertising.
- Understand how self-regulation works.
- Know what is socially responsible advertising.

The ads for Kamasutra condoms that appeared on television in the early 1990s, featuring Pooja Bedi and Marc Robinson, were in the news, provoking a lot of discussion. When the second TV commercial came along in 1998 starring Viveka Babaji, it could be shown on satellite channels at select timings. Soon, competing brands like Durex began featuring similar ads. Added to this was the fact that the permitted broadcasting times were limited, and Kamasutra condoms ads needed a change in design.

In a campaign starting 2002, the agency Ambience D' Arcy came up with a campaign featuring a number of everyday situations with slightly suggestive overtones, followed by a voice-over saying, "So what are you thinking of?" as a character breaks into a grin and the screen splits to show a pack of Kamasutra condoms on one side.

A number of questions are thrown up by the entire scenario:

- *Do you think it is socially responsible to market condoms without referring to advantages such as birth-control or prevention of AIDS?*
- *Do you think ad campaigns similar to the "So what are you thinking of?" one would affect young viewers?*
- *What do you think would be the ideal media strategy (in what media and at what times) that a campaign for condoms should choose?*

Source: *The Strategist, November 11, 2003. raymondindia.com.*

IMPACT OF ADVERTISING

Advertising has become a ubiquitous world surrounding us, virtually all the time and everywhere. If you count the number of advertisements you encounter each day, the number might reach an astonishing figure. Many a times ads create the need of the products, which customers actually don't need. "Advertising is a non-moral force, like electricity, which not only illuminates but electrocutes. Its worth to civilization depends upon how it is used", said William Bernbach

Many of the products hawked at us are trivial, self-indulgent and sometimes, even harmful. Even if advertising doesn't literally create wants, it seems undisputable that ads often exploit and manipulate our existing psychological needs and desires like security, conformity, sex, power, etc. So by manipulating our needs and desires, are advertisers controlling so as to violate our autonomy?

The Benefits of Advertising

Numerous material and human resources are devoted to advertising. It is practically everywhere today. No one can escape the influence of advertising. Even when an individual is not directly exposed to a particular form of advertising, he confronts the society which is highly influenced by good and ill of advertising messages. Many critics condemn advertising as waste of time, talent and money, as it is essentially a parasitic activity. This is not true. Advertising has significant potential for good, but it depends on the realization. Following are the benefits of advertising:

Economic benefits

Advertising plays a significant role in the economic system guided by moral principles, which contributes to human development. It is a necessary part of the functioning of modern market economies, which exist and are emerging in the rest of the world conforming to the moral standards so as to do good to the human kind.

In such a system, advertising can be a useful tool for sustaining honest and ethically responsible competition that contributes to economic growth in the human development. Advertising helps by informing people about availability of rationally desired new products and services, and improvements in existing products. This abreast them of the information about the product and let them take the prudent decision, contributing to efficiency and the lowering of prices, thus stimulating economic progress through expansion of business and trade. All this contributes to the generation of new jobs, higher incomes and comfortable and humane way of living.

Political benefits

Political advertising can make contribution to democracy analogous to its contribution to economic well-being in a market system guided by moral norms. It can quash monopolization. Political advertising makes a significant contribution by informing people about the candidate along with the policies and party proposals, including the new candidates who had not contested before. Citizens can make their political choices and can be assured that the candidates are accountable and can be replaced through peaceful means when appropriate. The 'India Shinning' campaign by BJP had updated Indians about their motto.

Cultural benefits

Advertising has tremendous impacts on media that depend on it for revenue. Advertisers have an opportunity to exert positive influence on decisions about media content. This is done by supporting material of excellent intellectual, aesthetic and moral quality presented with the public interest in view, and by encouraging and making media presentations, which are oriented to minorities whose need might otherwise go unreserved.

Moreover, advertising can contribute to the betterment of society by uplifting and inspiring people and motivating them to act in ways that benefit themselves and others. Advertising can brighten lives simply by being witty, tasteful and entertaining. It is an art with vivacity and élan of its own.

Moral and religious benefits

In many cases, benevolent social institutions including those of religious nature use advertising to communicate messages of faith, patriotism, tolerance, compassion, charity, health and education. Sometimes advertising generates constructive and helpful messages that educate and motivate people in a variety of beneficial ways.

Nevertheless, the obverse side of it can't be neglected. Though there is nothing intrinsically bad or good about advertising, it is an instrument and much depends on how it is used. It can have positive and beneficial results or a negative and harmful impact on individuals of society. According to Ogilvy, "Advertising is pretentious and incomprehensible nonsense. It is designed only to win creative awards".

We all know that advertising has become an indispensable commodity and its need is steadily increasing in the modern society. There are other areas of study as well which fall under the criticism like news media, journalism, cinema etc., but most conspicuous of all is advertising. The nebbish lot of audience has already accepted advertising as incorrigible. But then, the scenario is not so lugubrious. If enough attention is given to the harm done by advertising to different strata of society, adequate action to rectify it can also be initiated.

Advertising exists mainly for two purposes: to provide customers with the information of price and availability of goods and the other, also the most important, is to introduce customers to new products which they either need or want. Advertisers exploit this second purpose so much that they go the extent of exaggerating the information.

Even if they do not create non-existent needs, it is generally agreed that advertisers exploit people's existing psychological needs. It is here that the critical aspect of responsibility comes into the picture. There are ads which are socially irresponsible, and yet others that are responsible, emphasizing certain admirable values in a viewer, if only subconsciously.

Although ads have a number of benefits, they are a tool in the hands of the advertiser, and so, much depends on how they are used. Therefore, it is important for the public to be generally sensitive to how ethical or responsible ads are. Regulatory bodies also exist to check that ads adhere to responsible limits.

One of the areas where responsibility in ads is required is that which concerns children. The new-age children are avid followers of the mass media and are very likely to be influenced by it. Children are an increasingly influential section of consumers, while at the same time being susceptible to influences by advertising. The impact of ads on children, therefore, is an important area of concern.

THE IMPACT OF ADS ON CHILDREN

It is generally understood in today's world that children form a major segment of the customers of many companies. It is said that they have greater purchasing power—both in terms of pocket money and their ability to convince their parents to make a purchase for them.

As a consequence, a large number of ads are aimed at children and focus on the parent-child relationship. Because children lack the analytical abilities and judgement of adults, advertising directed to children raises special concerns. For instance, children may be unable to evaluate the accuracy of information they view, and judge the difference in entertainment and marketing, because the content and advertising are seamlessly integrated.

Children are Impressionable

An advertisement for *Thumbs Up* showing bungee jumping was talked about when some children got encouraged to emulate the stunts. The recent *Chatar Patar* ad shows a young girl—having had the sweet and getting into the mood for straight talk–tells her grandmother that her mother would like to attend on her so that her property would be bequeathed to their family. While such ads may be clever and effective, they might send out wrong messages to children. An ad for kid stain from *Surf Excel* shows children soiling their dresses in such a manner that you cannot stop your children doing the same.

The Hero cycles ad focussing on children.

Suggestive ads that are seen by children who are not old enough to understand what they are seeing might create confusion in their minds. In short, children are impressionable and therefore, admen should be extra careful about what they're saying in their advertisements. In countries like Sweden, UK, USA, Norway, Germany, Finland Greece, England and France, strict guidelines exist for ads targeted at children. Advertisers are expected to:

- Take into account knowledge, sophistication, and maturity levels of the target audience
- Not exploit the imaginative quality of children
- Communicate information truthfully and accurately
- Capitalize on the potential of advertising to influence social behaviour in a positive way
- Contribute to the parent-child relationship in a constructive way.

Such stringent guidelines would be useful in India as well.

However, some socially responsible groups may advertise for good causes. For example, look at the ad that exhorts the world to save children.

A socially responsible advertisement for an organization for children's welfare.

An ad of this sort is socially responsible. It features children in a realistic sense, creating awareness about the condition of children in certain places and highlighting the need for everyone to play an active part in helping them.

WOMEN AND ADVERTISING

The importance of advertising is evident in Steuart H. Britt's statement where an analogy is driven with the help of women, i.e. "doing business without advertising is like winking an eye at a girl in dark, only you know what you are doing and no one else". The advertising world has portrayed the woman in numerous ways and forms over a period of time. The impressions of woman have changed, depending upon the business scenario, the marketer, the creative instinct of advertising agencies and the customer. As we know today, advertising governs our lives to a great extent. It won't be an exaggeration if we say that advertising generates the need of the product, which we otherwise do not require, through its soft sell strategy. We have more penchant for the advertisements which depict women. It has been observed that women endorse 80 per cent of the advertisements.

The new genre of advertising has metamorphosed image of the woman. She is at the centre of all advertisements launched on electronic, print or outdoor media. If we close our eyes and recall any advertisement, myriad of ad will conjure up with innumerable images of women, be it an advertisement for automobiles, dress materials, cologne, toiletries, etc. Some directors have a gut feeling that an advertisement endorsed by women accelerates the chance of making it successful. Some lambaste by calling it an answer to prurient desire; others call it beauty. The interpretations vary but undoubtedly, the role of women is indispensable in advertisements. Earlier, the woman was considered as a weak sex, dominated by her male counterpart, and therefore remained hidden in her carapace. Even if required, she was only depicted as an ornament and object of decoration, further labelling her emotionally weak. She was hardly encouraged to cross the threshold of home, and her desires were quashed in the boundaries of four walls.

Today, woman is not only considered as the epitome of alabasterine beauty, but her demand in advertising is rapidly increasing as well. Glamour is best coruscated by women. She is an embodiment of tradition and no ad is complete if the emotional appeal is underscored without a woman, as she plays a pivotal role in the family affairs.

Portrayal of Women in Advertising

Each advertisement reflects the limpid projection of the ideal man or the ideal woman. A man is usually depicted as brawny, powerful, rich, confident and athletic. Contrarily, for women messages share a common theme, that is, she must be beautiful. Advertising, of course, did not invent the notion that the woman should be valued as ornaments; women have always been measured against cultural ideals of beauty. However, advertising has joined forces with sexism to make images of beauty ideal, more pervasive and more unattainable than ever before.

The Iron Maiden

Naomi Wolf, in her book, *The Beauty Myth,* compares the contemporary ideal of beauty to the Iron Maiden, a medieval torture device that enclosed its victims in a spike-lined box painted red with a woman's image. Like the Iron Maiden, the beauty ideal enforces conformity to a single, rigid shape. And both cause suffering, and even death, to their victims. The immaculate depiction of the Iron Maiden is, in fact, an illusion created by infucation done by artists, photographers and photo retouchers. Each image is painstakingly worked over. Teeth and eyeballs are bleached white, and blemishes, wrinkles and stray hairs are airbrushed away. In some cases, a picture is actually an amalgam of body parts of several different models—a mouth from one and limbs from the other. By inviting women to compare their unimproved reality with the Iron Maiden's honed perfection, advertising erodes self-esteem and then offers to sell it back for exorbitant price.

Women come in an endless array of shapes and sizes, but you'd never know it by looking at advertisements. In every generation, advertisers issue a new paradigm of female perfection. The very rigidity of the ideal guarantees that most women will fall outside of it, creating a gap between what women are and what they should be. This gap is very lucrative for the purveyors of commercialized beauty. Tragically, millions of women sacrifice their health and even life to conform to the shape of the Iron Maiden.

Circumscribed Views of Women

Advertisements present unrealistic images of women's faces and bodies just as insidiously as they present highly circumscribed views of women's lives. Even the time when women were entering the workforce in unprecedented numbers, advertisements failed to depict a significant increase in women's employment outside the house. It was felt that women in advertisements were apt to be portrayed in traditional female roles: cooking, cleaning and caring for children.

A quarter-century after the rebirth of the women's movement, women in advertisements are still depicted as housewives obsessed with ring around the collar and spots on the dishes. If they work outside the home, they are presented as super moms who cook, clean, take care of the kids and then slip into something sexy with the help of the brand advertised.

Object of Desire

Perhaps the most banal sexually exploitative advertisements are those that display women's bodies to sell products. The advertisements are ubiquitous. The use of women's bodies in advertisements is essentially a cheap ruse that marketers use instead of making more thoughtful arguments on behalf of their products. The mechanism used in these advertisements is quite simple. The svelte attractive figures are employed to grab attention and stimulate desire, which advertisers expect to be transferred to the product. You have preposterous preposition to buy the beer and get the girl. The women's bodies are equated with commodities, and presented as the rewards of consumption.

By instructing men to regard women's bodies as objects, advertisements create an atmosphere that devalues women as people, and encourage sexual harassment; plethora of advertisements take the dehumanization of women, a step further by focusing on body parts, for example, a pair of shapely female legs emerges from a box of cereal. A woman's torso is juxtaposed against a photo of a new Skoda Octavia rider, where you are invited to admire the curves of both. Women in these advertisements are not even whole objects rather they have been reduced to an assemblage of dismembered parts. Advertisements of this nature degrade women, and men are demeaned too. For one thing, exploitative advertisements insult men's intelligence.

Men's bodies too are no longer immune from exploitation in advertising. Recent years have seen a veritable deluge of exotic photos in advertisements glorifying men's muscles, torsos, backs and thighs. Women are accepting that they like men's bodies and that is represented in the advertisement of *blue Riband*. Now men have to be more vigilant and conscious to keep themselves in shape. Many men are queasy about being held to the standard presented in the advertisements, the same way women have been presented for generations. Women's nudity has proliferated in advertisements and other media, but male nudity has remained off-limits. However, the partial nudity is certainly visible in the *Jockey* advertisement.

The Role of Indian Women Vis-à-Vis Men

The battle of the sexes ended long ago. That's what it seems with advertising being neutral for both. Is advertising different for men and women? If it is, what has led to it?

India is a patriarchal country, with almost everything centred on the adult Indian male—even communication. This is evident in beauty cream advertisements where there has to be a male to appreciate beauty. Hasn't all this changed? The roles have. With the woman stepping out of the house and beyond, it wasn't long before marketers started revamping their ad campaigns. In the earlier talcum powder advertisements there used to be a woman coming out the shower and casually applying the talc. A woman now steps out of home carrying the talc in her purse and using it whenever she feels like. This is just one of the changes that advertising has undergone.

To put it empathetically, Women were stereotyped in advertising. They were featured in Nycil or Dettol advertisements taking care of children's wounds and soothing them. This was true in other media vehicles as well. If we ever paid attention to radio advertisements there was always a lilting feminine voice endorsing a brand. As for television, women view it for longer hours. No wonder that cosmetics and grocery brands are heavily advertised during the daytime. Based on this, we might as well assume that shaving creams advertisements are aired at night. That is a wrong assumption because it is the woman who purchases even toiletries for men.

Women make up over two-thirds of the adult viewing audience on weekday afternoons, the programmes that traditionally include soap operas. The only time of the week when men routinely form the largest proportion of the viewing audience is during sports telecasts on weekend afternoons. Prime time evening audiences are more evenly divided, but women viewers still outnumber men.

Complementary to the concept that television viewing is a gendered activity, is the advertisers' awareness that consumer behaviour is also gendered. Men and women have been conditioned to purchase different products in different ways for different reasons. As a result, most advertisers carefully purchase time for their commercials during programmes watched by the particular target audience they consider most likely to buy. For example, during cricket matches and other sport events you would see advertisements of Kingfisher and Foster. On the other hand, during a cookery show like *Khana Khazana*, you would see advertisements of Everest masalas, cookware or groceries like Pillsbury atta, Dhara, Mawana sugar, etc.

It is quite evident that the roles of men and women have changed. The world of the Indian woman is no longer limited to the four walls of her house and the Indian male has his role in household chores. Advertisers are taking notice of this metamorphosis as depicted in the Ariel and where a father is shown cleaning his child's dirty t-shirt or take for instance "the woman of substance" as portrayed by Femina advertisements–independent and head on!

Advertisements have taken a step forward by identifying what women view as masculinity and vice versa. This is what can be called **Gendered advertising**–smaller in some respects to customized advertising. Advertisers want viewers to enjoy their commercials and to associate the advertised products with a comfortable reinforcing picture of mainstream cultural values. As a result, commercials are designed to take optimal advantage of gender-specific fantasies, myths and fears. The 'Raymond Man' is almost a dream come true for a woman. The ad plays out her fantasies and becomes aspiration for men.

Portrayal of Women in Indian Advertisements

We cannot allow ourselves to be taken in by clever advertising where the woman is portrayed as a decision-maker for the kind of food the children should eat, for the kind of cereals the family takes at breakfast or the brand of clothes they wear. How often do we see an advertisement where the woman makes choice for herself? It is only when she is single and does not have a family to think of, that she thinks of herself, about her choice of soft-drink, her brand of clothes or her toiletries. Once she is married and becomes a mother, there is no room for her to make a choice for herself. Even the brand of balm that she should use for her backache has to be literally forced upon her by her mother-in-law and in turn, her husband.

Actually, Indian women have been traditionally groomed to take all pains and problems with a smile on their lips. It is considered a divine task to take care of one's family. The traditional Indian grooming makes women think that if they put that small little problem of headache, backache or the chest pain into the darkest corner of their minds, they will be able to chase it away with their will power. But will power does not work without medical help as in the case of all other human beings. Women often live in a fools' paradise believing that mere grit and will power will fade all pains and problems into oblivion.

This unquestioning and docile image of a woman where she should not think of her own comfort has been brought about by our inherent traditions, but it is time women began to realize that they owe it to themselves and their families to take care of themselves.

Stereotyping

Many ads tend to stereotype women—portraying them either as objects of attraction or in the role of mother, wife, etc. Also, many a time women in business are depicted to have as masculine characteristics, which denies them their specific gifts of insight, compassion and understanding.

Calvin Klein: An ad that tends to objectify and stereotype woman.

The irrelevant featuring of skimpily dressed women in ads for products ranging from biscuits to ice creams stereotypes women. Another effect of such ads is to give undue importance to attractiveness, creating anxiety in women who feel that they aren't as attractive as the women in the ads.

There are also a few ads which objectify women. Ads of Calvin Klein have invited criticism for portraying women in suggestive postures. Likewise, the Hindware ads featuring skimpily-clad women—totally irrelevant to the product—use women to sell the product.

Women's Self-image

The anxiety girls and women experience from feeling unattractive is arguably one of the most pervasive and damaging consequences of advertising. It is widely acknowledged that the body type glorified in most ads (a body type almost unattainable by most women) is an unhealthy one, and that in trying to achieve it women may become anorexic. Further, photographs of models used in ads are digitally or otherwise altered to achieve "perfection". This creates an endless demand for cosmetics and other such products, as the buyers get desperate to achieve that unattainable perfection. It is not hard to imagine that a woman's self-esteem might suffer when faced with these images of "perfectly" beautiful women day in and day out.

The "perfect" body type portrayed by most ads is difficult for most women to attain and may therefore, harm their self-image.

One study revealed that women who view the media's image of beauty as ideal are more likely than any other group to have a very negative body image (Pinhas et al. 1999). Still, relatively responsible ads may exist. For example, Donna Karen the ad is quite fair to both men and women, working against a stereotype that style is a "girl-thing".

An ad going against a stereotype relating to women and style.

ETHICS IN ADVERTISING

Advertising is a competitive world and the ethics involved will always be debated on. Some controversial aspects of advertising are discussed below:

Puffery

Puffery is the exaggerated fantastical or impossible claims. These claims are usually meant to appeal some hidden psychological need. This is legal and generally a successful ad technique. For example, a cosmetic ad says: "So beautiful that other women would want to kill you!" In a way, this technique is a harmless hyperbole. By definition, puffery does not mislead reasonable consumers.

Now, does the FIAT ad guarantee that the driver never gets hurt if an accident happens or it just means that it's probably safer than other cars?

The Nivia ad which says, "There are only three steps between you and beautiful skin", is just an exaggeration as beauty is only natural and cannot be achieved by any steps whatsoever!

Besides exaggeration, puffery entertains. Consumers know better than believing a sunscreen lotion ad trying to prove that the lotion is as good as an umbrella against the sun. Even if puffery's only function were to entertain, that would be a sufficient reason not to discourage it.

Puffery also informs consumers as well as promotes product quality. Before a consumer can buy a product, he/she must be made aware of the product. One function of advertising is to create such awareness. In this age of vivid video images and electronic sounds, sellers must compete hard for consumers' attention. Puffery is one benign means that the advertisers use to grab that attention. If firms are discouraged from placing in their ads the most dry factual claims, consumers will be forced to spend more time and resources discovering which products are available.

One consequence will be diminished product innovation. Because consumers are more familiar with established products than with the new one, puffery is pivotal to the marketing of new products. Fewer resources will be devoted to product innovation if firms encounter greater legal risks in bringing new products to consumers' attention. As fewer products are introduced into the market, established products will face less intense competition.

Shock Ads

As the name suggests, these ads try to captivate the audience with a shock, usually by a picture and sometimes just a shocking message. Shock advertisers tend to measure success by the controversy their campaigns generate. Whether the ads turn people on or off is immaterial. It should essentially succeed in gathering their attention and sales that follow.

Advertising deliberately appeals to motives such as envy, status and lust. Some advertisers consciously seek to shock and titillate by exploiting content of a morbid, perverse pornographic nature. This type of advertising was launched in the late 1960s. It was found that the hoi polloi was unaffected by the advertisement based on the old school of ad making. Those ads establishing the product's unique selling proposition and carefully building brand loyalty were at the moribund. The advertisement tried to paralyze the psyche of people by being sharp and trenchant enough to puncture the viewer's consciousness and arresting him fully. Cocktail of thousands of messages were repeated to aggregate the effect, but still they failed to be understood. Commercial messages came faster and more obliquely, but the modern media consumer was hard to impress. This attitude gave rise to the so-called **shock advertising**. For ads to work, the ad men conceded that they are to be rare and juicy to leave the audience hornswoggled.

Shock advertisers tend to measure success by the controversy their companies generate. Shock advertising least cares for morality. They advertise for the sake of provocation. The advertisement for United Colour of Benetton showing a priest kissing a nun on the lips—hovering between the chaste kiss of friendship and something sexier–or a new born child covered in blood and mucus, still with its umbilical cord intact, provoked controversial reactions. The shocks received from the advertising can be at three levels: visceral shock, intellectual shock and soul shock. In visceral shock, the advertisement is projected in a way to shock the viewer at the gut level. It bypasses the brain and evokes an involuntary response. It either scares, sickens or turns the consumer on. Few years ago, portraying skimpily dressed woman could shock the public, but now concepts of have changed drastically; you can see nude models on billboards and it doesn't affect the public. The fashion retailer French Connection recently discovered that while you can't use the four-letter word in a mainstream magazine, the word *fcuk* is just fine. And everyone reading the word know what it means, so you can produce commercials that say, "fcuk fashion" and "fcuk advertising". However, visceral shock is getting harder to create the desired effect in a culture where surreal, violent and erotic imagery blend in all advertisements.

Now the current trend in advertising is to not to go for gut but for the head. This is what is called **intellectual shock**, which upsets the expectations of readers and viewers. Selling to the current generation requires real finesse so that the viewers are temporarily paralyzed and unexpected mixed messages create great effect. The advertisement for 'Death Cigarettes' fall into this category where the visual is all black and the outcome of smoking it is inevitably death.

The third category of shock advertising is **soul shock** which goes beyond titillation. These advertisements are not just clever or coy, but deeply unsettling Horde of advertisements for United Colors of Benetton–an African guerrilla holding a Kalashnikov and a human leg bone, a boat overcrowded with Albanian refugees, a car with a corpse burning inside it after a Mafia bombing rock our values. There is probably something immoral about such ads that inure people to the suffering of other people. Today the shock advertisement has crossed the threshold of human psychology as now we can be titillated and amused but never really be shocked, since to be shocked requires innocence which is rarely found in people today.

This ad by United Colours of Benetton has a picture of Albanian refugees trying to board an already overcrowded ship. For people who are not aware of its cause, this could just be a picture that captured their attention, but for Albanians it could be both touching and an infuriating ad.

Weasel Claim

A **weasel claim** is a claim that contains a weasel word or a word that practically negates the claim that was intended for the product.

The word 'probably' is a weasel word and the entire claim hinges on it. Hence an overall impression is created of an extremely successful opening for the car.

Another, subtle example of a weasel claim is shown in the beano ad. The word 'helps' is the weasel word here.

A weasel claim that hinges on the word 'probably'.

A weasel claim—Note the word "helps".

Subliminal Advertising

The term 'subliminal' means 'below the limen' or below the threshold of consciousness. The idea is that certain things are heard, seen or felt that never reach our conscious thought processes, but may still be recorded somewhere in our subconscious mind and have an impact on our decisions and behaviour. Advertising professionals use this concept to hide images within advertisements, and that these images manipulate our behaviour without our even realizing we have seen them. Psychologists have studied this phenomenon since the late 1800s, and originally called it **subception**. However, while this is a real psychological phenomenon, all research on this topic indicates that subliminal stimulation is incapable of affecting our purchasing behaviour.

Kingfisher: A subliminal ad.

While these ads are a fun topic of discussion, there is no evidence that advertisers embed hidden images in advertisements. Moreover, such efforts would be a waste of time.

The subliminal adverts are unethical and can be considered to breach professional guidelines. In some countries they may also be illegal. Legal restrictions tend to apply to TV transmissions rather than to printed ads. The ads in question can be sexy, cheeky, rude, disturbing, distressing, crude, cynical, depressing and occasionally humorous. Quite often, if one looks at them superficially, they appear boring.

The ad is one of the most popular examples of subliminal advertising. Whether the ad actually has what it claims in the ad is a mystery to this day. Nevertheless, it is possible. There have been such ads time and again despite of the warnings of the regulatory authorities.

Surrogate Advertising

In India, according to the seventh rule of the Cable Television Networks Rules, 1999, no ad shall be permitted which promotes directly or indirectly the sale or consumption of cigarettes, tobacco products, wine, alcohol, liquor or other intoxicants, infant milk substitution, feeding bottles or infant food.

Surrogate advertising uses a promotion for a particular product but evokes associations of another product for which the brand may be more famous.

Brands like Aristocrat whisky, 8 PM, Whitehall, Smirnoff vodka, Hayward's, Royal Challenge, Kingfisher and Charms cigarettes have been selling a range of products from audio cassettes and CDs to darting kits, golf accessories and water under these brand names. For example, Royal Challenge is one of the most popular brands of beer in India and in its ads it sells mineral water under the same brand name. A viewer would automatically associate the ad with the other product, i.e. the beer.

Though some broadcasters had decided to withdraw surrogate ads of liquor and cigarette brands, sources say that the liquor lobby has been working overtime to prevent a ban on surrogate advertising.

Royal Stag: Mega movies is mentioned in the ad, but the associations evoked are different.

Another instance of surrogate advertising is the Royal Stag mega movies. The point is that advertising that encourages consumption of alcohol, cigarettes and other intoxicants can be harmful to society even if it is suggesting rather than explicitly advocating the consumption of the same. Young viewers are susceptible to such suggestions and may get addicted to such products.

Social and Economic Effects of Advertising

Advertising is viewed as a mirror of society, influenced and shaped by the culture and society. Technological developments, social, economic and political conditions influence the society and, as a consequence impact what is contained in advertising. For example, economic conditions have been regarded as important historic forces that have influenced society, industry, educational system, politics and religion. Advertising is part of the changing social, economic and cultural environment, and its visuals are created in a way that they reflect those changes which people would want to adjust themselves to. Another way of linking advertising and its visuals to society and culture is the cultural approach to advertising. Cultural historians argue that advertising is an important window through which different aspects of society and culture can be explained. Also, the advertising itself can be explained to determine how it might have been shaped by society. This approach recognizes advertising not only as a window to culture, but also as a mirror that reflects the culture, or rather cultures.

Advertising should be recognized as an important social influence and should be identified with one of the most pervasive forces in our life, the force of economic abundance. With this the most critical point on the functioning of society shifts from production to consumption. So, the culture must be reoriented to convert the producer's culture into consumer's culture. Advertising appeals primarily to consumer's desires. The social effect of advertising, is, in parallel but broader sense, to make the individual like what he gets–to enforce already existing attitudes, to diminish the range and variety of choices, and, in terms of abundance, to exalt the materialistic virtues of consumption. Customers argue that advertising should be directed to the stimulation or even the exploitation of materialistic drives and then to the standardization of these drives as accepted criteria of social value. In other words, advertising is part of the social, cultural and business environment, and its achievement depends on the ability of the advertiser to predict and react to a changing society.

The mass media have an important role in modern democratic society as the main channel of communication. The population relies on the news media as the main source of information and the basis on which they form their opinions and voting decisions. Any selection of messages in the mass media has a profound effect on the entire society.

CODES OF ETHICS

Ethics are systems of moral principles that help us determine right from wrong, good from bad. Following are a few guidelines to help people working in advertising agencies do the right thing in daily life or when faced with a conflict of interest:

- Advertisement carried shall be so designed as to conform to the laws of the country and should not offend morality, decency and religious susceptibilities of the viewers.
- Advertisements must not be directed towards any religious or political end.

- No advertisement shall contain references, which are likely to lead the public to infer that the product advertised, or any of its ingredients has some special or miraculous or supernatural property.
- The picture and the audible matter of the advertisement shall not be excessively 'loud'.
- No advertisement which endangers the safety of children or creates in them any interest in unhealthy practices or shows them begging or in an undignified or indecent manner shall be carried out.
- Indecent, vulgar, suggestive, repulsive or offensive themes or treatment shall be avoided in all advertisements.

Regulatory Bodies

All advertisements have to pass through the norms laid by the regulatory authorities. Regulation affects virtually every step in the advertising process, including protecting the product with a trademark, creating the message, showing the product in action and announcing a special sale. The following regulatory bodies provide an important check on advertisers, seeing to it that they do not advertise in ways that are deceptive or otherwise socially irresponsible.

- Federal Trade Commission
- Food and Drug Administration
- Federal Communication Commission
- Advertising Review Council
- Children's Advertising Review Unit
- Advertising Standard Authority

Federal Trade Commission

The Federal Trade Commission (FTC), established in 1915, is an independent agency of US Government with its main objective to keep American business competition free and fair. It constitutes of five-member jury, under the supervision of other governmental agencies. It was part of the programme to check the growth of monopoly and preserve competition as an effective regulator of the business.

The main duty of FTC is to promote competition through the enforcement of certain antitrust laws, to prevent the dissemination of false and deceptive advertising of goods, drugs, curative devices and cosmetics, and to investigate the workings of business and keep Congress and the public informed of the efficiency of such distrust legislation as exists as well as the practices and situations that may call for legislation.

The FTC enforces federal antitrust and consumer protection laws by investigating complaints against individual companies initiated by consumers, business, inquiries or report in media. The commission seeks to ensure that the nation's markets function comparatively by eliminating unfair or deceptive practices.

Food and Drug Administration

Under the jurisdiction of the Department of Health and Human Services, the Food and Drug Administration (FDA) has authority over the labelling, packaging, branding, ingredient listing and advertising of packaged foods and drug products. The FDA is authorized to require caution and warning labels on potentially hazardous products, and also has limited authority over nutritional claims made in food advertising. This agency has the authority to set rules for promoting these products and the power to seize food and drugs on charge of false and misleading advertising. Another regulatory area where the FDA has been heavily involved is the advertising and promotion of tobacco products.

Federal Communications Commission

The Federal Communications Commision (FCC), founded in 1934 to regulate broadcast communication, has jurisdiction over the radio, television, telephone and telegraph industries. The FCC has the authority to license broadcast stations as well as to remove a license or deny renewal to stations not operating in public's interest.

Advertising Review Council

As a part of the Entertainment Software Rating Board's self-regulatory mission, the Advertising Review Council (ARC) monitors all advertising, promotional and marketing materials for interactive entertainment software products that are released to the public. This includes print ads, packaging, radio and TV spots, Internet advertising, online stores, posters and demos.

The ARC's goal is to ensure that interactive entertainment software publishers follow standardized requirements for the display of rating information and that advertising content is responsible, appropriate, truthful and accurate. The council also implements marketing guidelines that prohibit game publishers from targeting audiences for whom products are not appropriate. Some of the principles adopted by the ARC are as follows:

- An advertisement should accurately reflect the nature and content of the product it represents and the rating issued.
- All advertisements should be created with a sense of responsibility towards the public.
- No advertisement should contain any content that is likely to create serious or widespread offense to the average consumer.

Children's Advertising Review Unit

Children's Advertising Review Unit (CARU) is recognized as the primary self-regulatory body with a success rate of over 95 per cent in resolving issues regarding advertising to children. In fact, CARU has received high praise from the FTC, whose Deputy Director for the Bureau of Consumer Protection, C. Lee Peeler, has stated: "As an advertising law enforcement official, I have always found it remarkable that, in the name of self-regulation, major national advertisers would voluntarily modify or discontinue their advertising to meet CARU's standards that sometimes go beyond existing law. CARU's twenty-five years of success demonstrates a sustained commitment to effective self-regulation".

CARU reviews and evaluates advertising claims for truth and accuracy, and compliance with CARU's guidelines, which, because of children's developing cognitive abilities, set standards that are higher than the law requires. It helps to ensure that commercials or advertisements directed to children contain responsible and positive social messages.

CARU has traditionally systematically monitored only English language advertisements directed to children. Now, with its new capability, CARU will be conducting the same systematic monitoring in Spanish language media.

Advertising Standards Authority

Advertising Standards Authority Inc. (ASA), previously known as Committee of Advertising Practice, was formed early in 1973 and incorporated in late 1990. In March 1988, ASA established a separate self-regulatory body called the Advertising Standards Complaints Board (formerly known as the Advertising Standards Council) to administer the Codes of Practice in New Zealand. Its three main functions are to:

- Adjudicate on complaints received about advertisements which may be in breach of the codes of practice.
- Advise the ASA on interpretation of the codes and possible improvements in them.
- Report to the ASA on any aspect of advertising which is causing concern.

The Complaints Board comprises four public representatives with no connection to media or advertising groups, one of whom is the chairperson with a right to exercise a casting vote, and four persons nominated by the ASA, representative of media, advertising agencies and advertisers.

Indian Regulatory Bodies

In addition to the above-mentioned authorities, there are a few Indian regulatory bodies which enforce rules and regulations for the benefit of the public at large.

Advertising Standard Council of India

The Advertising Standard Council of India (ASCI) is a voluntary self-regulatory body set up by the advertising community to ensure that all advertising in India is fair, truthful, safe and legal. Members of the Board of Governors are drawn from various companies. The ASCI code is applicable to press, TV, radio, films and even promotion messages on packaging. During the year ended March 31, 2002, 196 complaints were reviewed by the council, of which 92 were upheld (the ads were found to be in contravention of the ASCI code). Seventy three of the advertisers concerned assured compliance with the council rules.

Information and Broadcasting Ministry

The government and the Information and Broadcasting Ministry may also play a role in regulating advertising on television and other media. According to a recent report (September 2004), the then Censor Board chief Anupam Kher expressed concern about the unrestricted telecast of unsuitable material on prime time television. Another regulatory body in India is the Indian Broadcasting Federation.

Some regulations on advertising of various kinds of products are listed in Table 2.1.

TABLE 2.1 Regulations on advertising of various kinds of products

Products	Regulations
Beverages/alcohol	• Not permitted. • Print and outdoor do allow indirect advertising. • Satellite television accepts alcohol directly.
Cigarettes	Not permitted on air media, including satellite.
Pharmaceuticals/drugs	Rules vary with every college, clinic, institute, laboratories, and many such inititutions.
Advertising to children	Restriction of direction/attitude is placed on children's commercials.
Others	No infant food advertising is acceptable • Overseas commercials are accepted. • No language restrictions exist.

Self-Regulation

Though there exist regulatory bodies in advertising, it is important that advertisers themselves be conscientious and responsible as professionals. Since all human beings have freedom of speech and communication, it is largely up to the advertisers to ensure responsible practices in their profession. In this context, it is also important that viewers be aware and alert to unethical or irresponsible practices in advertising and raise concerns in such cases.

In 1971, a number of professional advertising associations in collaboration with the Council of Better Business Bureaus established National Advertising Review Council (NARC). The main purpose was to withdraw those advertisements which were considered as deceptive. The National Advertising Division (NAD) of the Council and National Advertising Review Board (NARB) are the two main operating bodies of the NARC.

National Advertising Division

The National Advertising Division (NAD) of the Council for Better Business Bureaus is the primary self-regulatory body for dealing with advertising issues in the United States America. The NAD is trying to establish new ground in issues of advertising where it has no jurisdiction. It established a first-of-a-kind principle which requires that lifecycle impacts must be included in any environmental benefit advertising claim. The NAD applied this lifecycle test even though the Federal Trade Commission's advertising guidelines say that the FTC "lacks sufficient information on which to base guidance on such claims".

National Advertising Review Board

The Board reviews the cases forwarded by NAD. This constitutes of five-person panel, which includes three advertisers, one agency person and one public representative. The NARB panel reviews the charges and the NAD staff holds hearings and let the advertiser present the case. The panel has full authority to ask the advertisers to make changes, but if they refuse then the NARB can reveal the information about the case and handover the case to FTC or other regulatory bodies.

Self-Regulation by the Media

Many sections of the media practice self-regulation in some form. For example, The *Reader's Digest* magazine does not accept tobacco or liquor ads. Several publications refused to feature some of the Benetton's shock ads. The television networks have their own standards for an admissible ad. Different ads are shown on different time slots, based on the suitability for different types of viewers. For examples, TV networks may have guidelines for children's advertising. For instance, on the ABC, ads for children among other things must not

- Use language like "Ask mom to buy..."
- Over-glamorize the product.
- Have celebrity endorsements.

CORPORATE SOCIAL RESPONSIBILITY

Corporate Social Responsibility (CSR) relates to how the companies manage the business processes to produce an overall image and create a positive impact on society. There is a continuous commitment by corporate firms to behave ethically and contribute to economic development while improving the quality of life of employees and their families as well as the society at large. CSR is about the corporation's obligation to the society for social amelioration and developments.

The need for CSR arises because to every company there exists interplay between society and businesses. Society and businesses are quite interdependent and companies need to consider the various forces operating in this interdependence.

Many big firms are facing tough competition to launch their products. Some of them have spent crores of rupees on advertising and publicity. However, it is also their responsibility for the proper development of society in general. Many of the companies are taking relevant steps for developmental activities, but more should come up in this direction. Recently, MRF tyres have launched a publicity campaign on safe driving, which is in the interest of the public. Another example quoted in this direction is the Benetton advertisement on the condom, which directly addresses the public for population control. The Benetton firm has nothing to do with this issue, but they take it as their responsibility to spread strong awareness regarding population control.

Public Service Advertising

Public service advertising, popularly called PSA, takes up the issues related to some good cause such as preventing child abuse, anti-smoking, stopping drunk driving, etc. Advertising professionals do not charge for creating PSA and media too donate space and time. Somethimes networks and publisheres find it difficult to run a deluge of public service announcements during prime time. Therefore, they are mostly aimed during the time when the viewership is low.

Most of the public service advertising compaigns that we see in the printmedia and television are created by the advertising council, a non-profit organization.

The standard of PSAs are like other commercials as the ad agencies donate their expertise to design them. Moreover, because of the service competition, the non-profit organizations are forced to do excellent job so that they can compete well with the paid commercials. Often make public service advertising appealing, superstars like Amitabh Bachchan and Jennifer Lopez are called to endorse advertisements.

Some significant issues dealt with in PSAs are as follows:

- No tobacco
- Take polio drops
- Educate your children
- Adult education
- AIDS awareness
- Save water

- Pay income tax
- Family planning
- Self-employment
- Girl child not a burden

Corporate Advertising

When corporate houses advertise to uplift their image on a viewpoint it is called corporate advertising. They do not sell products but take up a theme in which the corporate houses are involved. This kind of advertising sprouts in the public relation department rather than advertising department. The example of such advertising are the ads done for Tata, Birla and Amway. They take help of position statements directed at public.

Corporate identity advertising is yet another type of advertising that the grant houses use to maintain their reputation among the public or very specific audiences to spread the company's name and the nature of business. When MRF launched a campaign 'Go Green, Go MRF', they used corporate identity advertising.

Advocacy Advertising

To signal a corporate personality or image, opinionated messages are delivered, that communicate the corporate house's position on public issues. This is called *advocacy advertising*. Earlier, advocacy advertising targeted issues that were related with the organization's line of business. It is different from public service advertising as in such cases advertisers pay for the space and media.

A notable example of advocacy advertising is the ad campaigns used in Thailand to combat Aids. These promoted the use of condoms and within years there was a dramatic decline in the number of Aids cases in Thailand.

Shell is a company which tries to promote awareness about the environment with its ads on the theme of profits versus principles. Another example of successful advertising for a socially responsible cause is the Big Brother ad campaign.

CASE STUDY

The Big Brother organization in Vancouver, Canada, was facing a problem. Not enough mentors were signing on to spend time with fatherless boys who needed a big brother or a father figure. The Glennie Stamnes Strategy agency (Vancouver) was given the task of creating a campaign that would remedy the situation on a low budget.

The agency decided to depart from the previously used appeals—warm and fuzzy—to a more direct one, portraying the situation as a crisis, which indeed it was. Their ads showed young boys in a listless mood, with the captions "Two years is too long" and "Be a Brother Now". (Two years was the average time for a boy to wait to be matched with a brother.)

The ad campaign worked extremely well and a number of fence-sitters signed up for the programme. In time, there was a waiting list of would-be brothers!

Thus, it is seen that advertising principles can be used not only for increasing business and sales, but also for socially responsible causes.

SUMMARY

Advertising has close proximity with society. It influences people a great deal to buy a product. Sometimes it creates a want without making the consumer realize the same. It has economic, political, cultural, moral and religious benefits. Although advertisements have deluge of benefits, but it is very important how they are handled by the advertisers. There is a great concern on the impact it creates on children and women. It is generally understood that in today's world children constitute a major segment of the customers. They have great influence on parents' buying decision.

In advertising industry, women have been portrayed in numerous ways and forms over a period of time. Her dominance in advertisements is alarming and the issues of negative depiction and as a sexual object, are to be dealt with consciously. Whether the advertising people have obligations to society beyond their own organizational objects is a part of debate about relationship between organizations and society. Puffery, shock advertisements, weasel claim, subliminal advertisements and surrogate advertisements are some of the ethical concerns in advertising. Ethics are systems of moral principles that help us determine right from wrong and good from bad. That is why there are number of regulatory bodies. All advertisements have to pass through the norms laid by these regulatory authorities. Some of the bodies discussed in this chapter are FTC, FDA, FCC, ARC, CARU, and ASA. The prominent regulatory bodies in India are ASCI and India Broadcasting Federation. These bodies have issued several regulations, which an advertisement has to go through before being launched in the market.

Though there exist regulatory bodies, it is important that advertisers should be conscientious and responsible as professionals. There are co-opted self-regulatory bodies like NAD and NARB who review advertisements. Apart from following the ethical norms, ther are a few companies that take a step ahead. They create a positive image of themselves by improving quality of life of their employees and their family. They also launch campaigns, which are good for the society, for example, taking up issues of population, Aids, environment, etc. Public service advertising, popularly called PSA takes some issues related to good cause such as child abuse, anti-smoking, stopping drunk driving, etc. When corporate houses advertise to uplift their corporate image it is called corporate advertising. Advocacy advertising is another form of advertising which communicates the corporate houses' position on public issues.

QUESTIONS

1. In your opinion is society a reflection of advertising or advertising a reflection of society? Elucidate.
2. Is it justifiable to use puffery in advertising? Should there be a limit drawn for the use of puffery?
3. Trace the beginning of shock advertising. Give examples to support that shock advertising is a better way to captivate.
4. What do you understand by corporate social responsibility? How is it different from advocacy advertising?
5. What are ethics in advertising? Explain the role of ethical bodies in India. Are they effective in implementing their policies?
6. Why should the advertisement laws for children be more stringent? What should be done so that they are not exposed to the advertisements, which create negative impact on them?
7. Justify the role of women in advertising? Is her portrayal positive or negative?
8. What do you understand by self-regulation in advertising? Explain the role of NARB and NAD.
9. In 1998, the *Hartford Courant* declined to carry an ad for a Janet Jackson tour which they felt might be inappropriate for "the homes of readers with young children".

   There has been a debate on whether the media should practice such censorship or if it should be up to the watchdog bodies. What is your opinion on the issue?
10. What do you think should be the main focus of regulatory bodies in India? Do you believe there is a strong need for regulatory bodies in advertising or that it should be up to the media and networks to follow their own standards?

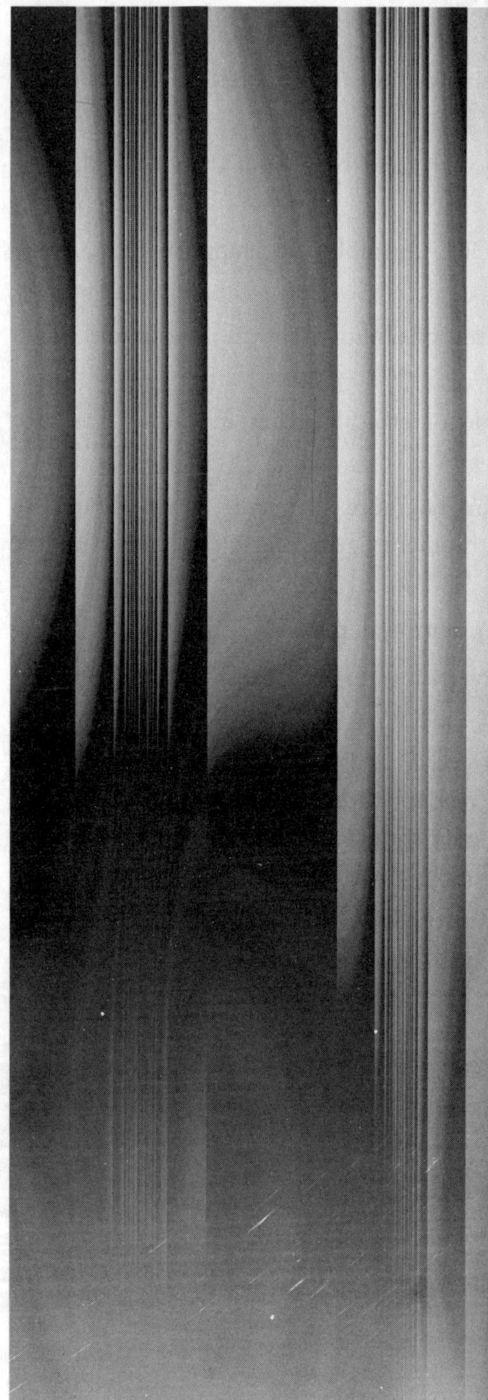

CHAPTER 3

Advertising: A Marketing Tool

LEARNING OBJECTIVES

After reading this chapter, you will be able to:

- Understand the concept of marketing.
- Understand the marketing process.
- Know the various elements of marketing mix and its interaction with advertising and promotional strategy.
- Understand the role of segmentation and target marketing, and the importance of positioning.
- Know that a sucessful relationship between an advertiser and an advertising agency is important for results.
- Understand that the selection of an advertising agency is a complex series of steps.
- Know how advertising plays an important role in achieving marketing objectives.

In this chapter we will take a closer look at the various concepts of basic marketing to understand the complete marketing process. This includes identification of marketing opportunities and threats, market segmentation, target marketing and positioning, and development of complete marketing programmes. We would also examine briefly the marketing mix decisions that a marketer makes for achieving success at the market place. Later part of the chapter is devoted to the advertising agency, its role, functions and its contribution to the business organization in achieving its objectives.

The tremendous growth in promotional budgets the world over in the last decade recognizes the value and importance of advertising and promotions. Promotional strategies are playing an important role in the marketing programmes of companies in the highly competitive and free markets across the world. To understand the role and importance of advertising and promotions let's examine the marketing process and its related concepts.

Different people end up defining marketing in different ways. Some people primarily term it as selling and others call it advertising and promotions. For some others, even pricing and product decisions may form part of the marketing definition.

The American Marketing Association (AMA), which represents marketing professionals in the US and Canada, defines marketing as: "The process of planning and executing the conception, pricing, promotion and distribution of ideas, goods and services to create exchanges that satisfy individual and organizational objectives". It can also be defined as "the process of identification and satisfaction of customer needs profitably".

MARKETING CONCEPTS

Exchange

Exchange is the core concept of marketing which means the exchange of a product between the seller and the buyer. For exchange to take place there must be at least two parties: each party has to have something that is meaningful to the other party, and each of them feels that it is desirable to deal with the other party. Each party is free to accept or reject the exchange offer and is capable of communication and delivery.

Transaction

When the agreement is reached between the two parties, a transaction takes place. Thus, transaction is a trade of values between two or more parties.

Needs, Wants and Demands

It is important for the marketer to understand and interpret the needs, wants and demands of the target market. *Need* is the basic human necessity. It is the basic human requirement in the form of food, shelter, clothes and air to survive. When the needs are directed towards specific objects that may satisfy the need it is termed as want. For example, a young college student needs food but wants French fries, a burger and a soft drink. *Demand* is a want for specific product supported by an ability to pay. When a young collegiate expresses the desire to have his French fries and soft drink in a five star deluxe hotel, he indicates the demand for a luxury hotel and restaurant.

Value

It is the customer's feeling that as long as what he gets (benefit) is greater than what he gives (cost), he gets a value for his money. Thus, it is a ratio between what the customer gets and what he gives:

$$\text{Value} = \frac{\text{Benefits}}{\text{Costs}} = \frac{\text{Functional benefit} + \text{Emotional benefit}}{\text{Monetary cost} + \text{Time cost} + \text{Energy cost} + \text{Psychic cost}}$$

The above equation shows that a marketer has several ways to increase the value by varying his total offering.

Value Proposition

The product offer consisting of the best possible benefits/value is put forward as a value proposition, explaining how the offer matches the customer's requirements and how it works out to be the best among all the competing offers.

Marketplace and Marketspace

The marketplace is physical, for example, like we go to a store to buy; marketspace is digital as we access the Internet for purchase. A large amount of purchasing has already shifted to marketspace and this shift is increasing fast.

Metamarket

Metamarket is a cluster of complimentary products and services that are closely related in the minds of the customer and is spread across various kinds of industries. For example, electronic metamarket comprises electronic equipment manufacturers, dealers, financing and insurance companies, component manufacturers, spare parts dealers, service stations, technicians, electronic magazines and Internet sites.

Segmentation

It is an impossible task for a marketer to satisfy everyone in a market. A given brand of soft drink, sports shoes, TV, automobile, toothpaste, soap, etc. may not be liked by everyone as each customer has different reason for his choice of brand. Therefore, the marketer divides the entire market into groups based on homogeneity or similarity on certain predefined factors.

Segmentation can be done based on demographic, psychographic and behavioural differences among buyers.

The marketer then identifies most potential segments based on factors like accessibility, profitability, size and sustainability. The segments that measure well against these factors form the target market.

Relationship Marketing

Every transaction between the company and customer, supplier and distributor costs the company. Thus, maintaining a long-term and enduring relationship is more advantageous. Relationship marketing aims to build mutually satisfying enduring relations with the key stakeholders. The philosophy is to retain the existing customers through continued contact and greater value addition. Relationship marketing builds strong economic, technical and social ties with the stakeholders.

Network Marketing

When marketers fundamentally use snowballing effect to spread their customer base it is called network marketing. Its main aim is to cut down on marketing cost by removing the intermediaries and minimizing various marketing activities. The company begins with identifying few customers who in turn identify few more and so on. The companies like Amway, Oriflame, etc. are the examples of network marketing.

MARKETING PROCESS

The marketing process model has four major stages: the marketing environment analysis, the target market and positioning process, marketing mix decisions and the ultimate consumer (see Figure 3.1).

The marketing process begins with the analysis of external environment factors like economic, social, political, legal and technological, which provides a statement of various opportunities and threats. Depending upon the internal strength and weakness profile, the marketer decides what opportunities to seek and how various relevant threats are to be avoided. At the same time, the marketer also turns his attention to the competitors and their offerings so as to arrive at an appropriate marketing mix decision.

Having identified opportunities at the marketplace, the marketer looks for the customer base and the occupation of space in his mind for the brand. The marketer must answer the following questions:

- Where and whom to sell broadly?
- On what basis to disaggregate the broad market?

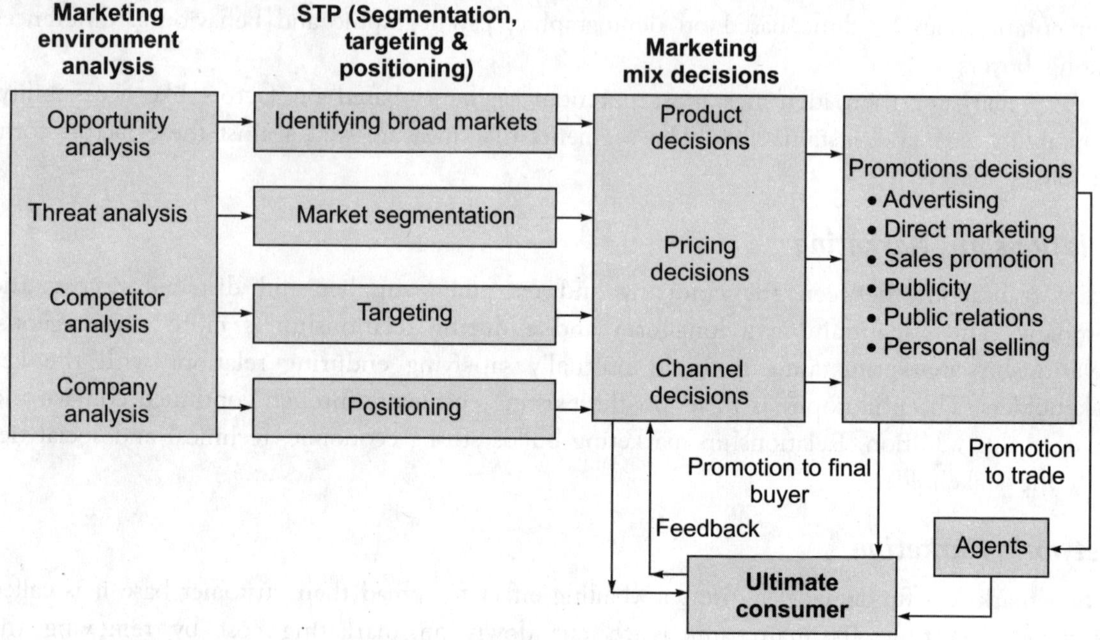

Fig 3.1 Marketing process model.

- How to select the homogenous groups of customers?
- How to differentiate the brand from many others in the market?

Having found the answers to the above questions, the marketer then makes critical decisions for marketplace battle with the competitors. These are termed as **marketing mix decisions**, broadly known as Four Ps of marketing, which have since been extended to Seven Ps:

- Product
- Price
- Physical distribution
- Promotions
- Packaging
- People
- Process

The concept of Four Ps was given by McCarthy and was popularized by Philip Kotler as four broad tools of marketing.

In fact, the Four Ps represent the sellers' viewpoint of marketing tools available with the marketer to influence the buyers. From a buyer's point of view, each marketing tool is designed to deliver customer benefit. Robert Lauterborn has given customers' Four Cs and Four As corresponding to sellers' Four Ps. See Table 3.1.

TABLE 3.1 Four Ps vs four Cs

Four Ps	Four Cs	Four As
Product	Customer solution	Acceptability
Price	Customer cost	Affordability
Physical distribution	Convenience	Availability
Promotion	Communication	Awareness

Some of the winning companies strive to meet customer needs economically and conveniently, and have effective communication strategies. These companies emphasize on customers' Four Cs while designing their marketing mix.

Assembling the Marketing Mix

Assembling the marketing mix means identifying and creating the best possible combination of Four Ps. It involves the process of the choices of appropriate marketing activities and the allocation of adequate marketing efforts and resources to each of the P. It arrives at different marketing mix combinations with varying levels of expenditure on each marketing activity and tries to identify the effectiveness of different combinations in terms of possible sales volume and net profit. It then uses its judgement to arrive at the mix of product, price, place and promotion decisions.

Thus, marketing mix is the set of marketing variables that the firm uses to achieve its marketing objectives in the target market.

It is the marketer's main task to build a marketing plan or programme to attain the company's objectives. The marketing programme consists of numerous decisions on the marketing mix variable.

A marketer needs to take into account the following factors while assembling the marketing mix:

- Mix has to be worked out separately for every brand.
- Deciding the weightage for each P.
- Marketing mix decision has to be customer/market oriented.
- Marketing mix has to be dynamic.
- Marketing mix is the most visible part of marketing strategy.

The Components of Marketing Mix

Each of the marketing P has numerous variables to be considered for the marketing programme. (see Table 3.2)

TABLE 3.2 Components of marketing mix

Product		
• Ingredients	• Colour	• Packaging
• Quality	• Size	• Services
• Design	• Product variety	• Warranties
• Features	• Brand name	• Replacement and return
• Installation	• Customer education and training	• Customer relationship management
Price		
• List price	• Allowances	
• Discounts	• Payment mode	
• Credit terms		
Physical distribution		
• Channels	• Assortments	
• Coverage	• Locations	
• Inventory	• Transportation	
• Warehousing		
Promotion		
• Advertising	• Personal selling	
• Direct marketing	• Publicity	
• Sales promotions	• Public relations	

While assembling a marketing mix, the marketer has to clearly organize marketing variables under a well-thought out philosophy of efficiency, effectiveness and social responsibility.

MARKETING TOOLS

Marketing tools are those techniques and support elements of marketing that help the marketer to design the most appropriate marketing programmes to attain organizational objectives. These tools provide a deep insight and understanding into various complexities and issues in the field of marketing and related aspects. Every professional marketer should know these tools thoroughly and must be able to use the same in real marketing situations to assure success at the marketplace. A brief description of each of the tool is given in the following paragraphs:

Product Life Cycle (PLC) Curve

A company's product offering must change as the product, market and competitors change over time. A product life cycle (PLC) shows sales volume of a product over a period of time. The PLC concept can be used to analyze a product category (soap), a product form (liquid or cake), a product (bathing soap) or a brand (Liril or Lux). The PLC is normally presented as a sales curve spanning the product's entire life from introduction to phase out.

Most product life cycle curves are bell-shaped as indicated in Figure 3.2.

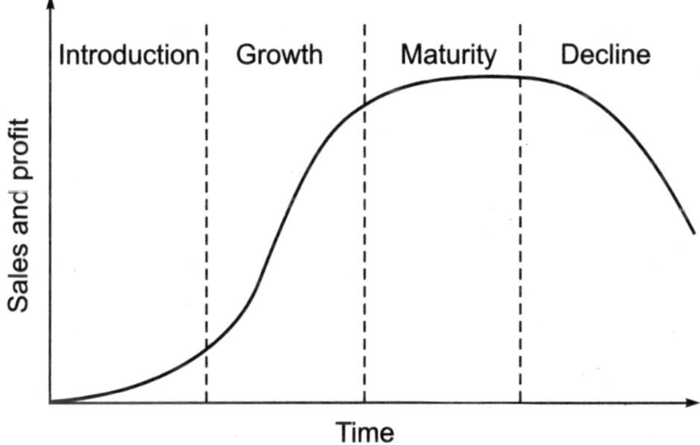

Fig. 3.2 Marketing process model.

However, not all products exhibit a bell shape. The three common alternate patterns are shown in Figure 3.3:

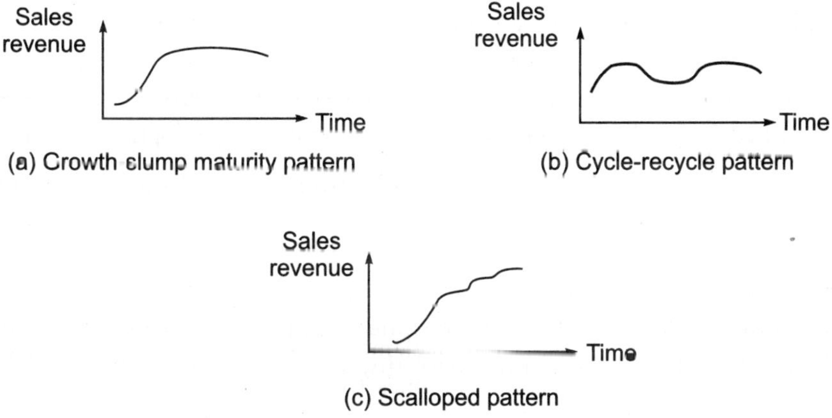

Fig. 3.3 Alternate patterns of product life cycle.

Invariably, every product passes through certain distinct stages during its life. However, it is not essential that every product has to pass through all the stages. Some of the products get phased out even at the introduction stage itself.

The importance of PLC concept lies in the fact that each stage in the cycle is characterized by a typical market behaviour. Therefore, each stage requires a distinctive market offering. Thorough understanding of the PLC concept and managing the same effectively can help in prolonging the profitable phases of a product's lifespan.

To say that every product has a life cycle is to say that:

- Products have a limited life.
- Product sales pass through distinct stages, each offering different challenges, opportunities and problems to the marketer.
- Profits rise and fall at different stages of the PLC.
- Products require different marketing, manufacturing, financial and purchase strategies in each life cycle stage.
- The competitive environment is different at different stages.

Stages of PLC

The PLC curve can be divided into the following four distinctive stages:

Introduction

This is a period of slow sales growth as the product is introduced in the market. Profits are negative as heavy expenses are incurred in R&D and launch of the product. The competition is non-existent and buyers are innovators in the market. Premium pricing is charged from the customers during this phase.

Growth

A period of rapid growth follows as acceptance of the product increases in the market. The competition increases as growth and profit potential is high. The competitive pricing sets in as copied products are brought in the market with low levels of expenses. There is substantial improvement in profits due to higher sales volume. Generally, early adopters and early majority are the buyers.

Maturity

This is a slowdown period in the rate of growth of the product as it has achieved acceptance by most potential buyers. Profits stabilize or decline because of increased competition. The competition is heightened. Lot of innovative marketing programmes are introduced for survival at this stage.

Decline

Lastly, it is the period of declining sales and the profits erode. Very few competitors are left behind. The laggards are the buyers. The investment is stopped. It is the stage of harvesting.

SWOT Analysis

The overall statement of company's strengths and weaknesses and assessment of opportunities and threats at the marketplace is called the SWOT analysis. It is done in two stages.

External Environment Analysis (Opportunity and Threat Analysis)

Every business unit fighting for a customer's pie at the marketplace should create a marketing intelligence system to track trends and important developments in the general business environment, because every change or new development in the external market has a potential to impact the profit earning ability of a company over a long run. The understanding of these changes will help the company to adopt its marketing programmes so as to take advantage of opportunities and avert threats. Generally, a company monitors both key macro and micro environmental factors.

Macro environmental factors are non-controllable factors. The impact of changes in these factors affect business units in the long run. The business units have to adapt or reorient themselves to the changes in these factors, which are as follows:

- Social
- Legal
- Economic
- Political
- Technology

Micro environmental (also termed task factors) factors are again non-controllable factors and impact the company in medium run. The following factors have comparatively more direct impact on the performance of the company:

- Customers
- Employees
- Competitors
- Distributors
- Creditors
- Suppliers
- Other stakeholders

Internal Environmental Analysis

Each business needs to evaluate its strengths and weaknesses before embarking on any strategic decision. It should develop a strength-weakness profile so as to identify a matching opportunity and avert a threat. All weaknesses need not be corrected and similarly, all strengths also may not be of much use. It must look into the relevance and match the two analyses to develop a profile of the key issues to be dealt with. The components for internal analysis are basically related to functional areas such as:

- Marketing
- Finance
- Manufacturing
- Purchase
- R&D
- Information technology
- Human resource
- Leadership
- Image

Marketing Plan

A company has to develop a total game plan to fight successfully at the marketplace. Marketing plan is a definitive and detailed statement of actions to be implemented at the marketplace. It is a well-documented and structured piece of information for all concerned people in the organization, and it requires proper communication to all the parts of the organization. See Figure 3.4.

A marketing plan helps to:

- Provide assessment of current situation and position
- Focus efforts in an identified direction
- Give clear cut performance targets
- Identify ways to achieve targets
- Allocate resources
- Direct all towards the common objectives

Fig. 3.4 Hierachy of components of a marketing plan.

A marketing plan should be a written document because it ensures effective execution of strategic marketing programmes.

It spells out clearly what actions are to be taken, when, by whom and what resources are available. Written marketing plans are crucial in larger organizations as the marketing manager's proposal has to be evaluated and approved by the top management. The approved plans then provide benchmarks against which the marketing function and marketing programme's performance will be evaluated. Marketing plans can vary a good deal in content and organization, but they generally follow a format which is indicated below:

Contents and Structure of a Marketing Plan

- Executive summary
- Current situation analysis
- Performance review (for an existing product or service only)
- Key issues
- Marketing objectives
- Marketing strategy
- Marketing action plan
  - Target market
  - Marketing mix variables (4 Ps)
  - Who is responsible for each action?
  - When and where the action will be?
  - How much is the budget for each action?
- Projected profit and loss statement
- Controls
- Contingency plan

Tools for Estimating Market Demand

Two kinds of tools help the marketer in estimating the market demand. These are:

- Qualitative tools
- Quantitative tools

Qualitative Tools

These tools involve opinion surveys.

Survey of buying intention

In this, a survey of the buyers is done to assess their intentions to buy the product. It is of great help in estimating the market demand for consumer durables and new products. It can also be used to measure the demand for a product at a different level of marketing effort. It is a very important tool for industrial marketing. The purchase intention of the buyer is measured on a seven point scale from a "definite buy" to a "definite no buy". The responses so obtained constitute purchase probability for a given product and hence, an index of purchase probability can be made.

Composite of sales force opinion

This method involves the opinion of entire sales force. Each sales personnel is asked by the company to give an estimate of a given product in his territory. These estimates are then combined and a national level forecast of sales is obtained. The major deficiency of this method is that there may seem to be a tendency to give a below average estimate to change their annual targets.

Delphi technique

In this method a panel of experts is formed and each expert is asked to estimate the market demand for a given product. Individual experts have no idea about other members on the panel. As each expert works independent of others, there is no chance of getting any influence over other experts. Once the estimates are ready, the marketer removes extreme values. He reverts to the concerned expert, giving them the assumptions others have made. However, the marketer does not reveal the estimate to others. The purposes of sending back the opinion is to get the estimates smoothened and arrive at consensus. If the experts choose not to revise their opinions, the marketer will have to leave it at that. This method can study different scenarios, and is particularly useful in estimating demand for a new product or technology.

Quantitative Tools

These tools are used for:

- Extrapolation
- Time series analysis
- Correlation
- Econometrics models

A lot of books on statistics give good, detailed account of these methods.

Ansoff's Product-Market Expansion Grid

It is a useful tool for strategic planning. Generally, every company has three possible routes for achieving growth: Intensification, integration and diversification. The Ansoff's model helps the company to achieve growth through intensification, i.e. through existing businesses. In the intensification strategy, a firm spots and utilizes opportunities for improving products and market penetration of its existing businesses. See Figure 3.5.

		Product: New	Product: Existing
Market	New	Diversification	Market development
	Existing	Product development	Penetration

Fig 3.5 Ansoff's product-market matrix.

Three strategies available for achieving growth through intensification are:

- Market penetration
- Market development
- Product development

The market penetration strategy tries to achieve growth through existing product in the existing markets. The emphasis is on achieving higher market share by enhancing total offerings to the customer. Market development, on the other hand, finds new markets for the existing products. It requires efforts in new markets. The product development strategy tries to bring a new or modified product for the same customers.

ADVERTISING AGENCIES

Advertising agencies play a major role of closing the distance between the advertiser and the media. Depending upon the size and the nature of the agency, it offers numerous services to the advertiser. Before describing the role and functions of advertising agencies it's important to revisit and understand the role and function of advertising.

The role and function of advertising is to:

- Acquire enhanced volumes of sales of products and services.
- Generate awareness about offerings.
- Induce trial of a new product or service.

- Motivate and impress trade channels.
- Change perception and create reassurance.
- Change or create attitude towards product or service.
- Influence staff.
- Support sales promotional, sponsorship and public relations activity.
- Comply with the statutory requirements of relevant legislation.
- Make announcements in the public interest such as product recalls.

Purpose of Advertising Agency

Most advertisers use the services of advertising agencies. Advertisers can have more than one advertising agency for different services at any given time. They use advertising agencies for various purposes such as to:

- Advise and counsel on marketing strategy.
- Advise and counsel on advertising and media strategy and tactics.
- Prepare and develop print, outdoor and electronic advertisements.
- Carry out collateral designs of various items such as display material, PoP material and other promotional material.
- Help and counsel on sales promotion and other communication task.

Generally, an advertising agency starts its operations from buying space and time for the clients and gradually attains a full or composite agency status.

Various Types of Agencies

There are different types of advertising agencies depending upon their functional areas as shown in Table 3.3.

TABLE 3.3 Various types of advertising agencies

Types of agencey	Role
Full Service Agency	It offers all marketing communication services. Develops ad copy and design, provides collateral art work, research services facilitating decision-making, and offers media buying and production facilities.
Creative Agency	Provides writing of ad copy and design service.
A Media Independent	It offers buying space and time, and may offer related research and audience measurement data.
A Composite Agency	Offers both creative and media buying services with accompanying research.

A large number of advertisers employ the services of many agencies, some generalist and others specialist. Since marketing communications are vital for the success of the company, it requires the attention of senior managers.

Structure of Advertising Agencies

The structure of advertising agency depends upon the range of services it offers and size of the agency. Every agency has a well structured job profile depending upon the services it offers. Generally, the agencies have the following personnel to take care of the tasks in a full service agency:

Account executive

There can be many individuals in this position depending upon the size of the agency. An account executive acts as the interface between the agency's many services and the client's many managers.

It's the best paid and the hardest job in the agency. It is where the pressure coming down from the client management meets the pressure coming up from the media and creative people in the agency.

An account executive gets the briefing from the client's marketing manager or product manager or brand manager on the nature of issues affecting the product or services, which may arise due to competition, change of market share, new consumer research, new product formula or packaging; or a new product in its own right.

It is the responsibility of the account executive to handle all matters within the agency and the place related to that particular client.

The account executive organizes the resources of the agency to solve the problems of the client.

The creative team

The team basically comprise a writer and a designer. The account executive discusses the client's problem on all aspects with the team. The writer and designer will work and rework on the problem until they come up with a workable solution of the problem in terms of a print or electronic advertising campaign.

The account planner or researcher

It is this executive who is responsible for the data and market intelligence on the account. The account planner gathers the necessary information related to the client's problem. Collecting data and market intelligence is important for the agency to ensure that its advertising campaign and media plans are rooted in the sound market understanding and ground realities.

The media planner and buyer

This is the team that actually makes the campaign come live. Depending upon the briefing the accounts executive has received from the client and the mutually agreed objectives, this team prepares the media budget, carries out the segmentation of audiences and decides the target audience. The timing, cost and design constraints are worked out with the client. If the plans are agreed, the team purchases the space and time in the chosen media vehicle.

Account director

The individual who holds overall responsibility of servicing effectively the entire clientele of the agency.

The creative director

The individual who is responsible for the over all creative and the art work of the agency's clients.

The media director

The individual who is responsible for media planning and buying activities of the agency.

Production house

The department which brings alive the creative and art work of creative team. It makes TV films, Press and Magazine advertisements, cinema films, radio recordings and other promotional material. This is the budget other than the space and time.

Release to media

All finished creative and art work related to advertising should be with the media at least several days before it is due to appear in normal circumstances. A lead time of few days is necessary so as to have approval from the broadcasting authorities or editors.

How Agencies are Paid for Their Work?

All systems of compensation in agencies ultimately depend on some method of allocating time to work on the account. In this way, it is possible to determine the profitability or otherwise of a piece of business and hence, the most suitable charging method.

- Ad agencies are paid a commission on the basis of percentage (which varies from medium to medium and from time to time) on the value of the space and time that they buy from the media on behalf of their clients.

- It is also a practice to charge a commission of about 20% on production costs to compensate for the additional administration and supervision involved in the production of advertising films and art work.
- Technologically, agencies are paid by the media and not by the client.
- Initially, the agencies were found to sell space and time for newspaper and radio and were rewarded commission on sales. Later, they helped prepare material appearing in media and the shift was towards their customers, but the method of payment remained the same.
- If a client goes bust, the agency has to pay the outstanding bills to media as the agency buys the space and the time as principals in law and not as agents for their clients.

How To Select an Advertising Agency

An advertising agency plays a great role in implementing the corporate's chosen strategy successfully. As advertising agency advises a corporation on marketing promotional activities, choosing a right agency is very important. Hence, selecting a new advertising agency is one of the most important strategic decisions for a corporation engaged in marketing operations.

The advertiser wishing to appoint an advertising agency should invite a good number of agencies who meet the predetermined minimum criteria. The purpose of application is to seek required information on the following format to evaluate their suitability.

Checklist for the selection of an advertising agency

The following details are to be acquired from the advertising agencies for short listing by the company.

- Name, address, telephone and fax nos.; e-mail and map
- CMD and Directors
- Average age of senior team of directors
- Agency history
- Year of establishment
- Ownership pattern
- Take over and mergers if any
- Size of turnovers and growth trends over last five years
- Revenue and billing for last five years
  - Commission
  - Fees
  - Forecasts

- Clients won in last three years
- Clients lost in last three years
- Client list (at present)
- Billing by clients
- Billing by products
- Minimum size of the account required
- Agency mission or philosophy if any
- Accounts
  - New products from existing clients
  - New products from new clients

Media-related information (in space and time)

- Percentage on TV
- Percentage on national press
- Percentage on other press (regional and local)
- Percentage on radio
- Percentage on outdoor and transportation
- Percentage on sales promotion
- Percentage on other significant media and services

Staff turnover

- Appointed in last two years
- Quit in last two years

Key personnel

- Length of service
- Relevant experience
- Account team
- Organizational structure

Agency annual report and accounts

Payment methods used

- Commission only
- Production cost payment method

- Fees only
- Expenses involved
- Fees plus commission
- Credit terms

Following the submission of checklists and initial visits the authenticity of information will be ascertained. A shortlisting of agencies will be made based on predetermined criteria. The shortlisted agencies will be invited to 'pitch' for the account(s). The interested agencies will have to make a competitive presentation of their creative and design work and other services on offer.

Working of an Advertising Agency

The agency has to develop a timing plan which sets out the steps of the programme from brief to the finished advertisement. This includes things like when the client can see the finished copy and layout, first edits of commercial television films, copy dates for magazines, commitment dates for buying space and time, presentations to senior managers, sales conferences, shots of new packaging for trade brochures and so on.

A mutually agreed timing plan is important in advertising business because it operates under high pressure of time. Decisions have to be made quickly and accurately, and the consequences of those decisions on the rest of the programme have to be recognized and dealt with.

The first stage in the making of an advertisement is when the account executive or manager translates the brief from client into the precise instructions to the creatives and the media planners and media buyers.

The creative and media briefing includes a summary of the environmental and the market background along with the more precise extracts for the creatives and media people to work on.

Then comes the question, "What response do we want from the target audience for the advertising?" Considering this, the account executive will provide the team of writers, designers and media executives with as much information about the product or service as he or she feels is helpful. It is important for the creative writers and designers to know where and how the product or service is differentiat from its competitors so that they can seek distinctiveness in the advertising.

The copy for a brand sets out the essential elements that must be present in all advertising communications material. For example, the requirement to show the package, logo or symbol of the advertiser.

Lastly, the account executive needs to provide a detailed brief to the different organs of the agency so that the campaign is well-coordinated. The client brief, media brief and creative brief are three types of brief that allow the information needed for a successful campaign to be passed around those who need it.

SYNERGY BETWEEN MARKETING AND ADVERTISING

Advertising planning and decision-making takes place in the context of an overall marketing plan. The marketing plan is based on the overall corporate plan and it helps achieve overall corporate objectives. The plan includes a statement of marketing objectives and will spell out particular strategies and tactics to reach those objectives. Figure 3.6 shows a synergistic flow between marketing and advertising.

The marketing objectives need to identify the segments to be served by the organization and how it is going to serve them. The needs and wants of consumers on which the firm will concentrate are identified and analyzed in a marketing plan.

There are several marketing tools that can be used to attain marketing objectives. Advertising is one of the important tools that help an organization to achieve its marketing objectives. The relationship between the two is strong and acts as an influence over the other.

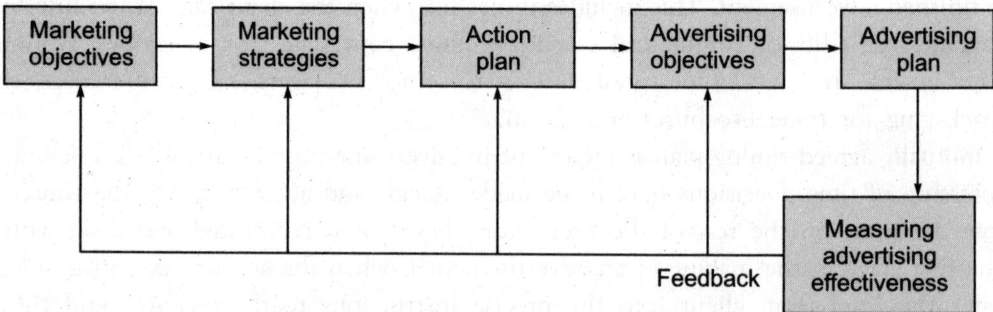

Fig 3.6 Synergistic flow between marketing and advertising.

Marketing plan is the outcome of the specific problems or opportunities uncovered for the brand through situational audit. It is the response to those problems or opportunities through the allocation of the marketing budget and the development of specific plans for the numerous variables of the marketing mix.

Advertising is that important variable of the marketing mix which is developed on the basis of the marketing objectives. In marketing mix advertising is the visible, action-oriented component that generates interest in the target market. In advertising all decision are based on a single criteria of attainment of marketing objectives.

An advertising plan should be developed once the overall marketing plan has been created and the role of advertising within it has been assessed. Advertising plays a crucial role in generating awareness, creating interest and changing attitude of the customer towards a brand. Unless this task is achieved, the other components of marketing, however strong these may be, fail to achieve the marketing objectives.

Marketing planning focuses on four important aspects—deciding marketing objectives, target market, developing appropriate mix of marketing variables and allocation of resources, whereas advertising planning focuses on advertising objectives and target selection, message strategy and tactics, and media strategy and tactics. Advertising planning process should be integrated with the marketing planning. The synergy in marketing operations is possible only if advertising decisions are embedded in marketing plans.

The marketing manager must take care to develop a marketing programme in which the component parts work in a coordinated manner instead of at cross-purposes. For example, when a firm develops a premium product and intends to charge premium price, it is important that advertising reinforces the idea of premium quality and high-end market. This can be done by choosing brand ambassadors of such image and situations and events of high repute and importance. The use of advertising copy and advertising media that is incompatible with the image of brand jeopardizes the whole marketing programme. Alternatively, when the firm offers a low priced product, the job of advertising might be to stress the price differential by using a compatible ad copy.

Depending upon the overall marketing strategy, the advertising effort may be primarily either directed to the trade or the consumer. In the case of trade directed advertising the dealer and distributor network is motivated to push the product to customer, as the emphasis is on providing better returns for their efforts. In case of consumer directed advertising the consumer is "pulled" to the dealers' place through various attractive offerings made available to him.

SUMMARY

Exchange is the core concept of marketing, which means obtaining a desired product from someone by offering something in return. It is important for the marketer to understand the need, want and demand of the target market. Need is deprivation of something. When needs are directed towards specific objects to satisfy the basic necessities of life it is termed as want. Demand is the need for specific object supported by an ability to pay.

Marketing is a process of satisfying customer needs profitably. The process begins with situational analysis which provides a statement of opportunities and threats, and strength and weaknesses. Based on these opportunities the marketer identifies the broader market. Since it is not possible to serve the entire market, therefore, segmentation needs to be done, which means identifying a homogeneous group which has similar needs. Out of the various segments a target market has to be chosen based on accessibility, size and profitability. A total market offerings is then developed for the target market. A total market offerings is the assembly of marketing mix which is particularly known as 4 Ps: Product, Price, Physical distribution and Promotion. A marketer uses numerous marketing tools to develop an appropriate marketing mix to achieve marketing objectives. The various marketing tools are: Product life cycle (PLC), SWOT analysis, marketing plan, composite of sales force opinion, Delphi technique, survey of buying intention and Ansoff's product-market grid, etc.

Advertising agencies have numerous roles to play which help the marketer to achieve its marketing objectives. Advertising agencies are different types such as creative service agency, media buying specialist, full service agency and composite agency.

An agency offering full services has many important people who help it in providing effective and efficient services to its clients.

An advertising agency consists of account executives, the media planner and buyer, the creative team, the account planner or researcher, the account director, the creative director, the media director, the production house and media release.

Agencies are paid for their work by the media and not by the client. Advertising agencies are paid a commission on the basis of percentage of the value of space or time that they buy from the media on behalf of their clients. There is also a practice to charge a commission of about 20 per cent on production costs to compensate for the additional administration and supervision involved in the production of advertising films and art work.

Selection of a proper advertising agency is a crucial decision for any marketing organization. A checklist of selection criteria is prepared, and the agencies who are interested to pitch for the account are asked to apply on the given format. The shortlisted agencies are then called for presentation and capability assessment.

There should be a synergy between the marketing and advertising. Advertising decisions should be based on marketing objectives and the two should work hand in hand rather than at cross purposes.

QUESTIONS

1. Clearly explain through examples, the difference between need, want and demand.
2. Can relationship marketing help a company gain advantage over its competitors. If yes, how?
3. Understanding and assembling the marketing mix is crucial for the marketer to gain and maintain its market position. Discuss the statement in the light of current market situation.
4. Describe the importance of promotions mix. Explain in brief each component of a promotions mix.
5. What are various stages of PLC? How will marketing activities vary from one another in case a firm has two different product categories at maturity and introduction stage?

6. Why is it important to develop a marketing plan? Describe briefly various components of a marketing plan.
7. Ansoff's Matrix gives an important insight to a marketer to develop an appropriate action plan for its brand at the market place. Justify the statement with illustrations.
8. What is the role of an advertising agency for the advertiser? Describe in brief various types of advertising agencies.
9. Identify various ways of bringing energy between advertising and marketing. How does advertising help in achieving the marketing objectives?
10. What are the various tools that can be used for estimating market demand? Describe each briefly.

Part Two

Advertising Research and Strategy

CHAPTER 4

The Consumer Behaviour

LEARNING OBJECTIVES

After reading this chapter, you will be able to:

- Understand consumer buyer behaviour concepts and its importance.
- Know various internal and external factors that influence the buyer behaviour.
- Know how consumers make purchase decision.
- Know and establish the relationship between advertising strategy and consumer behaviour.

The understanding of consumer behaviour is applied to develop appropriate marketing strategy. Knowledge of consumer behaviour is critical for influencing not only product purchase decisions, but also how much to purchase, where and what to purchase. It is important to note that the consumer is learning faster than ever before. The ever-changing environment has great impact on the needs, wants and desires of the consumer. Today, we cannot take our business for granted. We have to learn and anticipate consumer behaviour to provide important and critical inputs to planning and managing in this highly dynamic business environment.

The purpose of buyer behaviour is to understand the buyer and create a customer out of him through this Understanding. It is never easy to understand the consumer. It is a complex and multi-dimensional process. Customers may say one thing and do another. They may respond to influences and may change their minds at the last minute. But, not understanding customers' motivation, needs and preferences can hurt because understanding and knowing consumers provides the necessary information for developing new products, product features, choice of channels, price levels, media decisions and messages, and many other marketing variable decisions.

Before we get into the various aspects of consumer behaviour, it is important to understand that there are two categories of buyers—the individual buyer and the organization buyer. Individuals buy for their personal and family consumption; organizations buy for manufacturing other products, reselling or for use in running of enterprises.

These distinctions are substantial as these two categories are separate in buying motivation, attitude and purchase behaviour.

Consumer behaviour refers to how individuals, groups and organizations select, buy, use and dispose of goods and services to satisfy their needs, wants and desires.

Studying and understanding consumer behaviour is basic to marketing decisions. Marketing decisions will be based on the answers the marketer gets for the questions like:

- What motivates the buyer?
- Why does he choose a specific brand over others?
- Why does he buy from where he buys?
- What makes him shift from one brand to another and from one shop to another?
- What are his reactions to newly introduced product or a piece of information addressed to him?
- What are the various stages he passes through before he makes the decision to buy?

Answers to these questions will actually lead to various decisions on marketing mix elements. In his strategies and plans, the marketer keeps in mind how the buyers would behave and how they would respond to his marketing programme.

Therefore, it is important to note that all marketing decisions are based on assumptions about consumer behaviour. Whenever a marketer happens to make any change in marketing variable, it is for sure that his assumptions about the various aspects of the consumer have changed.

A marketer would do a better job if he could understand what influences the consumer behaviour. Basically, there are four important influencing factors: internal factors, external influences, self-concept and personality, and buying decision process. A research in each of these factors would provide a great insight into consumer behaviour that helps the marketer to serve the consumers better.

To understand how consumers actually make buying decisions, marketers must identify who makes or/and gives input into the buying decision—people can be initiators, influencers, deciders, buyers or users—so that different marketing campaigns can be made for each kind. Marketers must also examine buyers' levels of involvement and the number of brands available to determine whether consumers are engaging in complex buying behaviour, dissonance-reducing buying behaviour, habitual buying behaviour or variety-seeking buying behaviour.

CONSUMER BEHAVIOUR AND MARKETING STRATEGY

Understanding consumer behaviour is important for a marketing manager, as he/she wants to obtain usable managerial understanding about the consumer. Managers who have sound understanding of consumers can gain competitive advantage for their corporations. As discussed earlier, all marketing strategies and tactics are based on explicit assumption or implicit beliefs about consumer behaviour. Decisions based on explicit assumptions, sound theory and information derived from research are likely to be more successful than decisions based solely on implicit beliefs. Figure 4.1 shows how understanding consumer behaviour is an important part of marketing strategy.

NATURE OF BUYER BEHAVIOUR

As discussed earlier, consumer behaviour is complex and multi-dimensional. It is very difficult for the marketing manager to comprehend and explain certain reactions or lack of it to their market offerings. It is even difficult for the consumer to explain his own decisions. Understanding deeper or below the surface level beliefs is difficult. Do you remember your own decisions related to certain purchases? Can you explain why you had to change those decisions at the last moment or under the influence of salesmen or friends or others? It's truly not easy. Though on the surface consumer behaviour appears to be simple, structured, conscious, mechanical and linear, but a quick analysis of your own behaviour or that of other people around us will show us that it is a case of perceptual error, which may be fatal. Often consumer behaviour is complex, disorganized, subconscious, organic and circular.

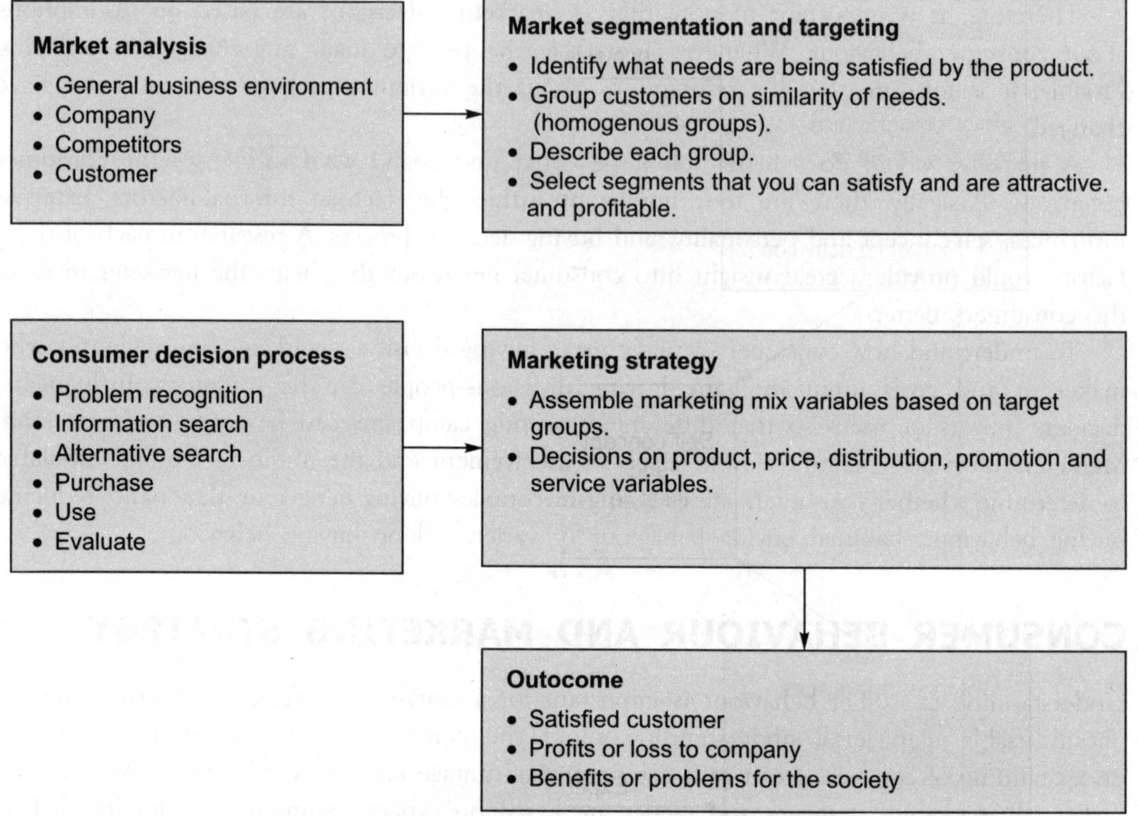

Fig. 4.1 Marketing strategy and consumer behaviour

It is, therefore, necessary to develop a framework of consumer behaviour for easy understanding and application. A conceptual model is developed to show the general structure and process of consumer behaviour (see Figure 4.2). It does not contain sufficient detail to predict particular behaviours, but it does reflect our beliefs about the nature of consumer behaviour.

The model of consumer behaviour is not only simple and easy to understand, but it is also conceptually sound and intuitively appealing. Each individual has a view of the self (self-concept) and try to live in a particular way depending upon one's resources (lifestyle). The individual's view of the self and the way one tries to live is actually determined by internal characteristics (such as values, emotions, personality, attitude, etc.) and external factors (such as individual's culture, age, family, friends, social status, etc.).

The individual's view of the self and the living habits give rise to needs and desires in everyday situations. Many such situations lead to a consideration for purchase. The decision one makes and the process used in making decision causes learning and may affect many internal

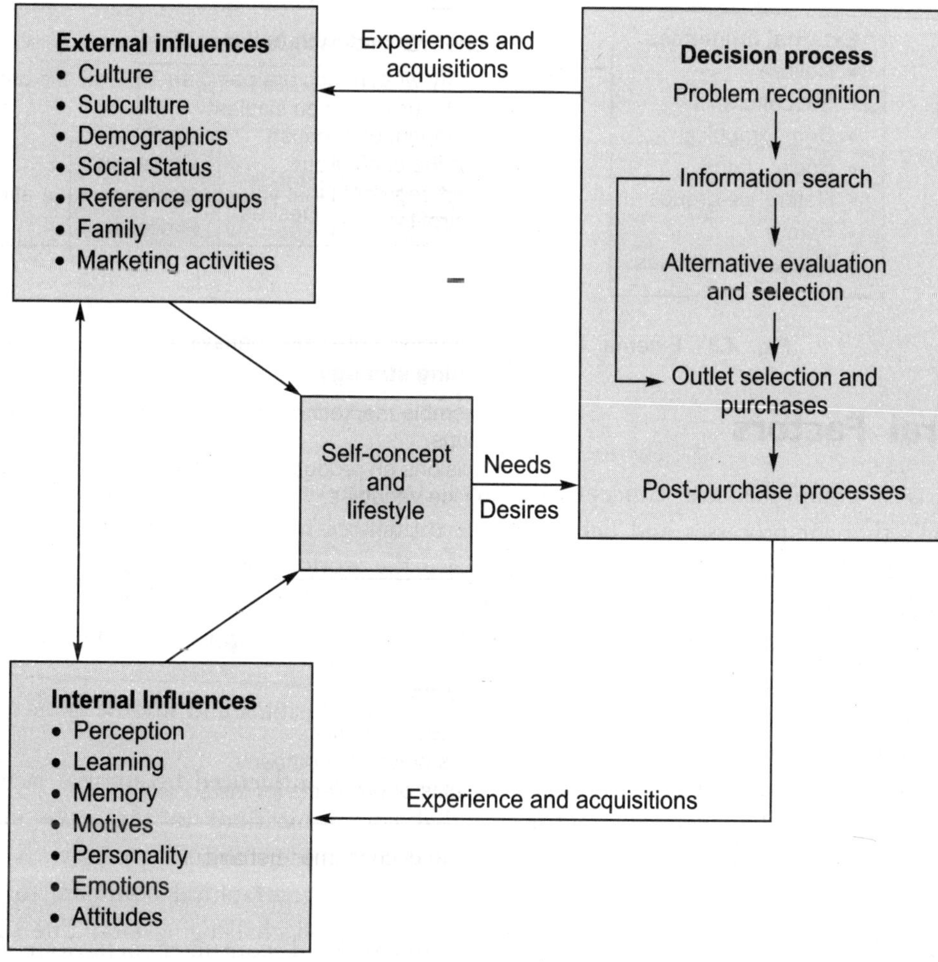

Fig. 4.2 Conceptual model of consumer behaviour.

characteristics and external factors that will either change or reinforce one's current self-concept and lifestyle.

External Factors

It is important to understand the functioning of the various external groups because learning actually involves external influences such as family, reference groups and peers (see Figure 4.3).

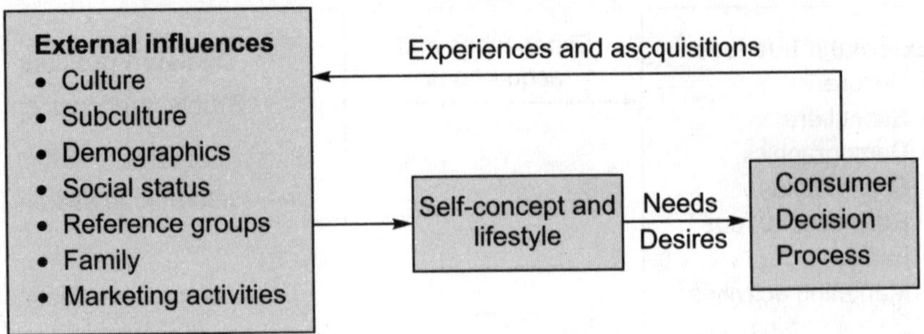

Fig. 4.3 External factors influencing consumer behaviour.

Cultural Factors

Culture is a comprehensive concept that includes almost everything that influences an individual's thought processes and behaviours. It influences not only our preferences, but also how we make decisions and even how we perceive the world around us. Most of the culture is acquired. It does not include inherited responses and predispositions. However, as we know that much of the human behaviour is learned rather than innate, culture does affect a wide range of behaviours.

Thus, culture is a set of norms, values, beliefs, morals, customs and knowledge acquired by humans as members of society.

As indicated in Figure 4.4, marketing strategy is heavily influenced by cultural factors such as values, language, demographics and non-verbal communication. In turn, the marketing strategy also influences these factors. It must be clearly understood that cultures vary from country to country as these factors differ widely from one geographical boundary to another. Hence, marketing across cultural boundaries is a difficult and challenging task. The success of a company depends upon how well it understands the cultural differences and its adaptability to these differences.

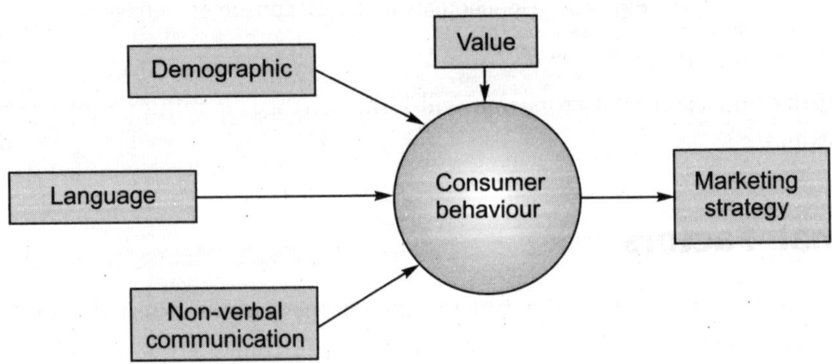

Fig. 4.4 Cultural factors affecting consumer behaviour and marketing strategy.

Culture provides the framework within which individual and household lifestyles evolve. The boundaries that culture sets on behaviour are called norms, which are simply rules that specify or prohibit certain behaviours in specific situations. Norms are derived from cultural values, or widely held beliefs that affirm what is desirable. Violations of cultural norms result in sanctions or penalties ranging from mild social disapproval to banishment from the group. Thus, cultural values give rise to norms and associated sanctions, which in turn influence consumption patterns.

There are numerous values that vary across cultures and affect consumption. The cultural values that have the most impact on consumer behaviour are classified as: other-oriented values, environmental-oriented values and self-oriented values.

Other-oriented values

These reflect a society's view of the appropriate relationship between individuals and groups within that society. These relationships have a major influence on marketing practice.

Environmental-oriented values

These values prescribe a society's relationship to its economic and technical as well as its physical environment.

Self-oriented values

Such values reflect the objectives and approaches to life that the individual members of society find desirable. These values too have strong implications for marketing management.

There is a great debate over the extent to which cross-cultural marketing strategies, especially advertising should be standardized. There is always trade off between standardization and adaptation. Since every adaptation results in extra cost to the company, the consumer response to the standardized campaign and to potential individualized campaigns must be considered.

Considerations for cross-cultural market operations

The factors discussed below will provide a framework necessary for deciding whether or not to enter the market and to what extent an individualized marketing strategy is required.

- Is the geographic area homogenous or heterogeneous with respect to culture?
- What need this product or a version of it fulfil in this culture?
- Can enough people afford it?
- What values or patterns of values are relevant to the purchase and use of this product?
- What are the distributions, political and legal structures of the product?
- In what ways can we communicate about the product?
- What are the ethical implications of marketing this product in this country?

Group Influences on Consumer Behaviour

The consumer or the family makes the purchase decision for most products or brands. The basic purchase motive is to satisfy the individual's need, but there are purchases in which the consumer buys more than the product or a brand. Membership in a group is also being purchased, for example, the purchase of Mercedes. Most customers acquire not only the car and some aspect of the image associated with Mercedes, they also join a group or subculture. While there may be a number of distinct 'Merc' groups, most share a core ethos or value system. People, the owners of other cars and general public, have certain expectations about the style and behaviour of Merc owners. So, purchasing a Mercedes is clearly a group-based process. It is to say that group memberships and identity are very important to all of us and while we do not want to think of ourselves as conformists, most of us conform to group expectations most of the time.

What we wear depends upon the occasion. Similarly, the behaviour also depends on the kind of party we are attending, whether it is brother's marriage or sister's marriage or grandparents' anniversary celebrations or New Year party. Hence, these behaviours are responses to group influences and expectations.

Ads showing different dresses based on occasions.

Most people belong to numerous groups at any given point of time. When we are actively involved with a particular group, it generally functions as a reference group. A *reference group* is a group whose presumed perspectives or values are being used by an individual as the basis for his or her current behaviour.

As the situation changes, we may base our behaviour on an entirely different group, which then becomes our reference group (see Figure 4.5).

We may belong to many groups simultaneously, but we use only one group as our primary point of reference in any given situation.

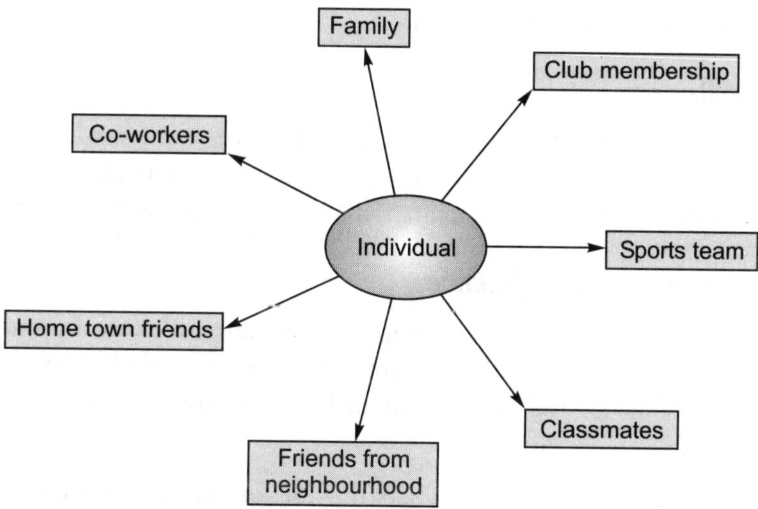

Fig. 4.5 Reference groups change as the situation changes.

Individuals tend to behave differently in diverse situations because reference groups change according to situations. Reference groups tend to exert a strong influence on one's purchase decision. Individuals frequently purchase products thought to be used by a desired group in order to achieve actual or symbolic membership in the group.

The nature of reference group influence

A reference group can have three types of influence on an individual: Informational, normative and identification. It is important to understand the type of influence each consumer is under, as the type of influence determines the marketing strategy.

Informational influence

It occurs when an individual uses the behaviour and opinions of reference group members as potentially useful information. In this, an individual may see several other members of the reference group using a specific brand of sports shoes. He or she may then decide to try that brand simply because there is evidence, as it is used by friends that it may be a good brand.

Normative influence

It also termed as utilitarian influence, which occurs when a group member fulfils group expectations to gain a direct reward or to avoid sanction. You may buy a particular brand of cigarette to win approval from a colleague. Or you may refrain from using a particular brand of jeans for fear of disapproval or teasing from friends. It is especially important when the group is very strong and the product involved is socially conspicuous. This influence appears particularly important to younger generation.

Identification influence

Also termed as value-expressive influence, this influence occurs when individuals have internalized the group's values and norms. There is no fear of reference group sanctions and rewards as the individual behaves in a manner that is consistent with the group's values.

Degree of reference group influence

Reference group influence is situational. It may not have any influence in a given situation or it may influence the usage of the product category, the type of product used or the brand used.

The following are some of the factors that make the reference group influence greater or lesser on an individual:

- Group influence is the strongest when the use of product or brand is visible to the group.
- The higher the reference group influence, the lesser is the necessity for decision making in a purchase situation.
- The more commitment an individual feels to a group, the more that individual will conform to the group norms.
- The more relevant a particular activity is to the group's functioning, the stronger is the pressure to conform to the group norms concerning that activity.
- The individual's confidence in the purchase situation will affect the degree of reference group influence.

Internal Influence

These are the processes that occur primarily within the individual and are different from the ones that are external to the individual. The interaction of these forces, i.e. external and internal, within an individual helps form self-concepts and lifestyle, which are central to the model of consumer behaviour (see Figure 4.6). **Self-concept** refers to the way individuals think and feel about themselves as well as how they would like to think and feel about themselves. Their actual and desired lifestyle is the way they translate their self-concepts into daily behaviours including consumption behaviours.

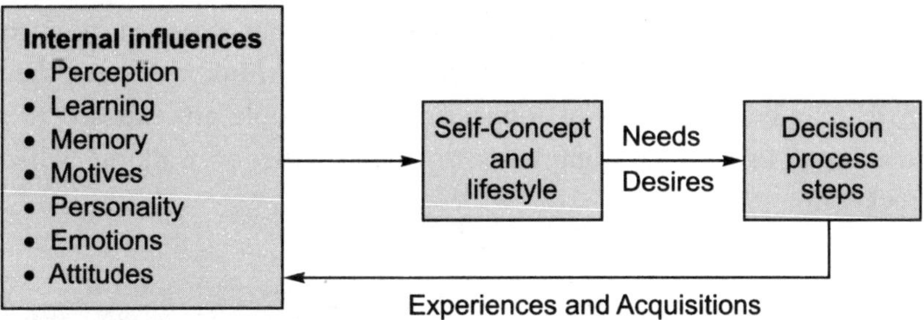

Fig. 4.6 Internal influences on consumer behaviour.

The clutter at marketplace forces advertisers to use humour, attractive models and other factors to attract the attention and interest of the audience. If an advertisement has not done well, the marketer may end up attracting the attention of audience to the models or humour in the advertisement rather than the message. Therefore, a marketer would want to communicate something about the product. For this it is essential that the marketer understands how an audience processes information so that his/her message is effectively communicated (see Figure 4.7).

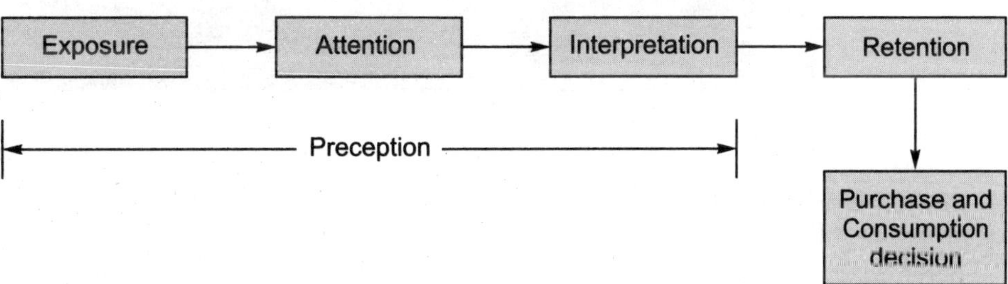

Fig. 4.7 Information processing by consumers.

Before a purchase decision is made by the consumer, the stimuli given by the marketer is processed in four different stages. The first three stages combined together constitute *perception*.

Exposure occurs whenever a stimulus such as a banner, TV advertisement or a hoarding advertisement comes within the range of a person's sensory receptor nerves–vision or auditory. This can happen deliberately or randomly. Therefore, it is important for the advertiser to place the stimulus within the person's relevant environment. Most of the stimuli to which individuals are exposed are "self-selected", i.e. people deliberately seek out exposure to certain stimuli and avoid others. Generally, people seek information that they think will help them achieve their goals. These goals may be short-term or long-term. Also, people are exposed to a large number of stimuli on a more or less random basis during driving or walking, which they do not purposefully seek out.

Attention catching advertisement.

Attention occurs when stimulus is seen, i.e. the receptor nerves pass the sensations into the brain for processing. People are exposed to innumerable stimuli way beyond than what they can process. Therefore, consumers have to be selective in attending to marketing as well as to other messages. This selectivity has major implications for marketers and others concerned with communicating effectively with consumers. Therefore, anyone interested in communicating effectively with consumers must understand how to obtain attention after getting the exposure. The important point is, how to obtain the attention.

How can a marketer assure that its advertising message is being attended to? Also, one must remember that attention always occurs within the context of a situation. The same individual may devote different levels of attention to the same stimulus in different situations.

Attention is determined by three factors. These are:

(a) **Stimulus factors** are physical characteristics of the stimulus itself. A large number of stimulus characteristics have the capability to attract our attention irrespective of individual and situational characteristics. Some of the stimulus factors are:

- Sizes and intensity (loudness, brightness, length)
- Insertion frequency
- Format

Ads using physical characteristics to attract attention.

- Colour and movement
- Contrast/expectations
- Position
- Interestingness
- Isolation
- Information quantity

(b) **Individual factors** are the characteristics of the individual (audience/consumer). Interest and need are the two major characteristics that influence the attention of the consumer.

Interest is a reflection of the overall lifestyle and result of long-term and short-term goals and plans.

Also, individuals differ in their ability to attend to information. They seek (exposure) and examine (attend to) the information relevant to their current needs and interests. Thus, an individual who is thinking of joining an MBA programme is likely to attend to a MBA admission-related advertisement.

(c) **Situational factors** include stimuli in the environment other than the local stimulus and temporary characteristics of the individual that are induced by the environment such as time pressure or a crowded store. Another factor is the **programme** itself. In general, the audiences are attending to the medium because of the programme or editorial content and not the advertisement.

Interpretation is the attachment of meaning to the stimuli. The meaning we assign to a stimulus is not a direct meaning of the words and the situation in which a consumer finds himself. For example, our attitude towards a brand is influenced by the company that is producing it, by the personality it is being endorsed, its price, country of origin and the store in which it is sold.

Consumers assign meaning to the tone and feel of the message as well as the actual words and symbols.

A given message can be subjected to different interpretations by different people in different situations. Basically, interpretation is of two types:

Cognitive interpretation is a process whereby stimuli are placed into existing categories of meaning. It is an interactive process. The addition of new information to existing categories also alters those categories and their relationships with other categories. Thus, it is the marketer who provides appropriate information and knowledge through advertising to facilitate the consumer to assign a particular category or alter the category of the product.

It is the individual's interpretation, not objective reality, which influences behaviour. For example, a company may bring a new high quality, low price brand among the existing brands because of its better production process and marketing efforts.

However, if consumers interpret this lower price to mean lower quality, the new brand will not succeed at marketplace irrespective of the objective reality.

The above example indicates the importance of differentiating between the semantic meaning–the conventional dictionary meaning, assigned to a word–and the the psychological meaning–which is nothing but a specific meaning assigned to a word by a given individual or a group of individuals based on their experiences and the context or situation in which the term is used.

Marketers must be concerned with the psychological meaning. For example, semantic meaning of the term on sale is "a price reduction from the normal level." However, psychological meaning which the consumers may derive is that the product is not selling or that it is out of fashion.

Affective interpretation is the emotional response or feeling triggered by a stimulus such as an advertisement. The emotional responses to stimuli vary from culture to culture. For example, a picture of a young child with kittens may draw a feeling of warmth from an American consumer whereas a person allergic to cats might have a negative emotional response to such a picture. Thus, consumers faced with new products or brands often assign them to emotional as well as cognitive categories.

Marketing stimuli have meaning only as individuals interpret it and individuals are not passive interpreters of marketing and other messages, but actively assign meaning based on their needs, desires, expectations and experiences.

An individual's interpretation of stimuli is mainly influenced by personal variables such as learning and expectations.

LEARNING, MEMORY AND MOTIVES

A lot of campaigns are designed to teach some specific aspects of a product or a brand. Its success depends upon how well the marketing team understands and uses the learning principles. Firms and business organizations want consumers to learn about the positive features of their products and services. Non-profit organizations are interested in teaching consumers about the consequences of their consumption choices.

Consumer behaviour is largely learned behaviour. The brands we buy, the place from where we buy and the criteria we use for choosing a brand are all learnt from our friends, relatives or family members. Therefore, we may say that people acquire most of their attitudes, values, tastes, behaviours, preferences, symbolic meanings and feelings through learning (see Figure 4.8).

Learning as a term is used to describe the processes by which memory and behaviour are changed as a result of conscious and nonconscious information processing. A large number of organizations attempt to help consumers learn "appropriate" attitudes and behaviours about issues such as racial discrimination, pollution, environmental protection, smoking, AIDS, drinking, proper nutrition and human rights. Learning is any change in behaviour which is a result of information processing.

Ads that help in learning pre-defined behaviour.

Learning may occur in either a high involvement or a low involvement situation. A high involvement learning situation is one in which the consumer is motivated to process or learn the material, for example, an individual reading through the user's guide dealing with various mobile phones. The buyer is highly motivated to learn various features and advantages of different brands. A low involvement learning situation is one in which the consumer has little or no motivation to process or learn the material. For example, a consumer viewing a news programme comes across a commercial for a product, which he/she does not currently need, use or has a desire for and thus has little motivation to learn the material of the commercial.

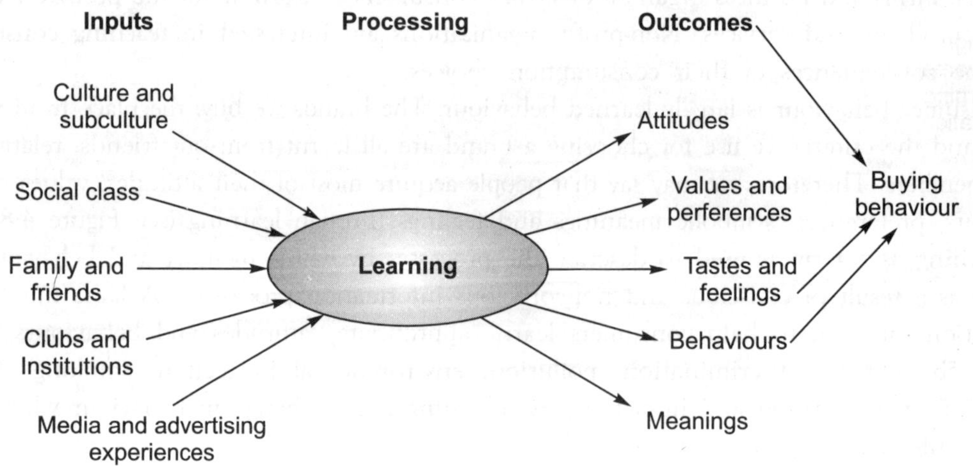

Fig. 4.8 Learning and consumer behaviour.

The processing of various inputs from the environment in which the consumer exists results in learning of certain values, preferences, attitudes, tastes and feelings as shown in Figure 4.8. This outcomes of learning then determines the buying behaviour. Thus, learning is a continuous change resulting in modifications or new learning outcomes.

Theories of Learning

It is important to understand the principles and underlying assumption of learning. The level of involvement is the primary factor in learning of a material. The way a communication should be structured differs depending on the level of involvement the consumer is expected to have. The involvement of the consumer with a stimulus is a function of the interaction between the individual, the stimulus and the situation. In other words, an important judgement in designing an advertisement must be the level of involvement the audience will have. Moreover, the involvement will be determined by the interaction of the characteristics of the target markets, the situation and the advertisement itself or other marketing stimulus. A marketer has to find answers to the following questions to develop an effective communication. Why does one ad assume a highly involved audience and the other a low-involvement audience? What difference do you notice between those two ads? Do these differences make sense?

Figure 4.9 indicates two general situations and five specific learning theories that help in understanding the learning behaviour of consumers. The solid lines in the figure indicate that

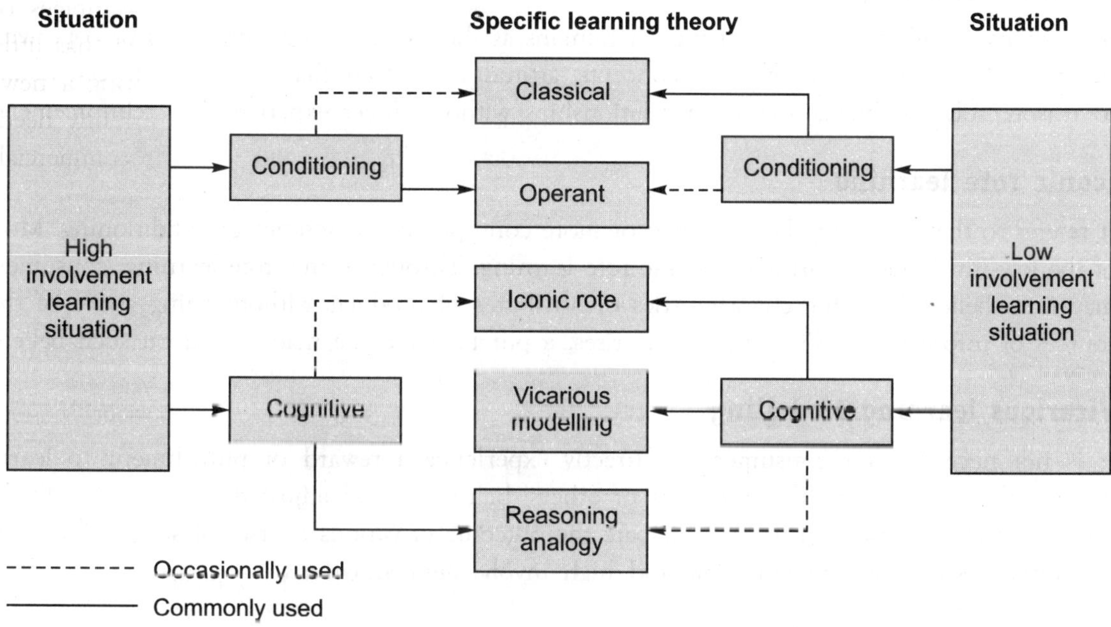

Adapted from: Hawkins, Best, Coney, *Consumer Behaviour: Building Marketing Strategy,* 9th ed., Tata McGraw-Hill.

Fig. 4.9 Learning theories in high and low involvement situations.

operant conditioning and reasoning/analogy are commonly used learning processes in high involvement situations. Classical conditioning, iconic rote learning and vicarious learning/ modelling tend to occur in low involvement situations.

Conditioning

It refers to learning based on association of a stimulus (information) and response (behaviour or feeling). It also means that through exposure to some stimulus and a corresponding response, one learns that they go together or do not go together. There are two types of learning.

- *Classical conditioning:* The process of using an established relationship between a stimulus and a response to bring about the learning of the same response to a different stimulus is called classical conditioning. The Classical conditioning is the most common in low-involvement situations.
- *Operant conditioning* also called instrumental learning, differs from classical conditioning primarily in the role and timing of reinforcement. Reinforcement plays a much larger role in operant conditioning. Since no automatic stimulus response relationship is involved, the subject must first be induced to engage in the desired behaviour. Then this behaviour must be reinforced. Operant conditioning often involves the actual usage of the product. Thus, a great deal of marketing strategy is aimed at securing an initial trial.

Cognitive learning

It encompasses all the mental activities of humans as they work to solve problems or cope with situations. It involves learning ideas, concepts, attitudes and facts that contribute to our ability to reason, solve problems and learn relationships without direct experience or reinforcement.

Iconic rote learning

It referes to the association between two or more concepts in the absence of conditioning. Most of the low involvement learning is iconic rote learning. Through iconic rote learning, consumers may form belief about the characteristics or attributes of products without being aware of the sources of information. When the need arises, a purchase may be made based on such beliefs.

Vicarious learning/Modelling

It is not necessary for consumers to directly experience a reward or punishment to learn. Instead, they can observe the outcomes of others' behaviour and adjust their own accordingly. Similarly, they can use imagery to anticipate the outcome of various courses of action. This type of learning is common in both low and high involvement situations.

Reasoning/Analogy

The most complex form of cognitive learning is reasoning. In reasoning, individuals engage in creative thinking to restructure and recombine existing information as well as new information to form new associations and concepts. Information from a credible source that contradicts one's existing beliefs will often trigger reasoning. Analogical learning occurs when a consumer uses an existing knowledge base to understand a new situation or object.

Theories of learning help us understand how consumers learn across a variety of situations.

Characteristics of Learning

Regardless of which approach to learning is applicable in a given situation, several general characteristics of learning are relevant and of interest to a marketing manager.

A few of the most important characteristics of learning are:

- Strength of learning
- Importance
- Message involvement
- Mood
- Reinforcement
- Repetition
- Imagery
- Extinction (forgetting)
- Stimulus generalization
- Stimulus discrimination
- Response environment

MEMORY

Memory is the total accumulation of prior learning experiences. It consists of two interrelated components: short-term memory and long-term memory. These are not distinct psychological entities.

Short-term memory

Short-term memory is that portion of total memory that is currently activated or in use. It is also known as *working memory*. People also have explicit memory, i.e. memory of specific events or objects, and implicit memory (i.e. generalized memory about events or objects).

Short-term memory has a limited capacity to store information and sensations. Consumers use short-term memory to hold information while they analyze and interpret it. Short-term memory is closely analogous to what we normally call 'thinking'. It is an active dynamic process and not a static structure. Basically, two types of information processing activities occur in short-term memory: elaborative activities and maintenance rehearsal.

Elaborative activities refer to the use of previously stored experiences, values, attitudes, beliefs and feelings to interpret and evaluate information in working memory as well as to add relevant previously stored information. Elaborative activities serve to redefine or add new elements to memory.

Maintenance rehearsal is the continual repetition of a piece of information in order to hold it in current memory for use in problem solving or transferal to long-term memory. Repetition of some line or formula before examination is an example of maintenance rehearsal.

Long-term memory

Long-term momery is viewed as an unlimited, permanent storage. It can store numerous types of information such as concepts, decision rules, processes, etc. Marketers are more interested in semantic memory as it concerns the basic knowledge and feelings an individual has about a concept. It represents the person's understanding of an object or event at its simplest level.

Episodic memory is another type of memory, which is of interest to the marketer. This is the memory of a sequence of events in which a person participated. This memory relates to events such as a birthday, graduation day, marriage day and birth of the first child, etc. Marketers are interested in episodic memory to associate their brand with the positive feelings such memory generates.

MOTIVATION, PERSONALITY AND EMOTIONS

These are two closely related concepts. *Motivation* is the energizing force that activates behaviour and provides purpose and direction to that behaviour. In fact, motivation is the drive within that causes behaviour. *Personality* reflects the common responses (behaviours) that individuals make to a given situation. *Emotions* are strong, relatively uncontrollable feelings that affect our behaviour. As observed among consumers, emotions can play an important role in consumer decisions. A good number of marketing strategies are designed to exploit emotions (strong feelings) of consumers towards an object.

Motivation and Marketing Strategy

Motivation is the reason for behaviour. A motive is an inner force that stimulates and compels a behavioural response and provides a specific direction to that response. A motive is why an individual does something. A consumer has a motivation for every purchase he makes. Therefore, it is important for the marketing manager to understand the type of motivation behind the purchase. But it is not an easy task. Motivations underlying the purchase decision even for a simple product are quite complex. There are plenty of motivation theories that give a good insight into why people do what they do.

We will discuss in particular two motivational theories that are relevant to consumer behaviour. Maslow's need hierarchy is important for understanding human behaviour in general terms. And McGuire's work is relevant because it uses detailed set of motives to understand specific aspects of consumer behaviour.

Maslow's hierarchy of needs

Maslow's theory divides all human needs into five different levels viz. physiological, safety, belongingness, esteem and self-actualization. These are further categorized as higher order and lower order needs.

Maslow's motivational theory is based on four premises:

- All human beings acquire similar set of motives through genetic endowment and social interaction.
- Motives have hierarchy, i.e. some are more important than others.
- The lower motives (needs) must be satisfied to a minimum level before higher-level motives (needs) are activated.
- As the lower order motives (needs) are satisfied, higher order motives (needs) come into play.

It is important to understand for the marketing manager that any given consumption behaviour can satisfy different needs at different times. The implications for the marketing manager are that before developing the marketing mix variables for the target market, he needs to know what level of needs the brand is satisfying or is perceived to be satisfying. Thus, the marketing mix variable decision on product, price, promotion and physical distribution would be based on the brand's perceived need level satisfaction.

McGuire's psychological motives

McGuire developed a classification system that organizes the various motives into 16 categories. The classification system helps the marketer to identify the motives associated with various consumption situations using two criteria:

- Is the mode of motivation cognitive or affective?
- Is the motive focused on preservation of the status quo or on growth?

The marketer divides all motives into four main categories. These four main categories are further subdivided on the basis of source and objective of the motive. The marketer therefore further identifies the motives by finding answers to the following:

- Is this behaviour actively initiated or in response to the environment?
- Does this behaviour help the individual achieve a new internal state or new external relationship to the environment?

Cognitive motives focus on the person's need for being adaptively oriented toward the environment and achieving a sense of meaning. *Affective motives* deal with the need to reach a satisfying feeling state and to obtain personal goals. *Preservation-oriented* motives emphasize the individual as striving to maintain the equilibrium, while *growth motives* emphasize development.

Each of the 16 motives given by McGuire has implications for the marketing manager. The categories are indicated below:

1. Cognitive Preservation Motives

- Need for consistency (active, internal).
- Need for attribution (active, external).
- Need to categorize (passive, internal).
- Need for objectification (passive, external) .

2. Cognitive Growth Motives

- Need for autonomy (active, internal).
- Need for stimulation (active, external).
- Teleological need (passive, internal).
- Utilitarian need (passive, external).

3. Affective Preservation Motives

- Need for tension reduction (active, internal).
- Need for expression (active, external).
- Need for ego defense (passive, internal).
- Need for reinforcement (passive, external).

4. Affective Growth Motives

- Need for assertion (active, internal).
- Need for affiliation (active, external).
- Need for identification (passive, internal).
- Need for modelling (passive, external).

The descriptions of both the theories show that motives are complex and difficult to understand. Once a combination of motives influencing the target market are understood, the manager's major task is to design an appropriate marketing strategy around the set of motives. It involves all decisions from product design and features, pricing, marketing communication to choice and location of channels.

If a consumer has more than one motive, the product must provide more than one benefit and the advertising must communicate these multiple benefits. While any given advertisement for a product may focus on only one or a few purchasing motives, the campaign needs to cover all the important purchase motives of the target market.

Personality

While motivations are the energizing and directing force that makes consumer behaviour purposeful and goal directed, the personality of the consumer guides and directs the behaviour chosen to accomplish goals in different situations.

Personality is an individual's characteristic response tendency across similar situations. These characteristic ways of responding to a wide range of situations should, of course, also include responses to marketing strategies.

There are large numbers of personality theories and all have two common assumptions:

- All individuals have internal characteristics or traits, and
- There are consistent and measurable differences between individuals on those characteristics.

Most of these theories state that the traits or characteristics are inherited or formed at an early age and are relatively static over the years. Differences between personality theories centre on the definition of which traits or characteristics are the most important.

A greater knowledge of the personality of the consumer help in satisfying him better. For example, a complain from the consumer can be handled accordingly whether the consumer is an extrovert or an introvert.

Generally, consumers use a particular product or brand to bolster an aspect of their personality. Thus, a weak and thin boy might drive a powerful bike to feel less weak and more powerful. However, another weak boy might forgo a powerful bike because of the "it's just not me" kind of feeling.

A consumer tends to match his human personality with that of the brand personality, a particular type of image that some brands acquire. Thus, **brand personality** is a set of human characteristics that become associated with a brand. Consumers perceive brand personalities in terms of sincerity, excitement, competence, sophistication and ruggedness.

Brands acquire personalities whether marketers want them or not, and these personalities influence purchases. Therefore, marketers need to manage the personalities of their brands, and need to reinforce them through appropriate advertising campaigns.

Emotion

We all experience a wide range of emotions every day. Emotions are generally triggered by environmental events. Anger, joy, cry and sadness are most frequently responses to a set of external events. However, emotional reactions may also be initiated by internal process called *imagery*. Thus, as defined earlier in the chapter, **emotions** are strong and relatively uncontrolled feelings that affect behaviour.

All emotions are accompanied by physiological changes, some of which are: rapid breathing, pupil dilation, increased perspiration, increased heartbeat and blood pressure and raised sugar levels. Another characteristics of emotions is cognitive thought, which is generally accompanied by thinking. However, the types of thoughts and our ability to think rationally vary with the type and degree of emotion. Also, extreme emotional responses are frequently used as an explanation for inappropriate thoughts or actions.

Emotions also have associate behaviours, which vary from individual to individual and with individual across time and situation. There are unique behavioural characteristics associated with different emotions like fear triggers fleeing response, anger triggers striking, grief triggers crying, etc.

Emotions involve subjective feelings. The feelings such as grief, joy, anger, fear and jealousy, etc. are at different levels in different individuals across times and situations. In addition to the feeling component, emotions carry an evaluative or a like/dislike component. Though emotions are generally evaluated (liked and disliked) in a consistent manner across individuals and within individuals over time, there are cultural, individual and situational variations. For example, some of us are scared of driving fast, yet we occasionally enjoy driving fast.

There are basically three dimensions-pleasure, arousal and dominance-underlying all emotions.

Understanding consumer emotions has implications for the marketer. The emotions have always been used for strategic decisions in the area of product positioning, sales presentations and advertising on an intuitive level.

It has been tentatively established through research that emotional content in advertisements enhances their attraction. Advertising messages that trigger the emotional reactions of joy, warmth or even digest are more likely to be attended to than those that are more neutral. Emotional messages may be processed more thoroughly than neutral messages and are remembered better than neutral ads. Repeated exposure to positive-emotion eliciting ads may increase brand preference through classical conditioning. Finally, emotional appeals can capture attention and enhance the retention of advertising messages. They can also help humanize the brand and associate feelings with it.

Attitudes

Business organizations often try to alter behaviour by changing attitude towards a brand, a product, a service or an organization. The experience and actions at the marketplace indicate that they succeed on numerous times. This change in attitude results in favourable consumption behaviour.

An **attitude** is a learned predisposition, a stabilized feeling that an individual holds toward an object, a person or an idea. Attitudes are more enduring and resistant to change.

Since attitudes are learned, we can change them, modify them and replace them with new ones. Attitudes also vary in direction and strength, i.e. an attitude can be positive or negative, reflecting likes or dislikes, or it can be neutral. Thus, an attitude is the way one thinks, feels and acts toward some aspect of his or her environment such as a retail store, television programme of a product, etc. We typically hold few strong attitudes, positive or negative. Strong emotional, social and political attitudes are most common. For example, people still hold a strong social attitude towards inter-caste marriage in India. Also, observe how apathetic Indian population is towards exercising their franchisee rights during elections.

Attitudes, generally, serve four functions:

- *Knowledge function:* Some attitudes serve as a means of organizing beliefs about objects or activities. For example, a consumer's attitude towards bikes that "they all are the same". This kind of consumer is likely to buy the cheapest and most fuel-efficient bike.
- *Value expressive function:* Some attitudes express an individual's central values and self-concept. Consumers who value nature and environment are likely to express support for environment friendly and green products.
- *Utilitarian function:* People tend to form favourable attitudes towards objects and activities that are rewarding and negative attitudes toward that are not.
- *Ego defensive function:* People form and use attitudes to defend their egos and self-images against threats and shortcomings.

Marketers need to be aware of the attitudes their brands fulfil for their target market. A given attitude may perform multifunction, though one may predominate.

Attitude components

Attitudes have following three components:

- *Cognitive component* consists of consumer's beliefs about an object. People have a number of beliefs about an object. As attitudes of a consumer get formed in the environment in which he lives, it is possible to change attitude through new learning. Changing cognitive component is the most effective way to change attitude. Following are a few steps that a marketer should take as part of the efforts to change attitudes:

- Change beliefs
- Shift importance
- Add beliefs
- Change ideal

- *Affective component* of an attitude represents feeling or emotional reactions to an object. The affective component or emotional reaction may change as the situation changes because products are evaluated in the context of a specific situation. Basically a marketer changes the liking of the brand through:

  (a) Classical conditioning
  (b) Affect towards the ad or website
  (c) More exposure

- *Behavioural component* of an attitude is one's tendency to respond in a certain manner toward an object or activity. As behaviour is directed towards an object, it is less likely to be specific than are beliefs and affective components.

Behaviour can lead directly to affect, to cognitions or both simultaneously. Consumers frequently try new brands or low cost items in the absence of prior knowledge or affect. Changing behaviour prior to changing affect or cognition is based primarily on operant conditioning. Therefore, the key marketing task is to induce people to purchase or consume the product while ensuring that the purchase or consumption will indeed be rewarding. Coupons, free trials, POP displays, tie-in purchases and price reductions are some of the common techniques to induce trial.

Individual and situational characteristics that influence attitude change

How much and in what direction the attitudinal change happens is determined by the individual and the situation as well as the activities of the firm or social agency. Individual difference matters a lot in attitude change as some people are more stubborn or narrow-minded or less subject to social influence than are others. Attitudes that are strongly held are more difficult to change than are those that are weakly held. Consumers are actively involved when marketers attempt to change their attitudes. The consumers infer the advertiser's intent and respond to the marketing communication in the light of this influence.

Self-concept and Lifestyle

In a way, lifestyle is an outward expression of one's self-concept. What an individual wears and the way he/she lives and spends his/her spare time, given the constraints and ability, is heavily influenced by that person's current and desired self-concept. Thus, self-concept is the totality of the individual's thought and feeling about the self.

Dimensions of a consumer's self-concept

Basically, a consumer's self-concept can be grouped as:

- Actual versus ideal and
- Private versus public

The actual vs ideal self-concept refers to the individual's perception of who he/she is and who he/she would like to be. The private self concept refers to what an individual is or what he/she would like to be. Public self-concept refers to how an individual is seen by others or how he/she would like to be seen by others.

Lifestyle is the way a person lives. The lifestyle of an individual is determined by his/her past experiences, and inborn characteristics and the current situation in which he/she is. The self-concepts of consumers get reflected through their lifestyles. Lifestyle is an important factor that influences all aspects of the consumer behaviour. The life style of an individual brings the self-concepts into action (see Figure 4.10).

Lifestyle determinants	*Lifestyle (How we live)*	*Impact on behaviour*
• Demographics	• Activities	**Purchase**
• Subculture	• Interests	• How
• Social class	• Likes or dislikes	• When
• Motives	• Attitudes	• Where
• Personality	• Consumption	• What
• Emotions	• Expectations	• With whom
• Values	• Feelings	**Consumption**
• Household life cycles		• Where
• Culture		• With whom
• Past experiences		• How
		• When
		• What

Fig. 4.10 Lifestyle and the consumption process.

Marketers can use lifestyle analysis with respect to specific area of consumer's life and relate to lifestyle with purchase and consumption decisions.

CONSUMER DECISION PROCESS

A marketer must understand how a consumer decides about what product he/she buys and what brand he/she prefers to satisfy his/her needs or find solutions to his/her problems. Understanding the process will help the marketer do right things for the consumer to make him/her purchase the brand and also assure repeated purchase.

The decision process used by the consumer will depend on two basic dimensions:

- Purchase involvement, and
- Type of decision making.

Purchase involvement is low involvement and high involvement. High involvement indicates greater concern and importance of the purchase and high interest shown by the consumer, whereas in low involvement concern, importance and interest are low.

There are three types of decision making:

- Nominal decision-making
- Limited decision-making
- Extended decision-making

Nominal decision-making involves no decision per se and it occurs when there is little involvement in the purchase. It is also called *habitual decision-making.* In this process, a problem is recognized, internal search (long-term memory) provides a single preferred solution (brand and store) that brand is purchased and an evaluation occurs only if the brand fails to perform as expected. Nominal decisions can be categorized as: brand loyal decisions and repeat purchase decisions.

Limited decision-making involves internal and limited external search, low alternatives, simple decision rule on few attributes and a little post-purchase evaluation. It involves organizing a problem for which there are several possible solutions. A few alternatives are evaluated based on a few dimensions using simple selection rule. There is very little post-purchase evaluation, unless there is a service problem or product failure.

Extended decision-making involves great internal and external information search followed by complex evaluation of multiple alternatives and a post-purchase evaluation. It is a high-involvement decision. These are relatively a few decisions that a consumer makes with this level of complexity.

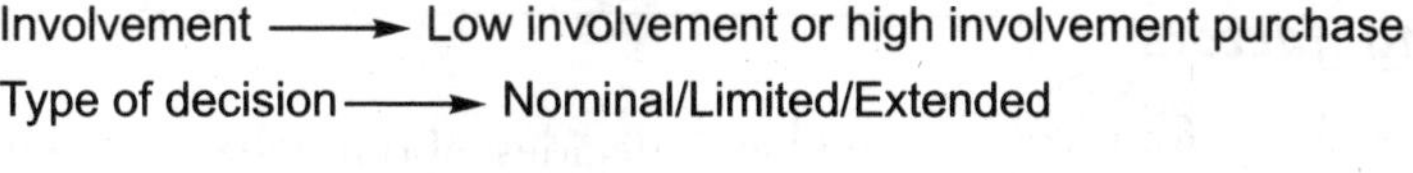

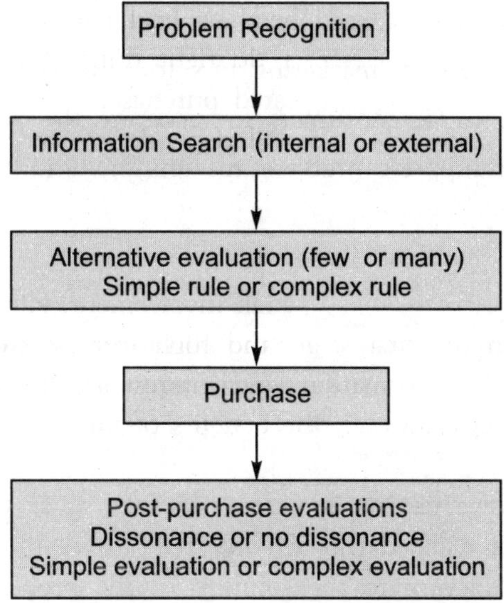

Fig. 4.11 Buyer decision process

Problem Recognition

Recognizing the problem is the first stage of consumer decision process. It is the difference between a desired state and an actual state that is sufficient enough to activate decision process. An actual state is the way an individual perceives his/her feelings and situation at present.

A desired state is the way an individual wants to feel at the present.

What action the consumer will initiate in response to the recognized problem will depend upon its importance to the consumer, the situation and the dissatisfaction or inconvenience created by the problem.

Problem recognition is stated to have occurred whenever the consumer feels a discrepancy between his/her desired and the actual state. The consumer's perception of the actual state that leads to problem recognition is not an objective reality as the perception of the actual state is also determined by a consumer's lifestyle and current situation.

Thus, discrepancy between what a consumer desires and what he/she has is the necessary condition for problem recognition. This discrepancy could be due to a large number of factors that influence consumer desires, perceptions of the existing state or both. These factors are beyond the control of marketing managers.

The factors that influence consumers' desires are both marketing and non-marketing in nature. The major non-marketing factors are: social status, culture and subculture, emotions, motives, previous financial status, expectations, reference groups, individual and situations.

Major marketing factors

Marketing managers have four concerns related to problem recognition. These are:

- They need to know the problems faced by the consumer
- They must know how to develop marketing mix to solve consumer problem
- They occasionally want to cause consumers to recognize the problem
- They sometimes desire to suppress problem recognition among consumers.

Information Search

Having recognized the problem in the first stage, the consumer now engages in information search both internally and externally. Information search requires mental and physical activities, which takes time, energy and money. However, the benefits of information search outweigh the cost associated with it.

Internal search requires extensive use of long-term memory so as to find if a satisfactory solution exists. If a solution is not reached through internal search, then the search process is focused on external information relevant to the solution of the problem.

External information includes:

- Opinions, attitudes, behaviours and feelings of friends, neighbours and relatives.
- Information provided by the company in pamphlets, articles, books, website and personal contest.
- Direct experiences with the product through inspection, trial and observation.
- Marketer generated information given in advertisements, websites and displays and by sales personnel.

What information does the consumer need?

A consumer decision requires information on the following:

- The appropriate evaluative criteria for the solution of a problem.
- The existence of various alternative solutions.
- The performance level of each alternative solution on each evaluative criterion.

The desired characteristics are the evaluative criteria. The evaluative criteria are the basis one uses for taking a decision to buy a particular brand.

One of the potential objectives of both internal and external search is the determination of appropriate evaluative criteria. Once an evaluative criterion has been decided, one would now seek appropriate alternatives for evaluations–this could be brands, stores, price, etc.

All such alternatives may fall in one of the following four types:

- Awareness set
- Evoked set
- Inert set
- Inept set

Awareness set comprises all those alternatives that the consumer knows about or is aware of. *Evoked set* is a collection of those brands or products that one evaluates for the solution of a particular consumer problem. It is also called a *consideration set*. *Inert set* comprises those brands which the consumer is aware of but is basically indifferent toward. *Inept set* comprises those brands that are actively disliked or avoided by the consumer.

Alternative Evaluation and Selection

We have all made numerous consumer choices and we know that those choices are not so logical, structured and rational as we made it seem in the preceding discussion. Consumer choices are rather frequently circular, emotionally incomplete and based on expediency rather than optimality. We also know that situation is an important factor in consumer choice.

A large number of marketing managers make assumptions about the consumer and consider him a rational decision-maker who has sufficient skills to calculate which option will maximize his value. This approach is known as **Rational Choice Theory**. But in reality all consumers have a limited capacity for processing information. In addition, for many decisions, consumers do not engage in strictly rational choice, instead they engage in a decision process that is suitable for the given situation.

However, a large number of consumers do not make any comparisons of brands or their features in their decisions. Such decisions are based on emotional responses to the brand or the overall impression of the brand.

While making buying decisions, a consumer makes any or a combination of the following consumer choice processes:

- *Affective choice* is more holistic in nature. Decisions based on affect use the "how do I feel about it" decision rule. The consumer imagines or pictures using the product or service and evaluates the feeling that this use will produce.
- *Attribute-based choice* requires the knowledge of specific attributes at the time of making the choice. It involves attribute-by-attribute comparisons across all brands.
- *Attitude-based choice* involves the use of general attitudes, summary impressions, intuitions or heuristics. No attribute-by-attribute comparisons are made at the time of choice.

The process of alternative evaluation and selection is depicted in Figure 4.12 below:

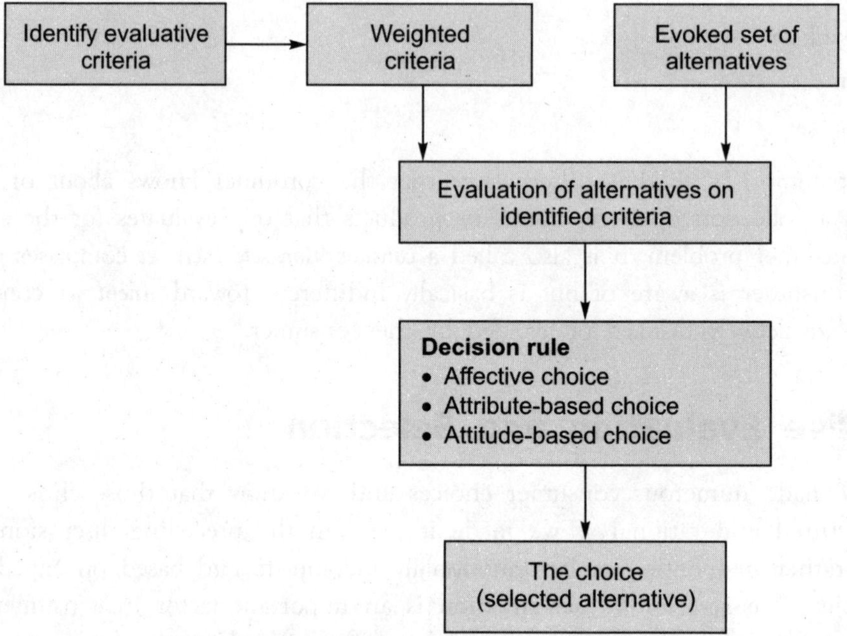

Fig. 4.12 Decision choice process.

Purchase

At the alternative evaluation stage, the consumer forms preferences among the brands in the choice set. Now, the consumer may form an intention to buy the most preferred brand. However, two factors can intervene between the purchase intention and purchase decision. These are:

- Attitude of others, and
- Unanticipated situational factors.

The attitude of others around the consumer may affect the preferred purchase intention. The extent to which another person's attitude reduces one's preferred alternative depends on the intensity of another person's negative attitude toward the consumer's preferred alternative and the consumer's motivation to comply with the other person's wishes.

A buyer's preference for a brand will increase if someone, whom he/she respects, strongly favours the same brand. The influence of others becomes complex when several people close to the buyer hold contradictory opinions and the buyer tries to please them all.

The unanticipated situational factors that may erupt to change the purchase decision are for example, a consumer losing his/her job, some other purchase becoming more urgent. etc.

A consumer's decision to modify, postpone or avoid a purchase decision is heavily influenced by the perceived risk. The amount of perceived risk varies with the amount of money at stake, the amount of attribute uncertainty and the amount of consumer self confidence.

While executing a purchase intention, the consumer may make up the following five purchase sub-decisions.

- Product choice
- Brand choice
- Dealer choice
- Purchase timing
- Purchase amount

Post-Purchase Behaviour

After making a purchase decision and consumption, the consumer experiences some level of satisfaction or dissatisfaction. The marketer's job does not end with the product sale. Marketers have to monitor post-purchase satisfaction, actions and product uses as well.

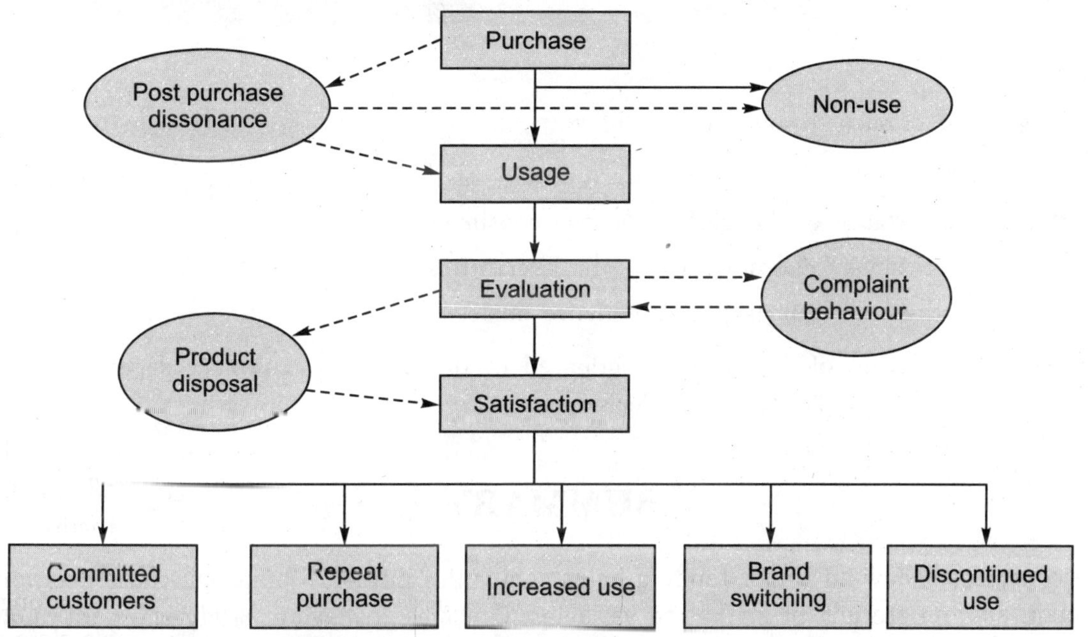

Source: Adapted from Hawkins, Best and Conay-Consumer *Behaviour Building Marketing Strategy*, 9th edition, Tata McGraw-Hill.

Fig. 4.13 Post-purchase consumer behaviour.

Some purchases result in non-use and some also result in post purchase dissonance which reflects a doubt or anxiety that might have come in the consumer's mind after he/she made the purchase.

Ads showing post-purchase behaviour.

The magnitude of such dissonance is a function of:

- The degree of commitment or irrevocability of the decision.
- The importance of the decision to the consumer.
- The difficulty of choosing among the alternatives.
- The individual's tendency to experience anxiety.

Therefore, the amount of dissonance experienced by the individual customer depends on the individual and the complexity of the decision.

SUMMARY

The consumer behaviour Understanding helps companies influence brand purchase decisions through appropriate mix of marketing variables. Consumer behaviour study is a continuous tracking of behaviour for the simple reason that the everchanging socio-economic and technology environment has great impact on the needs, wants and desires of the consumers. Studying and understanding consumer behaviour is basic to marketing decisions. All marketing decisions are based on assumptions about the consumer behaviour.

Individuals develop self-concepts and subsequent lifestyle under the influence of various internal and external factors. These self-concepts and lifestyles produce needs and desires, which can be satisfied through purchase decisions. Self-concept is the individual's view of the self. Lifestyle is the particular way in which one lives or the way an individual spends his spare time.

The decision process used by the consumer will depend on two basic dimensions:

- Purchase involvement, and
- Types of decision-making.

Purchase involvement may be low involvement and high involvement. Low involvement indicates low concern, importance and interest, whereas high involvement indicates greater concern and the importance of the purchase and the interest is high. There are three type of decision-making: Nominal decision-making, limited decision-making and extended decision-making. Nominal decision-making involves no decision per se. It is also called habitual decision-making. Nominal decisions can be categorized as brand loyal decisions and repeat purchase decisions.

Limited decision-making involves internal and limited external search, few alternatives, simple decision rule on few attributes and a little post-purchase evaluation.

Extended decision-making involves great internal and external information search followed by a complex evaluation of multiple alternatives and a post-purchase evaluation. Limited decision and extended decision are high involvement decisions whereas nominal decision-making is low-involvement decision.

Buyer's decision process involves five stages: Problem recognition, information search, alternative evaluation, purchase and post-purchase evaluation.

Problem recognition It is the difference between the actual state and the desired state. What action the consumer will initiate in response to a recognized problem will depend on the importance of the problem, situation and the inconvenience created by the problem.

Information search: The consumer engages in internal and external search, which requires mental and physical exercises.

Alternative evaluation and selection: The information collected by the consumer is used to evaluate every possible solution to the problem identified at stage one. The necessary criteria have to be identified and weighted. Each alternative then has to be evaluated on all chosen criteria.

Purchase decision: The third stage provides a clear-cut choice to the consumer.

Post-purchase behaviour. After the final purchase and consumption a consumer will experience some level of satisfaction or dissatisfaction. This is referred to as post-purchase behaviour.

Post-purchase dissonance: It refers to anxiety or doubt, which come in the consumer's mind after he has made the purchase.

QUESTIONS

1. How can the study of consumer behaviour help a marketing manager to develop an appropriate marketing strategy for the brand?
2. How can external factors influence the purchase decision of a consumer? Describe various external factors.
3. What are the various stages that a consumer goes through before deciding to buy a particular brand? Why is information search an important stage in decision-making_
4. What is buyer dissonance? Why does it occur? How can a marketer reduce it?
5. Describe various cultural factors that affect consumer behaviour. Through an example, illustrate how these factors impact marketing strategy.
6. How do internal factors affect consumer behaviour? How does perception and learning contribute to self-concept?
7. Personality and attitude are the important determinants of self-concept and lifestyle. Give an example to state clearly how these factors may affect the marketing strategy.
8. How does a consumer process the stimulus provided by the marketer? Explain the differences between exposure and attention through an example.
9. What should a marketer do to make the consumer take a favourable purchase decision towards the brand based on the knowledge of information processing by consumers?
10. What are the various choice decisions a consumer makes in the decision-making process? Distinguish the same through an example.

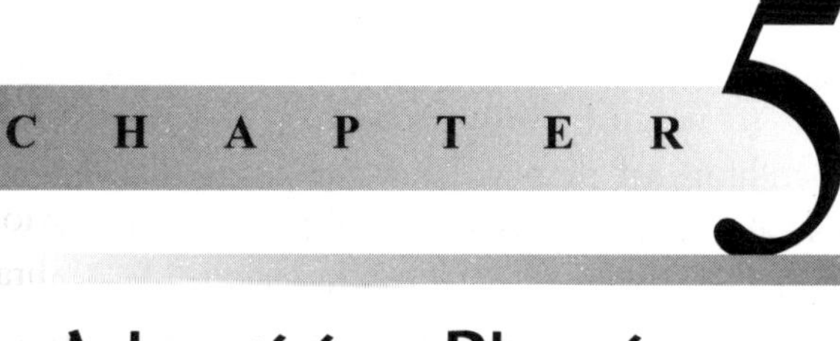

Advertising Planning

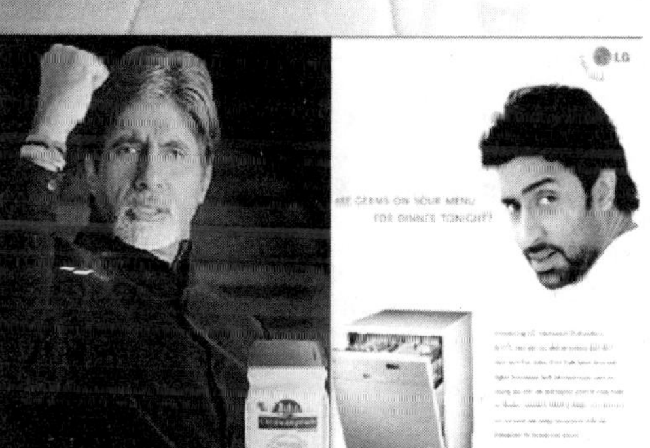

LEARNING OBJECTIVES

After reading this chapter, you will be able to:

- Identify the key elements of corporate strategic plan and marketing plan.
- Understand the link between marketing plan and advertising plan.
- Identify key elements in an advertising plan.
- Understand and develop an advertising campaign.
- Identify various elements of and understand a creative plan.
- Develop an effective media plan.

Advertising for a brand is not an outcome of whims or the fancies of the advertising or the brand manager. It is a well-thought, researched and stepwise process that leads to numerous decisions by the concerned managers. It is more so because every decision at this stage requires an expenditure of money. Therefore, a result-oriented action plan has to be developed and executed for achieving greater effectiveness of the advertising plan. A pertinent question may be asked here—why advertising planning? Planning is important because its essence is to identify alternatives and choose the best one that is expected to produce maximum results. Planning is also essential so that managers do not rely on whims and sudden flash of inspiration. It guides the managers as well as draws boundaries to operate within the plan. It is a well thought out future course of action to achieve desired results. Every plan needs to be documented and should offer sufficient scope for desired modification needed to encounter environmental dynamics. Advertising plan should be in synch with the marketing plan and the marketing plan should be in synch with corporate plan. This sort of synch is expected to produce maximum desired results.

The relationship between various plans is indicated in Figure 5.1.

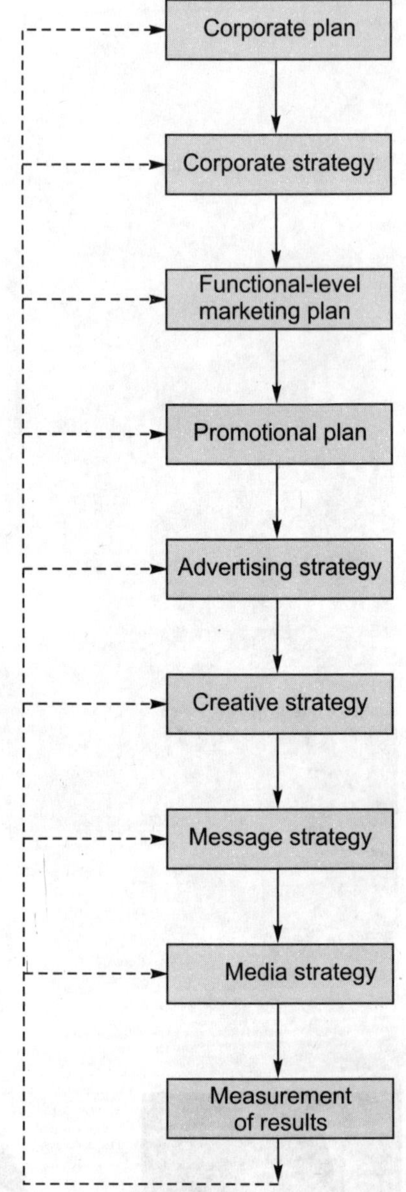

Fig. 5.1 Advertising plan linkages.

STRATEGIC PLANNING

Strategic planning is the process of deciding where to go, how to go and reaching the goal. In other words, it is the process of determining objectives (what you want to accomplish), fixing strategies (how to accomplish the objectives) and implementing the tactics (bringing the plan to life or making it action-oriented). A strategic plan for a business sets the tone for all other strategies. Figure 5.2 shows various steps in sequence and the relationship among them.

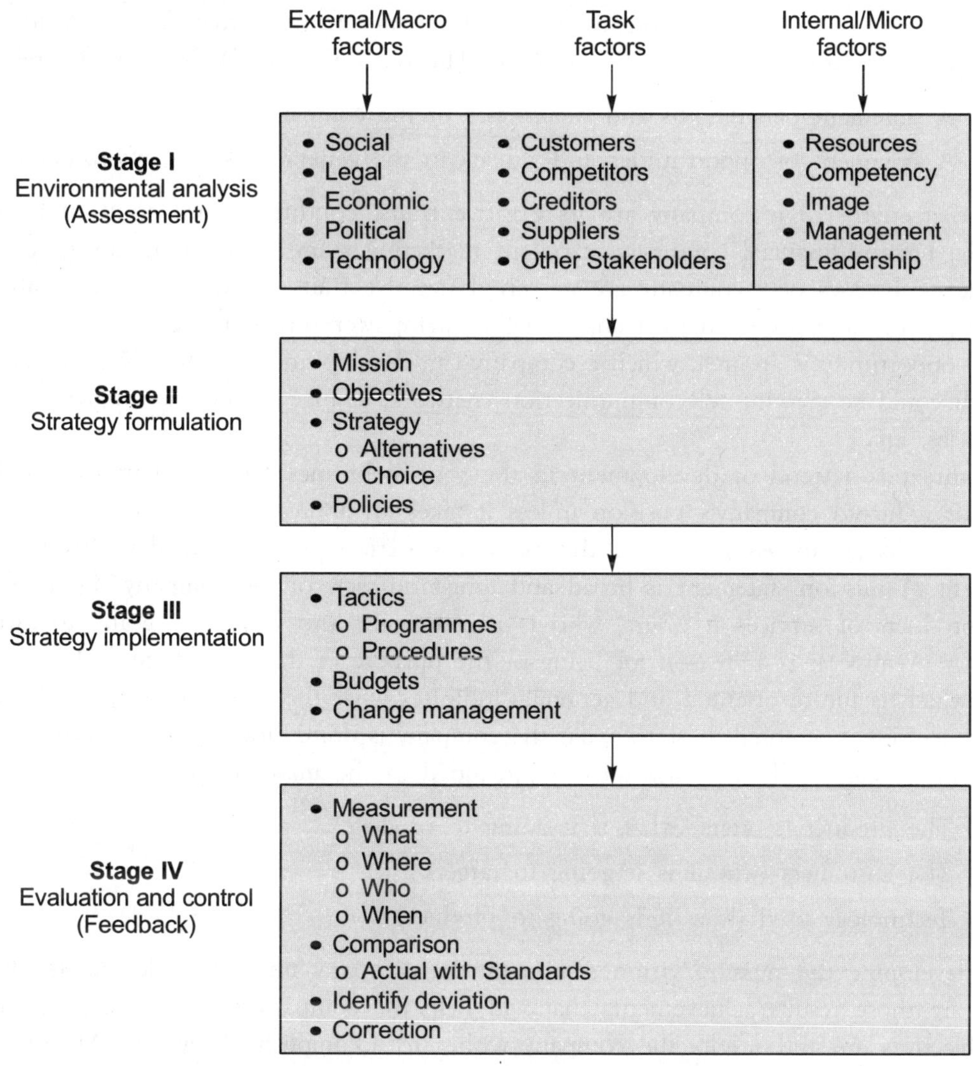

Fig. 5.2 Strategic planning process.

Strategic planning is a three-tiered plan. It starts with a corporate or business strategy, then moves to functional plans, such as marketing strategy or finance strategy or human resource strategy, etc. and then ends with a detailed tactical plan for each of the function and sub-function. Strategic planning process comprises four stages: environmental analysis, strategy formulation, strategy implementation, and evaluation and control. These stages are sequential and related to each other. It is a continual process beginning with assessing the current situational state of affairs in the organization and general business environment. A quantitative tool, SWOT analysis, is used for this purpose. The outcomes of SWOT analysis are:

- A statement of strengths and weaknesses of the company.
- A statement of opportunities and threats in the general business environment.

The strengths of a company are its positive traits, conditions and good situations, for example, healthy financial condition, excellent marketing team, great brand image, etc.

The weaknesses of a company are perceived negative traits, conditions and situations, for example, poor sales, losing market share, higher manpower turnover, etc.

An opportunity is an area, which a company can develop and take an advantage of over its rivals. It could be growing telecommunications network, change in lifestyle, higher expenditure tendencies, etc.

A threat is a trend or development in the general business environment that is likely to erode or reduce a company's position unless it takes an appropriate action.

After making an assessment of the current situation, a company develops its mission statement. A mission statement is broad and long-term view of the company about self-stating what products or services it offers, who is its customer and how it is going to satisfy the customer. A mission is a "reason for being or the purpose of the organization". It differs from vision which is future oriented and generally indicates what the company wants to be whereas mission is present oriented. It states what the company is doing, for whom it is doing and how it is going to do it. Three things must be included in the mission statement:

- The product it offers (what is it going to produce).
- The customers (whom is it going to target).
- Technology used (how it is going to produce).

After developing the mission/vision statement the company must now decide its objectives, which are those results/achievements that will help the company to accomplish its mission.

Objectives are end results the company wishes to accomplish. They are SMART–specific, measurable, attainable, resourced and timed. Objectives must be very specific and quantifiable. For example, Hyundai Motors wants to have 20 per cent increases in sales of Santro *Zing* for the year 2006-07.

Having decided what objectives are to be achieved, the company decides how they are to be achieved. In this, it chooses the ways and means to achieve its objective. In other words, it chooses a strategy to reach its goals. Strategy is a path or a way a company chooses out of many identified alternatives to achieve its objectives.

Choosing a strategy is a two-step process:

- Identification of alternatives.
- Evaluation and choice of alternatives.

Having decided the path it wishes to take, the company sets ground rules for carrying out action so that the strategy is implemented.

Policy is a set of guidelines and boundaries within which manager has to take decisions. Policies provide both freedom and restriction to the manager for implementing a strategy. The strategic implementation begins with detailed programmes and procedures. Also, budgets have to be formulated to assure that all programmes get implemented. However, it should always be kept in mind that the programmes implemented may not necessarily lead to achievement of objectives. The performance has to be continuously monitored and evaluated to assure that the actions initiated are on right path. At the stage of monitoring, the following things need to be decided:

- What to monitor?
- Where to monitor?
- When to monitor?
- Who to monitor?

Monitoring shall facilitate measurement of performance on various counts which would be compared with standards. Monitoring process will indicate deviations from such standards, if any. Following this an action has to be initiated to correct the deviations, and this can be done at any stage of the strategic process.

Thus, it is important to understand that once a business develops its key strategies for attaining its objectives, it must work out supporting programmes, known as tactics, for carrying out those strategies.

THE MARKETING PLAN

Marketing plan It is a functional level plan, which set out marketing objectives, particular strategies and tactics to attain organizational objectives. A marketing plan should be based on specific problems or opportunities identified at the stage of marketing environmental analysis. Therefore, a marketing plan analyzes the marketing situation, identifies the problems, outlines the marketing opportunities, sets the objectives and proposes strategies and tactics to solve those problems and meet objectives. To a large extent, a marketing plan parallels the business plan and contains many of the same components as shown in Figure 5.3. As is evident to advertising managers, the most important part of the marketing plan is the marketing strategy. It links the overall strategic business plan with specific marketing programmes, including advertising.

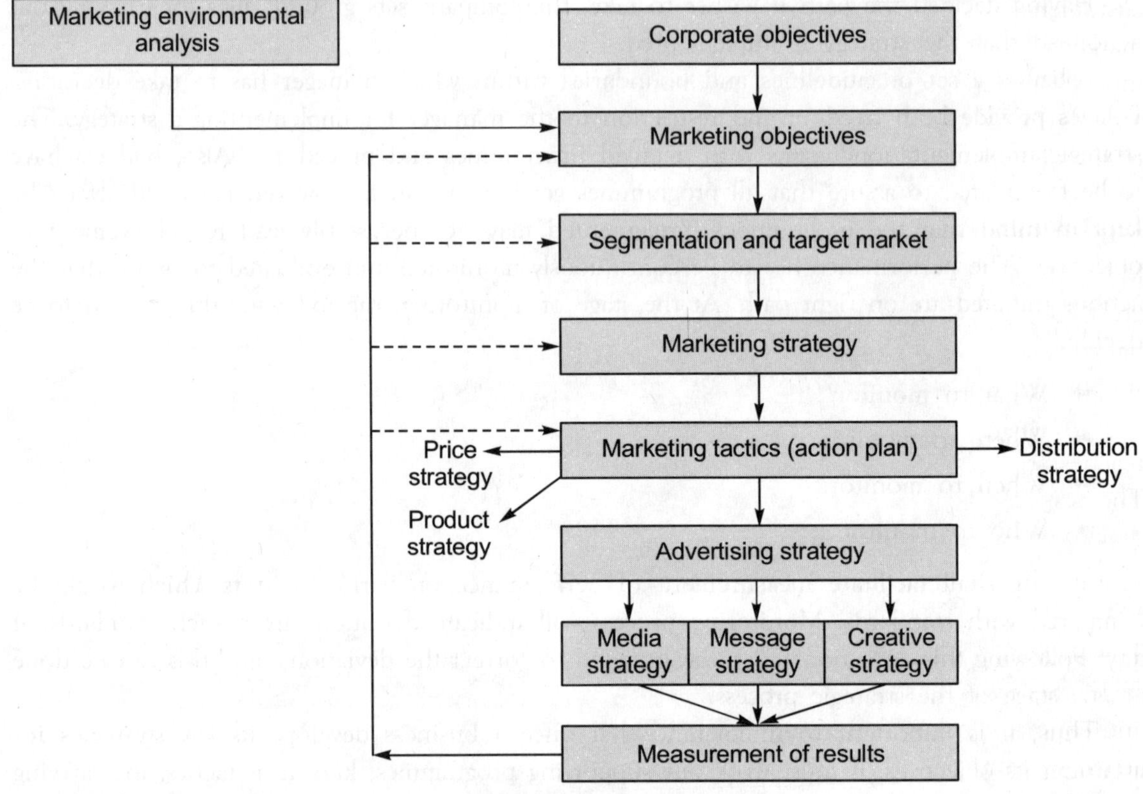

Fig. 5.3 Development of marketing plan.

The marketing planning process begins with the selection of marketing objectives, which are drawn from corporate objectives, and are outcomes of marketing environmental analysis.

A target market is one for which total marketing offer is made and it comprises a group of similar consumers of one or more characteristics.

For example, SONY TV has segmented its market based on capacity to pay, quality consciousness and trendy customers. Out of the numerous segments it selects few for its market offering. Some of the factors used as basis for target market selection are profitability, size and accessibility.

Developing Marketing Strategies

The most important part of the marketing planning is the identification of key strategic decisions that will not only help achieve the stated objectives, but also provide competitive advantage at the market place. The marketer has to make several assumptions about the customers and competitors before a marketing mix is developed for the target market. The marketer has to develop specific action plans or tactics for each of the element of the marketing mix. Moreover, the elements in the marketing mix are to be designed in such a way that it appeals to the target market, takes into account the limitations of the resources and proves profitable.

Implementing the plan

Merely having a great strategy is not sufficient; it has to be implemented very carefully and with great efforts. This would require a great number of decisions at the ground level. The marketer has to assure that the product reaches the warehouses and the sales team is in the field, training, supporting and motivating the dealer network.

The marketer also has to assure that the promotional material is dispatched timely and reaches at the point of purchase and also that the advertising campaign kicks off as scheduled. The responsibilities for various action plans have to be fixed and schedules for each plan are drawn, agreed and adhered.

Evaluation and control

This component is very important but often neglected for want of time and efforts. At this stage, the actual performance is continuously measured at a predefined point and interval time and compared with standard (planned) performance. The marketer then finds gap, if any, in the actual performance so that a timely corrective action is introduced to bring the performance as planned. As indicated in Figure 5.3, a feedback is introduced at each stage of the marketing plan so that reasons for poor performance could be identified and necessary corrective measures taken.

ADVERTISING PLAN

Generally, companies concentrate on campaign advertising, meant for or focusing on solving a particular marketing communication problem, rather than annual advertising plans. In fact, an advertising plan should only be developed once the marketing plan has been decided and the role of advertising has been clearly defined in it.

Advertising plan and campaign plan are similar in outline and structure. These plans are the responsibility of the account manager, who is responsible for every decision that is to be made in these plans. Advertising planning involves identifying objectives and target audience, theme selection and structure, message strategy, media choice and frequency and budgets. Every advertising plan should reflect planning, decision and commitment concerning each of these tasks.

Thus, an advertising plan matches the right message to the right audience through the right medium.

Developing an advertising campaign is based on two major factors:

- Identification of target market.
- Buyer motives (behaviour).

It is important to know and understand the characteristics of the target consumers before any decision is made on various issues related to advertising campaign. Ultimately, the potential buyer's lifestyle, motives, characteristics and demographic factors will influence various advertising variable decisions on message, theme, appeal, media and frequency.

Five major decisions that need to be made creating an advertising campaign are:

- What are advertising objectives? (Mission)
- What message should be used? (Message)
- How much money can be spent? (Money)
- What media should be used? (Media)
- How should the results be evaluated? (Measurement)

These are 5Ms that are essential in making a successful advertising campaign. A typical advertising plan outline is given in Figure 5.4.

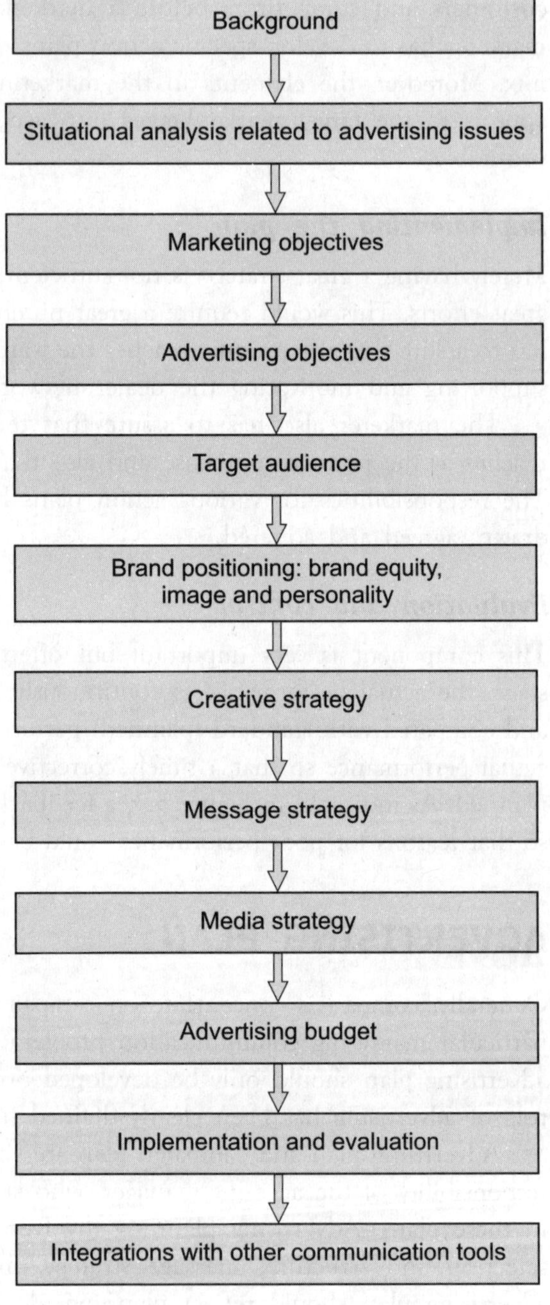

Fig. 5.4 Advertising plan outline.

BACKGROUND

The advertising plan should have a sound grounding in the background situation. The marketing manager must have full information on the problems, situation and competitive environment to develop the most appropriate advertising plan. The advertising strategy must be embedded in the organization's problem areas and opportunities that the organization seeks to exploit. In what situation the advertising campaign should be launched, what are the competitor's campaigns, what opportunities are likely to emerge at marketplace, specific problems faced by the organization are some of the background information the manager must collect to have the appropriate advertising strategy developed.

SITUATION ANALYSIS

It is basically a SWOT analysis at advertising level: A review of current state of the business that is relevant to the brand's advertising. This section details the search for and analysis of important information trends affecting the marketplace, the competition, consumer behaviour, the company, the product, and the brand.

The internal strengths and weaknesses of the company are determined through the analytical tools and the opportunities and threats profile is prepared as well. To take advantage of opportunities and avert threats, appropriate strengths are identified and weaknesses are corrected.

MARKETING OBJECTIVES

Depending on the corporate objectives and deeper insight into situational analysis the marketing objectives are formulated. These are the end results the marketing function wishes to achieve. Marketing objectives need to be consistent with corporate objectives. Some of the typical marketing objectives could be: to become market leader, achieving thirty per cent market share, achieving twenty-five per cent sales growth, etc.

ADVERTISING OBJECTIVES

Advertising objectives are set in such a way that they help in achieving marketing objectives. It is important for the advertiser to know what to expect from the advertising campaign given the huge money spent on advertising. Thus, every advertising campaign and the ads in it must be guided by specific advertising objectives. Basically, advertising objectives fall in four categories: perception, learning, persuasion and behaviour.

For an advertisement to be effective, it must be seen, read, understood believed and acted upon. Based on this, advertising objectives can be divided into the following three categories:

Sales objectives.
Communications objectives.
Behavrioural objectives.

Sales objectives

Advertising objectives, like organizational objectives, should be operational. This means there should be criteria for decision-making and standards with which results can be compared.

The most common advertising objectives in terms of sales are:

- Immediate increase in percentage of sales.
- Increase in market share.

These two measures are immediately available to evaluate the results of a campaign.

However, the objectives that involve increase in sales and market share may not be operational for two reasons:

- Advertising is one of among many factors influencing sales and it is difficult to isolate the influence of it on sales.
- The influence of advertising continues over a long time.

As indicated in Figure 5.5, advertising is only one of the many factors that influence sales. The other factors that influence sales include price, distribution, channel management and

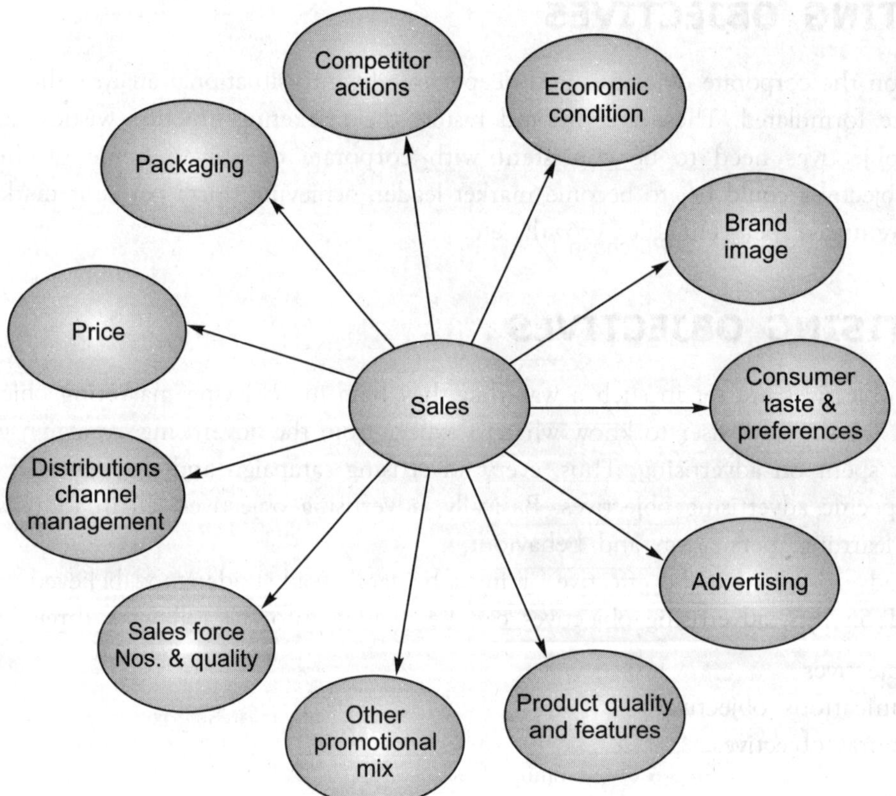

Fig. 5.5 Factors influencing sales.

motivation, the size and quality of sales force, product quality and features, the quality of packaging, role of other promotional mix—like sales promotion, public relations, direct and personal selling, etc.,—shifting consumer tastes and preferences, the brand image, general economic conditions prevailing in the country, planned and reactive competitor actions etc. It is extremely difficult to isolate the effect of advertising on the sales. This proves that when such quantifiable targets (increasing sales) are not achieved, it does not mean that the advertising has failed. For example, Sony TV launched advertising campaign in Rajasthan to increase its market share by few percentage point, but not many sets could be sold. This does not mean the campaign failed. The reasons were that dealers in Rajasthan were not interested in pushing sales as it offered them poor returns, the price range was much higher, other brands like LG and Samsung came up with better strategy and there was hardly any follow up service rendered to the dealers due to inadequate sales force in Sony.

Therefore, it is totally unfair and unrealistic to judge the advertising campaign by the number of sets sold, as it could have been influenced by many other factors.

Communications objectives

Advertising is most effective when it is used to obtain narrowly defined communication objectives. Shown in the Figure 5.6 are the various communication objectives that an advertising campaign must achieve.

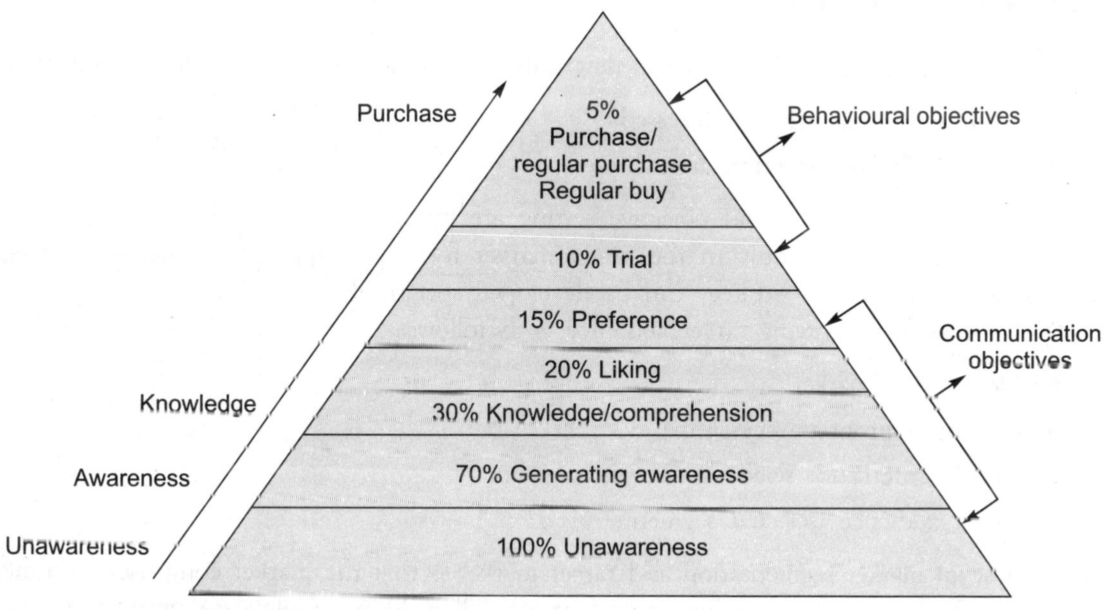

Fig. 5.6 Communication response pyramid.

For any advertising campaign, achieving lower-level communications objectives like awareness, knowledge or comprehension are paramount and basic. The subsequent movement will be towards achieving higher-level objectives such as liking and preference. It is easier to achieve lower-level communications objectives. The promotions manager should measure existing level of consumer awareness, knowledge, liking or preference for his brand. If the awareness and knowledge about the brand or its features is low among the consumers, he must concentrate on increasing this aspect. If the liking and preference for the brand is low, then he should try creating liking and preference for the brand by identifying right message and media strategy.

Behavioural objectives

To increase sales or achieve a particular market share merely by achieving communications objectives is not sufficient. It is important to induce action in the consumer through advertising.

Here, we require the consumer to act or show a specific behaviour. The behaviour could be trial of the brand or purchase of the brand.

The two specific objectives could be:

(i) Increasing company's brand usage rate among existing consumers.
(ii) Encouraging non-users to have trial consumption and/ or purchase the brand.

TARGET AUDIENCE

Basic questions that need to be replied in determining target audience and setting objectives are:

- To whom is advertising addressed?
- Where will the objectives be achieved?

Determining target audience and objective setting are intimately connected because identified objectives can be achieved only in the target market for which appropriate message strategy, media strategy and creative strategy can be developed specifically.

The process of identifying target audience is as follows:

- Identify the market
- Identify appropriate segments
- Decide criteria for selecting relevant segment
- Target audience (selected segments)

The premise of market segmentation and target market is that the market comprises customers who are heterogeneous in their needs and wants. Their liking, preferences and choices are different from others. Therefore, it is a difficult task for any company to satisfy such diversified needs.

Market segmentation is the process of disaggregating total heterogeneous market into relatively more distinctive homogeneous groups of consumers with similar characteristics and selecting few segments to target with distinctive market offerings.

The marketer has to decide how many characteristics to use for segmenting the market. The more the identifying characteristics used for segmenting the market, the more precisely defined are the segments. However, more the segmenting characteristics used, the fewer are the consumers in each segment. So, theoretically each individual consumer can be considered as a distinct segment. Thus, the marketer has to decide how far to go in the segmenting process.

Some of the basis used for segmentation are: Geographic, demographic, psychographics and behavioural.

The number of segments would now depend upon how many bases for segmentation have been used. It must be made clear here that all segments may not be attractive in terms of sales. So, the marketer has to identify and select those segments that are attractive and profitable not only now but in future as well.

A marketer needs to identify relevant criteria to determine the most attractive and profitable segments. Each of the segment will now have to be evaluated against identified criteria such as profitability, size, accessibility, sales potentiality, future returns, etc. The segment that measures well against those criteria will form the part of target market.

POSITIONING: BRAND IMAGE AND BRAND PERSONALITY

Positioning is the foundation upon which all other marketing mix decisions are built. A brand's position is the first thing that comes to mind when we hear a brand's name. For example, Volvo owns the safety position, while ESPN owns the sports information position.

Positioning strategy descriptions usually have an important role in advertising strategy. Positioning when combined with other marketing tools produces a unique perception in the mind of the consumer.

Positioning involves a decision to emphasize or highlight certain aspects of a brand.

The major decision in positioning is to let the consumer have a clear and definite idea of what the brand stands for in the given product category. Also, a brand cannot be distinctively and clearly positioned if it tries to do everything for everyone. A brand's marketing communications is the most important tool for acquiring such positioning. However, marketing variables such as price, distributions and product quality and features may also play major roles. Therefore, we may say that positioning is not what you do to the product, but what you do to the minds of the consumer through marketing communications.

Why Positioning?

Advertising efforts and other promotion tools attempt to communicate the brand's position to consumers. It is difficult to create brands in the given product category. Positioning provides necessary answer to what the brand is and attempts to create a brand identity to stand firmly against the competitors' efforts.

A product finds no place or does not exist unless it finds place in the consumers' perception. Consumers respond to products or brands as they perceive them rather than what these are in reality. The perception of individual product is subjective and called **perceptual identity**. The individual perceptual identity is determined by the individual's needs, values, beliefs, experience and environment.

The positioning concept has introduced the concept of "distance" and dissimilarity between brands in the "perceptual space" of the consumer. As Professor Levitt said that there is no such thing as a commodity, all the goods and services are differentiable. Therefore, the poisoning concept offers plenty of opportunities for perceived differentiation of products and brands. To be meaningful, a differential advantage has to be persuasive and sustainable.

The rapid advances made in technology and development has reduced differences among brands on functional aspects. The brand or product manager has to emphasize non-functional aspects to meaningfuly differentiate his brand from other brands.

According to Philips Kotler, positioning is the act of designing the company's offering and image to occupy a distinctive place in the target market's mind. Brands can expect loyalty only if they are perceived as distinct/different in some way which is meaningful and persuasive for the consumers in the target market.

Positioning Strategies

It is important to see that the positioning fits the target market. A brand must be positioned in a way that it is most effective in attracting the desired target segment.

Subroto Sengupta has suggested that a brand by answering the following questions itself can develop positioning strategies.

- Who am I? (Knowledge of the brand's identity and image, lineage or family),
- What am I? (The functional capabilities of the brand),
- For whom am I? (The consumer segment I serve best), and
- Why me? (Powerful reasons to choose me than any other alternative).

Similarly, Jack Trout and Al Ries suggest that managers should ask themselves the following six questions to create a position for a product or service brand:

- What position, if any, do we already have in the prospect's mind? (This information must come from the marketplace, not the manager's perceptions.)
- What position we want to own?
- What companies must be outgunned if we are to establish that position?
- Do we have enough marketing money to occupy and hold that position?
- Do we have the capability to stick with one consistent positioning strategy?
- Does our creative approach match our positioning strategy?

The strategy can be conceived and implemented in a variety of ways that may come from attributes, competitors, specific applications, the type of consumers involved or the characteristics of the product class.

Approaches to Positioning Strategy

Whatever is the approach used for developing positioning strategy, all of them have the common objective of either developing or reinforcing a particular image for the brand in the minds of the consumer.

Seven approaches to positioning strategy are:

- Using product characteristics or customer benefit approach
- The price-quality approach
- The use or applications approach
- The product user approach
- The product class approach
- The cultural symbol approach
- The competitor approach

Using product characteristics or customer benefit approach

It is the most used positioning strategy. It involves putting the brand above competitors, based on specific brand attributes and customer benefits. Many cars emphasize technical features such as: MPFI engine, power windows, fuel efficiency, safety and reliability, etc.

For example, Tata Indica is "more car per car". Volvo stresses safety and durability and it shows commercials of crash tests.

BMW car is the "ultimate driving machine" and similarly, Ford Ikon is "Josh Machine".

Gillette Satin Care.

Generally, marketers identify positioning in respect of product characteristics that have been ignored by the competitors.

Sometimes, brand managers attempt to position the brand along two or more characteristics simultaneously. For example, Aquafresh from Beecham was positioned on cavity-fighting and breath freshening benefits. Sometimes, different variants of a product may be positioned toward different segments by highlighting different attributes.

It is always tempting for a brand manager to position along several attributes or benefits because it might be very disheartening for the brand manager to have some of the characteristics that are not communicated. However, an advertisement trying to achieve multiple objectives by showing too many characteristics might confuse the brand image and thus hurt it.

Price-quality approach

Indian market is large and heterogeneous where consumer's quality and price expectations vary widely depending upon their socio-economic status. There are brands that deliberately attempt to offer more in terms of service, features, quality or performance. Manufacturers of such brands charge higher prices partly to cover the cost and partly to communicate the fact that they are of high quality. Conversely, in the same product category there are brands, though comparable in quality, that appeal on the basis of price. For example, in detergent product category the brands like *Surf* and *Ariel* are positioned on quality whereas brands like Nirma, though comparable in quality, is positioned on price. In watch category, brands like Rado and Timex use quality and price positioning respectively. It is difficult to use both quality and price positioning together because there is always a risk that high quality-low price campaign will smear such position, as people may infer that quality and low price don't go together.

Watches: RADO competes for quality; Timex competes on price.

The use and application approach

Yet another way to communicate an image is to associate the product with a use or application. AT&T associated long-distance calling with communicating with loved ones in its "Reach out and touch someone" campaign. Similarly, Campbell's soup for many years was positioned as a lunch-time product and used noontime radio advertisements quite extensively.

The recent campaign by LG is positioned as bacteria-free dishwasher.

LG: Intellowash dishwashers

The product user approach

In this approach, the brand manager identifies and determines the target segment for which the product will be positioned. Many brands use a model or a celebrity to position their product. Many sportsmen and filmstars have been used by various companies the world over. The expectations are that a model or a celebrity is likely to influence the product's image by reflecting the characteristics and image of the celebrity, communicated in the ad as a product user. Johnson and Johnson repositioned its shampoo from one used for babies to one used by people who wash hair frequently. It created a need for a mild shampoo for such users. The repositioning of the shampoo resulted in capturing a large market share by Johnson and Johnson.

Zandu special *Chyavanprash* is positioned for small children to build up their resistance against coughs and colds. However, Dabur Chyvanprash is positioned for all age groups. Both brands have similar ingredients but are positioned for different demographic segments.

Dabur: The Amitabh Bachchan ad reinforces that the product is useful for all ages.

The product class approach

This approach is used so that the brand is associated with a particular product category. This is a very bold positioning strategy and is generally used when a particular product category is too crowded. By this positioning, the brand manager would like the customers to perceive the brand in different context. For example, the Dove toilet soap from HLL is positioned as a cleansing cream product for young women with dry skin, thereby, finding a different position from other toilet soaps.

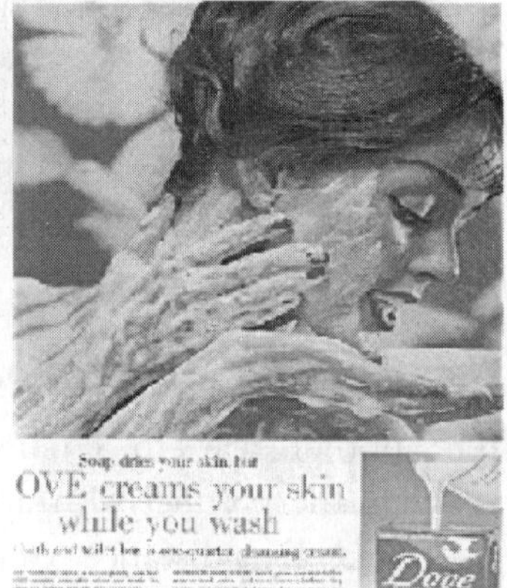

Dove soap ad positions the brand different from other toilet soaps.

One of the finest example of positioning by product class approach is that of 7up soft drink. The drink 7 up was positioned for long time as a beverage with "fresh clean taste". which was "thirst quenching". However, the research indicated that 7up was not regarded by people as a soft drink but a mixer beverage. Thus, a positioning strategy was developed to position 7-up altogether differently from the existing soft drink colas. Thus, the highly successful campaign "uncola" was born.

The 7up uncola ad.

The Cultural symbol approach

This positioning strategy is based on deeply entrenched cultural symbols. The use of such cultural symbols can help differentiate the brand from competitors' brands. A brand manager needs to identify something that is highly meaningful to the consumers and is not being used by competitors. The identified cultural symbol can then be associated with the brand. The positioning of Marlboro cigarettes is a classical example of using cultural symbol. The Marlboro cigarettes campaign used the American cowboy as its main focus to differentiate the brand from competitors.

Marlboro: Cigarettes that use typical American cowboy image.

The competitor approach

In many positioning strategies the frame of reference, implicitly or explicitly, is a competitor. Many brands use "competitor" as a dominant plank in their campaigns. This is an offensive strategy. It is very common in comparative advertising. One of the finest example of positioning by competitor is by Avis, the car rental company. Avis positioned itself as a No. 2 company behind the leader Hertz. It's positioning statement was, "We try harder because we are No. 2" This positioning succeeded because Hertz was No.1 company in US and thus, Avis related to Hertz.

Avis car ad: an example of positioning by competitor.

Avis is the second largest producer of used cars in the world.

In short, we're a giant in the used car business.

But we don't turn them over to you.

Apple computers. *Cox & Kings Ad.*

In India, lot of comparative advertising is done by automobile, electronics and airline industry to win customers.

Positioning by competitors is important for two reasons.

- Many times it is not important what customers think about you in absolute terms but it is important that they believe you are better than or as good as other competitors.
- The competitor image can be referenced, i.e. a competitor's image can be used as a stepping stone to communicate another image in reference to it. For example, if someone wants to know the address of Eros Cinema in Mumbai, it is better to say it is opposite church gate main entrance rather than describing the complete roads, lanes and bylanes that lead to Eros cinema.

Deciding the Positioning Strategy

The choice of taking up an appropriate positioning strategy is a difficult and complex task. However, it may be made easy if the company collects sufficient information through research and follow the nine steps as indicated in Figure 5.7.

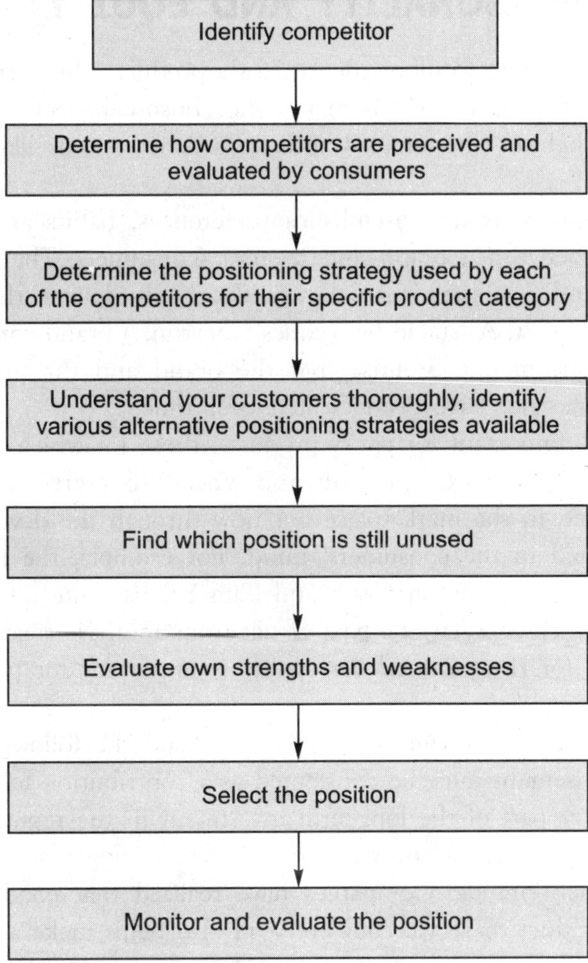

Fig. 5.7 Steps in positioning strategy.

Making the Positioning Decision

Some guidelines for getting a right positioning for the brand are as follows:

- An economic analysis should guide the decision.
- Positioning usually implies a segmentation commitment.
- Stick to the advertising theme if it is working. Do not change it for the sake of changing.
- Don't try to be something you are not.
- Use associations or symbols.

BRAND IMAGE, PERSONALITY AND EQUITY

Branding is the process of creating a unique identity for a product. This identity creates a feeling of familiarity with a known product, which makes the consumers feel comfortable to buy it again. This is the reason behind phenomenal success of some brands like IBM, Pepsi, Coke, HUL, Tata and Godrej.

Branding creates memorability and establishes preferences, habits and loyalties. It, thus, encourages a relationship between a brand and its user (consumer). The major ingredient in branding is trust. A brand promises that the product will deliver the same satisfactory performance as it has in the past. As stated by Jacques Chevron, a brand consultant, "The brand is a covenant with the consumer, a promise that the brand and the product it names will conform to the expectations that have been created over time."

Branding is particularly important for parity products, those for which there are few, if any, major differences in features. For example, salt and wheat flour are parity products. These products are undifferentiated in the marketplace but now through the development of a brand image, they are differentiated in the consumers' mind. For example, the image that comes to one's mind when one thinks of Captain Cook and Tata Salt is quite different.

What creates the difference between one type of salt from another—is advertising. Advertising can establish a personality for the product. Personality is important for positioning as well as building a brand image.

David Ogilvy, in *Confessions of an Advertising Man*, has said the following on brand image, "We hold that every advertisement must be considered as a contribution to the complex symbol which is the brand image, as part of the long-term investment in the reputation of the brand."

Today companies are heavily using advertising and other elements of the marketing mix to build up this equity in their brands. Companies have realized that good advertising doesn't simply make a sale of a product or service but every ad also helps make a brand image in the minds of the consumer. This imagery or personality of the brand then partly determines the price premium that the brands can command from consumers.

Brand Awareness

Brand awareness is the consumer's ability to recognize or recall (identify) the brand within a given product category in sufficient details to make a purchase decision. This also means that the consumer can propose, recommend, choose or use the brand. Objectives for most advertising are centred around creating and maintaining preferences. The first step towards making a consumer exercise his/her preference towards a brand is generating brand awareness. Generally, brand awareness is equated with recalling brand name. The creative ad copy, ad size and ad frequency contribute a lot in brand awareness and recognition. This is amply clear when brands like Lux and Hamam soaps, Bajaj scooter, Hero Honda motorcycle in India and Apple,

IBM, Pepsi and McDonald's in foreign markets have achieved great brand awareness and recognition through continuous and creative advertising for last many decades.

Brand Image

Professor Sid Levy, North Western University, in his article in *Harvard Business Review*, 1955, defined brand image as "the sets of ideas, feelings and attitude that consumers have about the brand". Thus, it is an image in customer's mind that reflects what they think and feel about a product and how they value it.

A brand has both physical and psychological dimensions. Physical dimensions are attributes, ingredients, design of the product, design of package and logo, the letters, shape, colours and art of the product. whereas psychological aspect includes the beliefs, values, emotions and personalities that people ascribe to the product.

Tools such as distinctive names, slogans, graphics and characters are used to transform products and lock them into memory.

Nikon camera ad: Excellent advertising reinforcing the image of the brand.

Joseph Plummer opined that there are three components to a brand image as given below:

- Attributes,
- Consequences, and
- Personality.

According to Plummer, brand image is inclusive of all associations that a consumer has for the brand, such as thoughts, feelings, imagery, sounds, colours, smells, etc. that the consumer links to the brand in his/her memory. Brand personality includes associations with specific characters, symbols, endorsers, users and lifestyles. Some consumers might relate intensely to a brand like owners of Harley-Davidson motorcycles in USA.

Brand Personality

The research indicates that when a consumer buys or uses a particular brand, he/she expresses his/her own self, an ideal self or some specific dimensions of the self through the use of a brand. This information about the consumer helps marketers to differentiate a brand in a product category.

Marketers visualize a brand in human terms, i.e. the brand is viewed on the dimensions of human personality. For example, the personality profile of Pepsi is: Youthful, cool, extrovert and anti-establishment.

Brand personality of Bajaj Pulsar: Definitely male.

Advertising and marketing managers talk of brand image, brand character and brand personality. These terms are often confusing and are used interchangeably.

Differentiating brand image and brand personality, Christine Restall has said that the brand personality is made up of the emotional associations of the brand while the brand image comprises physical features and benefits.

According to Subroto Sengupta, brand personality is the sum total of all characteristics, psychological and physical aspects. According to him, brand personality represents that part of the brand image which in the consumers' mind is associated with the brand's emotional aspects and symbolism.

Advertising can create associations with users and endorsers. For example, one of the oldest ads of Rajdoot motorcycle shows Dharmendra (the famous filmstar of Hindi Cinema) riding the bike and saying "*Jordar logon ki shandar savari*".

A brand that has acquired a well-known and favourable personality over a period of time is more like an old friend and consumers would prefer to buy such a brand rather than a new one. A brand's personality is often unique and cannot be copied. For example, 7Up's personality as the un-cola soft drink and *Maggi's* personality as 2-minute quick food has successfully faced competitors and could not be dislodged from their dominant positions.

Brand personality associations are important from the marketer and the consumer's point of view.

Importance to the marketer

It helps the marketer to differentiate the brand from competition. Easy availability and access to technology has brought all brands near parity on functional aspects, and these are also perceived to be so by the consumer. So, the only differentiating element between the brands is the personality that is associated with them. By creating a favourable and pleasing personality a marketer can set his brand apart, which often enables him to gain market share or charge premium pricing. Brand personality is unique and non-preemptible. Though competitors can match a brand's features and price, but they can't copy a brand's personality.

Brand extension

A lot of brand extension decisions are taken by marketing managers for obvious reasons. Examples of brand extensions are plenty in Indian and foreign markets. Companies like Sony, Godrej, Tata, IBM and Videocon have used brand extension to great advantage. Because brand extension decisions do not require huge budgets that is otherwise required to launch a new brand name, it helps the company find ready trial and acceptance by consumers of its new product launch, because the well-known name behind the new product probably reduces the level of risk for the consumer and the retail trade.

Importance to consumer

Knowingly or unknowingly consumers regard their possessions as part of self. They acquire or reinforce their sense of self through the goods they buy and what those goods symbolize both to themselves and others they come in contact with Brands encapsulate social meaning, for example, masculinity, intelligence or sophistication. So, by acquiring specific brands we also acquire for ourselves the meaning that they symbolize.

Implementing a brand personality strategy

Implementation of a brand personality strategy through advertising is done in three stages:

- Researching the brand personality associations: The symbolic associations that currently exist with the product category and competing brands.
- Targeting a brand personality: Deciding upon the brand personality which is going to be most valuable to target audience.
- Executing brand personality: Develop advertisements that create, reinforce or change that target personality. The important advertising elements are: Endorser, using imagery, executional elements, symbols and consistency.

Brand Equity

According David Aaker, brands have equity because they generate awareness, they have many loyal consumers, a reputation for quality, own patents, have good access to distribution network and associations, etc. For example, Tata Tea acquired the brand *Tetley* tea of UK by paying $130 million mainly for the goodwill of the brand most of which is built through brand's advertising. Also goodwill is one major way to assess the intangible value of a brand. Also, Volkswagon paid $780 million for the assets of Rolls Royce, and $65 million for the brand Rolls Royce.

Brands vary in their power and value that they enjoy in the market. Some brands are hardly known to consumers while others have a very high level of recognition. Some of the brands are highly acceptable to consumers and some are highly preferred from among the acceptable ones. Finally, there are those brands that command a very high degree of brand loyalty among consumers, i.e., consumers do not accept substitutes of that brand.

The brand that has high equity is likely to have higher brand loyalty because consumers find it easier to interpret what benefits the brand offers, feel more confident of it, and get more satisfaction from using it. Because of such preferences the brand can charge a higher price, can afford to offer lower retail incentives, can invest less to launch brand extensions and have more effective marketing programmes.

The factors associated with the brand indicate that main objective of an advertisement is to increase brand equity by increasing awareness, familiarity, favourable meanings and associations with the brand. Thus, the brand is what the consumer thinks, feels, visualizes when he/she sees the brand name or its symbol. A schematic representation of brand equity is shown in Figure 5.8.

Fig. 5.8 Brand equity: an overview.

The framework shown in Figure 5.8 defines a brand as having equity not only with consumers (through high awareness and strong associations), but also with the distribution trade, brand personality and other proprietary associations.

Kevin Keller has argued that a brand has equity if the knowledge that the customer has about the brand—in terms of greater familiarity with it, and more favourable, strong, congruent, unique and leverageable associations with it—leads to greater consumer preference.

The framework suggested by Keller is shown in Figure 5.9. Notice that the associations can either be about the brand's attributes or benefits (functional, experiential and symbolic) or attitudes towards it.

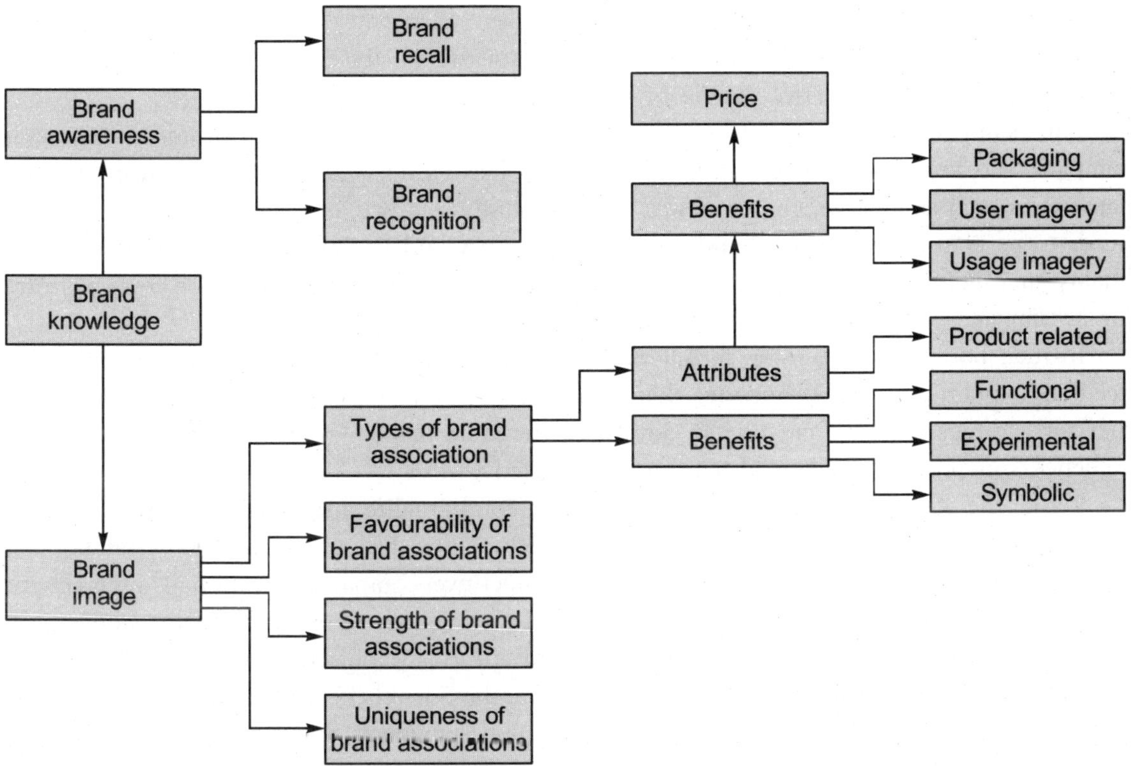

Fig. 5.9 Consumer knowledge about a brand.

Both frameworks, shown in Figures 5.8 and 5.9, show that one of the main tasks of advertising in increasing brand equity is to increase consumer's awareness of and familiarity with it.

Brand knowledge gets enhanced through brand awareness and brand image. The nature of associations that advertising creates with the brand is what actually shapes the brand image.

Let's recall that a brand is not a physical entity but instead it is what the consumer thinks, feels and visualizes when he/she sees the brand's symbol or name. Stronger brands have more shape and substance, they evoke richer, stronger and more consistent favourable meanings and associations.

CREATIVE STRATEGY

The present day advertising is quite different from the past. A large number of commercials of modern times seem to be completely unrelated to selling any particular product. There appears to be great emphasis rather obsession with feelings, emotions and images in the advertisements and no claims are made about the product.

Once the advertiser has decided on the content of the ad, the task of creating the ad itself is usually given to the creative people of the ad agency.

For example, Ford Fusion has come up with a big campaign in print media where it compares the brand with other competitive brands like Honda City and Hyundai on various parameters such as mileage, engine power, price, ground clearance, etc. An advertising campaign needs to be planned well. The brand manager, ad agency and its creative people need to spend quality time before hitting with a great idea which can be the central theme or copy platform for a campaign.

In their book *Creative Strategy in Advertising*, Jewler and Drewniany say that an advertisement needs to contain a persuasive message that convinces people to take action. They suggest further that for a campaign to be creative an advertisement must make a relevant connection with its audience and present a selling idea in an unexpected way.

Before the writers and art directors move on to conceptualize and create the ad, it is always helpful to decide the broad framework within which the ad has to be created: What kind of appeal should the ad utilize? Whether it is a competitive comparison (rational) approach or emotional appeal (fear or humour) or uses an endorser (expert or a likable personality).

Creative strategy is driven by the marketing and advertising objectives and is a reflection of the product category. Some of the products like clothes, jewellery and cosmetics are fashion items and their advertisement needs to make a fashion statement. Some product categories are just naturally difficult to advertise. In this case, lot of copy testing may be required.

Some other product categories such as products used in homes, for personal care or for sustenance are in commodity markets where it is difficult to differentiate the products based on their features. In these cases, the creative strategy is designed to build a distinctive brand personality.

In addition to product category, the creative strategy is also driven by targeting strategies. For the creative, targeting means being able to identify with the target audience. Creativity in advertising requires empathy and a keen awareness of the audience, i.e. how they think and feel, what they value and what makes them take notice. This ability to identify with the target audience delivers consumer insights that often lead directly to the creative idea. That's why account planners are helpful for the creative team as they have greater insight into the consumer that lead to great creative strategies. An analysis of the winning ads in the Annual Communication Arts Award indicates that agencies using account planners were more successful in winning awards than other agencies.

Creative strategies blend the elements of creative mix: the target audience, the product and its positioning, the communication media and advertising mix. Advertising and creative strategy address target audiences to effectively communicate the product positioning through selected media.

Creative strategy determines what the advertising messages will say or communicate and creative tactics determine how the message strategy will be executed. The most important aspect of creative strategy is to find or determine the big idea that will be used as central theme of the advertising campaign and translated into attention getting, distinctive and memorable messages. Creative specialists find it difficult to come up with big idea that will break through the clutter. Some of the well-known examples of campaign with big ideas are:

Brand	Big idea or theme
Timex Watches	"It takes a licking & keeps on ticking"
Thumps Up	Taste the thunder
Nike	Just do it
Hallmark Cards	When you care enough to send the very best
Coca Cola	*Matlab thanda*
Intel	Intel inside
BMW	Ultimate driving machine

A good creative strategy and execution is central to determining the success of a product or service or reversing the fortunes of a struggling brand. Conversely, an advertising campaign poorly conceived and executed can be a liability. An advertising campaign is a set of interrelated and coordinated marketing communication activities that centre on a single theme or idea that appears in different media across a specified time period. Determining the unifying idea around which the campaign will be built is a critical part of the creative process, as it sets the tone for the individual ads and other forms of marketing communications that will be used.

A campaign theme should be a strong idea, as it is the central message that will be communicated in the advertising and other promotional activities. Advertising campaign plans are short-term in nature and are generally done on annual basis. However, some themes are usually developed for a longer period of time, for example, 'Intel inside' of Intel.

Like any other area of marketing, creative theme is guided by specific goals and objectives. A creative strategy that focuses on what must be communicated will guide the selection of the campaign theme and the development of all messages used in the ad campaign. The creative strategy is based on several factors such as:

- Identification of the target audience,
- The basic problem issue,
- Opportunity that advertising must address,
- The major selling idea or key benefit the message needs to communicate, and
- Any supportive information that needs to be included in the ad. Once these factors are determined, a creative strategy statement should describe the message appeal and execution style that will be used. The flow diagram in Figure 5.10 shows the sequence of events and interrelationships.

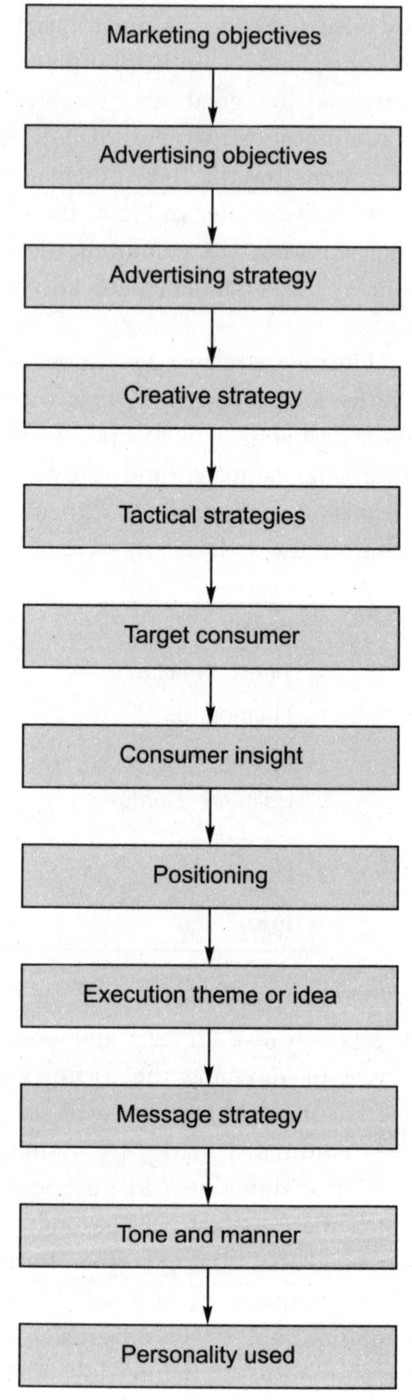

Fig. 5.10 Creative strategy elements.

The above indicated elements and the key execution details are spelled out in a document called creative brief (also called creative platform, worksheet or blueprint). The brief is the document prepared by the account manger to summarize the basic marketing and advertising strategy. It gives direction to the creative team as they search for the theme. Generally, a copy platform is prepared by the account planner and it is approved by the marketing manager from the client's side. Figure 5.11 shows a sample copy platform outline prepared by an accounts executive. It is prepared to guide the creative process. Just as there are different names for the copy platform, there are variations in the outline and in the level of details included.

The copy platform should be understood and agreed upon both by advertising agency and the client team. It is a simple written statement of the most significant issues to consider and guide the creative team in developing an advertising campaign. The copy platform

1. Basic problem the advertising must address
2. Advertising and communications objectives
3. Target audience
4. Major selling idea or key benefits to communicate
5. Creative strategy statement (campaign theme, appeal, and execution technique to be used)
6 Supporting information and requirements.

Fig. 5.11 Copy platform outline.

outline is indicated in Figure 5.11 can be transformed into a more elaborated form with the use of six Ws as indicated:

- **Who:** Who is the potential customer in terms of geographic, demographic, behavioural and psychographics qualities? What is the personality profile of a typical prospect?
- **Why:** Does the consumer have specific needs and wants that the ad message should focus upon and appeal to? There are two broad categories of appeals: Rational and emotional. Rational appeals are directed at the consumer's practical and functional need for the product or service, whereas the emotional appeals aim at the consumer's psychological, social and symbolic needs.
- **What:** Are there any special features of the product or service to satisfy the consumer's needs? What factors support the product claim? How is the product positioned? What image or personality of the brand can be/has been created? What perceived strengths and weaknesses of the brand need to be addressed?
- **Where, when and how:** In which market area, what time of the year and through what media will these messages be delivered?
- **What:** What style, approach or tone will the campaign use? What will the copy say and how will it say (tone conveys quality, beauty and sophistication, and brand character statements relate to long-term descriptions of the brand's values.)

The creative process may help the creative team bring out unique and innovative advertising campaign. According to Alex Fosborn, former head of BBDO, creative process involves the following seven steps:

- **Orientation:** Pointing out the problem.
- **Preparation:** Gathering pertinent data.
- **Analysis:** Breaking down the relevant material.
- **Ideation:** Piling up alternative ideas.

- **Incubation:** Putting the problem aside to invite spontaneous ideas at later time.
- **Synthesis:** Putting the pieces together.
- **Evaluation:** Judging the resulting idea.

What constitutes creativity in advertising is probably somewhere between the two extremes of the continuum:

Creative team		*Account planners and marketing managers*
Those who judge the creativity of an ad in terms of its artistic or aesthetic value and originality. They contend creative ads can break through the competitive clutter, grab the consumer's attention and have some impact.	⟵⟶	Those who judge the creativity of an ad in terms of promotional tools whose primary purpose is to communicate favourable impressions to the market. They evaluate the creative ads in terms of maximizing the impact of the message.

However, irrespective of the agreement on the definition of an creative ad, it is imperative that everyone involved in planning and developing an advertising campaign must understand the importance of balancing the "it's not creative unless it sells" perspective with novelty, uniqueness and impact position. Brand managers or account executives must recognize that imposing too many sales and marketing-oriented communications objectives on the creative team can result in mediocre advertising, which is often ineffective in today's competitive, cluttered media environment. At the same time, creative team must realize that the goal of advertising is to assist in selling the product and good advertising must communicate in a manner that helps the client achieve this goal.

Thus, advertising creativity is the ability to generate fresh, unique and appropriate ideas that can be used as solutions to communications problems. To be appropriate and effective, a creative idea must be relevant to the needs, wants and aspirations of the target audience.

Advertising creativity is not the exclusive domain of the creative team. The modern business requires that creative thinking should come from all those who are involved with the promotional aspect of the product.

The D'Arcy, Masius Benton and Bowles agency has developed guidelines to achieve superior creativity. The agency views a creative advertising message as one that is built around a creative core or power idea and uses excellent design and execution to communicate information that interests the target audience. It has used these principles for developing outstanding advertising campaigns for P&G, Norelco and many other popular brands.

D'ARCY, MASIUS BENTON AND BOWLES UNIVERSAL ADVERTISING STANDARDS

Does this advertising position the product simply and with unmistakable clarity?

The target audience must be able to understand immediately about the product, whom it is for and what's in it for them. Creating this clear vision of how the product or service fits into their lives is the first job of advertising. Without a simple, clear and focused positioning no creative work can begin.

Does this advertising bolt the brand to a clinching benefit?

Advertising should be built on the most compelling and persuasive consumer benefit, not on some unique-but-insignificant peripheral feature.

Admen must be sure they are saying the right thing. If they do not know what the most compelling benefit is, they must find out before doing anything else.

Does this advertising contain a power idea?

Power idea is the vehicle that transforms the creative strategy into a dynamic and creative communications concept. It is the core creative idea that sets the stage for brilliant executions to come. The ideal power idea should:

- Be describable in a simple word, phrase or sentence without reference to any final execution.
- Be likely to attract the prospect's attention.
- Revolve around the clinching benefit.
- Allow us to brand the advertising.
- Make it easy for the prospect to vividly experience our client's product or service.

Does this advertising create a brand personality?

Great brands tend to have something in common: the extra edge of having a brand personality. This is something beyond identifying what the brand does for the consumer.

Is this advertising unexpected?

Should our clients pay good money to wind up with advertising that looks and sounds like everybody else's in the category? They should not.

We must dare to be different, because sameness is suicide. We can't be outstanding unless we are different. The thing is not to emulate the competition, but to annihilate them.

Is this advertising single-minded.

If we want people to remember one big thing from a given place of advertising, let's not make it more difficult than it already is in an over communicated world. The advertising should be all about that one big thing.

Does this advertising reward the prospect?

Let's give audience something that makes it easy and even pleasurable for our message to penetrate: a tear, a smile, and a laugh. An emotional stimulus is that special something that makes them want to see the advertising again and again.

Is this advertising visually arresting?

Great advertising is unusual to look at: it is often a compelling, riveting and nourishing feast for the eyes. If you need a reason to strive for arresting work, create something "catching or holding the attention, thought, feelings, or gripping.

Does this advertising exhibit painstaking craftsmanship?

Lighting, casting, wardrobe, direction—all components of the art of advertising are as important as the science of it.

Source: Adapted from Advertising and Promotion: An Integrated Marketing Communications Perspective, 5th edition, by George E. Belch and Michael A. Belch, Tata McGraw-Hill.

MESSAGE STRATEGY

The way marketing communications are presented is very important in determining their effectiveness. The message is often considered as the most vital component in the communications process. "Message is the thought, idea, attitude, image, or other information that the advertiser wishes to convey to targeted audience".

Brand managers must focus on what will be the message content, how the information will be structured for communication and what kind of message appeal would be appropriate. Message structure refers to how the elements of a message are organized.

Advertisers go through the following three steps for developing a message strategy:

- ***Message generation:*** It revolves around major benefits and brand offers. A customer derives four types of rewards/benefits from the product. These are rational, sensory, social and ego satisfaction.
- ***Message evaluation and selection:*** Every advertising campaign would have to generate a number of alternative suitable messages. Each message would then have to be evaluated and the most appropriate would be selected. The message needs to be rated on factors like desirability (interesting), exclusiveness (distinctive) and believability.
- ***Message execution:*** The message's impact depends not only upon what is said, but also on how it is said. Some ads use rational positioning and others use emotional positioning.

Designing message

The message should be developed using AIDA model. The message should gain attention, hold interest, arouse desire and elicit action. Formulation of a message requires four essential factors:

- What to say (message content).
- How to say logically (message structure).
- How to say symbolically (message format).
- Who should say it (message source).

Message content

It is also called appeal, theme, idea and the unique selling proposition (USP). It amounts to formulating some kind of benefit, motivation, identification or reason for the audience to think about or investigate the product.

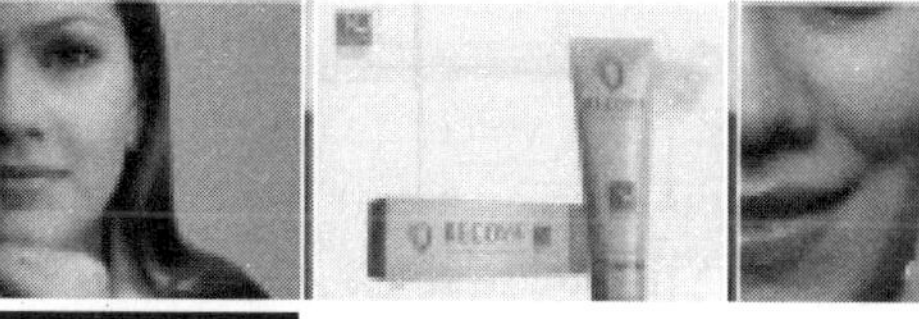

Recova—30 days formula.

The following are the three basic types of appeals that can be used:

- **Rational:** This kind of appeal is based on audience's self interest like benefits in terms of quality, economy, value, performance, saving time, etc.
- **Emotional:** These appeals stir up positive or negative emotions that motivate purchase. Negative emotions are fear, guilt and shame while positive emotions are love, humour, pride and joy.

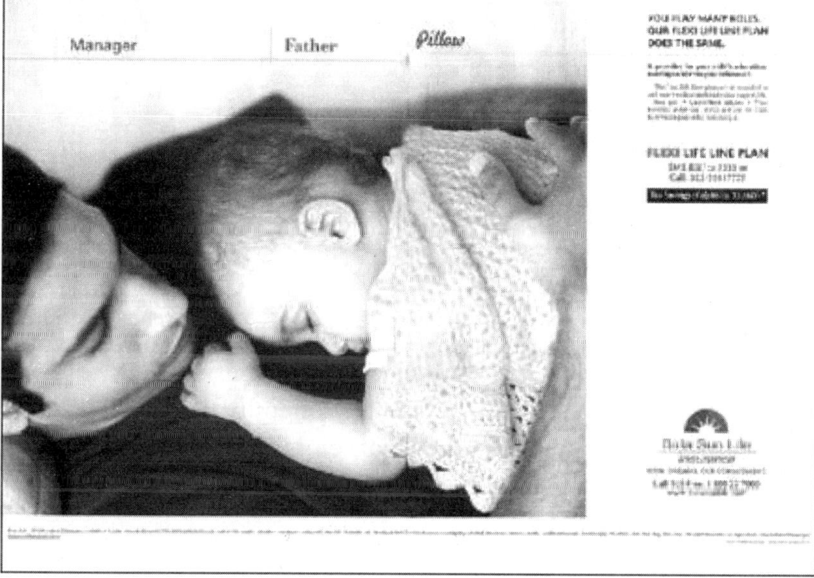

Birla Sun Life Insurance Ad with an emotional appeal.

- **Moral:** These appeals are directed at audience's sense of what is right and proper. They are used more for social causes.

Kohinoor condoms: An ad promoting use of condoms for social cause.

Message format

A message format is the sequence and the manner in which message has to be presented for its maximum effectiveness. The message format depends on the type of medium to be used.

In print media, the communicator has to decide on the headline, copy, illustration and colour.

In radio words and voice quality (speech rate, rhythm, pitch, tone, articulation) and vocalization (pauses, sighs, yawns) matters.

In TV, words, voice quality, vocalization, body languages (non-verbal clues) are important. The presenters have to pay attention to their facial expression, gestures, dress, posture and hairstyle.

Message source

Message delivered by attractive sources achieves higher attention and recall. Advertisers often use celebrities as spokesperson. Messages delivered by highly credible sources are more persuasive. For example, Pharma products testified by doctors have high credibility. Three factors that mainly underlie source credibility are expertise, trustworthiness and likeability.

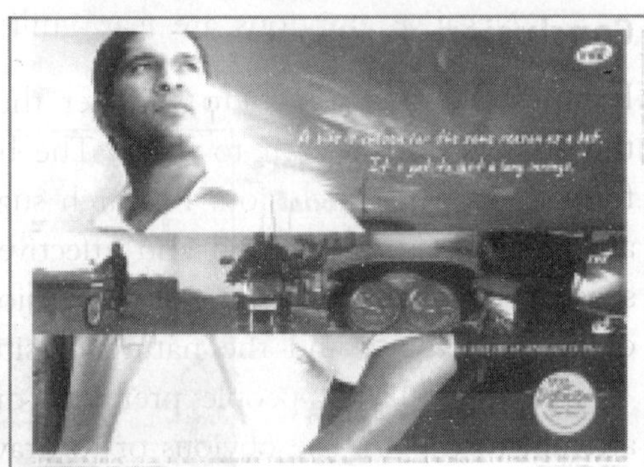

TVs Victor: A motor bike ad by renowned circketer Sachin Tendulkar.

Message structure

Message structure is an important aspect of message strategy. It is the way to communicate the various message points and overcome any opposing viewpoints that the audience may hold. The message structure comprises order of presentation, conclusion drawing, message sidedness, refutation and verbal versus visual message characteristics.

Order presentation

A basic consideration in the design of a persuasive message is the argument's order of presentation. The decision needs to be taken on whether the most important message points be placed at the beginning of the message, in the middle, or at the end. In two-sided messages, the issue is whether to present the positive argument first (**primacy effect**) or last (**recency effect**). The decision depends on several factors.

- If the target audience is opposed to the communicator's position, presenting strong points first can reduce the level of counter arguing.
- If the target audience is not interested in the topic, the strong points of the message put first create better impact on the target audience.
- If the target audience is predisposed toward the communicator's position or is highly interested in the issue or product, the strong points could be saved for the end of the message.

The order of presentation can be very critical when a long detailed message with many arguments is presented. Most effective sales presentations open and close with strong selling points and bury weaker arguments in the middle. There are many product and service messages that are received by consumers with low involvement and minimal interest. Thus, an advertiser may present the brand name and key selling points early in the message and repeat them at the end to enhance recalling and retention.

Conclusion drawing

It raises the question as to whether the communicator should draw a definite conclusion for the audience or leave it to them. The best ads ask questions and allow readers and viewers to form their own conclusion. Research suggests that, in general, messages with explicit conclusion are more easily understood and effective in influencing attitudes. However, some other studies suggest that the effectiveness of conclusion drawing may depend on the target audience, the type of issue or topic, and the nature of situations.

Highly educated people prefer to draw their own conclusion and may be annoyed at an attempt to explain the obvious or to draw an inference for them. But drawing a conclusion may be appropriate for lowly educated audience, who may not draw any conclusion or may infer wrongly. For highly personal or ego-involving issues, message recipients may want to make up their mind and resent any attempts by the communicator to draw conclusions.

The complexity of the topic is also a factor whether the audience would like the message with conclusions drawn. Even a highly educated audience may need assistance if the knowledge level in a particular area is low. If the marketer wants immediate action then the message should draw definite conclusion.

Message Sidedness

The marketer is faced with the decision whether it is going to be a one-sided or two-sided message. Message sidedness raises the question of whether the communicator should only praise the product or also mention some of its shortcomings.

One sided messages mention only positive attributes and benefits. It works best when audiences are initially predisposed to the communication's position. It also works better with less educated audience.

Two-sided message present both good and bad points. Two-sided messages are more effective when the audiences are opposed and are better educated. Two-sided messages may enhance the credibility of the source. A better educated audience usually knows there are opposing arguments, so a communicator who presents both sides of an issue is likely to be seen as less biased and more objective. W.K. Buckley Ltd. of Canada uses two-sided message for its brand of cough syrup "Buckley's mixture. It taste awful. And it works".

Refutation

In two-sided message, the communicator presents both sides of an issue and then refutes the opposing viewpoint. Since refutation appeals tend to inoculate the target audience against a competitor's counterclaims, they are more effective than one-sided messages in making consumers resistant to an opposing message. Refutation messages may be useful when marketers wish to build attitudes that resist change and defend against attacks or criticism of their products or the company.

Verbal vs. Visual Messages

The non-verbal and visual elements are a very important part of an advertising message. Many ads provide minimal information and rely heavily on visual elements to communicate. Pictures are commonly used in advertising to convey information or reinforce message claims. Both verbal and visual portions of an ad influence the way the advertising message is processed. Consumers may develop images or impressions based on visual elements such as an illustration in an ad or the scenes in a TV commercial. Pictures affect the way consumers process the accompanying copy.

A recent study said that when verbal information was low in imagery value, the use of pictures increased both immediate and delayed recall of product attributes. When the verbal information was already high in imagery value, the addition of pictures did not increase recall.

MEDIA STRATEGY

In these paragraphs, we would study the media planning and buying functions, where they fit in the advertising process and how media planners set objectives and develop media strategies.

Over the last decade media planning has acquired significant role in developing advertising campaigns. The proliferation of media choice and increased cost has made the task of media planners very intricate. Today, the advertisers expect greater efficiency and creativity in media buying decision so as to derive maximum advantage.

It must be remembered that the product or service being advertised affects the media planning decisions. Some products are suitable to be advertised on certain media vehicles only because of their nature and audience reach.

Basic terms and concepts related to media planning

Media planning is the process of determining how to use time and space of the media to achieve advertising objectives. It is the series of decisions involved in delivering the promotional message to the prospective buyers of the brand.

Media plan is the guide for media selection. It contains specific media objectives and media strategies (plan of action) designed to attain media objectives.

Medium is a single form of communication (TV, billboards, radio, online media) or it is the general category of available delivery system.

Media mix is the combination of media to be used for delivering message to the target audience.

Media class is a type of medium such as TV, radio, newspapers, magazines, direct mail, etc.

Media vehicle is a single programme, magazine or radio station. It is the specific carrier within a medium category. *Times of India* or *Business Today* in print media, *Office Office* of SAB TV, *Geetmala* of AIR are the examples of media vehicle.

Media option is the detailed description of an ad's characteristics other than the copy and the artwork used. It specifies media vehicle and other advertising characteristics such as size (full page or half page), spot length (15 seconds or 60 seconds), colour (black-white or four color) and location (front page, back page or interior positions).

Above-the-line media are such as broadcast, press, outdoor, cinema and posters in which the advertising agency gets commission.

Below-the-line media are such as direct mail, sales promotion, exhibitions, merchandising, sales literature, etc. in which the advertising agency does not get any commission.

Reach is the measure of the number of different audience members exposed at least once to a media vehicle carrying the advertising message within a given time period.

Coverage refers to the potential audience that might get exposed to the ad message through a media vehicle.

Frequency refers to the number of times the audience is exposed to the advertising message in a given period of time.

Scheduling and timings specify how media options are scheduled over time. Among the strategy alternatives are:

- **Flighting**: A period of total inactivity. It is on and off schedule,
- **Continuous:** Advertising spread evenly through out the time,
- **Pulsing:** A continuous base augmented by intermittent bursts of heavy advertising. Pulse pattern has peaks and valleys.

Timings decisions include the selection of specific issues or time slots. The media schedule will also specify the number of planned insertions in each media vehicle. A more detailed media schedule also specifies other details of media option such as size or length and the timings of the advertisement insertions.

Developing a Media Plan

We have discussed in the previous topics about the situational analysis and its importance. We discussed broadly the internal and external factors, competitive strategies and the customers. While developing a media plan, a market analysis will again be performed focusing on the media and delivery of message. The key issues to be analyzed at this stage are:

- To whom shall we advertise?
- What internal and external factors may influence the media plan?
- Where (geographically) and when should we focus our efforts?

Figure 5.12 indicates various stages involved in developing an effective media plan.

The media planner works with the account planner, marketing manager of the client and the creative director to decide which target markets to be focused for message delivery. A variety of information can help the media planner to arrive at this decision. Some of this may be primary data collected through research and more can be had from secondary (published data) sources. A large number of organizations publish variety of data on consumers and products used by them.

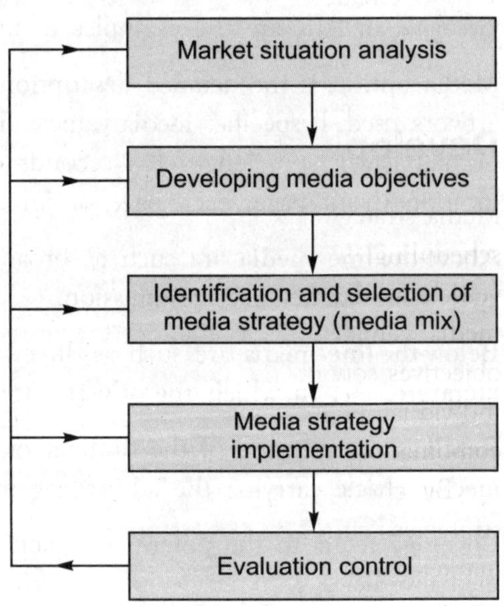

Fig. 5.12 Developing a media plan.

The analysis of internal and external market factors provides a good assessment of opportunities and the client's strengths and weaknesses, which is then used for developing the most suitable media plan. Internal factors are size of the media budget, and managerial and administrative capabilities of the agency itself. The external factors are the economy (rising cost of media) and competitive factors.

Companies often find it difficult to decide where to promote the brand. It relates to geographic considerations. Some geographical areas give excellent sales and some give poor sales of the brand. Thus, the problem of allocating media budget whether it should be proportionate to sales figure or according to the market potential. The media planner can make use of some of the techniques for making this decision. He/She may use some of the following indexes:

- The survey of buying power index (BPI)
- The brand development index (BDI)
- The category development index (CDI)

Establishing media objectives

Market situation analysis should lead to development of media specific objectives, which are designed to lead to attainment of communications and marketing objectives. Thus, media objectives are the end results that must be accomplished through media plan and programmes. Some of the media objectives can be:

- Create 80 per cent awareness in the target market
- Create favourable attitude in the 40 per cent of the target market.
- Make 15 per cent of the target market purchase the brand.

Developing Media Strategy

Media strategy relates to the choice of media category, media vehicle, deciding reach and media scheduling. It must be kept in mind that an advertiser has a wide variety of media and media vehicle available to him. In the first step, he identifies various alternative media categories and media vehicles. Then the choice of the media and media vehicle is made on the basis of objectives sought, the characteristics of the product or a services, the size of the budget and the individual preferences. These factors contribute in the decision whether a single media or a combination of it will be used.

By choosing a media mix strategy advertisers can add more versatility to their media strategies, since each medium contributes its own distinct advantage. By combining media, marketers can increase coverage, reach and frequency levels while improving the likelihood of achieving marketing and advertising objectives.

The following criteria need to be considered in media execution plan:

- The media mix
- Target market coverage
- Geographic coverage
- Scheduling
- Reach
- Frequency
- Creative aspects and mood
- Flexibility
- Budget considerations

Like all other plans, media plan also needs to be evaluated to assess its performance. Having decided on various issues such as media mix, coverage, frequency, reach, scheduling and budgets, the advertiser and the media planner set the media plans rolling. The action takes place and the consumer is exposed to the brand message. Putting media strategies in action where the consumer is, the marketer and the media planner must know how far they have been successful.

The measures of success or failure will be considered on two factors: How well did these strategies achieve media objectives and how well did this media plan contribute to attaining the communications and marketing objectives.

If the media strategies were successful they must be used as base for future media plans. If not, then they should be analyzed for shortcomings.

However, the performance parameters of media strategy need to be monitored regularly. It must be measured and compared with standards. Any deviations observed must then be corrected immediately rather than waiting for the complete duration of the plan.

The media plan helps the marketer decide in advance what he wants to achieve and how he is going to achieve it. The marketer, thus, decides the base against which he measures his advertising performance at the marketplace.

There are a large number of activities and decisions that are required to be made in the process of developing and executing media plan. As the media plan unfolds, events may occur that require changes. Many advertisers find it necessary to alter and update their media objectives and strategies frequently.

The activities required to be undertaken in a media plan are given in Figure 5.13.

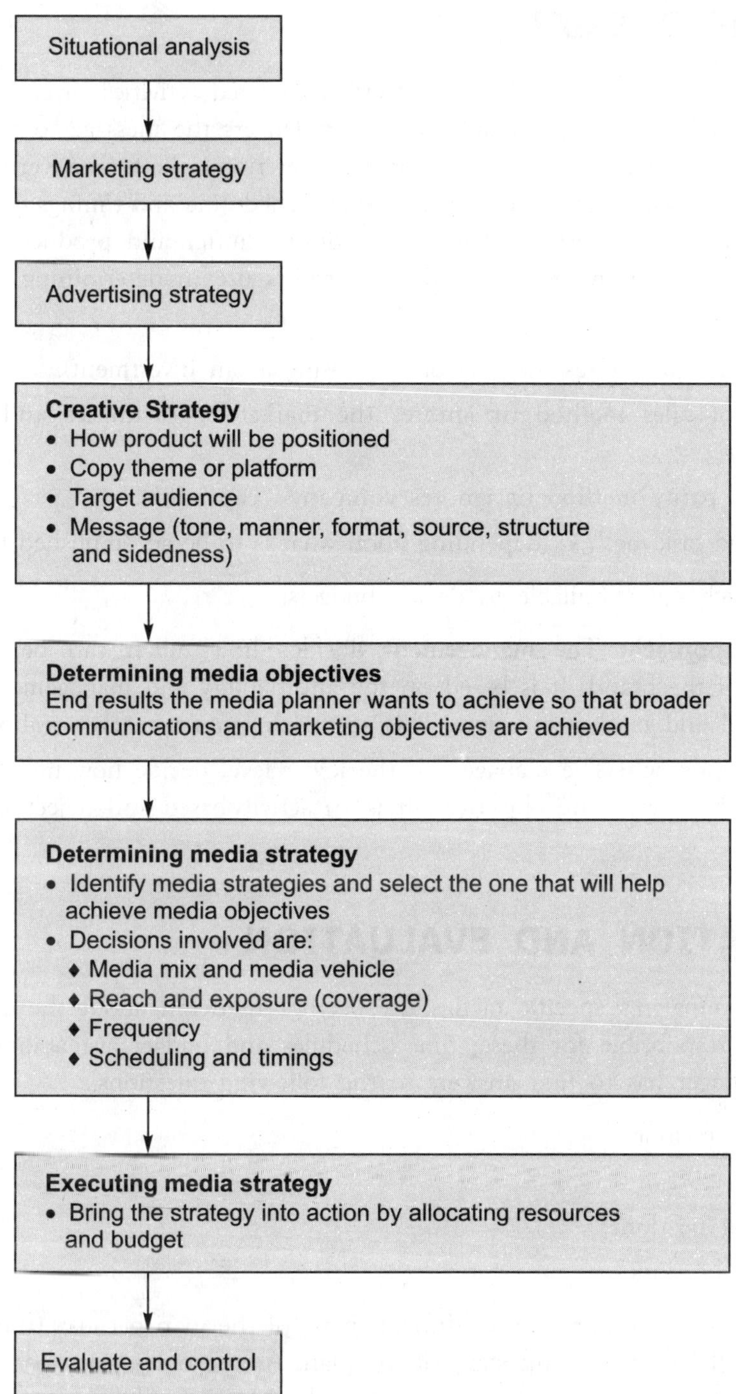

Fig. 5.13 Activities in a media plan.

ADVERTISING BUDGET

The budget brings the media plan and other advertising related activities alive. The value of an advertising strategy can be determined by how well it delivers the message to the audience in the lowest cost. There is a large number of factors that determine the total advertising cost, such as media mix decision, source person, reach, frequency, scheduling and timings, stage of product life cycle, market share and consumer base, competition, clutter and product substitutability.

There are generally four methods that the advertisers use in determining the advertising budget.

- Affordable rate (it ignores the role of advertising as an investment).
- Percentage of sales method (it ignores the market opportunities and objectives of advertising).
- Competitive parity method (it ignores company's capability).
- Objective and task method (depending upon what is to be accomplished by advertising).

Broadly, two approaches are available to decide budgets:

- **Top-down approach:** The management decides how much can be given for the promotion of the brand. It is based on the affordability and management's perception of the brand and market situation. This approach ignores market reality.
- **Bottom-up approach:** The managers at the lower level decide how much they need to accomplish their respective objectives. It is an activity-based and object-oriented budget approach.

IMPLEMENTATION AND EVALUATION

It deals with the campaign's specific tactics. It specifies in detail about the activities to be undertaken, people responsible for these, time schedules and budget availability.
The advertising manager has to find answers to the following questions:

- What is to be done?
- Who will do it?
- When will it be done?
- How will it be done?

Execution of the plan is one of the most difficult parts of the plan because if anything wrong has to happen, it will happen, at this stage of the plan. As the old saying goes, "Success is in details", and there are innumerable details in a typical advertising plan.

For successful execution of the plan, the advertising manager has to authorize individuals responsible for execution, for expenditure so as to bring the plan into action.

As the plan goes into action, activities start happening and results pour in from various points. The advertising manager should now evaluate the results. Evaluations of the advertising plan are based on how well the advertising plan meets its objectives. Essentially, the evaluation of the plan is done midway so that necessary corrections may be introduced to achieve desired objectives.

INTEGRATING ADVERTISING WITH OTHER MARKETING COMMUNICATION TOOLS

For many years, promotional activities/functions in majority of companies were dominated by advertising. Companies, generally, relied heavily on advertising agencies for guidance in all areas of marketing communication. However, most marketers did use other promotions and marketing communication tools but in an isolated and fragmented way. Other marketing communications were handled separately and independently with different budgets, different views of the market and different objectives. As a result, each of the promotional activity communicated different image of the brand. It could not present a common communication and a consistent image. The returns on the promotional expenditure were therefore low.

The marketers later realized the importance of integrated communication approach. They wanted seamless communication to achieve synergy between various promotional tools. Though promotional tool has specific objective to achieve, it should also help in achieving common marketing objectives. Advertising, however creative it may be, can't achieve desired results as a stand-alone promotional tool. It must be understood that though we are targeting homogenous groups, still there exist a lot of heterogeneity among customers who are influenced by different promotional tools such as sales promotions, publicity, personal selling, direct marketing, public relations and advertising. Each of these promotional tools is dealt with extensively in the later chapters of the book.

It is now evident that a systematic approach to advertising can bring far better results for every paisa spent by the brand manager.

SUMMARY

Advertising for a brand is well thought, researched and stepwise process leading to numerous decisions by the brand manager. In order to create maximum impact or achieve desired results, the advertising plan should be in synch with the marketing plan, and the marketing plan should be in synch with the corporate plan.

A typical marketing plan should contain marketing objectives, identified target market and strategies related to product, advertising, media, message, creative, pricing and distribution.

An advertising plan is developed for solving a marketing communication problem. It involves numerous tasks such as objectives determination, target audience selection, choosing a theme, creating a right message, media choice, arriving at correct frequency and budget formulation. Therefore, it is a plan to say the right things (message) to right people (target audience) through the right medium.

An advertising campaign is developed to achieve advertising objectives. Major decisions in advertising campaigns are related to advertising objectives, message, money, media and measurement.

Positioning strategy influences advertising strategy significantly. It acts like the foundation upon which all major marketing mix decisions are made. Marketing communications is the major weapon for acquiring a given positioning for the brand. Positioning helps in creating a brand identity or a unique space in the minds of the consumer. Positioning is developed through many ways such as customer benefit, price-quality, applications, product user approach and cultural approach.

Creative strategy of a brand is driven by marketing and advertising objectives, product category and target market. A creative strategy determines what the advertising messages will say or communicate and creative tactics determines how the message strategy will be executed.

A message strategy involves selection of message appeal, message content, message structure, message format and message source.

Media strategy is a very important component of advertising planning because it involves outgo of funds and brings the brand in contact with potential buyers. It requires the advertising agency and the brand manager to make various decisions related to media mix and media vehicle, reach and exposure, frequency, and scheduling and timings.

Advertising budget brings the advertising plan into action. Budget can either be determined by top-down or bottom-up approach. Various methods used for determining the budget are affordable rate, percentage of sales, competitive parity and task method.

QUESTIONS

1. Why is advertising planning important for achieving marketing objectives? Does advertising planning help in getting better returns on advertising budget? How?
2. What are the key factors that must be kept in mind while developing an advertising plan? Briefly describe various components of advertising planning.

3. Using appropriate illustrations, differentiate advertising strategy from advertising tactics.
4. What is the basis of determining advertising objectives? List out possible advertising objectives for Maruti Ltd. which has decided to increase its sales by 20 per cent for the current year.
5. What is the role of positioning in advertising of a brand? Describe various positioning approaches.
6. Differentiate between brand equity, image and personality through appropriate illustrations.
7. What are the components to creative strategy? "Creative is the heart of advertising." Discuss this statement in the light of intense competitive market situations.
8. Discuss message strategy and its relevance to the creative strategy.
9. What are the various appeals that can be used in a copy platform? Discuss it by taking examples of some advertisements from Indian corporate sector.

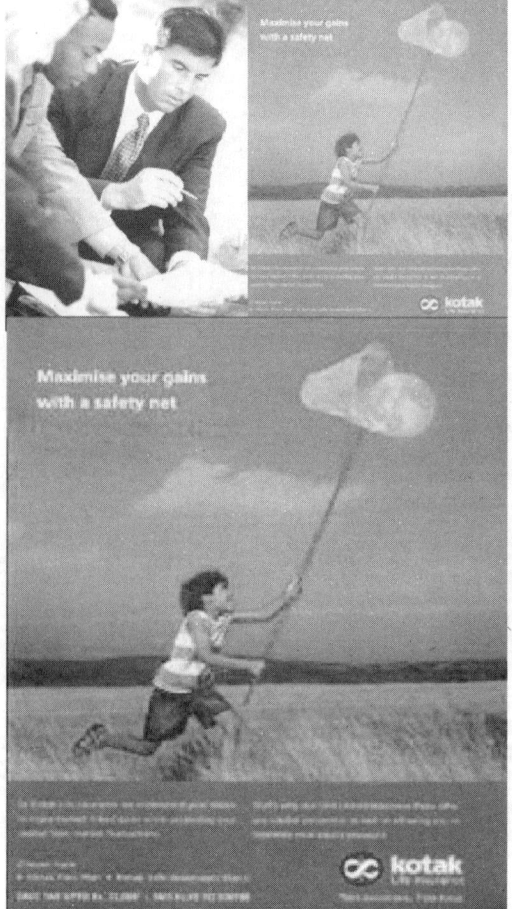

CHAPTER 6

Advertising Research and Account Planning

LEARNING OBJECTIVES

After reading this chapter, you will be able to:

- Understand the concept of advertising research.
- Learn various tools of advertising research.
- Know and understand media research.
- Know and understand account planning.
- Know and understand role and function of account planning in developing and executing an advertising campaign.

Huge sums of money are being spent by companies on marketing communication efforts in the hope that this expenditure would benefit their businesses by influencing consumer choices. Too much of money is at risk and advertisers need to have relevant, updated and complete information about who their customers are, what they want and like, and where they spend their media time. Research is needed to get the required information for marketing and advertising decisions.

For conducting marketing research, companies develop systematic procedures for collecting, recording and analyzing data from secondary and primary sources to help managers in making decisions. Marketing research helps in identifying customer needs and market segments, furnishes information that is necessary for developing new products and formulating marketing strategies, it enables managers to measure the effectiveness of marketing programmes and promotional activities, develops forecasting and helps in financial planning and quality control.

Advertising research is a subset of marketing research. It systematically gathers and analzses information to help develop and evaluate advertising strategies, individual ads or an advertising campaign. The advertiser needs to know how consumers perceive its products or services, what are their views about the competition and what image of the brand or the company would be the most appropriate to build.

Advertising research primarily relates to three critical decisions that have to be made to develop an advertising programme:

- Setting objective,
- Selecting the message, and
- Choosing appropriate media vehicles.

As to objectives, managers would ideally want to see the payout in terms of sales or profits or both.

In case of selecting message, advertisers decide what their message should be. How should they present it? What copy should they use? What headlines? What pictures and/or symbols? What situations?

In case of choice of media vehicles, advertisers decide what they should use: TV, newspapers, radio, magazines, billboards, etc. or a combination thereof.

The choice is made on the following:

- What programme?
- What days of the week?
- What time of the day?
- How many times?

To answer all these questions, it is necessary to know the number and kinds of people making up the market and to have detailed information about audiences of alternative media vehicles.

PURPOSE OF ADVERTISING RESEARCH

Advertising research serves numerous purposes.

- It helps in arriving at an appropriate positioning decision for the brand.
- It helps in selecting target markets, advertising messages and media vehicles.
- Creative concept research is used to find out the acceptability of creative ideas at the concept development stage itself.
- Pre-testing of ads is done to diagnose any possible communication problems before beginning an ad campaign.
- Post-testing of ads is done to find out effectiveness of the advertising campaign.

RESEARCH OBJECTIVES

The advertiser has to find out:

- Who are the customers?
- Who are the customers of the competing brands?
- What do these customers like and dislike about the company's brand and the competitors' brands.
- How the company's brand is currently perceived among customers?
- What must we do to clarify and improve the customer's existing perceptions?

The statement clearly defines the specific and measurable problem that the researcher had to address. All the five questions raised above relate to relevant objectives for which the research should provide answers needed by the decision maker. The information generated through these questions help the marketer decide on new positioning strategy. This would facilitate the company in developing appropriate marketing plans, advertising and promotion strategy to communicate the new positioning to the target market.

We have seen and discussed that the advertising research is a part of marketing research. Advertising research if performed scientifically helps avoid wasting money on ineffective advertising by doing pre-launch test and a means of monitoring the effectiveness of a campaign while and after the campaign has ended.

Advertising research is not limited to testing creativity. There is huge data available through independently-researched statistical information on sales, readership and audience figures regarding all media so that one can select the most economical and effective media. Also, it is possible to decide the duration of appearance of an advertisement by addressing when enough people have had the opportunity to see the advertisement a sufficient number of times.

Advertising research can help achieve the advertising objectives effectively and economically. The advertising is defined by IPA as "the most persuasive selling message to the right prospects for the product or service at the lowest possible cost".

Let's revisit the advertising objectives that will help in better comprehension of why advertising research is a necessary element in marketing decisions.

Advertising research is more specialized in that it focuses on all the elements of advertising including advertising design, media planning and evaluation. We have discussed in the preceding paragraphs that information play a big role in every major advertising campaign. The information gathered from research is always assimilated, combined with and altered and added by the professional and personal experience of those who plan, execute and approve the advertising.

The research process

An effective research involves the following steps that advertisers take to collect the relevant information:

(a) Problem definition
(b) Exploratory or informal research
(c) Determining research objectives
(d) Research design:
- Sampling methods and sample size
- Scaling
- Data collection methods

(e) Data collection
(f) Data Tabulation and analysis
(g) Interpretation conclusion and reporting

ADVERTISING OBJECTIVES

Ideally, advertising objectives should be stated in terms of sales or profits. This is difficult or impossible given that advertising is only one of the input variables and it interacts with other controlled and uncontrolled variables that also impact sales and profits.

The advertising objectives must somehow relate to consumer's behaviour since this is what must be influenced to obtain a sale. But, behaviour is a function of a complex process. It is not enough to say that the objective of advertising is to trigger behaviour that will lead to sale. Rather, what is needed is a measurement of the process by which the desired response was achieved; i.e. the communication must attract the attention of the target group, be understood and convince all those concerned that the product can meet their needs better than alternative products.

COMPONENTS OF ADVERTISING RESEARCH

Advertising research can be strategic or evaluative by nature. Also, it has different purposes. Strategic research is an information gathering process that enhances the design at a creative strategy level. It covers all the issues that lead to the actual creation of advertising. Strategic research can be thought of as collecting relevant background information needed to make a decision. Figure 6.1 shows components of advertising research.

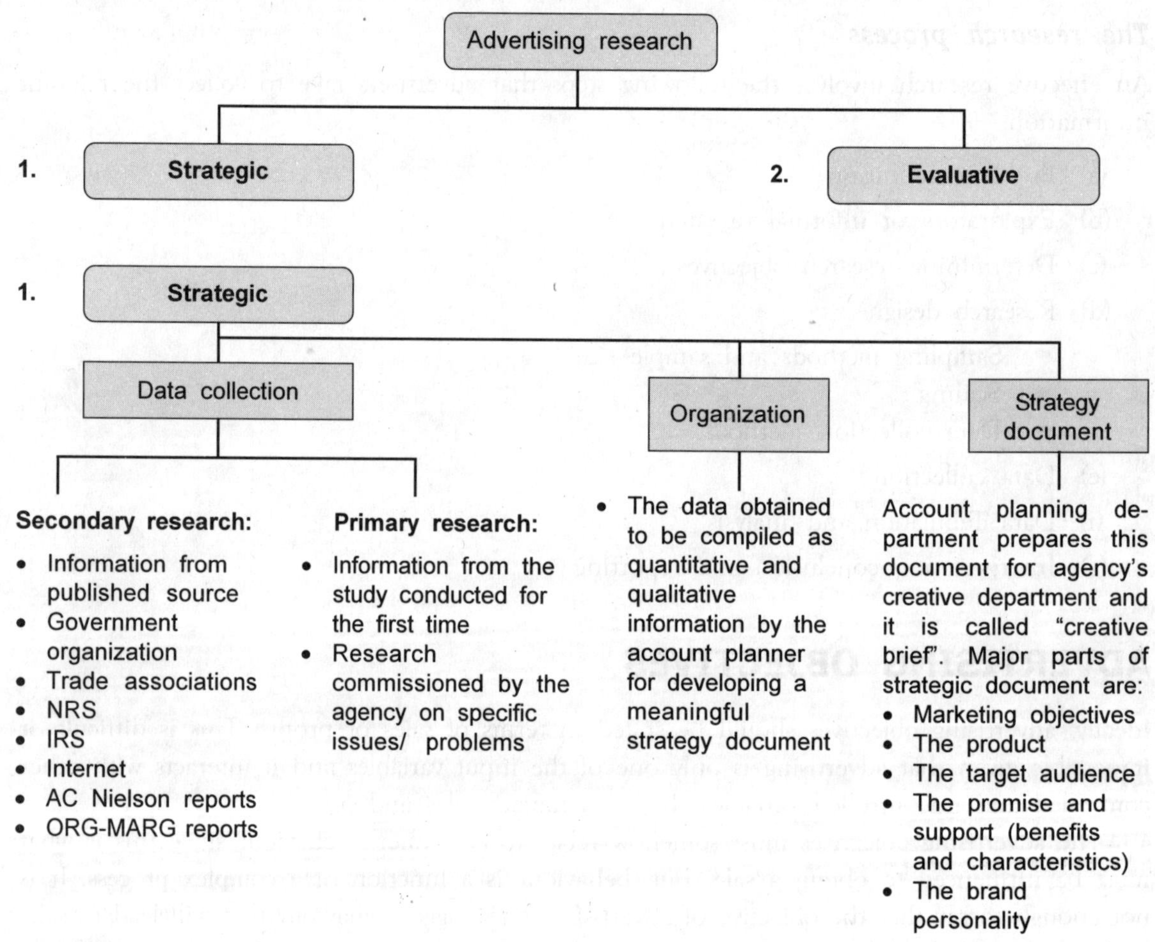

Fig. 6.1 (*Contd.*)

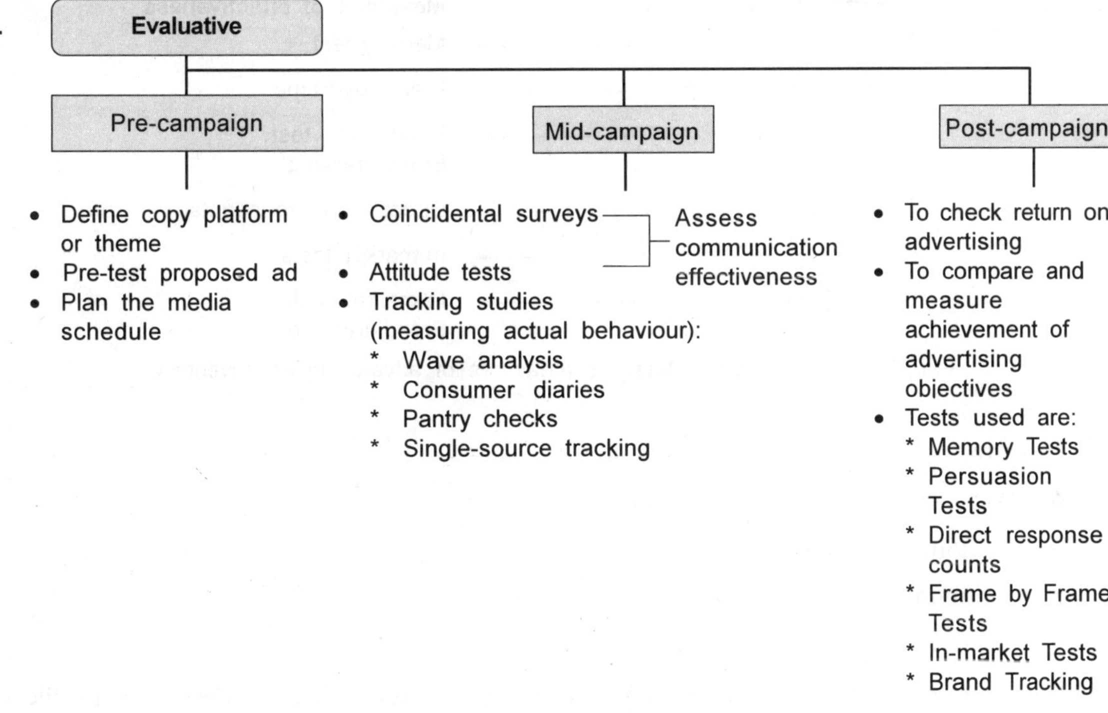

Fig. 6.1 Components of advertising research.

The information related to consumers regarding what, where, why and how consumers purchase; competitors, brand, sales, price, etc. is collected to facilitate decision making for copy platform and media choice. Evaluative research assesses the effectiveness of advertising decisions. An advertisement goes through various stages of development and evaluation takes place at each of the stage. In evaluative research, the advertising copy is tested before it is released to the media to judge the acceptability of the advertising campaign. The test is conducted whether the advertisement gives the message, which the advertiser intends to give to the target audience. Post-test evaluates whether the advertising objectives have been achieved or not (refer to Figure 6.2).

ADVERTISING STRATEGY RESEARCH

Advertising strategy is developed by carefully blending the creative mix for the target audience to attain an appropriate "positioning" through the use of right media mix.

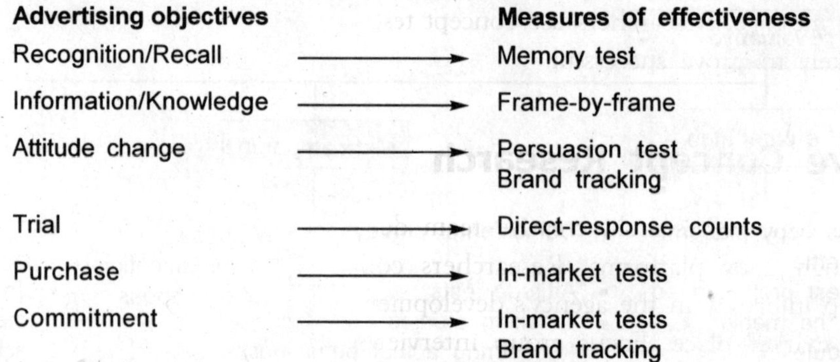

Fig. 6.2 Post-campaign tests as measures of advertising effectiveness.

The advertising strategy components are:

- Target market
- Positioning
- Communication media and
- Creative concept

The main reason behind conducting "target market" research is to develop a profile of brand's consumers/buyers. It is very important to know the primary users of the product category and carefully study their geographic, demographic, psychographic and behavioural characteristics. The research may reveal the most potential market segments and target them to achieve advertising objectives. It is very true while introducing new products. Companies may have budget constraints and might prefer to launch the product first in the most potential markets and subsequently spread to lesser potential markets.

The advertiser has to know how, the brand is perceived by the consumers. He also has to know how competitor's brand is perceived by the same set of consumers. The brand/ advertising manager should have information about what qualities, features or benefits associated with the product or service lead to initial purchases and ultimately to repeat and consistent purchases (brand loyalty). This set of information will help him/ her to develop an effective positioning strategy for the brand.

Media choice is an important decision because this stage in advertising strategy leads to outgo of funds and delivers the message to the desired target market. Therefore, communication media research helps develop media strategies like choice of media vehicle from among different media class (TV, newspapers, magazines, radio, outdoor, etc.). Lot of information on reach, audience profile and effectiveness of different media vehicles can be had by subscribing syndicated research services like IRS and NRS.

Advertisers undertake research to study and identify what the consumer's likes and dislikes are with respect to brands or products and hope to find the big idea and develop an effective advertising message. Researchers use concept testing to determine which message-element option is most likely to prove successful.

Creative Concept Research

In creative concept research, creative team develops several rough copy platforms. Researchers conduct focus group interview in the agency's development lab or at the market place. Focus group interviews are combined with other quantitative techniques. A discussion leader moderates the discussion of focus group and each focus group is made to view the roughs (copy platform). The reactions of these groups are measured, videotaped and observed by researchers from behind a one way - mirror. This helps in identifying the most promising creative concept from among many that have been seen and discussed by the focus groups.

Creativity at its best.

OTHER OBJECTIVES

There are many specific communication objectives:

- Closing an immediate sale (buy now because of price)
- Creating near-term sales by moving the prospect closer to a purchase (combating competitive claims)
- Building a long-range consumer franchise (establish brand recognition and acceptance)
- Contribute towards increased sales (convert non-users of the product type)
- Emphasizing a specific step which leads to a sale (induce prospects to sample the product)
- Imparting information needed to close a sale (where to buy it)
- Building confidence in the company (past and present profitability)
- Building images (product quality and corporate citizenship)

Objectives may also be classified in terms of:

Informing → making consumers aware of a new product, announcing a new price and explaining how a product works

Advertisement introducing the "New Lux- Aqua Sparkle".

Persuading → attempting to build brand preference and loyalty and changing a consumer's attitude towards a particular brand's characteristics

Advertisement persuading customers to increase their gains by investing with Kotak.

Reminding → Telling consumers where and when to buy

Advertisement reminding people about the slash down of prices and also inviting them to join the revolution before it is too late.

ATTITUDE MEASURES

In recent years, the use of attitude maintenance or shift as a measure of advertising effectiveness has grown in importance. This has resulted from recent work dealing with product positioning in which product benefits serve as the basis for market segmentation.

To achieve any attitudinal objectives, the communication must satisfy several requirements like attracting attention, being understood and being convincing. Awareness (both aided and unaided) is often used as a summary measure of advertising's success in attracting attention and being remembered and thus, can be used as an objective.

Measuring the attitudes of target audience towards products and then attempting to determine the effect of advertising on those attitudes, more than a single measurement is needed since marketer need to evaluate attitudes towards their product's salient characteristics as well as toward those competing brands. Such a set of measurements should give some indication of what specific attitudinal changes must be brought about in order to obtain sales. The goal of advertising can be stated in terms of changing consumer attitude with respect to selected product characteristics that means, attitudes are predictors of behaviour and that they can be measured with some reasonable degree of accuracy.

Idea of using attitudes as the focus of advertising effort has great appeal because of its presumed link with behaviour. In lieu of measurements of attitudes per se, purchase intention measures are often used as a way of testing advertisements that seek to increase the likelihood of purchase by changing beliefs and evaluations.

COPY TESTING

Research seeks to evaluate alternative ways for advertisers to present their messages.

Body/copy: I reflect. I absorb. I change. I blend into progress. Getting smarter all the time. For me, life refreshes at 7 am. I am my newspaper.

Body/copy: Fitness for a smarter life. And like my lungs need oxygen, my brain needs inspiration. My newspaper is my jogging track. Every morning, I run for my mind.

The word 'copy is perhaps unfortunate, since it seems only to refer to print media and more specifically to the headline and text of the ad message. Here copy refers to an entire advertisement, including the verbal message, pictures, colours and dramatizations, whether the ad appears in print, on radio or television or via some other medium.

Copy-testing Measures and Methods

The methods used for copy testing depend upon the following:

- What assumptions are made about how advertising works?
- What are its objectives?

If objective is to persuade, then a measure of purchase intent will be used.

If objective is attitude shift, then a measure of scales will be used.

If objective is exposure to message overtime, then in market controlled experiments will be used.

To test an ad copy, the researcher must know both what the copywriter is trying to accomplish and what assumptions are being made as to how the various copy components will contribute to this end.

To judge an ad effectiveness, the measures dealing with recognition, recall, comprehension, believability, persuasion and attitude change are the most typical measures.

Copy testing is divided into two parts:

(a) Tests made before the copy is released on a full-run basis (before testing or pre-tests)

(b) Tests done after the copy is run (after testing or post-tests)

Pre-tests are designed to determine what weaknesses exist in the copy before too much money has been spent on the ad. After testing or post-testing attempts to measure the combined effect of the advertising, the media used, the scheduling, the product's distribution, and competitive advertising.

Before discussing these copy-testing methods, let's see the research needed to determine which creative strategy to adopt.

Creative Strategy Research

A product's creative strategy is concerned mainly with determining which message can elicit the desired response from members of the target audience. Product's target audience and desired response can be specified by using attitude and market segmentation studies. First, take a decision as to what ideas the message needs to communicate that requires the use of marketing research to measure the impact of the idea on which the message is based.

Concept sort tests are used to select one or few ideas from a large number. The ideas can be written in the form of one or two statements and typed on a 3 × 5 card. Respondents proceed to sort these cards into piles based on some evaluation criterion such as:

- Intention to purchase or some descriptive scales like uniqueness
- Importance or believability

Concepts having the highest box score are developed further. Focus group discussions can often provide insights into the relative importance of various concepts. A skilled moderator may gain insights into why consumers prefer one brand to another as well as how consumers feel and think about advertising for a given product class or type.

Pre-tests may be conducted as early as during idea generation to rough execution to testing the final version before its implementation. There is no sure-fire way of predicting the success of an advertisement campaign. Advertisers and advertising agencies often use more than one type of pre-tests to examine possible problems before large amount of money is spent on communicating the actual message. By using pre-testing techniques, a number of variables can be evaluated such as the ability of the ad to attract attention, message comprehension by the audience, recall of copy points and the probability that the consumer will buy the product or service. Pre-tests should be used as guide and not as final indicators of success.

Methods for Pre-testing Advertising

Print advertising

- Direct questioning
- Focus group
- Portfolio tests
- Paired comparison test
- Order-of-merit test
- Mock magazine test
- Direct mail test
- Psychological test
- Word association
- Sentence completion
- Depth interview
- Story-telling

Physiological tests

- Pupillometer
- Eye-movement camera
- Electro thermal response
- Voice-pitch analysis
- Brain pattern analysis
- Hemispheric lateralization

TV and radio advertising

- Central location test
- Clutter test
- Trailer test
- Theatre test
- Live telecast test
- Sales experiment

Before Tests (Pre-campaign Tests)

(i) Consumer jury

It provides a "rating" given to an ad by a group of consumers who represent potential buyers of the product. In this test, potential consumers are found. Personal interviews may be used or a group may be assembled and the members asked to vote on the alternatives. The ad copy may be made up in dummy form or the major theme placed on cards. Respondents are then asked to rank the alternatives according to their preferences or interest in buying the product. It is assumed that respondents will always like at least one ad. A variation of these is sometimes used to analyse TV programmes and commercials.

The first step is as follows:

- Expose the audience to the programme or commercial.
- Let members record at specific intervals whether they liked, disliked, or are indifferent to, what they had just heard or seen.
- The same may be accomplished using an electronic machine known as the program analyser.
- The machine has two buttons; respondents press one when they find the program interesting, the other when the program is uninteresting for them and neither when they are indifferent.

- A record machine summarizes the data and charts the continuous reaction of the audience.
- This machine does not measure the extent of feeling or reasons for liking or disliking.

(ii) Rating scales

It may be used by advertisers or ad agency personnel for rating alternative ads. Their use require the establishment of standards for effective copy and numerical weights for each standard. The weights indicate a standard's relative worth in the overall success of the copy. Ads are then rated in accordance with the scale values and a numerical score obtained. If the total weight for one item, for example, is 10, analysts might give one ad 8, if they think it above average on that item. The total of the individual scores provides the numerical rating for an ad. The major advantage of a rating scale is that it provides a list against which to check an ad and helps to single out the elements of an ad. that are good and bad. A variation to the above has been developed by the Leo Burnett agency to quantify the consumer's subjective reaction to a TV commercial. It is called VRP (Viewer Response Profile). It is different from other copy-testing methods in which it seeks to measure a viewer's "experience" with a commercial on several dimensions. Scale items are evaluative statements made by consumers about commercials in general. The VRP focuses on the emotional component of communication effects and provides information relative to such questions as: "Do viewers see the commercial as confusing, entertaining or empathize with the character and situations in commercial. Various dimensions included in the scale are entertainment, confusion, relevancy, brand reinforcement, empathy, familiarity and alienation.

(iii) Portfolio tests

Ads that are to be tested are packaged.

A group of ads (usually a mixture of test ads and control ads) are in portfolio. Sometimes these ads are actually placed as dummy copies in newspapers or magazines. In this test, respondents (being representative of the target audience) are given the folio and asked to go through it, reading whatever interests them and taking as much time as they want. Then, the respondents are asked to recall (with the folio closed) the ads that they can remember. Such recall may be on a completely unaided basis or the interviewer may aid the recall by asking about specific ads or ads for specific products. For each recalled ad, the respondent is asked to play back as much of the ad as possible. This information is recorded verbatim. Further, additional questions may be asked about such things as the believability of the claims in the ad, the general reaction to the ad, and whether the respondent uses the product. Portfolio test is used to test the merits of two or more alternative ads. Experimental design is used in which two or more sets of folio are prepared. The only difference between folios is that one set contains the test ad A and another set contains the test ad B and so on. The non-test ads (control ads) are the same in all folios and positioned in the same order. Using small matched samples and comparing recall and play back scores among the various groups obtain a "winner".

(iv) Psychological tests

These tests are same as other tests mentioned above but differ in methods used. Ad effectiveness depends on the results achieved by the ad in the mind of the individual. Ideally, one could set up a list of the reactions that might result from a given ad. such as self-pity, security, fear, or nostalgia. Alternative ads could then be rated on how readers responded with respect to these reactions. The variety of research techniques used is word associations, sentence completion, depth interviewing and story telling. The idea is to know what respondents see in various ads and what it means to them. Such studies can be taken either before or after the copy has run.

(v) Physiological tests

In these tests, use is made of special lab equipment, which records an individual's physiological responses to an ad. It helps achieve objective responses to identifiable stimuli. Two important physiological tests are galvanic skin response and the eye movement tests.

Galvanic skin response test uses a device similar to polygraph machine used in lie-detection work. In this test, respondents are linked by electrodes to a monitor and are exposed to a number of stimuli in the form of test and control ads. The monitor records the impact of these ads on the nervous system by measuring the amount of perspiration occurring on the hands. Advertising effectiveness is judged on the basis of the "arousal" registered on the monitor. The problem with the test is the small sample size and what is being measured, since arousal does not necessarily mean favourable reaction.

The eye movement test uses the eye camera, which is a device that records continuously the activity of the eye both horizontal and vertical as it reads printed material. By analyzing the route "taken" by the eye, researchers can determine what part of the ad attracted the initial attention, what was interesting in it, and whether there was any part which appeared confusing. In this method, the interpretation of the result is difficult as it is impossible to correlate eye action with what readers are thinking -for example, when the eye lingers at one point in the ad. Does this indicate interest or confusion?

A new machine **"the pupil reader"**, permits both finished ads and those in rough draft form to be tested in a real world setting. The machine resembles a lamp, and when respondents sit in front of it, they are not aware that it is recording both their eyes and the reading material at the same time. Another machine that is used measures **pupil dilation**. The basis of this test is that the pupil dilates when the respondents receive an interesting or pleasant stimulus. Conversely, the pupil contracts when individuals receive uninteresting or unpleasant stimulus. This machine is also called pupillometer. By comparing the changes induced by a message against the base line produced through the use of neutral stimuli, a measure of effectiveness can be obtained. A disagreement exists about what the pupillometer is measuring. A pupillary change may reflect an emotional response to a stimulus or may result from an increase in mental activity, regardless of whether it is pleasant or unpleasant.

Another device, the **tachistoscope**, permits researchers to control the amount of time (in fraction of a second) that an advertisement (either in rough or finished form) is exposed to a group or to an individual. This permits researchers to study perception and comprehension under rigid time conditions. Thus, for example, the ability of outdoor billboard copy to impart a message can be tested under simulated exposure conditions.

Post-testing Methods (Post-campaign Tests)

Post-testing occurs after the advertising campaign has run and is commonly undertaken both by advertisers and advertising agencies. Once the campaign has "run", it is impossible to measure the effects of message separately as results are confounded by the frequency of media schedule, impact of medium used and other market factors:

- Inquiry test
- Sales test
- Recall test (aided recall or unaided recall)
- Recognition test

Inquiry test

Some ads. are designed to produce direct results, such as sales or inquiries. In such cases, a basis exists for measuring accurately the advertisement's worth.

Inquiry tests may be handled in the following ways:

(a) The same offer may be placed in different pieces of copy placed in different issues to the same medium.

(b) The offers are so keyed that they can be traced to the specific advertisement copy. Assuming that all other factors remain constant between issues–a difficult assumption to make–the difference in the number of inquiries received should indicate the "pulling power" of the different pieces of copy.

(c) The same offer is placed in different ad copy that appears in different magazines or newspapers. The assumption is that differences between media are either negligible or can be corrected (say, on the basis of the circulation), and that the adjusted return will indicate the best copy.

(d) The same offer is placed in a medium that provides a split run service. This is a procedure whereby half the copies of the magazine or newspaper contains one piece of copy and half contains another piece of copy. This is accomplished in a systematic way so that the two pieces of copy reach similar audiences.

(e) A large number of inquiries do not mean that the advertising is successful unless inquiries are the sole advertising objective. If the ad's objective is to help the long term build up of a general attitude, the number of inquiries may not necessarily be a sound basis for judging the ad's effectiveness.

Sales tests

This test measures only short term effects.
The measuring instruments may not be sufficiently sensitive to detect relatively small differences in sales; they are time consuming, it is hard to hold all other factors constant and they are quite expensive.

Some of the sales tests are:

(a) Use of alternative pieces of copy

In this test, consumers are exposed to **alternative pieces of copy** through points of purchase displays or direct mail.

In case of POP displays, the need to test two ads would require two matched store samples. Product sales will be measured in each store before and after the introduction of the appropriate display. The changes in sales between the two periods for the two store samples would be compared, and that group with the largest increase would be presumed to have the best copy. Similar experimental design studies can be conducted by mail using coupons.

(b) Use of two matched groups

In this test, one group of respondents are shown a group of TV commercials in a trailer located next to a supermarket. Another does not see a commercial. Both groups are given tickets with a redemption value that group members use in the supermarket to buy whatever brands they wish in the product category involved in the test. The store, through its check out electronic machine records the purchases made by each group, thereby providing the data needed to measure the effect of test commercials.

(c) Behaviour scan (a service operated by information resources inc)

It measures the effectiveness of TV advertising in a similar fashion as described at earlier paragraphs. Such companies install UPC scanners in all supermarkets in test areas. The company doing such a scan identifies a panel of households. Members of a panel of households in each of these test market areas have their purchase recorded electronically by presenting their ID cards to the cashier. The panels are representation of the total market and serve as the basis for studying trial and repeat buying, purchase rates and brand loyalty.

Recall tests

This test measures the proportion of a sample audience that can recall an ad. There are two types of recall–**aided recall and unaided recall**. It provides the cue to the respondents about the media vehicle involved, product class and ad sponsors. In aided recall, the respondent is prompted by showing a picture of the ad with the sponsor or brand name blanked out. Whereas, in unaided recall, only the product or service name may be given.

Day–after recall

It is applied to TV commercials. An exposure of the finished commercial is given to audiences in one or two cities. After this, several hundred viewers are interviewed by phone to determine if they can recall the message. Based on their answers, a recall score is derived, which is then compared with a standard or a normative score (derived from similar studies). On this basis, a commercial is either accepted or rejected. One major problem with such scores is that they are an inappropriate measure of emotional commercials.

Problem of reliability

When commercials were retested, the score varied often substantially. The scores are affected by the type of the programme that carried the commercial.

The straight recall test described above can be modified to provide more discriminating data pertaining to copy effectiveness.

Recognition test

Recognition test measures whether a respondent can recognize an advertisement as he or she has seen before. This test is more suitable to print media. This test is done by mail survey in which questionnaires are mailed to large number of households. In recognition test, three measures are generated for each advertisement in a media vehicle. These measures are noted, seen, associated and read the most. Studies show that recognition depends on the product class, the involvement of the consumer segment in the product class, and on variables such as size, colour, position, copy approach, and the nature of the magazine or media. Recognition is a necessary condition for effective advertising. If the advertising can't pass this minimal test, it probably will not be effective. It may be appreciated that high recognition scores are easier to achieve than high recall scores, since recognition requires only a judgement about the climates and does not require as much retrieval of information from memory as is required by recall.

MEDIA RESEARCH

It is very important as it requires outgo of funds and provides exposure to the target audience. Any decision that is not based on proper information can spell disaster for any advertising campaign. The information collected through media research shall be able to provide answer to the following questions:

- What class of media should be used?
- What media vehicle and media option should be used?
- What should be the exposure level and how schedule it?

The major areas of research are media selection and media scheduling.

Media selection

The goal is to select a media schedule from among the many alternatives that will maximize same combination of the number of people reached and the frequency with which they are reached. This decision presupposes that advertisers have specified the market segments they want to reach.

They must then decide the following:

1. What frequency of message exposure is desired in order to bring about a change in behaviour that will affect the sales of their brand favourably
2. Maximum numbers in the market segment that can be reached with that frequency.

Not only the type of media selection but also the vehicle selection is a problem.

Media selected affects—recall of ad message, ratings of its sponsors and coupon return.

The Advertising Research Foundation suggests that following the elimination of non-prospects, the media analyst pay attention to the five levels at which the media vehicle operates to contribute to the effectiveness of the ad message.

1. Vehicle distribution

It refers to the individual medium's circulation—the process by which, it becomes available.

2. Vehicle exposure

It refers to exposure of audience to the vehicle-reading a given issue of a magazine or watching a particular TV programme

3. Ad exposure

It is like the vehicle exposure but involves the ad. It requires that the message physically come within the audience's attention range.

4. Advertising perception

Audience has conscious awareness of the ad. Perception of print advertising is affected by the size, colour and position of the ad. as well as the thickness. The vehicle measures are also influenced by product interest, past and present usage and prospect status.

5. Advertising communication

The audience receives the message in a desired context.

Media scheduling

The purpose is to determine the appropriate level of repetition. Since advertising is forgotten (wears out) over time, there is also the question of whether a pulsed or burst schedule should be used in contrast to one using constant spending.

Market and sales analysis research

It includes market potential analysis, sales forecasting and sales analysis.

Market potential analysis

It involves development of potentials for individual markets. Market potential is used in establishing sales territories, allocating marketing effort and setting sales quotas. It may be estimated in two ways–through direct data or through corollary data.

Sales forecasting

Sales forecasts predict company's sales of a specific product in a specific market or region during a specific time period. These serve as a guide for planning within the company. Methods of forecasting are executive or sales force judgement, trend analysis and regression analysis.

Sales analysis

It is useful for identifying strong and weak points in company sales programme. Sales analysis is performed by comparing the sales and selling costs associated with different territories, products, customers, or order size.

Measuring advertising effectiveness

Every advertising campaign has to achieve specific objectives. The ad agency and the advertiser have to assure that the given campaign achieves its objectives so that every rupee spent is utilized most effectively. The research can help in providing right information so that right decision is taken.

Research may be applied at four different stages:

(a) A continuous analysis of past advertising experience, in search of guidelines for an analytical framework, is a very useful first step except in the case of new advertisers or products. Such an analysis can provide a valuable basis for reviewing and developing advertising strategy.

(b) Surveys of buyer behaviour and consumer preferences are helpful in developing advertising objectives and strategy. Such research will also be useful in monitoring changes in the target segment.

(c) The third area involves pre-testing advertisements before their release. Pre-testing provides an indication of the likely acceptance of an advertisement or a campaign by the target audience. Results of pre-testing will be used for making improvement and changes as suggested by research.

(d) Post-test research involves testing of the reach and impact of advertising after it has been released. Pre-production research and post-testing are complimentary. The former is diagnostic and is concerned with evaluation of noticeability, recognition, recall, comprehension and behavioural changes, if any, brought about advertising.

Pre-placement Evaluation of Advertising

Although past experience and a 'feel' for the market would always remain valuable aids for advertising executives, a systematic and methodical approach for estimating the possible effectiveness of the advertising before its release would be a worthwhile effort and might also be helpful in avoiding possible adverse effects later.

The first advertising decision may require searching and screening of suitable advertising ideas:

- Quest for new ideas or for new expressions of old ones
- Collection of facts about what people know or feel about a company
- Prediction of how people will probably react to a new advertising idea

The themes, product ideas, brand names, slogans and other elements to be included in an advertisement can thus be evaluated by using the following methods:

(i) Concept testing

It is the basic communication concept around which a campaign may be developed. Lipton Green Label campaign emphasized the environmental features of the areas such as the shade of the Himalayas and the cool mountain winds where this tree is grown. Liril and Thumps Up concept testing would usually involve not more than 50 to 100 respondents, using techniques such as qualitative interviews, free association tests and various statement comparison tests.

(ii) Theme testing

The advertising themes are as follows:

- **Utilitarian**–emphasis on the value of the product and for service directed towards providing satisfaction for the money or efforts spent on obtaining the product/service.
- **Focused**–an extension of utilitarian themes, which will appeal to specific market/ audience segments.
- **Informative**–emphasis only on information about the product/service being advertised. No explicit selling message is present.
- **Non-specific**–a vague or diffused message which contains only passing reference to the product or advertiser.
- **Achievement orientation**–highlighting the achievements in terms of sales, profits or awards won by the advertisers.
- **Descriptive and projective**–a combination of informative and achievement oriented themes.
- **New product, service scheme or idea**–a new entry in the market.

(iii) The media factor

The best of messages may fail in achieving their objectives if the message vehicle is inappropriate or inadequate in terms of its reach and coverage. In addition to having a major bearing on the cost of advertising, media types and advertising effectiveness, the media factors help in the following ways:

1. They determine in large measure the size and characteristics of the audience exposed to advertising, i.e. how many and what types of persons would have an opportunity to see or hear the advertising and how often.
2. They provide an environment that is favourable, unfavourable or neutral for advertisement to be seen or heard.
3. In interaction with copy and the audience, they determine the overall impact of an advertising campaign–the information communicated, attitudes formed or changed or action that may be taken as a result of advertising.

(iv) Copy research

The basic purpose of pre-testing various possible advertisements is to establish whether the message content and presentation are likely to perform their allocated task efficiently, and what changes or improvements may be helpful.

Sources of Statistics for Media Research

(a) Independent Media Surveys

A number of research organizations produce regular independent media studies. They are independent in the sense that they have tripartite sponsorship representing the three sides of advertising through bodies serving the advertisers, advertising agencies and the relevant media bodies. Some surveys are conducted continuously with press and TV, or periodically with radio, or occasionally with outdoor. In addition, individual media owners such as publishing houses and TV contractors conduct their own surveys.

(b) Readership and Circulation

These provide press media data. **Readership** is the estimate of the number of people who read newspapers and magazines and the figures result from surveying a sample of the reading public. **Circulation** is the average audited net sale, or the number of copies actually sold at the full cover price (free copies not included).

Readership is estimated by means of extensive readership surveys. Readership is not found by multiplying the circulation figure by a given number.

Circulation figures are based on audited net sales, not field research. In their absence, there are sometimes publishers' statements as well. The IRS (Indian Readership Survey) and NRS (National Readership Survey) provide these figures every year.

(c) Audit Bureau of Circulation (ABC)

Audit Bureau of Circulation (ABC) was found to inform advertisers and advertising agencies of the number of newspapers or magazines, which are sold. It was created because publishers were selling advertisement space on the basis of spurious circulation figures, which were actually total print orders rather actual number of copies sold.

National Readership Survey

All most all newspapers and magazines that are registered with Indian Newspaper Society (INS) are included in the readership survey, plus certain other specialist journals from time to time and a very large sample of people is interviewed.

During the continuous survey, questions are asked about individual's TV viewing, listening to radio, cinema going, related to readership and purchasing habits, etc. The respondents are divided into A, B, C, D and E socio-economic classes so as to produce demographic profile of the readership of each publication. The NRS figures are issued every six month.

Poster

Structured power audience traffic studies are carried out by Poster Audience Research (POSTAR). It was set up in 1996 to provide independent on-going research into audiences for outdoor advertising.

POSTAR provides on-going data on poster audience traffic, coverage and frequency estimates. These indicate:

- How each site is located and panel positioned;
- How many people pass each panel
- How they see it

This information is obtained through;

- Computer-modelled traffic counts; advance visibility studies;
- Extensive travel survey

ACCOUNT PLANNING

Account planning is a process that involves conducting research and gathering all relevant information about a client's product or service brand and the consumers in the target market. Account planning facilitates the creative process. It provides necessary inputs to the creative process. Without inputs from the account planning, it may be very difficult for the creative team to proceed with its work. Account planning is an important link between the client and advertising agency's creative team. Many a times, the account executive is the real face of the client because the kind of inputs he/she provides becomes the basis for the creative team's creative work.

Account planning started in England during the 1960s and 70s and has eversince spread across the globe including the US, Europe and Asia. The concept has been very successful during the last two decades, as many agencies have experienced higher success rate with the campaigns that were developed with the help of account planning. For example, Goodby, Siverstein and partners who have used account planning extensively had developed many successful advertising campaigns for many clients such as Polaroid, HP, Sega and Nike. One of most popular ad campaign "got milk" for California milk processor Board was also developed by the same agency.

In his book entitled *Truth, Lies, and Advertising: The Art of Account Planning,* Jon Stell, Vice President and Director of Account Planning, notes that the account planner's job is to provide the key decision makers with all the information they require to make an intelligent decision. According to Stell, "Account planners may have to work very hard to influence the way the advertising turns out, carefully laying out a strategic foundation with the client, handing over titbits of information to creative people when, in their judgement, that information will have the greatest impact, giving feedback on ideas and hopefully adding some ideas of their own."

An account planner uses research (both primary and secondary) to gain more information about the brand in its market place, the consumer's perspectives, competitor information and shares this information to contribute directly or indirectly to develop an appropriate advertising campaign.

Small agencies may not afford to have account planning department or if they have the department, it may lack the expertise for certain aspects or problems related to brand promotions. In such situation, small agencies depend on external research suppliers. In some of the cases, this agency-supplier relationship becomes so strong, lasting and productive that the external supplier fulfils most of the roles of an internal account planning and research department.

An account planner discussing the advertising campaign with company managers.

Many advertising agencies create and maintain specialized libraries often known as information and intelligence centres that provide access to dictionaries, encyclopedias, atlases, cookbooks, book of famous quotations and trade, business and general newspapers. A typical information and intelligence centre (specialized) library must be equipped with people and material to answer numerous and variety of questions as indicated below.

An Information Processing Centre (IPC).

A sample of questions to be answered by a typical intelligence centre (library) of an agency

- What are the trends in soaps and detergents?
- What information regarding the fourth of September 2004 is available at the intelligence centre?
- We want to shoot our commercial at Ooty (India)? What is the average temperature and rainfall in the months of August and September and what is the best way to reach there? Check the availability of hotel accommodation as well.
- Who are the leading detergent players? Provide sales and market share data
- How many Indian families have children under the age of 6 and family income above Rs 03 lac annually?
- How big is the detergent market in India?
- We need pictures of brand characters—original and revised ones of Ariel, Nirma and surf.

A typical advertising campaign might be influenced, directly or indirectly, by information from many sources. Both outside research suppliers and agency's own account planning department are the major sources of information for any ad campaign. It is surprising to note that the account planner faces the problem of plenty rather than scarcity, i.e. he/she has too much of information available with him from various sources. His difficulty is to sort it out and identify meaningful and useful information out of this heap. He has plenty of qualitative information, which provides insight into how consumers behave and why, and the quantitative information which has numerical information such as exposure to ads, purchases, and other market-related information.

The account planner must sort out the potentially relevant material from irrelevant material and put the findings into a format that decision makers and the creative team can use. The research task usually falls to account planners in case of agencies with internal account planning or research departments. An account planner is responsible for the advertising strategy formulation and implementation in the creative work. The account planners must thoroughly understand the client's target market, brand and other market-related information to develop an effective advertising strategy. One of the most important skills possessed by the account planner is the ability to organize huge amount of information in relevant and useful form so as to solve the problem related to the brand.

A large full agency will have an account planning department to develop a meaningful interface with the client. However, agencies in small towns and newly-formed agencies in large towns, many of the specialist's jobs may be carried out by the same person.

A typical organizational structure of a large agency with its departments and functions is indicated in Figure 6.3. Various positions shown in Figure 6.3 indicate how different specialist

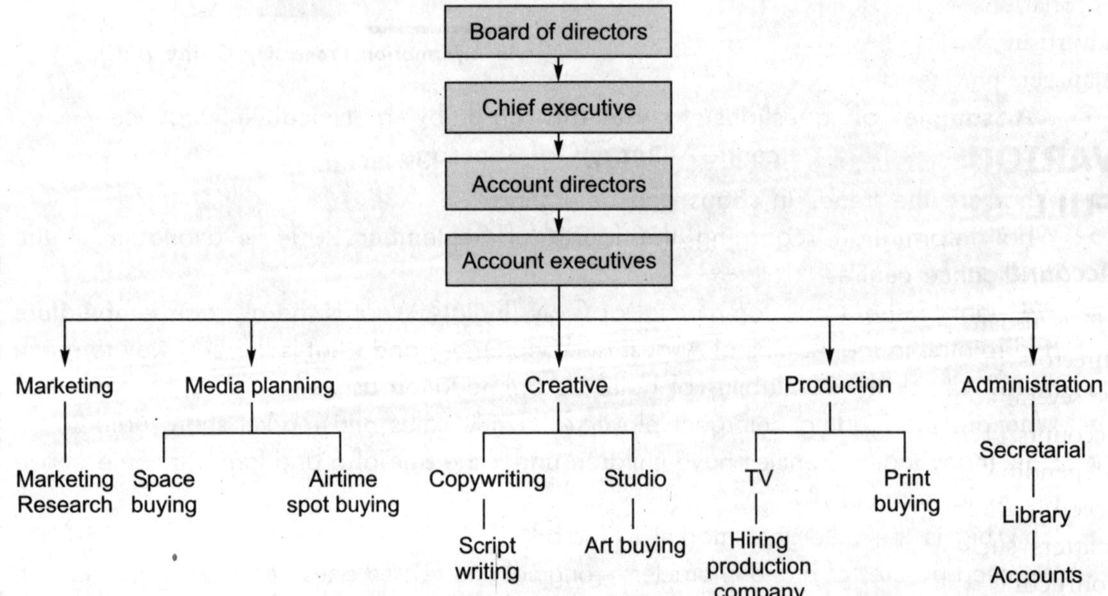

Fig. 6.3 A full service agency: departments and function.

jobs are performed in a full service agency. Advertising agencies may vary in size and structure. They may operate according to plans board system (consisting of account executive and heads of agency departments; an account executive introduces new account and submits his/her report to all heads who in turn discuss and a campaign is agreed upon) or have overall account planner who integrates the work of departments and personnel. Working closely with the account executive, the account planner prepares the creative brief and gets associated throughout the campaign. Whatever may be the structure and interrelationship, the general flow and control of work will be similar, with the account executive maintaining liaison with the client, the agency, and the production manager.

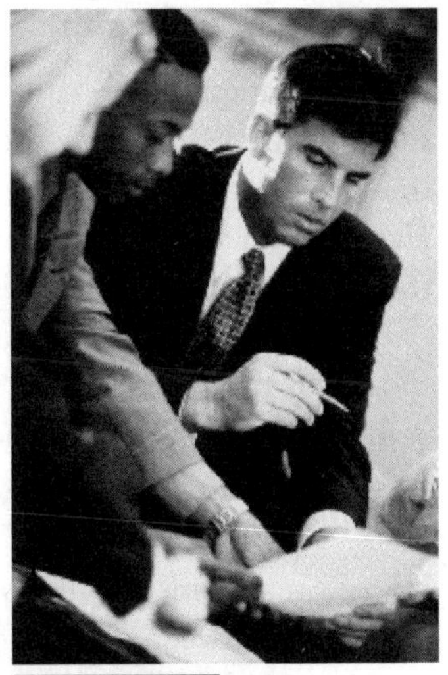

An account planner interacting one to one basis with the individuals and the department.

An account executive also acts as a controller to ensure that each stage of the campaign is completed on time so that advertisements reach the media by the deadlines or copy dates and the schedule of release to media is adhered. It must be appreciated here that a number of different campaigns will be progressing simultaneously at the agency so there will be great variety of work. The account planner has to remain constantly in touch with various departments and accounts executives so that no confusion and interchanging arise.

A common mistake is to assume that advertising manager works in the agency. He/she is, in fact, in charge of the client's advertising department. The agency - client relations and negotiations will be conducted between the agency account executive and the company's advertising manager (or somebody else on the client's behalf. It may be marketing manager, sales manager, product or brand manager or any senior manager, etc.).

VARIOUS POSITIONS AND FUNCTIONS IN A FULL SERVICE AGENCY

Account director

He is usually one of the partners or directors of the agency. He/she (may be several account directors in very large agency) will be responsible for a group of accounts (clients). There shall be several account executives working under him/her. Each of the executive handles one or more accounts. The account director will be responsible to Chief Executive or Board of Directors (depending on agency structure) and his/her main concern is profitability of the agency. The account director will lead negotiations for new and renewal business. He decides on policy matters such as whether or not to accept certain accounts–the accounts that are risky or conflicting with existing accounts.

Competing accounts

It is not unethical for an agency to handle competing accounts. Contrarily, it might provide some advantage both to the client and the agency if it has experience in handling accounts in the fields such as banking, insurance, automobile, telecommunications and electronics, etc. However, an agency may not handle competing accounts on the grounds that it is objected by the rival for security or greater intensity of rivalry.

There are problems of conflicting accounts. It may be undesirable to service two mutually substitute products such as tea and coffee, and road transport and rail transport etc. There is a difference between conflicting and competing clients.

Account executive

He/she maintains the liaison with the agency and the client. It does not mean that he/she is just a go-between or performing the post-office function; the account executive has to understand the client's needs, the business and the industry and market situation. He has to interpret these needs and market realities and feed it to the creative department of the agency. Conversely, the account executive has to present the agency's proposals, ideas and work to the client (account). It is a delicate, diplomatic job and with the responsibility to keep and acquire accounts.

The account executive should have a broad knowledge of advertising and be able to work with everyone in the agency, directing his or her efforts in the interest of the client.

Contact report

This report is also termed as call report, which is essential to good management of an account. After every client meeting the account executive quickly submits to the client a special form of minutes of the meeting called contact report. It contains details of the meeting like when and where the meeting was held, who were present, what was discussed and what decision were arrived at and to whom in the client's organization and the agency the report is being distributed. The report gives a brief statement of items reported and decisions taken. It must be immediately distributed after the meeting, so that there is an opportunity to make any necessary revisions and misunderstandings, if any, are avoided. The reports are filed in the facts books, which become a record for constant reference and also the basis of the agency's annual report to the client.

Role of Account Planning in development and execution of an advertising campaign

This part of the chapter will discuss in detail the role of account planning in successfully managing a complete campaign from initial briefing to the final assessment of the results.

Initial briefing

As discussed earlier, before anything can be planned an account executive from the agency must obtain complete current information about the client's company and the product or service to be advertised. The client to be serviced may be regular for whom the next campaign is to be prepared or a potential client for whom a competitive proposition has to be assembled. In the later case, information required may be both in width and depth. For giving clearer picture of the client to his colleagues in the agency the account planner would generally require the information on the following:

- The Budget
- The company, product or service
- Market
- Distribution
- What is the name
- Price
- Packaging
- Competition

The budget

How much is the decided marketing budget and what portion will be spend on advertising?

- What is ratio of budget spending on above-the-line and below-the-line media?
- Is the agency responsible for one of the media or both or any part of the each, etc.?
- The agency needs to know that it has to plan the campaign within the set financial limits.
- There may be occasions when the agency may be asked to undertake a campaign with certain defined objectives. In this case, the agency has to develop the budget to achieve the predetermined objective.

The company, product or service

- Understand the company, its background and how it operates. Some of this may be got from annual report but each company is unique and has its own character.
- The product has to be seen, understood and used or operated for obtaining first-hand experience and detailed information (wherever possible, take the product to the office to show other colleagues in the agency).

The market

- At whom the product or service aimed?
- Who is likely to buy it?
- Was it created to satisfy a particular market need?
- What are the buying motives?
- How satisfied or dissatisfied is the customer?
- Does the client require marketing advice?
- Is the agency expected to conduct market research?

Distribution

- How does/will it reach to the consumer?
- What is the distribution channel?
- What is the client's relationship with channel partners?
- Is distribution extensive or intensive?

What is the name (brand)

- Has this been decided or agency has to find a name. Usually advertising agency must be consulted as early as possible for giving a name to the product

Price

- Has this been decided or the agency's help needed for arriving at the best selling price?
- What is the selling price?
- Is it a psychological, market, bargain or competitive price or is the product pitched at a certain price bracket allied to market.

Packaging

- Has this been decided or does it have to be designed by the agency? Is research necessary? This may concern the actual container, its type or material, the labelling, and any other form of container like a bottle is packed in a box.

Competition

- Is the product unique or does it compete within an established product group? Or
- If it is expensive, what sort of discretionary income expenditure does it compete with?

In many cases, it may be possible, the client would have prepared a marketing mix and done all the marketing research. But very often, marketing is introduced by the advertising agency, there are specialist product development agencies which start at the beginning. Moreover, it may be good idea to bring in the agency at the earliest possible so that the agency could advise throughout all the stages of the marketing mix, beginning with the new product.

Report to the agency head

Whatever may be the case, the account executive obtains all the relevant and needed information and reports it to senior people in the agency, may be to the managing director, accounts director or account manager. This is essential for policy decisions. The senior managers also need to know the progress of work, the need for additional staff and the financial implications of the new or renewable business, in addition, the suitability of business in terms of ethics and business conflict is also examined by the senior managers.

Report to the departmental heads

If the account executive gets go ahead on his/her report. A detailed report is now submitted to the departmental heads that comprise the plans board. Each one will study the report submitted by the account executive and discussions take place. This is done to prepare the proposal for presentation to the client.

Preparing the campaign

The plans board meeting takes place where the product, the company and client needs are discussed thoroughly. Lots of ideas start flowing from various departmental heads of the agency. The campaign starts taking shape with the assimilation of discussions by the account executives. Even the client's advertising manager may be asked to join at this stage to provide initial feedback on the campaign.

The account executive now presents the initial campaign details to the plans board. The discussions take place; additions and alterations are made at this stage. Once the ideas have been agreed upon, the campaign is now assembled for presentation to the client. Copy platform and visuals are prepared to be shown to the client. The media schedules are drawn and even tentative bookings for space and slots are made wherever there is a requirement for the lead time.

The presentation of the campaign is made to the client. It is the campaign that has to be sold to the client. In his/her presentation, the account executive has to justify the copy platform, the visual treatment, layout, the choice of media and date, sizes and spot duration recommended, media vehicle chosen, etc. At this stage, client has to be convinced that the scheme will achieve the desired results or at least contribute effectively to the sales target, which may depend on many other factors. With large companies and big accounts, the presentation could take all day, especially, if it is a complicated campaign covering perhaps more than one product and making use of a variety of media. It can be an occasion of great argument. Everyone thinks they know all about advertising at this stage. Account executive may find an ally in the advertising manager of the client company if they have worked closely from the proposal stage itself.

Once the client has given approval (which involves a contract of service), the creative work and media buying can go ahead. At this stage, time schedules for each activity is drawn elaborately like finalization of copy, production of finished layouts, completion of artwork and typesetting, submission to clients, return by clients, amendments made and final copy in the desired form being dispatched to the media. The account executive will work closely with agency departments to oversee the preparation and production of the campaign to assure the adherence to the time schedules.

Both the agency's account executive and the client's advertising manager will study the actual appearance of the ads. Has it been reproduced well? Has it appeared in the right position the right day and time? What are the audience ratings (TVRs) for the programmes when the commercial appeared on TV? The problems such as wrong insertions, poor printing quality, missing part of the copy, wrong spellings, etc. are to be taken care of before the ad is released to media. The campaign has to be monitored to make sure that the media schedules have been met.

The effectiveness of the advertising has to be measured through recall research to test whether people saw, remembered or responded to the ad. Later, dealer audit research will record what effect the advertising had in moving sales and also the effect it had on brand share and position in the product group.

The account planning has a great role to play in acquiring the client for company and maintaining the client through client satisfaction. Therefore, accounts executive becomes a key link between the ad agency and the client. There needs to be a close rapport between the client and the account executive for providing the quality service.

SUMMARY

Advertising research generates current information on the consumer profile, market, competition and brand, etc. Information generated by advertising research can be used for brand positioning, developing advertising copy, media decisions and knowing advertising effectiveness.

Advertising research components are strategic and evaluative. Strategic component comprises of data collection and organization and preparing a strategy document. The evaluative component consists of three-stage evaluations of advertisements at pre-campaign, mid-campaign and post-campaign.

Various methods are used for pre-testing of advertisements which are media specific. For print advertising, methods like direct questions, focus group, portfolio tests, paired comparison test, order of merit test, mock magazine test, direct mail test, psychological test, word association, sentence completion, depth interview and story telling are used. Also various physiological tests like pupillometer, eye-movement camera, electrothermal response, voice-pitch analysis, brain pattern analysis and hemispheric lateralization, etc. are also used for the purpose. Methods used in TV and radio advertising are central location test, clutter test, trailer test, theatre test, live telecast test and sales experiment.

Account planning is a process that involves conducting research and gathering all relevant information about a client's product or service brand and the consumers in the target marketing. It helps creative process by providing necessary inputs. Account planning is a phenomenon of large advertising agencies because small agencies may not afford to have account planning department. Small agencies depend on external research suppliers. An account planner uses research (both primary and secondary) to gain more information about the brand in its market place, the consumer's perspectives and competitors and shares this information with the creative team to develop an appropriate advertising campaign.

QUESTIONS

1. Why advertising research is needed? What are its objectives?
2. Identify various components of advertising research and discuss each in short.
3. What do you mean by creative concept research? How is it important for an advertiser?
4. How does an advertiser decide the message to be sent to the audience? Discuss various methods of pre-testing an advertisement. Why is pre-testing important.
5. Can you use the same methods for pre-testing in case of an ad copy being released in the print and in the television? Justify your decision.
6. Do you agree or disagree with the statement "Physiological tests are not the true indication of one's mind". Justify your answer.
7. How can post-testing an ad copy help the advertiser? Describe various methods used in post-testing.
8. What do you mean by media research? How can you measure advertising effectiveness?
9. Describe account planning and its importance for an advertising agency.
10. What is a full service agency? Describe various organs of such an agency.
11. Describe the importance of initial briefing. What does it cover?

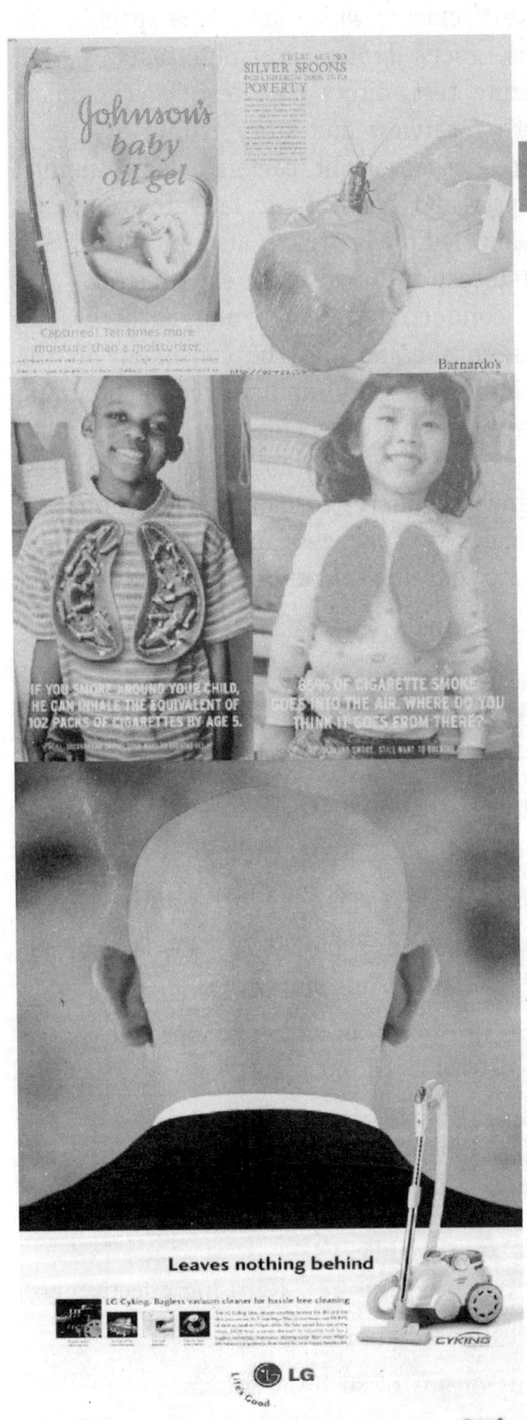

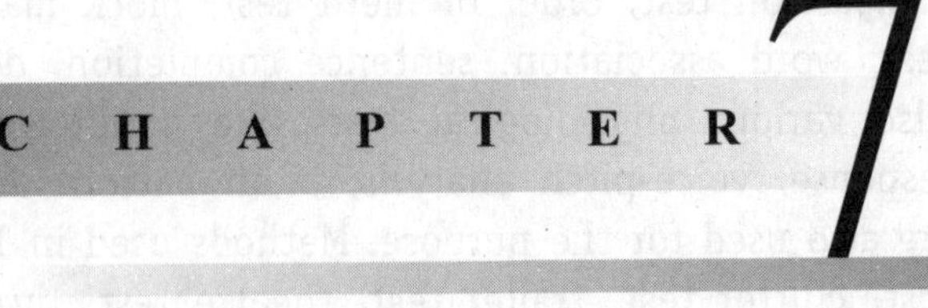

CHAPTER 7

Working of Advertising

LEARNING OBJECTIVES

After reading this chapter, you will be able to:

- Review research work on how advertising works.
- Understand communication process.
- Know and understand various communication (response) models used in advertising.
- Know and learn what makes an effective advertisement.

Before an ad campaign is planned and launched, it will be worth the efforts to spend sometime on thinking about what exactly the advertising objectives are. Advertising is a communication sent from the advertiser (brand) to the receiver (customer/purchaser). Thus, to create an effective advertisement, the advertiser needs to decide what kind of communications effect it needs to achieve.

As will be discussed in this chapter in the following paragraphs, advertising can affect consumers in various ways, and the mechanism or "route" of affect sought in any particular situation needs to be: clearly specified and understood before creating an ad. An advertiser has to specifically decide the consumer elements to be influenced by advertising. Should the elements be: generating awareness about the brand, changes in attitudes or the feelings associated with the brand? Should certain kinds of thoughts be evoked in the consumer's mind or some changes in the social norms concerning the brand? Should it be inducement for some kind of action? All these questions can be answered better if we develop an understanding of how "advertising works" in different types of situations. A lot of research findings are available in the literature. The insight gained from such research findings can change our very basic understanding of how consumers process advertising.

Advertising objectives can be set with ease if one acquires complete understanding of various response models. The hierarchy of response model suggests that in the first place advertisers should always create advertising to increase awareness, follow up with a campaign to change attitude, and subsequently strive to induce trial action. A point of debate arises here: is this always true. If not, what implications might it have for how we design ads. Another hierarchy model, DAGMAR (Defining Advertising Goals for Measured Advertising Result), suggests that clear advertising objectives need to be set for measuring the results of an ad campaign. In this approach, advertising objectives involve a communication task that is specific and measurable. Communications objectives based on hierarchical model are awareness, comprehension, conviction and action. The other models like AIDA (Attention, Interest, Desire and Action), Innovation-adoption model and information processing model also suggest the communication effect as hierarchical. These models are explained in detail in later part of this chapter.

We will now discuss about what kind of effect an ad should try to create and in what kind of situation.

Early studies suggest that advertising repetition may in some situations lead to preference, even if consumers don't absorb information on product benefits. Thus, keeping brand awareness at a high level should often be considered as a possible advertising objective. This kind of brand salience or top-of-mind awareness is especially important when the advertising is aimed not so much at getting new customers, but at making existing customers buy a particular brand even more frequently. The brands like ASC Ehrenberg, Gerald Tallis and others have indicated that, for most mature brands, advertising serves mostly to reinforce (rather than create) brand preference, in the face of competitive advertising, and that one way of reinforcing, it is to have high levels of reminder advertising that use frequent repetition.

A related view of the exposure effect suggests that repeated exposure creates a conscious sense of familiarity with the brand, which then causes liking. The concept here is that familiar, known objects are evaluated more highly than are unknown objects with associated uncertainty. Perhaps, uncertainty creates tension, which is undesirable, or familiarity may create positive feelings of comfort, security, ownership, or intimacy.

Advertising researcher H.E. Krugman has pointed out that a product is often preferred not because it is indeed better but because of "the pleasure of its recognition–sheer familiarity". The research review seems to suggest that a high level of ad repetition is especially important when consumers don't process ads with a view to extract much information from them. When ads are likely to be processed in such a shallow manner, a high level of ad repetition can lead to brand preference simply because that brand is now top-of-mind, preconsciously liked, perceived to be more believable and feels safer, and more trusted, familiar and comfortable.

Plenty of research has been done on the concept of involvement and its importance in determining the way in which advertising shapes consumers attitude and behaviour. Some researchers equate involvement with the amount of attention paid to the brand information in the advertisement, others measure it by the extent to which the message is personally relevant to the consumer, or the degree to which the consumer's thoughts, while viewing the ad, concern the brand instead of the way the ad is made. Regardless of these conceptual differences, there is substantial agreement that the degree to which the consumer is "involved" is of critical importance in determining which part of the advertisement will shape the consumer's final attitude towards the brand. It is also commonly agreed that consumers are more involved when they consider the message content more relevant (high motivation), when they have the knowledge and experience to think about that message content (high ability), and when the environment in which that message content is presented does not interfere with such thinking (high opportunity). The motivational involvement factor is determined both by the individual's intrinsic level of interest in the product category (enduring involvement) as well as more temporary factors, such as how close the consumer is to a purchase in that product category and the degree of perceived risk in making a purchase in that category (situational involvement).

Finally, for advertising managers seeking to make decisions about objectives, the overall implication of this research on involvement is that when consumers are in a high involvement situation, with the consumer seeking rational or problem-solving benefits, the advertisers ought to have as their objectives the communication of product benefits through message content, for only that can lead to the attitude change necessary for behavioural effects. Low-involvement situations should lead to the targeting of greater awareness as a primary objective rather than the communication of attitude-enhancing arguments about why the brand is better. Research by Wayne D. Hoyer and Stevan P. Brown has shown that when subjects prefer to economize on time and effort in making a brand choice, they give great weight to the fact that they are already aware of a brand instead of probing quality differences in detail.

One of the models of advertising that focuses on the role of such involvement is the **Elaboration Likelihood Model (ELM).** According to this model, a basic dimension of information processing and attitude change is the depth or amount of information processing. At one extreme, the consumer can consciously and diligently consider the information provided in the ad in forming attitude towards the advertised brand. In this way, attitudes are changed or formed by careful consideration, thinking and integration of information relevant to the product. This type of persuasion process is termed the central route to attitude change. In contrast to this processing, there also exists a peripheral route to attitude change in which attitudes are changed or formed without active thinking about the brand's attributes and its pros and cons.

An advertiser who is setting objectives needs to predict whether, in a given context, the central route is feasible and whether audience members will actually exert the effort involved to process an advertisement with strong arguments deeply. If this is unlikely, the consumer is more likely to form attitude peripherally. Then the advertiser is better off creating an ad with likeable or credible spokespeople, rather than relying on strong, logical arguments. Consumers are more likely to process centrally when both motivation and ability to process information are high. When either is low, peripheral processing is more likely.

From the advertising planning point of view, the key implication of this research stream is that the motivation and ability of the target audience are both high, and central processing is most likely. It makes sense to try to focus on changing attitudes through strong "reasons why" the brand is better. Thus, an ad selling expensive office product might not be best served by using a celebrity endorser, which will be peripheral cue. When consumers don't really know much about the differences between brands, it makes sense to use an endorser for the brand.

To recapitulate the research findings:

- In low-involvement situations, it may be more appropriate to create ads that raise awareness and change brand attitudes through executional liking and credibility.
- In high-involvement situations, it may be better for ads to provide strong reasons, "why" the brand is superior.

Some TV commercials become very popular among the audience but such commercials do little to affect the brand sales. So, are these creative commercials effective if they fail to sell the product? Most people pay only a limited amount of attention to a TV commercial or print ad, so the ad may create little impact if the message is complicated or the brand links are unclear, even though it is well remembered and well liked.

In this chapter, we are going to discuss and address some of these issues and find answer for these questions. How do we decide whether an advertisement or other marketing communication message is effective? What these messages accomplish and how do they work to create impact?

HOW TO DEVELOP AN EFFECTIVE ADVERTISEMENT AND UNDERSTANDING OF HOW ADVERTISING WORKS

Understanding of concepts related to how advertising works shall help create an effective advertising campaign. It requires complete understanding of various steps that are essential part of creating a workable advertisement. Figure 7.1 indicates various sequential steps that an advertiser must follow for creating an effective advertisement campaign.

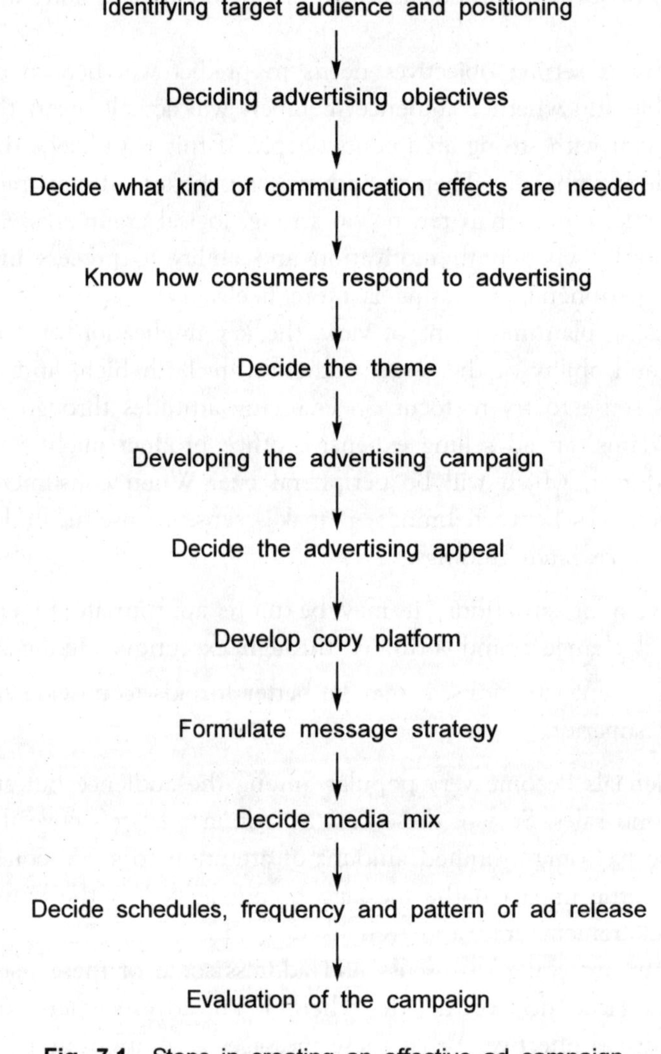

Fig. 7.1 Steps in creating an effective ad campaign.

The first step in developing an effective campaign is finding who are the target audiences or for whom the campaign is and how do you want them to perceive your brand (positioning). Thereafter, decide what do you want to accomplish through advertising. The next step is about deciding the communication objectives, which may be awareness, interest, desire or action. It is important for the agencies and account executives to understand how consumers respond through a series of steps to these ads.

Knowing about what the advertiser wants to achieve and how generally consumer responds to advertising, will facilitate the development of an effective campaign. Deciding the theme will help bring together various elements of the campaign. A *campaign is a complex set of activities designed to meet certain defined objectives and solve some critical problems within a specified time period of less than a year.* It is designed around a creative theme covering a time period, different advertising vehicles or marketing communication activities and focuses on a specific product attribute or one set of audience or may cover variety of attributes and reach all the audiences. A campaign basically comprises of creative strategy and tactics, media plan and other marketing integrated communication tools.

The creative strategies in a campaign will require decision on ad appeal, copy platform and message. This aspect of advertisement requires a lot of thinking and brainstorming to come out with the most appropriate output that is expected to have desired response from the consumers. A good ad copy without good media strategy may not get desired results. Identifying the right type of media that can carry the message to the target audience with required exposure. Depending upon the advertising objectives, the schedule and frequency decisions have to be taken.

Finally, the results of the campaign must be measured for comparison with the advertising objectives.

Before discussing how to design an effective ad, it is important to discuss how communication works? Advertising is a form of communication. In a way, it is a conversation with a consumer about a product. It gets attention, provides information and a little bit of entertainment and tries to create some sort of response like a trial or a sale.

HOW COMMUNICATION WORKS

Mass communication (which is impersonal) is a process depicted in a communication model in Figure 7.2. The model outlines the important players and steps in the communication process.

The model begins with a source (S), a sender (the advertiser) who encodes the message (M), puts it in words and pictures. The prepared message is presented to the audience through channels of communications (C) such as TV, radio, newspapers or magazines. The message is received and interpreted (M) by the target audience. The feedback is obtained by the source (advertiser) by monitoring the response of the receiver. However, this is a one-way

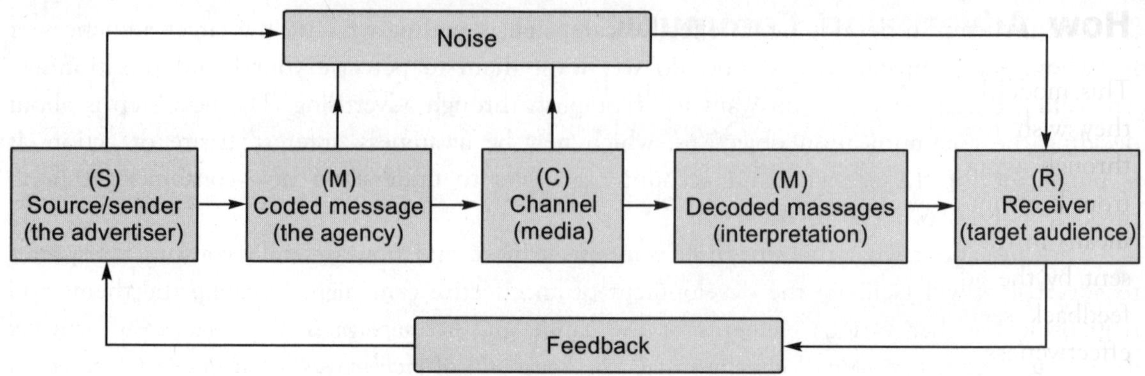

Fig. 7.2 A basic communication model.

communication (mass media). What is needed nowadays is a two-way interactive communication in which source and receiver exchange positions as message bounces between them. The noise in the model is due to the sender who may be tired or garbles the message. A 'noise' is any factor that interferes with or distorts the delivery of the advertising message to the target audience. It may be due to channel or the agency itself.

The two-way (interactive) communication model is depicted in Figure 7.3.

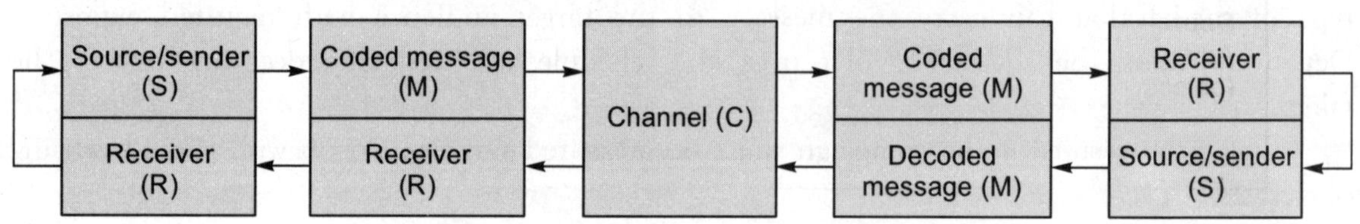

Fig. 7.3 An interactive (two-way) communication model.

Adapted from *Advertising Principles and practice* by Wells, Burnett and Moriarty; Prentice-Hall of India, 2005.

This model suggests that if advertiser wants to address the limitations of one-way communication model (it does not provide opportunity for questions and feedback and hence no dialogue takes place), they need to listen to as well as send messages to customers. This may be done partly by using more interactive forms of marketing communication (personal selling, telemarketing, and online marketing). The advertiser can also achieve more interactivity by providing such response devices as toll-free numbers and e-mail addresses to open opportunities for dialogue.

How Advertising Communication Works

This model begins with the source or advertiser and its agency and advertising objectives (what they wish to accomplish through advertising). The advertisers usually deliver their messages through a variety of tools termed generally as media mix. Accompanying the message is 'noise' from both internal and external sources - internal means internal to the consumer and external means in the environment. The next stage is message reception and response where the message sent by the advertiser is seen, understood, interpreted and responded. This step is followed by feedback section in which the source finds out what happened to the message sent. The effectiveness of the communication is measured through this action. The advertising communication model is depicted in Figure 7.4.

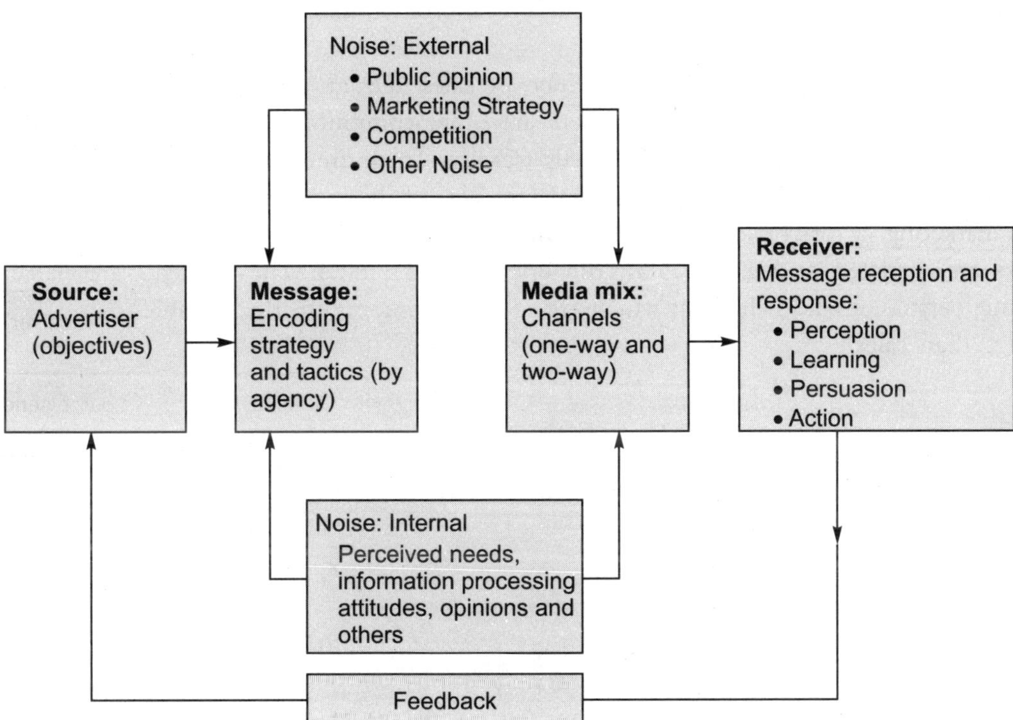

Adapted from: Advertising Principles and Practices, 6th ed., Wells, Burnett and Morlarty, Prentice-Hall of India, 2005.

Fig. 7.4 Advertising communication model.

Source

The advertiser and the advertising agency are the sources. Combined together, they decide the objectives for advertisement campaign in terms of impact they want the message to have on the consumer. In customer-oriented marketing, all communications are evaluated in terms of consumer response. The consumer's response is measured to determine whether the message have met its objectives and was effective.

The question here is: how do advertisers and their agencies evaluate the impact of advertising. In our mind, it is the ultimate result advertising brings. It hardly matters how creative the ad is; how attractive, funny, entertaining it looks or if it has won some awards. It also doesn't matter which media we chose, the bargain we got, the frequency and reach we planned and the endorser (personality) we used. It is simply the results that matter. We would like to measure and assure whether the communication delivered the desired results. Did it meet its objectives? If not, it has failed.

One of the effects of advertising is to increase sales. It is an important behavioural objective to get consumers to buy the product. There are other communication effects that may also be important and may lead directly or indirectly to sales. There are other effects that are drivers of sales and may be a better indicator of the effectiveness of the message than sales (there are many other marketing factors besides advertising that have an impact on sale). These communication drivers are depicted at Figure 7.5 in the effectiveness model. These effects are perception, learning, persuasion and behaviour which are sometimes more directly traceable to an advertising message than sales.

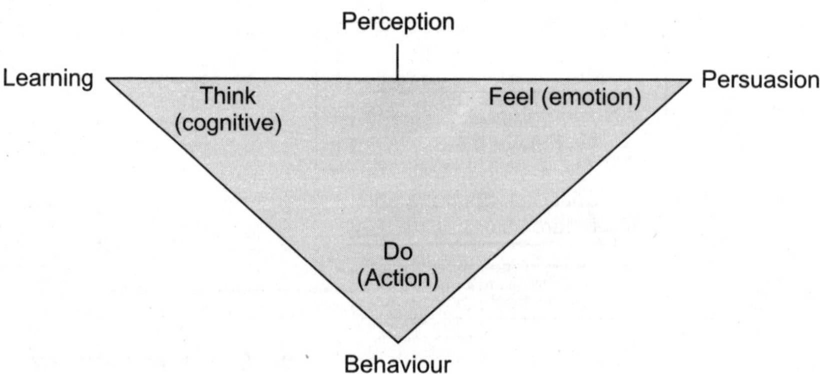

Fig. 7.5 A model of key effects.

These key effects may lead to sales. At first, advertisers try to get consumers to perceive (at least notice) the ad. Then, the advertiser hopes consumers will either learn something or be persuaded by something in the ad. Finally, the advertiser tries to get consumers to behave in a certain way ideally to buy the product in the ad.

Table 7.1 explains how to determine the effectiveness of the ads and which tools are used for creating these communication effects. In the first column, the key categories of message effects are mentioned. The next column, labelled "surrogate measures" refers to the way advertisers evaluate how well the advertising has worked. The last column indicates the communication tools that may be the most appropriate for achieving the objectives.

Table 7.1 Message effectiveness factors

Key message effects	Surrogate measures	Communication tools
Perception	Exposure	Advertising; public relations
	Attention	Advertising; sales promotion
	Interest	Advertising; sales promotion; public relations
	Memory: recognition/recall	Advertising; sales promotion; public relations
Learning	Understanding	Public relations; personal selling Direct marketing; advertising
	Image and association Brand links	Advertising; public relations, point of purchase ads
Persuasion	Attitudes: form or change	Public relations; personal selling
	Preference/intention	sales promotion
	Emotions and involvement	Advertising; public relations personal selling
	Conviction: belief, commitment	Personal selling and direct marketing
Behaviour	Trial	Personal selling; direct marketing
	Purchase	Sales promotion, personal selling; direct marketing
	Repeat purchase, use more	Sales promotion; personal selling; direct marketing

Source credibility

Another source-related factor that affects ad effectiveness is source credibility. It is a very important factor in persuasion–you believe messages you hear from some people more than that from others because they are simply more credible. That's why doctors and authority figures are used.

Noise: External and Internal

The advertising communication process is also affected by the noise, i.e. the message to be communicated is also hindered by the noise present in the external environment and within the customers (internal). Noise is any factor that interferes with or distorts the delivery of the advertising message to the target audience. The external factors that distort or interfere with the message are the marketing strategy, other marketing communication by competitors, general patterns of consumer trends (interest in healthy food and exercise) and public opinion. Other external factors could be poor quality picture or unreadable newspaper ad, lots of noise in the room where consumer is and due to advertising clutter (audience sees an excessive number of commercial messages).

Internal factors include those personal factors that affect the reception of an advertisement. These factors are target audience's needs, purchase history, information-processing abilities and level of avoidance of advertising in general.

Message and Media Mix Factors

What to say to the audience and then how to reach to the audience is an important step in entire advertising communication process. The process of deciding what to say or creating an advertising message begins with analysis of the marketing and advertising strategy and target audience. To execute this, the creative team designs the actual ads and produces them. The next decision is related to media mix, which will determine the ability of a particular advertising message to reach a target audience. The reach will depend on the effectiveness of the media plan. The media plan indicates the media mix decisions (media choices) that have the best chance of delivering the advertising message to the right target audience at the right time and place. Advertisers may require different media mix to reach different target audiences.

The Receiver: Message, Reception and Response

The last two stages of the advertising communication process are message reception and response and feedback. The effectiveness or success of an advertisement depends on the target audience receiving and processing it as accurately and completely as the advertiser intended. But it must be remembered that no two people respond to an advertisement in exactly the same way. So how does advertising work to create a response. It is evident that advertising may communicate messages in number of ways and cause different types of simultaneous responses. For example, you may understand an ad's copy (the learning effect) and at the same time form an opinion of the advertised product (the persuasion effect).

In the following paragraphs, you will see how advertising meets the challenges of perception and then examine the two responses that happen simultaneously–the learning (cognitive) response and the persuasion (emotion and feeling) response–and finally we look into the behaviour, or action response. These three responses are commonly referred to as think/feel/do. This framework is very helpful in planning advertising objectives.

The message reception and response process is depicted in figure 7.6. Even though no two people respond to an advertisement in exactly the same way, there are three general responses ads elicit once perceived. These are learning, persuasion and behaviour.

Perception

Breaking through perception takes place when a person notices something, the message gets registered and it has broken through the defenses and disinterest of the consumer and made an impression. The biggest challenge faced by the advertiser is to get consumers notice their messages. Ads have better chance of being perceived if they are intrusive and original. Let's look

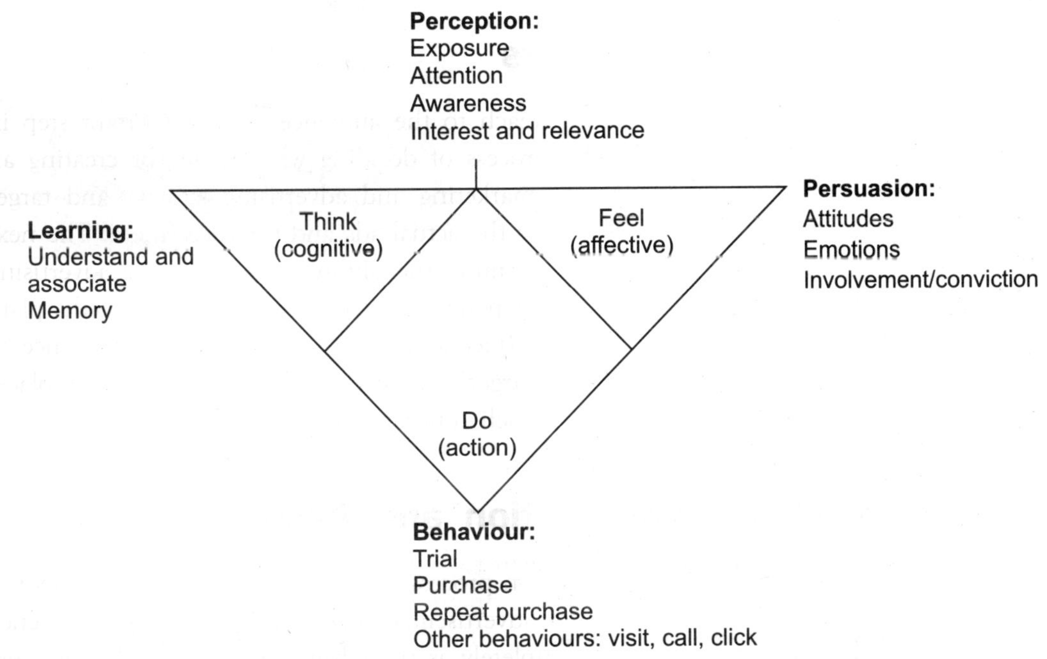

Fig. 7.6 Message reception and Response.

at the perception process and how it works. The steps in perception (communication drivers) are exposure, attention, awareness and interest.

Exposure (making contact)

For the advertiser, exposure is mainly a media-buying task. At first, the advertiser has to place the message in a medium that the target audience listens to, sees, reads or watches. So look for the media vehicle used by your target audience. For the choice of sound medium for your ad exposure is the first requirement. However, great the message be, if your target audience never sees or hears it or the target audience changes the channels or skips the page, it is not at all effective.

Attention (creating stopping power)

Once the audience is exposed to the message, the next task is to get and keep its attention. This will lead to the state of awareness. Attention means that the mind is engaged; it is focusing on something. A trigger, something that catches the target's interest, arouses attention. It can be something in the message or something within the readers or viewers that makes them get attracted to a particular message. In print ads it may be large headings, a starting illustration or a large blank space with small and crisp message. On television, the trigger may be sound effects, music, an action-oriented or visually-interesting scene or a captivating idea. The advertising message also has to compete with other messages in the same medium whether it is print, electronic, outdoor or internet, etc. If the objective is only a brand reminder, then the attention level doesn't need to be as high as it does when the objective is the understanding of a copy point.

Awareness (making an impression)

Once the message has been perceived and has caught the attention of consumers, the perception process moves to the next step—awareness of the brand message. Awareness means that the message has made an impression on the consumer, and the consumer can identify the advertiser. When you ask a consumer in the departmental store what comes to his/her mind when he/she thinks of soap and the response is "Lux", then that brand has top-of-mind awareness.

Although the awareness of advertisement gets generated first, that is not the ultimate objective of the advertiser. As far as the advertiser is concerned, the ultimate objective is awareness of the brand, not the advertisement. Being aware means that the receiver has impression of something. Awareness can evolve through public opinion, just as consumer trends catch the attention of the public.

Interest and relevance (creating pulling power)

The next step in perception process is interest. It provides the pulling power to an advertisement; it keeps people tuned in to the message. One of the most important drivers of interest is personal relevance. People might have interest in many things like the product advertised, model or star in the ad, promises made by the ad. graphics, etc. they will pay attention to advertising only if it is relevant to them.

Learning (Making it clear)

The second major category of effects is learning, which is an important factor in how people receive advertising messages. There are two types of learning that are particularly important to advertising—cognitive learning, which refers to understanding, and classical conditioning, which explains how association works. Through cognitive learning, advertisers want people to know something, new after they have read, watched or heard the message. Some campaigns are specifically plan to increase understanding. In case of new products, advertisers try to get consumers to understand how to recognize and use the product. Whereas perception is a passive process, understanding is an active response from the consumers and it requires conscious mental effort to make sense of information. A cognitive response to advertising is a series of steps. First the consumer should find the ad interesting, then he/she learns something about it and finally form it part of his/her memory.

Understanding is particularly important for ads that present a lot of information (brand characteristics and features, price, how it works, when and where to use it). The advertiser must keep in mind for the informational advertising that the large amount of information must be clear, precise and make relevant explanation so that the reader or viewer is able to follow the logic, make choices, compare points of view, comprehend reasons and arguments, synthesize and organize facts. Conditioned learning helps make connections in mind and linking ideas termed as association.

Advertisements use association to try to get consumers to like the product with something they aspire to, respect, value or appreciate, such as a personality or type of person, a pleasant experience or situation, or a specific lifestyle.

Persuasion (changing attitudes)

Persuasion is to encourage people to believe or feel something. A persuasive message tries to establish, reinforce or change an attitude, touch an emotion or anchor or conviction firmly in the potential customer's belief structure.

Arguments

Its a line of reasoning in which one point follows from another, leading to a logical conclusion. The reasons behind a statement or claim are particularly important in persuasive communication. Ads generally focus on logic and proof when trying to persuade the consumer to buy a product. Other motivations, such as saving money or getting a good deal, are addressed by sales promotion and advertising that focuses on sale prices.

Every person has unique attitude and opinions based on individual experiences. Attitudes are underlying beliefs. Opinions are the expression of these attitudes. Advertising that seeks to persuade us by addressing our attitudes usually attempts to accomplish one of three things:

- Establish a new opinion where none has existed before
- Reinforce an existing opinion.
- Change an existing opinion.

It is a common knowledge that consumers form opinions of new products and they modify or confirm their opinions as they use the product. No amount of

advertising and good messages can help in case a customer has had bad experience with product. To win back the consumers, the marketer has to try very hard by distributing sample to make them use it, by using celebrities and experts whose opinion people trust.

Emotions can be used for persuasion. Advertisers who touch people's emotions with their messages have greater success in getting consumers to remember that message.

The result of persuasion is conviction—a strong belief, such as that which drives national allegiance and religious fervour. Attitudes, reasons, logic, and emotion are all parts of the persuasive package that leads to belief. For many people, seeing is believing. So a product demonstration tends to remove doubt and increase consumer belief and conviction in the sales message. Believability is an extremely important concept in advertising and other forms of marketing communication. Do consumers believe the claims made by the advertising? Do spokespeople particularly the authority figures, have credibility? So when all other tools of integrated marketing communication (IMC) fail to create conviction, use public relations to build conviction.

Action (motivating behaviour)

The fourth category of response to advertising is action. Every advertiser hopes that the advertising used will lead to some behaviour, such as trying, sampling or buying a product, which could lead to increased sales. Although it is often difficult to prove that the advertising led to an increase in sales because there are other marketing and situational factors that might have contributed to the increase in sales.

The strategies used for increasing sales are to increase the usage level, encourage repurchases and find new customers. This can happen if the advertiser can give sufficient and valid reasons for buying. Ultimately, most marketers strive to get customers to repurchase their products regularly. The goal is to build strong brand loyalty, which is best measured by repeat behaviour. Customers become loyal to company's brands that are known for their product quality, innovative initiatives and market leadership.

ADVERTISING RESPONSE HIERARCHY MODELS

We have discussed in the earlier part of the chapter how advertising communication works. Advertiser's intention to get a response from the target audience follows certain steps. We identified these stages as exposure, attention, interest and behaviour. Understanding this response process (various stages) is very important for the advertiser in developing an effective advertising programme. The objectives of the advertiser (responses of the consumer) may be cognitive, affective or behavioural. A number of models have been developed to explain how consumers pass through various stages in eliciting some behaviour.

There are four response hierarchy models:

- The AIDA model
- Hierarchy-of-effects model
- Innovation-adoption model
- Information processing model

AIDA model

The AIDA (Attention, Interest, Desire and Action) model was developed by E.K Strong (1920s). This model suggests that an effective advertisement should be able to draw/attract attention, be interesting, create desire and initiate action (purchase) from the consumer. Thus, the model suggests the desirable qualities of an effective ad. See Figure 7.7.

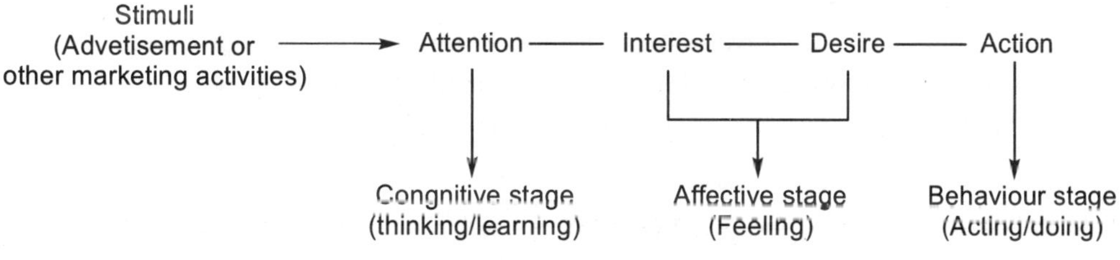

Fig. 7.7 AIDA model

Hierarchy-of-effects model

It was developed by Lavidge and Steiner who suggest that this model provides the basis for setting advertising objectives and measuring its effectiveness. It further suggests that advertising produces its effects on consumer by taking him/her through a series of stages in a sequence from generating awareness to ultimate purchase of the brand. The sequential order of effects indicates that the advertising effects are elicited over a period of time and the advertising may not get results immediately because series of effects must occur before the consumer moves to the next stage in the hierarchy as indicated in figure 7.8.

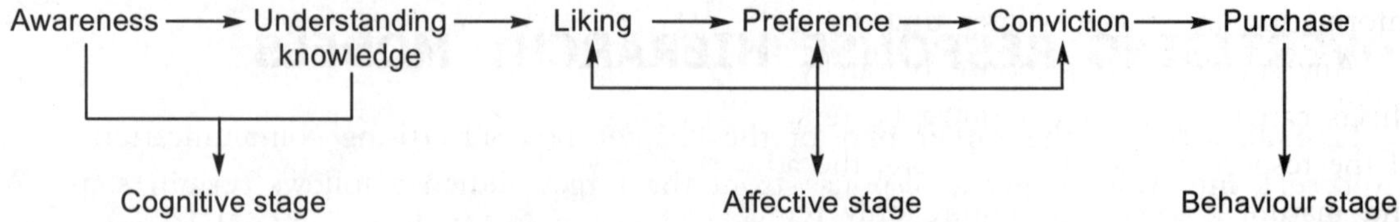

Fig. 7.8 Hierarchy-of-effects Model.

Innovation-adoption model

This model is based on diffusion of innovations. It depicts various stages through which a consumer moves in adopting a new product or service. The marketer's major task is to create awareness and interest in the product amongst the target audience. The marketer also has to ensure that the product is evaluated favourably so that a consumer is induced to a trial use. Based on the experience of the consumer with the product trial, it results either in satisfaction or dissatisfaction. If the consumer is satisfied the product is adopted, otherwise rejected. This model is depicted in figure 7.9

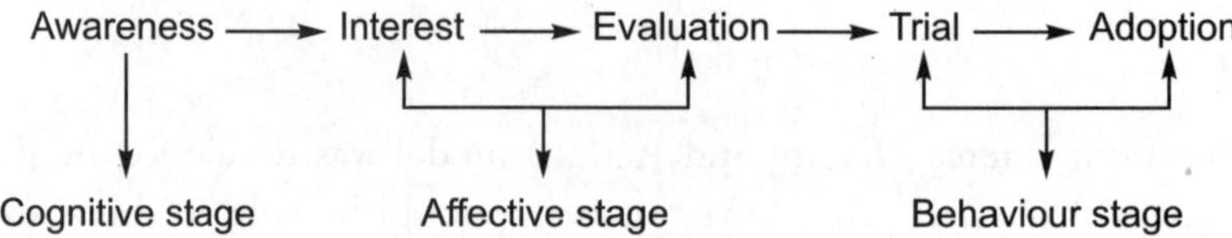

Fig 7.9 Innovation-adoption Model.

Information processing model

This model assumes that in advertising audiences are information processors and problem solvers. it was given by Willaim McGuire who divided the entire process into three stages– presentation, attention and comprehension. See Figure 7.10.

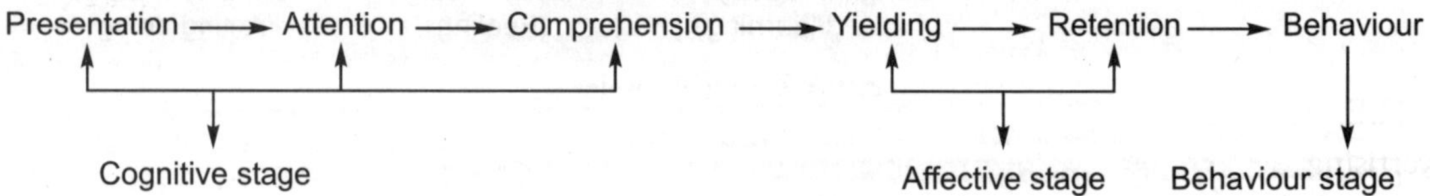

Fig. 7.10 Information processing model.

Yielding in this model means the liking. 'Retention' is unique in this model, which is not in any other model. Retention means, the consumer accepts and stores in memory the relevant information about the product or service. Retention of information is important because most advertising is done for not immediate action but for long time decisions. The retained information is used at a later time to make the purchase decision.

Any stage in the response hierarchy may serve to establish advertising objectives and the effects can be measured. It must be remembered that the target audience may be at any stage of the response hierarchy; therefore, the advertisers' task may be different at each stage. Popular and mature brands may require only reminder advertising to reinforce consumers' favourable perceptions. Now, you may realize that why such popular brands like coke, IBM, Colgate, Pepsi, Ariel, Surf and many more need to be advertised.

Before deciding advertising objectives, an advertising research must be undertaken to know at what stage of response hierarchy the majority of audiences are. If the research reveals that the majority of audiences have low level of awareness or knowledge about the brand and its attributes, then the advertising task is to design the ad in such a way, with such contents, and with such media decisions that the maximum awareness and knowledge occurs respectively.

The hierarchy-of-effects models are also referred to as standard learning models, in which the consumer is considered as an active participant who gathers information through active learning. This type of learning takes place when the consumer is highly involved in the purchase decision and perceives great differentiation among competing brands. Advertising for these types of products or services is usually very detailed and it attempts to furnish a great deal of meaningful and important information to the target audience. This detailed information about the brand facilitates the consumer to make brand choices. However, this may not hold true in different product categories where certain convenience products are consumed daily and purchased routinely.

All the four models start with cognitive stage and then move to affective stage and finally to behavioural stage. This is indicated below in Figure 7.11.

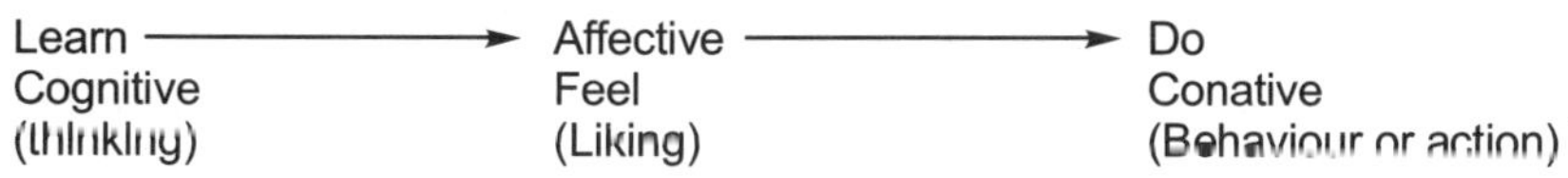

Fig. 7.11 Low involvement learning model.

H.E. Krugman of General Electric in his research work pointed out that comparative advertising on television is not feasible since the commercials on TV can't be slowed down or stopped for the consumer's convenience. Thus, the consumer has a very little opportunity to think deeply about them. Television is a low-involvement medium where consumer hardly has a chance to evaluate the commercial. So not much of meaningful information can be provided on the television but TV ads appear to enhance brand preference due to repeated exposure, such as brand name, ad slogan or the ad theme. This information is considered sufficient enough while making purchase decision whenever shopping occasion arises. In other words, repetitions of ads on TV can give reliability to a brand that can create preferences.

Research work done at Stanford university by Micheal Ray and others on low involvement learning revealed that when the products are of low-involvement category (low risk, inexpensive or low interest) for the consumer and ads are shown on television, this does not lead to change in consumer's attitude to induce to product trial based on information in the ad. In actuality, the ads are able to induce trial because of the top-of-mind recall or awareness. The product trial may then lead to a change in attitude depending upon the experiences with the brand.

The low-involvement sequence of advertising effect is different from the standard learning models. In low-involvement situation, consumers engage in passive learning and random information gathering. The ad agencies and advertisers must appreciate that music, symbols, endorsers, slogans etc. (non-message elements) are more important than actual message content.

Repetitions of 'simple product claims' advertisements increase consumers' recall and belief in those claims as found in a study by S. Hawkins and S. Hoch and they concluded that it may be highly advantageous for advertisers to go for repetitions of ad for low-involvement products rather than lengthy messages with plenty of information on features, technical and operational aspects.

To conclude, for low-involvement products, the advertisers' objectives must be to generate greater awareness rather than attempting to influence the consumers' attitude by rational basis. Wayne Hoyer and Steven Brown in their study have indicated that TV as a mass medium is not an appropriate choice for high-involvement products as information processing is passive. They have further added that brand awareness rather than comparative differences is given greater weightage when the consumer is short of time and effort.

Deciding the theme

Having decided what kind of communication effects the advertiser needs and then knowing how consumers respond to advertising, the next logical step is to choose a theme so that appropriate response from the consumer is elicited.

Advertising theme is the core advertising message or a great advertising idea about the brand that will place the brand in a better position vis-à-vis competitor brands. This core idea shall be used to develop the entire campaign.

How Do We Come Up with Such Ideas

It is the job of the creative department of the agency to generate alternative advertising ideas and ultimately to pick one or few that will go to the production. The creative process is concerned with taking the broadly stated marketing proposition, usually derived from marketing research and indicated in manufacturing specifications and turning it into powerful and persuasive idea to be conveyed to the consumer what the brand does for them and why it should matter to them.

A powerful "big idea" can add immeasurably to the effectiveness of an ad campaign, and the presence of such an idea must be the first thing you look for in evaluating a proposed ad campaign.

To get the big "Idea", the process could start as follows:

(a) Fact finding
  (i) Problem definition: picking out and pointing out the problem
  (ii) Preparation: Gathering and analyzing the pertinent data

(b) Idea finding
  (i) Idea production: thinking up tentative ideas as possible leads
  (ii) Idea development: selecting from resultant ideas, adding others and reprocessing by means of modification, combination and so on.

The process begins with fact finding—picking out and identifying the problem and gathering and analysing the pertinent data. The raw material for ideas is information—information from all sources. The creative team should become immersed in as much factual information about the company, the product, competition and the target audience (their language, needs, motivations, desires) as possible.

Sometimes, it is worthwhile to get first-hand knowledge of the consumer. The advertising agency people should go out in supermarkets and homes to meet consumers and discuss the products. Focus group interviewing can also help generate useful ideas and appropriate words and phrases for use in developing copy. The theme provides necessary ingredients to writing a creative copy and developing illustrations.

The following examples will provide an idea how theme can be a base for writing creative:

Theme		Creative copy
7-up is not a cola.	→	The un-cola (7up)
Milk is good for you.	→	Got milk? (US milk industry)
Our technology can help you do almost anything.	→	Where do you want to go today? (Microsoft)
No hard sell, just a good car.	→	Drivers wanted. (Volkswagon)
We don't rent as many cars, so we have to do more for our customers.	→	We try harder.

In creative process that brings a good theme and equally good creative copy alive, we go through the steps indicated below:

- Creating idea (idea generation)
- Generation of written copy (copywriting)
- Art work of various kinds (illustrations)
- A preliminary and comprehensive vision of ad (layout)

DEVELOPING ADVERTISING CAMPAIGN

A campaign is a systematic effort to accomplish some pre-determined objectives where as creative strategy concerns what message to deliver to the audience to accomplish the objectives.

Some of the big and successful campaigns launched by various companies are as under:

Campaign	Company/brand
Just do it	Nike
Intel inside	Intel
Yeh Dil Maange More	Pepsi
Coca cola enjoy	Coca-cola
Let's do the dew	Mountain dew

Compaines that create one ad at a time and constantly change the core message do not use a campaign.

A campaign is a complex set of interrelated and coordinated activities strategically designed to meet a set of objectives and to solve some critical problem within a specified time period, usually a year or less. A campaign is designed around a creative theme that extends across time and different advertising vehicles or marketing communication activities. A campaign may focus on the single specific product attribute or one audience or it may cover a variety of attributes and reach all the audiences.

A campaign plan summarizes the marketplace situation, the underlying campaign strategy, main creative strategy and tactics, media and other marketing integrated communication tools.

Advertising campaign plan differs from advertising plan in a way that it is more lightly focused on solving a particular marketing communication problem. The advertising plan and the campaign plan are similar in outline and structure. These plans are the responsibility of the account manager. An advertising campaign matches the right audience to the right message and presents it in the right medium to reach that audience consistently over a specified period.

The following three elements are the heart of an advertising campaign:

- Targeting the audience: Whom are you trying to reach?
- Message strategy: What do you say to them?
- Media strategy: When and where will you reach them?

An advertising campaign is guided by the promotion and advertising plans which evolve from marketing objectives and strategy. The ad campaign is normally a commitment to a creative strategy that usually lasts for one year.

The term campaign is used to describe many different systematic efforts such as a political election campaign, or a campaign to raise money for some social or charitable cause, or a systematic effort to promote a product or service. Thus, a campaign theme should be a strong idea, as it is the central message that will be communicated in all the advertising and promotional activities.

According to Dunn and Barban:

"An advertising campaign includes a series of ads, placed in various media, that are designed to meet objectives and are based on analysis of marketing and communication situations". (S. Watson Dunn and Arnold. M. Barban, *Advertising: Its Role in Modern Marketing*, 7th ed., p. 232, Dryden Press, New York).

Advertising campaign plans are short term in nature and, like marketing and IMC plans, are done on an annual basis. However, the campaign themes are usually developed with the intention of being used for a longer period. Unfortunately, many campaigns last only a short time, because they are ineffective, or market conditions or/and competitive developments in the marketplace change. Some successful campaigns have been there for years. Philips Morris has been using the "Marlboro country" campaign for nearly 40 years and BMW has used the "ultimate driving machine" campaign since 1974.

Like any other arena of marketing and promotional process, the creative aspect of advertising and the development of the campaign theme is guided by specific objectives as discussed earlier. A creative strategy that focuses on what must be communicated will guide the selection of the campaign theme and the development of all messages used in the ad campaign. The creative strategy is based on various factors like identification of the target audience, the basic problem, issue or opportunity the advertising must address: the major selling idea or key benefit the message needs to communicate and any other supporting information that needs to be included in the ad. Once these factors are determined, a creative strategy statement should describe the message appeal and execution style that will be used. Many ad agencies outline these elements in a document known as the copy or creative platform.

The two critical components of the copy platform—major selling idea and creative strategy statement—form the basis of the advertising campaign theme. For example, for a Polaroid ad, the major selling idea was "the picture is only the beginning", and the resulting campaign theme built around this idea was "see what develops". The creative strategy statement was to have each ad in the campaign tell a story in which a Polaroid camera sets off a chain reaction.

A typical advertising campaign development is shown as a series of steps in Figure 7.12.

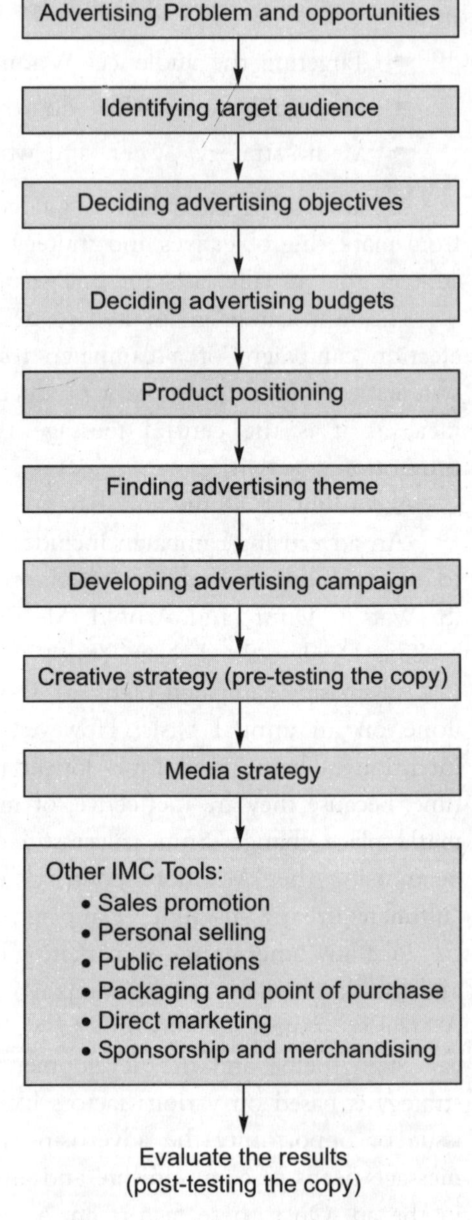

Fig. 7.12 A typical advertising campaign plan.

DECIDING ADVERTISING APPEAL

Advertising appeals are used to communicate and influence the purchase and consumption behaviour of existing and potential customers. Choice of a right appeal is one of the most critical decisions for creative strategy in advertising.

After an advertiser decides on the content of an ad –the "what to say" decision–the task of creating the ad itself is usually handed over to the creative people at the ad agency. Before the creative team proceeds to conceptualization and creation of the ad, it is pertinent to give a thought to the broad framework within which the ad should be created: What kind of appeal should the ad utilize? For instance, should the ad attempt a competitive comparison (a "rational") approach? Or, should it use some type of emotional appeal, such as fear or humour? Should it use an endorser, and if so, what kind of endorser-an expert in that product category, or a likable celebrity?

Thus, the advertising appeal refers to the approach used to attract the attention of consumers and/or to influence their feelings toward the product or their wants or needs and excites their interest. The creative execution is the way a particular appeal is transformed into an advertising message presented to the consumer. According to William Weilbacher: "The appeal can be said to form the underlying content of the advertisement and the execution is the way in which that content is presented. Advertising appeals and execution are independent of each other; that is, a particular appeal can be executed in a variety of ways and a particular means of execution can be applied to a variety of advertising appeals. Advertising appeals tend to adapt themselves to all media, whereas some kinds of executional devices are more adaptable to some media than others."

Types of Advertising Appeals

Basically all types of appeals can be categorized into three:

(a) Informational/rational/logical appeal
(b) Emotional appeal
(c) Moral appeals

Informational/rational/logical appeal

It focuses on the consumer's practical, functional or utilization need for the product or service and emphasize features of a product or service and/or the benefits or reasons for owning or using a particular brand. The contents of such messages emphasize facts, learning and the logic

News Appeal.

Feature appeal.

or persuasion. Rational appeals, through the use of information, attempt to convince the consumers that a particular product or service has particular attribute(s) or provides a specific benefit, which satisfies their needs.

There are large number of rational motives such as comfort, health, sensory benefits, quality, dependability, efficiency, performance, durability, convenience and economy etc., which can be used as a basis for advertising appeals. However, the particular benefits, features or evaluative criteria vary among target markets as well as from one product or service category to another.

Weilbacher identified various advertising appeals that can be put under the category of informational or rational appeal. Such appeals are feature appeal, competitive advantage appeal, favourable price appeal, news appeal and product/service popularity appeal.

Competitive advantage appeal.

Favourable price appeal.

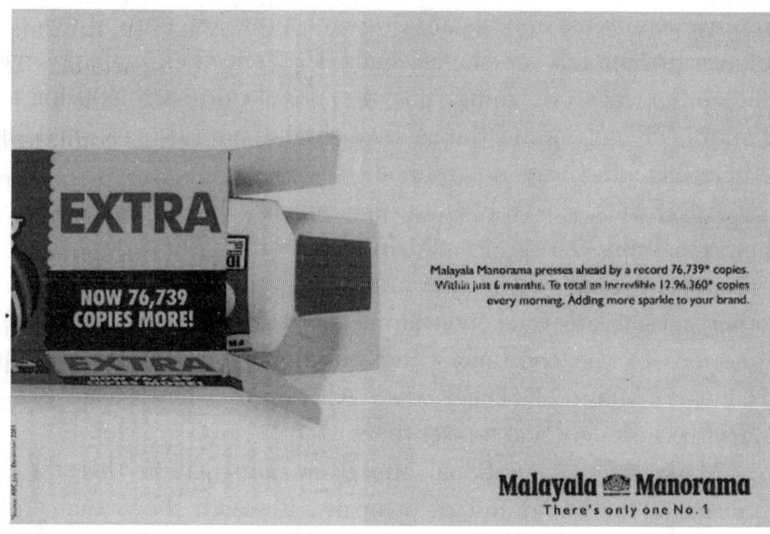

Product/service popularity appeal.

Emotional appeals

It is related to the consumer's psychological and/or social needs for purchasing a product or service. Many purchase motives of consumers relate to emotions and feelings about a brand, which can be more important than attributes, functions and features.

Emotional appeals can be put into two categories–positive emotional appeals and negative emotional appeals, depending on what kind of emotions are to be triggered. Some of the

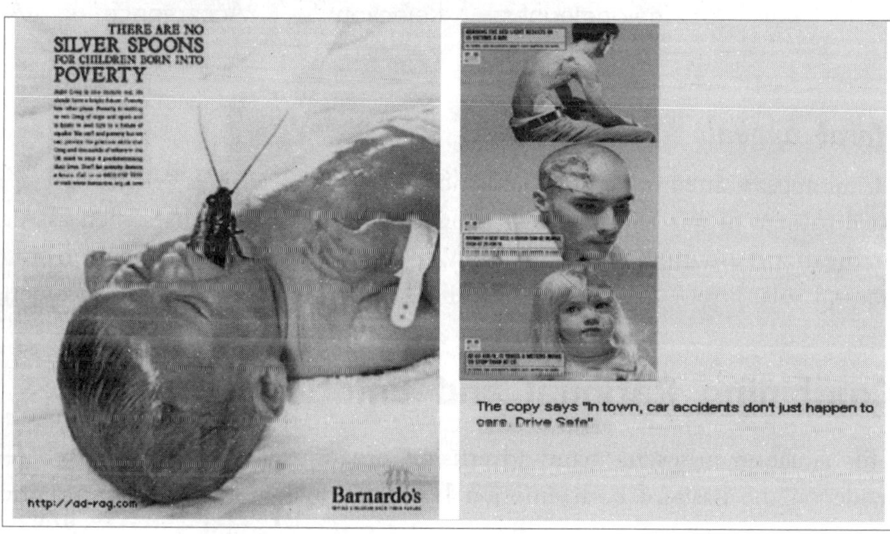

Emotional appeals.

positive emotional appeals are love, affection, joy, pride, humour, prestige, status, etc. Examples of negative appeals are shame, guilt, fear, rejection, embarrassment, etc. Such appeals motivate the consumers to do things that they should do such as using after shave lotion (Denim Shave Lotion), or stop doing things they should not such as smoking, chewing tobacco and eating edible oils which are not refined, etc.

Advertisers can use emotional appeals in their commercials by using the concept of emotional integration in which they portray the characters in the ad as experiencing an emotional benefit or outcome from using a product or service. Ads using humour, sex and many other appeals are very entertaining, arousing, upbeat, and/or exciting that can influence the emotions of the consumers and put them in a favourable frame of mind. The brands like Hallmark, Maruti, Nokia, Kodak, AT&T etc. often create commercials that evoke feelings of warmth, nostalgia and/or sentiment.

Marketers use emotional appeals in anticipation that the positive feeling they evoke will transfer to the brand and/or company. Research shows that positive mood and feelings created by advertising can have a favourable effect on consumer's evaluations of a brand. Studies also show that emotional advertising is better remembered than non-emotional messages.

Some of the feelings that can be used as emotional appeals are listed below:

Safety	Affection	Sentiment	Pride	Achievement
Pleasure	Security	Happiness	Excitement	Accomplishment
Ambition	Comfort	Fear	Joy	Arousal/stimulation
Self-esteem	Recognition	Status	Love	Nostalgia
Sorrow/grief	Actualization	Respect	Involvement	Embarrassment
Affiliation	belongingness	Rejection	Acceptance	Approval

Moral appeals

Moral appeals attempt to draw audience attention to what is "right". These appeals are generally used to urge people to support or show concern to social causes such as AIDS prevention, polio eradication, environment protection, population control, donation to support victims of natural calamity or prevention of child labour or equal rights for women, etc.

Combining Rational and Emotional Appeals

This situation arises in many advertising situations as consumer purchase decisions are often made on the basis of both emotional and rational motives. Thus, attention must be given to

Combining rational and emotional appeals.

both elements while developing ads. McCann-Erickson Worldwide along with Prof. Michael Ray developed a well-known research technique known as **emotional bonding** which evaluates how consumers feel about brands and the nature of any emotional rapport they have with a brand compared to ideal emotional state they associate with product category.

According to emotional bonding, consumers develop three levels of relationships with brand. The basic relationship is product benefits, which indicate how consumers think about brands in respect to product benefits. Consumers at this level often switch brand, as they are not yet brand loyal. This can be measured through how well advertising communicates product information.

In the next level, the consumer assigns a personality to the brand, say a brand may be thought as aggressive, proud, self-assured and modern, etc. rather than timid, outdated and poor. The consumer's judgement of the brand has, at this stage, moved beyond attributes and benefits. In most cases, consumers judge the personality of a brand on the basis of an assessment of overt or covert cues found in its advertising. The strongest relationship that develops between a brand and the consumer is based on feelings or emotional attachment to the brand. Consumers develop a positive psychological movement towards a brand once an emotional bond gets developed with it. Prominently used emotional appeals are fear, humour and sex.

Fear appeal

Fear is an emotional response to some actual or perceived threat or danger. It is used in certain situations to evoke the desired emotional response and motivate the audience to take certain action to remove fear. Some of the product categories that generally use fear appeal are life or general insurance, mediclaim policies, toothpaste, deodorants, helmets, water filters, edible oils,

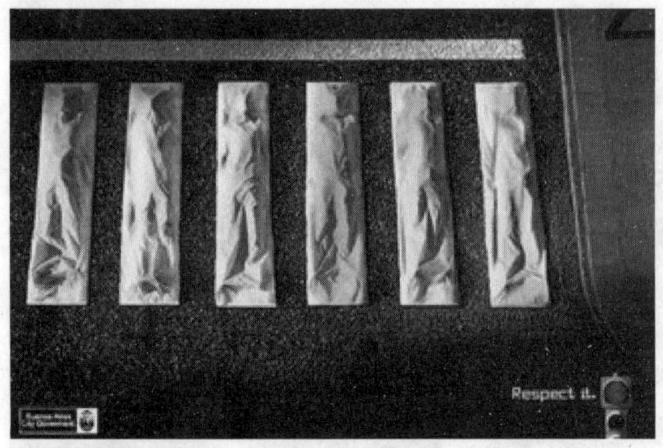

Fear appeals.

anti-dandruff shampoos. Ad appeals using fear has been used extensively for social causes as well in cases of AIDS, drugs, smoking and drinking, driving two wheelers without helmets, etc.

Fear appeals are, generally, useful for products or services that do not interest consumers, or are considered burdensome. The research points out that neither mild nor high intensity fear appeals generate any required response from the consumers. Only fear appeals of moderate level work because they provide sufficient motivation and do not activate perceptual defense mechanism leading to message acceptance and attitude change among consumers.

It is necessary for the advertiser to know how fears operate, what level of fear to use in advertising and how different types of audiences respond to fear appeals. However, there are number of factors that may influence how consumers respond to a given fear appeal. Some of them are source credibility, audience characteristics, the message context and the type of fear appeal used.

Humour appeal

Humour has the power to have an effect on information processing for making purchase decision by way of attracting attention, generating pleasant mood, improving brand name recall and reducing the chances of counter arguing. Since humour generates feelings of pleasure and amusement, it has potential for the feelings to become associated with the brand and may influence consumer attitudes towards the brand and probably its image. However, critics argue that humourous ads do draw attention to the amusement and funny aspect of the ad but it may also distract the audience from the brand and its better attributes.

Marc Weinberger and Charles Gulas have extensively reviewed ads using humorous appeals and concluded that humour in ads does enhance audience attention and liking for the ads but less likely to increase message comprehension and persuasion. Humour appears to work best for "low-involvement" and "feel" category of products but not for "high-involvement" and "think" kind of products.

Some of the positive aspects of humour ads are as follows:

(b) Humour enhances attention and liking.
(c) Humour enhances source credibility.
(d) Humour may also enhance audience attitude towards the ad.
(e) Humour may help diminish the chances of counter arguments because it distracts the audience from making cognitive responses.

The ads shown below are based on humour appeals.

Humour appeal.

While creating humour appeal, understanding of target audience is important because what appears humour to one person may sound silly or irritating to another person. Humour ads can be created by using jokes, anecdotes, satire, understatements, puns and irony, etc. The use of humour is culture bound and the taste for it varies considerably.

Sex appeals

Ads based on Sex appeals have attention-arresting magic. The sex appeal is coming to be used because there are too many advertising claims and increasing competition from new products. There is a tremendous advertising clutter. So, to draw audience attention sex is heavily used from blatant nudity to subtle devices. Advertising themes related to sex appeal may attract audience attention but they rarely generate any curiosity and interest in the product being advertised. It is believed that audience interest stops with sex only and the ad message is hardly, if ever, processed deeply.

The advertiser wishing to use sex appeal must ensure that the product, the ad, the target audience and the sexual message themes and other elements all match up. If sex is relevant to the product, it can be an extremely strong copy theme. The ads of Kamasutra and Moods condoms are excellent examples of ads using sex appeal in relation to product and their functionality.

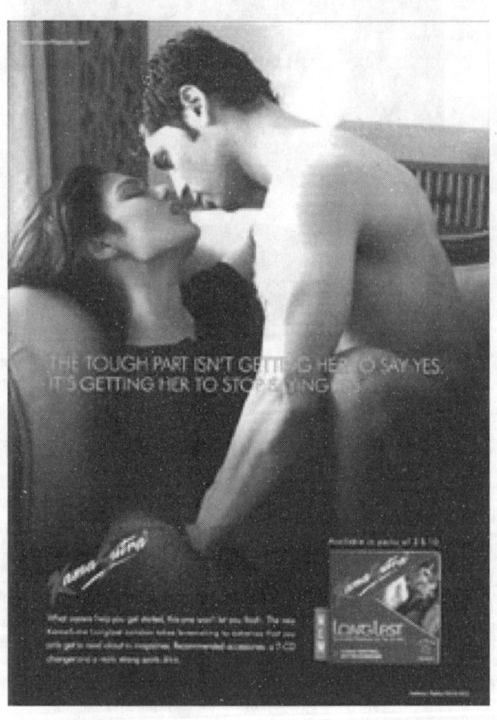

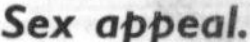

Sex appeal.

ADVERTISING EXECUTION

Once the advertising appeal, as the basis, for the message has been decided, the creative team begins its execution. **Creative execution** is the way or style an advertising appeal is presented.

In advertising, it is not just enough "what you say", but it is equally important how do you say what you say.

An advertising message can be presented or executed in numerous ways:

(a) Straight sell or factual message
(b) Animation
(c) Scientific/technical evidence
(d) Personality symbol
(e) Demonstration
(f) Fantasy
(g) Testimonial
(h) Dramatization
(i) Slice of life
(j) Humour
(k) Combinations

MEDIA MIX DECISIONS

The first step in media mix decision is to decide what media to be used. Whether it is going to be single media or combination. The next step is to choose media vehicle i.e. specific media that will carry the message. The media to be choosen depends upon the following factors:

(a) Target audience
(b) Type of product category
(c) Message appeal
(d) Execution style and
(e) Budget

Before discussing how to choose the most effective media, let's discuss some relevant terms that will help us in understanding media strategy and its related aspects.

Clutter

A large number of advertising messages are carried by media vehicle. Therefore, drawing attention is a big task. Clutter is number of advertisements in a medium. It is of concern because there are so many messages vying for the audience attention

Fleeting message

The commercials are becoming shorter and shorter because of the increasing demand for a limited amount of broadcast time. Increasing media costs are forcing advertisers to consider shorter commercials for keeping media costs low. The commercial duration of 30 seconds and 15 seconds is the order of the day. So nothing tangible is left for the audience to examine or consider. The commercial appears to be a fleeting moment in time.

Zapping

It refers to changing channels to avoid commercials. Zapping is likely to occur because commercial breaks are so long and predictable. Zapping has also been fuelled by the emergence of 24-hour continuous format programming on cable channels and DTH (Direct to Home).

Zipping

It occurs when customers fast-forward through commercials as they play back a previously recorded program.

Scheduling strategy

It is of three types–pulsing, continuity and flighting.

Pulsing

It alternates between high and low levels of advertising. It has peaks and valleys.

Continuity

It spreads the advertising continuously and evenly over the length of the campaign.

Flighting

It alternates between intense and no advertising.

How To Make Effective Media Choice Decision

The first thing is to establish media objectives and then to develop suitable media strategy to achieve the objectives. Examples of media objectives could be: use broadcast media to provide coverage of 80% of the target market in next 6 months, reach 60% of the target audience at least three times over the next 3 months and concentrate on the heaviest advertising in winter and spring and lighter emphasis in summer and monsoon. In modern times, plethora of media alternatives and media vehicles are available. Small companies generally use single media whereas large companies use a number of media alternatives and vehicles.

The media mix decision is influenced by factors such as:

(a) Product characteristics
(b) Media objectives
(c) Media budget
(d) Individual preference of the media planner

The Media planner's objective is to reach as many member of the target market as possible. So, the starting point for developing a media strategy is to define coverage in terms of geographic area and percentage of target audience.

The media strategy will decide issues such as reach, frequency, scheduling and media vehicle choice, etc.

How Scheduling Decision is Made

Media schedule is the calendar of advertising plan and is concerned with timing insertion of advertisements in the selected media. Scheduling decision is based on the assumptions regarding how the target audience will respond to the presence or absence of the advertising messages with respect to the set advertising objectives like brand recall or attitudes. Basically, there are three approaches of scheduling—continuity, flighting and pulsing. This decision is based on the product category and media planner's understanding of the promotional requirement of the brand, buying cycles, budget, advertising decay and competitive spending.

How To Decide on "Reach"

Achieving awareness requires reach, i.e. exposing potential buyers to the message. New brands or products need a very high level of reach, since the objective is to make all potential buyers aware of the new entry. High reach is also desired at the trial stage of adoption hierarchy, a promotional strategy might use discount coupons or free samples. The media planner calculates the reach of a media schedule according to research estimate that forecasts the unduplicated audience. If the ad is placed on two shows, the total number of exposed once is unduplicated audience.

Some of the research tools that can be used in "deciding reach" are disucssed below.

Programme rating

Programme rating is a number expressed as a percentage. It is a measure of potential reach of broadcast media industry such as TV or radios.

$$\text{Programme rating} = \frac{\text{Number of households viewing the programme}}{\text{Total number of households owning TV sets}} \times 100$$

For example, in the city of Jaipur there are total 1 million households that own TV sets and "*Ghar Ghar Ki Kahani*" on Star Plus is viewed by 3 lakh households. Then the programme rating is given by

$$\frac{3,00,000}{10,00,000} \times 100 = 30$$

Gross rating point (GRP)

The media buyer would like to know how many potential audience may be exposed to a series of commercials. The sum of the total exposure potential expressed as a percentage of the audience population is called gross rating point (GRP). The GRP is calculated by dividing the total number of impressions by the size of the audience and multiplying by hundred. It is a summary measure that combines the programme rating and the average number of times the home is reached during this period (frequency of exposure).

$$\text{GRP} = \text{reach} \times \text{frequency}$$

$$\text{Frequency} = \frac{\text{Total exposures}}{\text{Reach}} = \frac{\text{GRP}}{\text{Reach}}$$

Target rating point (TRP)

It refers to the number of people in the primary target audience that the media buy will reach and the number of times it will reach them. Unlike GRP, TRP does not include waste coverage. In other words, it refers to the number of times (frequency) and the number of individuals in the primary target audience that the media will reach. One TRP is equal to one percent of the total TV audience (here audience means the total number of members on the panel for research purpose who watch TV and record the data). If a TV programme has 50 TRPs, it means that 50% of the panel members watched the programme in that week.

Deciding Effective Frequency

The rate of exposure of a programme or number of times it is exposed, is called its frequency. "Effective Frequency" is the number of exposures, in an advertising cycle, assumed to be able to maximize the member of target audience members' disposition to act. In media planning, 'frequency' is the number of times one is exposed to the media vehicle, not necessarily to the ad itself.

No one really knows the exact number of exposures necessary for an ad to make an impact. There are three general approaches to problem. The first is "linear approach", according to which each additional exposure adds as much purchase probability as the one preceding it. This approach favours greater frequency. The second approach, "decreasing return approach", assumes that the first exposure is the strongest in terms of impact and each succeeding exposure is less effective. This approach favours low frequency levels. The third, "learning curve approach", suggests that the effectiveness of each exposure increases more than an equal amount only up to a certain point and any additional exposures beyond this do not add much.

Determining media budget

While evaluating media alternatives, the cost of media is an important component that is considered. The advertising manager tries to arrive at optimal delivery by balancing cost with reach, frequency and availability of media exposures. For evaluating alternatives, advertisers must compare the relative costs of media as well as vehicles within these media. **Relative cost** refers to the relationship between the price paid for advertising time or space and the size of the audience delivered. It is used to compare media vehicles. **Absolute cost** of the medium or vehicle is the actual total cost required to place the message. Some of the terms related to media budget are discussed below.

Cost per Thousand (CPT)

It is used for magazines as a media vehicle. It is a cost breakdown on the basis of cost per thousand people reached.

$$\text{CPT} = \frac{\text{Cost of ad space (absolute cost)}}{\text{Circulation}} \times 1{,}000$$

Even if the absolute cost of a magazine is higher, it may provide a more cost-effective buy. A comparison of two magazines, India Today and Business Today, is given below.

	India Today	Business Today
Per-page cost	Rs. 50,000	Rs. 40,000
Circulation	4,00,000	3,00,000
CPT calculation	50,000 × 1000/ 4,00,000	40,000 × 1,000/3,00,000
CPT	Rs. 125	Rs. 133

Though India Today appears to be a more costly magazine than Business Today in absolute terms, its relative cost is lower than that of Business Today.

Cost per Rating Point (CPRP)

The broadcast media provide a different comparative cost figure, referred to as cost per rating point or cost per point (CPP).

$$\text{CPRP} = \frac{\text{Cost of commercial time}}{\text{Programme rating}}$$

Daily inch rate

For Newspapers, cost effectiveness is based on daily inch rate. Earlier newspapers sold space in cm column. Nowadays, most of the newspapers sell space in cm square.

Where Do You Get Media Related Information

Presently, three major sources are available for media information. These are:

(a) National Readership Survey (NRS)
(b) Indian Readership Survey (IRS)
(c) Annual report of Ministry of Information and Broadcasting

National Readership Survey (NRS) is conducted every two years by the National Readership Council (NRC). This council comprises of Advertising Agencies Association of India (AAAI), Audit Bureau of Circulation (ABC) and Indian Newspaper Society (INS). The actual fieldwork is undertaken by research agencies like A.C. Nielsen and Indian Market Research Bureau (IMRB). Currently NRS is conducted every six months rather than every two years. Indian Readership Survey (IRS) is conducted by ORG-MARG. The annual data published by the Ministry of Information and Broadcasting contains information related to government-controlled media such as Aakashwani and Doordarshan.

The space in newspapers and magazines is bought based on the NRS and IRS data. The survey data can help find the most effective print media. TV time buying is different from print space buying. The main point to consider in time buying is selecting the right time period and appropriate programme to carry the ad message. Advertisers are more concerned about cost per rating point (CPRP) and not just the number of spots. The cost of television advertising time varies depending upon the time of the day and the particular programme.

There are few research agencies that supply data on audience measurement to facilitate the decision of selecting a particular channel and programme. The techniques used to gather audience measurement information include diaries, personal interviews and electronic meters or recorders (In India, the use of people meters is limited to less than a dozen cities including metros). These audience measures are important to media planners in deciding to buy commercial time on a programme.

Bringing an advertisement to life requires plenty of decisions by the advertiser, account planner, creative team and the media planner. An effective ad would be possible only if all these three put their heads together. In each of the areas of advertising, research plays an important role, as it provides accurate and timely information to the concerned manager for making decision. An effective advertisement or a working ad. can be created if all decisions are made right. The major areas of decision making are: deciding target audience, brand positioning, advertising objectives, communication effects needed, deciding theme and appeal, execution style, message strategy, media mix and scheduling decisions. If these decision are taken based on the information provided by research, it is more likely that an ad campaign will be effective.

SUMMARY

An advertiser should decide in advance what specific communication effects are desired on the target audience. All ads are created keeping the "desired effects" central to all decisions. An audience when exposed to the brand communication moves through a series of responses. Two important response models are AIDA (Attention, Interest, Desire and Action) and DAGMAR (Defining Advertising Goals for Measured Advertising Result).

An advertiser must understand the situation to determine the kind of advertising effect he/she wants to create. Repeated exposures create a conscious sense of familiarity with the brand which then causes liking and it is especially important when consumers do not process ads with a view to extract much information from them. In case of high involvement situation, consumer seeks rational or problem-solving benefits. The advertiser sets attitude-change as its communication objectives and highlights the product benefits in the ads.

Understanding of concepts related to how advertising works shall help create an effective advertising campaign. An advertiser needs to know series of steps essential before an effective workable advertisement is created. These steps are identifying target audience and positioning, deciding advertising objectives, deciding what kind of communication effects are needed, knowing how consumers respond to advertising, deciding the theme, developing an advertising campaign, deciding the advertising appeal, developing copy platform, deciding the message, making media mix decisions and deciding schedules, frequency and pattern of ad release.

Advertising theme is the core advertising message or a great advertising idea about the brand. The theme provides necessary ingredients to writing a creative copy and developing illustrations. An advertising campaign is a systematic effort to accomplish some predetermined objectives. A campaign plan summarises the marketplace situation, the underlying campaign strategy, main creative strategy and tactics, media and other marketing integrated communication tools.

Advertising appeal refers to the approach used to attract the attention of consumers and/or to influence their feelings towards the product or their wants or needs. All types of appeals in advertising can be broadly categorized as rational/logical appeals, emotional appeals and moral appeals. Advertising execution is the way or style an advertising appeal is presented (how to say what to say).

Media mix decisions involve choosing types of media and media vehicle. Media scheduling is the way ads are released. These are pulsing, continuity and flighting.

QUESTIONS

1. What do you mean by communication objectives? What are different types of communication objectives? How communication objectives are set?
2. High level of ad repetition is important when consumers do not process ads. Critically evaluate this statement.
3. What are various steps in creating an effective ad campaign?
4. Through illustration, explain how communication works. Also compare it with advertising communication.
5. Explain the model of key effects. How is it related to advertising communication objectives?
6. Compare and contrast the AIDA model from the Hierarchy-of-effects model.
7. What is an advertising theme? How is it different from creative copy? Bring out the differences clearly through examples.
8. How an advertising campaign is developed? What are different elements of an effective ad campaign?
9. What do you mean by advertising appeal? What are different types of appeals? Take few ads from Indian context and relate the same to various appeals that are used by advertisers.
10. What is creative execution? Explain in brief the numerous ways an ad campaign can be executed.
11. What do you mean by media mix decision? How do you select an appropriate media?
12. Explain the following terms:
    (a) Clutter
    (b) Zapping
    (c) Zipping
    (d) Fleeting message
    (e) Frequency
    (f) TRP
    (g) GRP
13. What do you mean by media scheduling strategy? Explain in detail various scheduling strategy.
14. What do you mean by media reach? How is "reach" decision made?

Part Three

Creativity and Advertising

CHAPTER 8

Role of Creativity

LEARNING OBJECTIVES

After reading this chapter, you will be able to:

- Examine the significance of creativity in advertising.
- Study the various elements of creative advertising.
- Explain the creative process.
- Describe the creative style of advertising.
- Illustrate the common appeals.
- Understand the development of creative strategy.
- List the elements of creative strategy.

CASE STUDY: MERCEDES-BENZ

Mercedes-Benz has developed a new concept, CAR inspired from the box fish.
The box fish: great rigidity and low weight—a growth principle designed by the nature.

Despite its boxy, cube-shaped body, tropical fish is, in fact, outstandingly streamlined and, therefore, represents an aerodynamic ideal. With an accurately constructed model of the boxfish, the engineers in Stuttgart were able to achieve a wind drag coefficient of just 0.06 in the wind tunnel.

The Boxfish, the aerodynamic model for the concept car, is also a prime example of rigidity and light weight. Its skin consists of numerous hexagonal, bony plates which provide maximum strength with minimal weight and effectively protect the animal from injury.

Daimler Chrysler researcheers examined this bionic structure and transferred this principle to the Mercedes-Benz bionic car study with the help of a special calculation process. The process is based on the principles of bone formation and for instance allows up to 40 per cent more rigidity to be achieved in the external door panelling than would be possible with conventional designs. If the entire body shell is calculated according to this bionic principle, the total weight is reduced by around one-third with undiminished strength and crash safety.

Now here is the car:

B. Krishna Kumar says in *The week*: **"Imagine a half-open matchbox as the logo for an international meet of highly creative brains.** A no-impact visual? Think again. There is so much packed into that little utility tool. Rub it the right way, it could light up a stove or a ciggy or dark pathways during those 'power-cuts'. In wrong hands, it becomes a deadly weapon to burn people and places."

This is what the power of creativity is. The ideas exist, but you give it a different perspective while interpreting an advertisement.

Advertising is the principal reason why the businessman has come to inherit the earth. The present day business is so heavily dependent on advertising that no one can afford to neglect it. But, even then, the advertising sector has never grown, compared to its proportion of importance in business, especially in India. Therefore, more importance is given to creative ideas by announcing special awards to highly creative ads.

The commercials we watch on TV or hear on radio and the print ads we see in magazines and newspapers are a source of entertainment, motivation, fascination, fantasy, information and sometimes irritation. Ads and commercials appeal to, and often create or shape, consumers' problems, desires and goals. From the marketer's perspective, the advertising message is a way to tell consumers how the product or service can solve a problem or satisfy desires or achieve goals. Advertising can also be used to create images or associations and position a brand in the consumer's mind as well as transform the experience of buying and/or using a product or service. Many people who have never driven or even ridden in a BMW perceive it as "the ultimate driving machine". It is only because of the impact of advertising.

BMW: The ultimate driving machine.

There are a myriad of ways to convey an advertising message. Underlying all of these messages, however, are a **creative strategy** that determines what the advertising message will say or communicate, and creative tactics for how the message strategy will be executed.

As Piyush Pandey, the Jury President at the Cannes Lions Festival and Executive Chairman and National Creative Director of Ogilvy & Mather, Mumbai, answered the question,

"What kind of advertising do you like? The great kind–something that delights the consumer first and the jury later."

A great ad is not only the source of enjoyment but it also informs the viewers aptly. The cost incurred on advertisement is huge. Many companies see this as money well spent. They realize that the manner in which the advertising message is developed and executed is often critical to the success of the promotional programme, which in turn can influence the effectiveness of the entire marketing programme. Good creative strategy and execution can often be central to determining the success of a product or service or reversing the fortunes of a struggling brand. Conversely, an advertising campaign that is poorly conceived or executed can be a liability. Therefore, the advertisers should be cautiously and meticulously work on an ad before launching it.

The recession of the early 90s slammed the advertising industry with over 13,500 layoffs. However, specialists in small, regional creative shops wer able to snatch away some large accounts during this period and produce ads for established corporations. This coca-cola and came from the clever minds at Creative Artists Agency in Hollywood (a talent agency!).

Many companies have solid marketing and promotional plans and spend substantial amount of money on advertising, yet have difficulties coming up with a creative campaign that will differentiate them from their competitors. For example, Burger King has changed its advertising theme 11 times in the past 15 years and changed agencies 6 times in search of a campaign that would give the chain a strong identity in the fast-food market. During many of these campaigns, market share dropped and franchises were unhappy with the company's inability to come up with an effective campaign.

Pioneer: Car Speakers.

Just because an ad or commercial is creative or popular does not mean it will increase sales or revive a declining brand. Many ads have won awards for creativity but failed to increase sales. In some instances, the failure to increase sales has cost the company a great deal. Let us find out first what creativity is

WHAT IS CREATIVITY

People tend to give different meanings for *creativity* based on the context. So let us start with the dictionary meaning of 'creative'.

Create: To cause to exist, Bring into being, Originate, To give rise to, Bring about, Produce, To be the first to portray and give character to a role or part (appropriate to creating fictional characters and writing stories).

Creation: An original product of human invention or imagination.

Creative: Characterized by originality and expressiveness, imaginative "Being creative is seeing the same thing as everybody else but thinking of something different".

There are many aspects to creativity, but one definition would include the ability to take existing objects and combine them in different ways for new purposes. For example, Gutenberg took the wine press and die/punch and produced a printing press. Thus, a simple definition of creativity is the action of combining previously uncombined elements from art, music and invention to household chores, this is part of the nature of being creative. Another way of looking at creativity is as playing with the way things are interrelated. Creativity is the ability to generate novel and useful ideas and solutions to everyday problems and challenges.

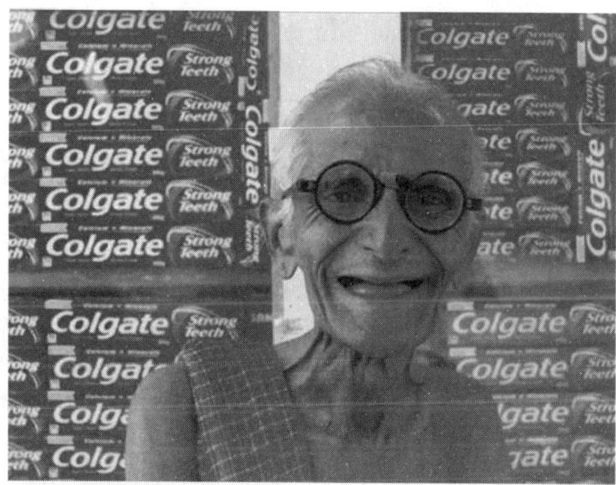

Colgate: Old idea in new bottle.

Creativity involves the translation of our unique gifts, talents and vision into an external reality that is new and useful. We must keep in mind that creativity takes place unavoidably inside our own personal, social and cultural boundaries.

The more we define our creativity by identifying with specific sets of values, meanings, beliefs and symbols, the more our creativity will be focused and limited. The more we define our creativity by focusing on how values, meanings, beliefs and symbols are formed, the greater the chance that our creativity will become less restricted.

In the creative process, there are always two different (but interrelated) dimensions or levels of dynamics with which one can create. The system consists of a particular medium (e.g. oil painting or a particular musical form), or a particular process (like a problem-solving agenda). The creative person manipulates that means to a creative end. The second dimension is described by the conceptual "content" which the medium describes. Again, the creative person depicts changes, manipulates and expresses somehow the idea of that content.

There is no definition of creativity that everyone can agree with. Creativity researchers, mostly from the field of psychology, usually claim that being creative means being novel and appropriate. Subsumed under the appropriateness criterion are qualities of fit, utility and value.

At least the following three aspects of creativity have drawn much attention:

- The creative process, receiving the most attention, focuses on the mechanisms and phases involved as one partakes in a creative act.
- The second aspect of creativity is the creative person. Here, personality traits of creative people are central. The environmental atmosphere and influence are concern of a third aspect, the creative situation.
- Lastly, the criteria or characteristics of creative products have been sought. This area is of particular importance because it is the basis of any performance assessment of real world creativity and may provide a window on the other aspects of creativity.

CREATIVITY AND ADVERTISING

"Creating a distinct message, new markets and creating innovation with results is what we call creativity. Creativity is at the heart of everything we do. Our ability to translate strategic thinking into ideas enables us to develop creative communications that work in the marketplace. Whether it's a print, radio or television ad, a corporate brochure or an annual report, creativity makes our work stand out in the crowd."–Pressman Advertising.

Advertising that people like and that wins awards is very satisfying, but advertising that sells the product is much better. Widespread scepticism exists concerning creativity in advertising, such as: "I know the ad looks great, but will it actually sell?" and "Are the award-winning commercials great advertising?" Often, great advertising concerns issues other than gold medals. Considering the ultimate objective of advertising–sales–creativity should not stand alone in advertising. Creativity must be harmonized with every element of advertising to achieve the final goal. See the ad of Coca Cola for instance.

Thanda matlab Coca Cola: An award-winning ad.

Perspectives on what constitutes creativity differ. At one extreme are people who argue that advertising is creative only if it sells the product. For them, an advertising message or campaign's impact on sales counts more than the fact whether it is innovative or wins awards. At the other end of the continuum are those who judge the creativity of an ad on the basis of its artistic or aesthetic value and originality. They contend that creative ads can break through the competitive clutter, grab the consumer's attention and have some impact.

To break through the clutter and make an impression on the target audience, an ad must be unique and entertaining. A major determinant of whether a commercial will be successful in changing brand preferences is its "likeability" or the viewer's overall reaction. TV commercials and print ads that are well designed and executed and that generate emotional responses can create positive feelings that are transferred to the product or service being advertised. Many creative people believe that this type of advertising can come about only if they are given considerable latitude in developing advertising messages. But ads that are creative only for the sake of being creative often fail to communicate a relevant or meaningful message that will lead consumers to purchase the product or service. Ultimately, everyone involved in planning and developing an advertising campaign must understand the importance of balancing the "it's not creative unless it sells" perspective with the novelty/uniqueness and impact position. We have to answer the question "Is there a direct correlation between creativity and success in the market place?"

To believe that creativity decides on the life and death of a brand is to take yourself too seriously. You are a team member in the process. Sometimes the team loses and you see that you scored a home run each time you went in to bat. Sometimes the team wins and you had actually done nothing to contribute. So keep doing the most relevant creative work and learn to keep quiet.

Advertising creativity is the ability to generate fresh, unique and appropriate ideas that can be used as solution to communication problems. To be appropriate and effective, a creative idea must be relevant to the target audience. Many agencies view a creative advertising message as one that is built around a creative core or power idea and uses excellent design and execution to communicate information that interests the target audience.

Master Card: Twist in the concept.

Creative people in advertising agencies, i.e., copywriters and art directors usually believe that creativity is necessary for effectiveness, that creativity can push the advertising message into the viewer's mind. However, there is also a negative opinion about creativity in advertising. Some critics define creativity as bothersome, costly, and time-consuming. Sometimes it is believed that creative advertising may be an award winner, but may have little to do with advertising effectiveness.

Despite these criticisms, conventional wisdom holds that there is a positive relationship between creative/award winning advertising and sales effectiveness. Creativity is still considered the most important element of the advertising business because it is almost impossible to get the consumer's attention with trite or commonplace advertisements. Creativity is the one area that can put a company far ahead of the fierce competition. From this perspective, it is valuable to stress creativity in the advertising business.

ELEMENTS OF CREATIVE ADVERTISING

A characteristic of the creative personality is an ability to appeal to consumers and to catch their attention. This is the conventional belief that most advertising people, both creative side and account side, are supposed to know. Nevertheless, it is not as easy as to say to execute real advertising plan since continuous conflicts exist between the advertising executives responsible for sales effectiveness and the creative people viewing the effectiveness as the outcome of creativity. There is no clear distinction between creativity and effectiveness. Some creative commercials are effective, some effective ads are creative, and other ads are neither creative nor effective.

Fevicol : An ad creating immediate impact.

Commonly, successful campaigns result from pinpointing an idea, a nuance, an insight, or a nugget of information gleaned from research or sometimes from an intuitive understanding or quickness of human nature. Successful creative strategies are based on such gems.

Unlike other businesses, advertising is ultimately a people's business. Thus creative advertising that sells is the result of three ingredients–people, information and environment.

KEY FACTORS IN SUCCESSFUL ADVERTISING

Team work, effectiveness and communication are the key factors in successful advertising campaigns, and the agencies must strive for a balance between them. 'Team Work' is essential simply because a group of creative thinkers put together can be more creative than a single one, even if he/she is a genius at that. Among the three factors, communication could be the most important factor from the consumers' point of view. For advertising to be useful, communication between the company that originates the advertisement and the potential customer must take place. The real communication is a two-way process requiring active participation by both the sender and the receiver of the message to facilitate the transfer of meaning.

Malboro hoarding: An ad with universal appeal.

When the recall communication occurs, the other two factors, creativity and effectiveness, could be worthy of it. Otherwise, no matter how great the creativity or effectiveness is, it won't be useful, at least in advertising business. This suggests several important characteristics of creativity in advertising. Most of all, it should be different from the creativity of universal meaning.

Here are four unbreakable rules of creativity:

1. Make the product relevant to the customer.
2. It should be promise to the customer.
3. Don't let it stand alone.
4. Always put the product in the center of the commercial.

PLANNING CREATIVE STRATEGY

Those who work on the creative side of advertising often face a lot of challenges. They must take all the research, creative briefs, strategy statements, communication objectives and other inputs and transform them into an advertising message, which should effectively communicate the central theme on which the campaign is based. Rather than simply stating the features or benefits of a product or service, they must put the advertising message into a form that will engage the audience's interest and make the ads memorable.

The job of the creative team is difficult because every marketing situation is different and each campaign or advertisement may require a different creative approach. As copywriter Hank Sneiden notes in his book *Advertising–Pure and Simple*:

"Rules lead to dull stereotyped advertising, and they stifle creativity, inspiration, initiative and progress. The only hard and fast rule that I know of in advertising is that there are no rules. No formulas. No right way. Given the same problem, a dozen creative talents would solve it in a dozen different ways. If there were a sure-fire formula for successful advertising, everyone would use it. Then there'd be no need for creative people. We would simply program robots to create our ads and commercials and they'd sell loads of products to other robots."

TAKING CREATIVE RISKS

Many creative people follow proven formulas when creating ads because they are safe. Clients often feel uncomfortable with advertising that is too different. Bill Tragos, former chairman of TBWA, the advertising agency, noted for its excellent creative work for Absolute vodka, Evian, and many other clients, says, "Very few clients realize that the reason that their work is so bad is that they are the ones who commandeered it and directed it to be that way. I think that at least 50% of an agency's successful work resides in the client."

It is important for clients to take risks if they want a breakthrough advertising that gets noticed. Not all companies or agencies agree that advertising has to be risky to be effective, however. Many marketing managers are more comfortable with advertising that simply communicates product or service features and benefits and gives the consumer a reason to buy. They see their ad campaigns as crores of investments whose goal is to sell the product rather than finance the whims of their agency's creative staff. They argue that some creative people have lost sight of advertising's bottom line—Does it sell?

Extra: Indeed memorable.

An example of a company that has begun taking more creative risks with its advertising is Wrigley. For many years, the company, which has long dominated the market for chewing gum, was very conservative with its advertising and relied on more traditional, attribute–focused messages. However, in recent years, Wrigley has taken a more dynamic approach in its ads. For example, advertising for the company's Big Red brand used the tried and true "Kiss a Little Longer" campaign, featuring smooching couples, for many years. However, in 2000, Wrigley decided to develop a new image for the brand and began using a new campaign that focuses on the product's bold cinnamon taste and little "wisdoms" regarding fresh breath.

THE CREATIVE PROCESS

Some advertising people say that creativity in advertising is best viewed as a process and creative success is most likely when some organized approach is followed. This does not mean that there is an infallible blue - print to follow to create effective advertising. Many advertising people reject attempts to standardize creativity or develop rules. However, most do follow a process when developing an ad.

James Webb Young, a former creative vice president at J. Walter Thompson agency, developed one of the most popular approaches to creativity in advertising. Young said, "The production of ideas is just as definite a process as the production of Fords; the production of ideas, too, runs an assembly line; in this production, the mind follows an operative technique which can be learned and controlled; and that its effective use is just as much a matter of practice in the technique as in the effective use of any tool." Young's model of the creative process contains five steps:

1. *Immersion*—Gathering raw material and information through background research and immersing you in the problem
2. *Digestion*—Taking the information, working it over, and wrestling with it in the mind
3. *Incubation*—Putting the problems out of your conscious mind and turning the information over to the subconscious to do the work

4. *Illumination*–Having the birth of an idea.
5. *Reality or verification*–studying the idea to see if it still looks good or solves the problem; then shaping the idea to practical usefulness

Models of the creative process are valuable to those working in the creative area of advertising, since they offer an organized way to approach an advertising problem. Many agencies are now using a process called account planning to gather information and help creative specialist as they go through the creative process of developing advertising.

Background Research

The creative specialist should learn as much as possible about the client's product or service, the target market, the competition, general trends, conditions and developments in the marketplace. Some informal fact-finding techniques have been noted as follows:

- Reading anything related to the product or market–books, trade publications, general interest articles, research reports
- Asking everyone involved with the product for information–designers, engineers, sales people, and consumers
- Listening to what people are talking about. Visits to stores, malls, restaurants etc.
- Using the product or service and becoming familiar with it
- Working in and learning about the client's business to understand better the people you're trying to reach

Qualitative Research Input

In addition to various quantitative research studies, qualitative research techniques such as in-depth interviews or focus groups can provide the creative team with valuable insight at the early stages of the creative process. Focus groups are research methods whereby consumers (usually 10 to 12 people) from the target market are led through a discussion regarding a particular topic. Focus groups give insight as to why and how consumers use a product or service, what is important to them in choosing a particular brand, what they like and don't like about various products or services, and any special needs they might have that aren't being satisfied. Another form of qualitative input that has become popular amongst advertising agencies is *ethnographic research*, which involves observing consumers in their natural environment.

Creative Strategy Development

Most ads are part of a series of messages that make up an advertising campaign, which is a set of interrelated and coordinated marketing communication activities that centre around a single theme or idea that appears in different media across a specified time period. Determining the unifying theme around which the campaign will be built is a critical part of the creative process. A campaign theme should be a strong idea, as it is the central message that will be communicated in all the advertising and other promotional activities.

While some marketers change their campaign themes often, a successful campaign theme may last for years. Philip Morris has been using the "Marlboro country" campaign for over 40 years; Santoor has positioned its bathing soap as "no one can guess my age from my complexion" for decades, and BMW has used the "ultimate driving machine" theme since 1974. Some popular themes are given below:

	Company or brand	Campaign theme
1.	DeBeers	Diamonds are forever.
2.	Nike	Just do it.
3.	Coca Cola	The pause that refreshes.
4.	Amul	Taste of India.
5.	Avis	We try harder.
6.	Colgate	The ring of confidence.
7.	BPL	Believes in the Best.
8.	Onida	Neighbours envy, owner's pride.
9.	L'Oreal	Because I'm worth it.
10.	Canon	Delighting you always.

Marketers have also developed their campaign themes based on another famous theme. One of immediate recall is the visual featuring a desolate cowboy standing next to his fallen horse. Piyush's creation for the Cancer Patient's Aid Association made more impact than the original 'cowboy-horse' ad and even die-hard nicotine addicts would stop to take a look and think about the consequences of a dalliance with the cancer-stick.

Anti-Smoking: Second hand smoking kills.

The Search for the Major Selling Idea

An important part of creative strategy is determining the central theme that will become the **major selling idea** of the ad campaign. For an ad campaign to be effective, it must contain a big idea that attracts the consumer's attention, gets a reaction and sets the advertiser's product or service apart from the competitions. The real challenge to the creative team is coming up with the big idea to use in the ad. Many products and services virtually offer nothing unique, and it can be difficult to find something interesting to say about them. The late David Ogilvy, generally considered one of the most creative advertising copywriters ever to work in the business, has stated:

"I doubt if more than one campaign in a hundred contains a big idea. I am supposed to be one of the more fertile inventors of big ideas, but in my long career as a copywriter I have not had more than 20, if that."

"Every Burnett employee knows that it is not enough to produce advertising that works. We have to stretch farther and deliver brand miracles." says Mr. Arvind Sharma, Managing Director of Leo Burnett.

It is difficult to pinpoint the inspiration for a big idea or to teach advertising people how to find one. However, several approaches can guide the creative team's search for a major selling idea and offer solutions for developing effective advertising. Some of the best known approaches are as follow:

1. Using a unique selling proposition
2. Creating a brand image
3. Finding the inherent drama
4. Positioning

Unique Selling Proposition (USP)

Rosser Reeves, former Chairman of Ted Bates agency, developed the concept of the unique selling proposition. Reeves noted the following three characteristics of unique selling propositions:

1. Each advertisement must make a proposition to the consumer. Not just words, not just product puffery, not just show-window advertising. Each advertisement must say to each reader: "Buy this product and you will get this benefit".
2. The proposition must be the one that the competition either cannot or does not offer. It must be unique either in the brand or in the claim.
3. The proposition must be strong enough to move the masses, that is, pull over new customers to your brand.

Creating a Brand Image

Benetton: An example of creating image.

In many product and service categories, competing brands are so similar that it is very difficult to find or create a unique attribute or benefit to use as the major selling idea. The creative strategy used to sell these products is based on the development of a strong, memorable identity for the brand through **image advertising**.

Image advertising has become increasingly popular and is used as the main selling idea for a variety of products and services, including soft drinks, liquor, cigarettes, cars, airlines, financial services, perfumes/cologne and clothing. Many consumers wear designer jeans or *Raymond* shirts or drink certain brands of beer or soft drinks because of the image of these brands.

Finding the inherent drama

Advertising campaign can be engrossing if it has an inherent drama in it. The advertisement of Mirinda revolves around the drama where the mother is so much fascinated by the taste of the drink that she doesn't even recognize her lost son. People believe the story as it doesn't cross the boundary. On the other hand, a notable opinion about advertising strategy and integrity is that advertising insults the intelligence of an average consumer. This lack of trust could affect consumers' response to advertising and the total creative environment.

Spa: An obfuscating advertisement.

This is an ad by *Spa*. The customer is supposed to figure out what the ad says through just a picture. Looks like it's definitely not for getting slim! Or is it that he is just playing with us by stating the opposite of usual purpose of a gym? Sometimes the real meaning is hidden in the name of creativity.

Of course, there are also some advertisements, which are vague and befitting, but that is not necessarily result of great creativity. However, when creativity exists without regard for the consumer, the creative ad might insult the consumer more easily than the ad using uncreative ideas. To some extent, creative advertising can be more dangerous than demonstration or testimonial advertisement. Therefore, advertising people must consider the intelligence of the consumer or suffer the consequence of building a less than desirable brand image.

As Mr. Sharma says, "I genuinely believe that human beings ultimately choose good sense. I'm, therefore, for freedom of speech. Internet is finally demonstrating the futility of censorship every day. Those who still don't buy it, will buy in a couple of years. Advertising is still the most fun you can have with your clothes on. It challenges a man's capability to solve amorphously defined problems in creative ways. It is the stuff of human life!"

Positioning

Any product creates a position of itself in the market. The process, which determines what place will be occupied in the given market with the ongoing products, is called positioning. This process, which creates a niche for the product makes a position similar to the segmentation process, which produces alternative market segments and finally target markets.

The markets can position a product, service and ideas in the following ways:

- By price (*Nirma* by claiming the same cleaning in lesser price).
- By attributes (*Surf Excel* can save two buckets of water).
- By its ability to surpass the competition (*Harpic* cleans better than other toilet cleaners).
- By application (*Fair and lovely* can make the skin fairer in fourteen days only).
- By product users (*Rasna* is a favourite drink of all children).
- By product class (*Tropicana* juice is the real fruit juice).

Fair and lovely: A well-positioned ad.

It is quite true that both marketing and advertising separately relate the product positioning to the target market. Hyundai positioned *Sonata* as high quality and high price product. Advertising certainly reinforces the campaign position through the choice of copy, music, media and spokesperson. The advertisement of *Titan* is a good example for choosing the appropriate spokesperson, music and media.

THE STYLE: HARD SELL OR SOFT SELL

The style of selling can be decided according to the nature of the product, the competition and the target audience. The style of each agency and individual campaign differs. Some want to be noticed without screaming. Leo Burnett emphasizes that their style is straightforward without being flatfooted, warm without being mawkish.

Hard sell advertising is almost, as it sounds, coaxing the receivers with the immediate demand to buy the product. This is done by using the phrases like 'buy now' or by promising being the exceptional, the best, amazing and the most wonderful product in the universe. The screaming of the house dealer is an appropriate example, which is used when the price is the most important criteria for buying decision. Remember not to confuse hard sell with well-crafted ads that have lot of persuasive and cajoling passion. The remarkable feature of hard sell ads is to put a unintermittent pressure to buy immediately.

Soft sell advertising is just opposite to the hard sell as it takes wider approach to persuade and motivate the reader to create a desire to buy the product. It does not bank on exhortations of 'buy now', in fact, not even urge people to buy at all but has a very subtle approach of advertising. It simply creates a situation in audiences' mind that will inadvertently lead them to buy the product. Soft sell advertisements are equally effective as the hard sell advertisement, in fact, sometimes more as they don't irk the customer.

Nizoral: An example of soft sell.

It is the market scenario which influences the advertiser's style choices. During the natural disasters, the gaudy style and luxurious style might be toned down to avoid offending people who might be facing financial crunch.

THE APPEALS

The most successful advertisement will be able to appeal the people who view, read or listen to it. The advertising appeal is a trial to draw some synergy between the product advertised and some desire that is felt by audience. This audience is motivated by reducing the gaps in their lives– the way they perceive thing to be and they way the like things to be. This appeal will announce that this product will meet your need and fulfill your desire. Therefore, to be successful, the appeal should be in congruence with the customer's buying process.

The appeals can be categorized into logical and emotional appeals. The logical appeal is also known as rational appeal as it is based on reasoning while emotional appeal tries to sell the product by giving the customer satisfaction after buying the product. Suppose, if you have to advertise for a Xerox machine, then logical appeal will be more appropriate. If you have to advertise for a talcum powder, it is safe to opt for emotional appeal. In fact, if you advertise for a product like diamond, the appeal strategy changes according to the audience need. If it is to be used as the jewellery, the obvious appeal used is emotional but if the purpose is for industrial use, the appeal will be logical.

Consider the tag like for *Amul* Chocolate which says 'a gift to some one you love' has a strong emotional appeal that draws a connection between the product and the need for love and commitment. On the other hand, the products, which are for industrial/business use like the advertisement for HP, have logical appeal.

The definitions do talk about these appeals separately but seldom will you find each appeal in isolation. Most of the advertisements will have mixture of both the appeals. For example, if you advertise for something you consider logical as a photocopier as a piece of office equipment, it will appeal to emotions. As a decision to buy this equipment might be intertwined up with the concern about the job performance, quickness of results or being mocked at if the results are not exact. Human beings will remain the same throughout the world and will have same sentiments and feelings. All have feelings of hopes, apprehensions, desires and dreams regardless of their profession. Even a highly technical ad can appeal to emotions as the perfection in the office can reduce the stress and increase the chances of success or satisfy your other emotions.

Bilt: Mixing emotions for the office product.

It is very important to put an emotional appeal in the product being advertised. It is not just enough to roil the emotions of love, anger, friendship and security but those feelings should be translated into purchase decision. Otherwise making an ad will be an exercise in sentiments and not selling. The *Vicks* advertisement has done it very well. When the child has gone out in the rains and caught cold, he just showed how much he loved his mother and had gone in awful weather conditions to get flowers for his mother. Mother in return gave him a hug and massaged *Vicks* to make him fine.

Advertisers can employ different kinds of appeals which can be named as logical, emotional or combination of the two. The most common types of appeal are based on price, quality star identification, ego, anger or fear or five senses, sex, love and novelty.

Price appeal

Dabur glucose-D is now 33% free, Now you will be getting 5% extra in the same price is what is the price appeal or the other way is to lower the price and give the same amount as was done by HLL for their detergent powder. In some situations, you keep the price and the product same but common people still try as the product is worth the price they pay.

Remember that price in isolation is not an effective appeal and no one would be ready to buy bad quality of goods in lower prices. If the quality is maintained then only the lower price can make an appeal. Price is used as the extra punch in appeal. When you offer good quality product at reasonable price, then may be it attracts the potential buyers.

Surf Excel: Attracting customers by reducing price.

Quality appeal

The obverse side to price appeal is the appeal to quality. An ad for Arvind Mills mentions its quality products for the last 100 years and also challenges the others. It cannot do unless it has quality of the right level. The audience is sceptical of such claims. Therefore, you ought to support it with right kind of information to build the trust.

Star appeal

The audience has great fascination for superstars in films and sports and that is why you will find every second advertisement being endorsed by the celebrity. Endorsement by a celebrity has become very popular these days in India and abroad. Amitabh Bacchhan, Aishwarya Rai, Sachin Teldulkar, Preity Zinta, Amir Khan, Rani Mukherjee, Sharukh Khan, etc. are seen in most of the advertisements. An ad with the star endorsement has a greater appeal and recall value.

A related appeal is testimonial, in which a real user of the product uses the product and claims it to be the best. It need not be a celebrity but can be any real user who will tell about the benefits got by using the product. For example, N. Kartikeyan, the fastest car driver, was given an ad for Bridgestone tyres. One ought to be careful about the legal issues involved in this type of appeal but if it is rightly executed, it becomes very powerful as the message comes from the satisfied customer.

Star endorsement: A common approach to have instant attention.

Ego appeal

An appeal to the personal quality of an individual always have an indelible effect whether it is related to intellect, appearance, sense of humour or any other trait. The appropriate example for the appeal is for L'oreal where Diana Hayden claims "b'coz I am worth it". At later stage, it, was changed to "b'coz you are worth it". She accepts that it is quite expensive but the statement touches the ego of the potential buyers goading them to think about the same product for themselves. The ego appeal is something that happens in private and, therefore, is not embarrassing.

Fear appeal

The greatest fear human beings have is the fear of death, distortion of figure and face, or mutilation of body parts. The extreme case of this appeal was used in antismoking ad where the complete advertisement is shown in black which depicts that you are embracing death, if you smoke. The other example is the advertisement for LIC policy, where a lady dreams that she is bereft of her husband and had nothing left to support her. It is very scary and that cajoles her to go for LIC policy. Certainly, it has a very strong appeal.

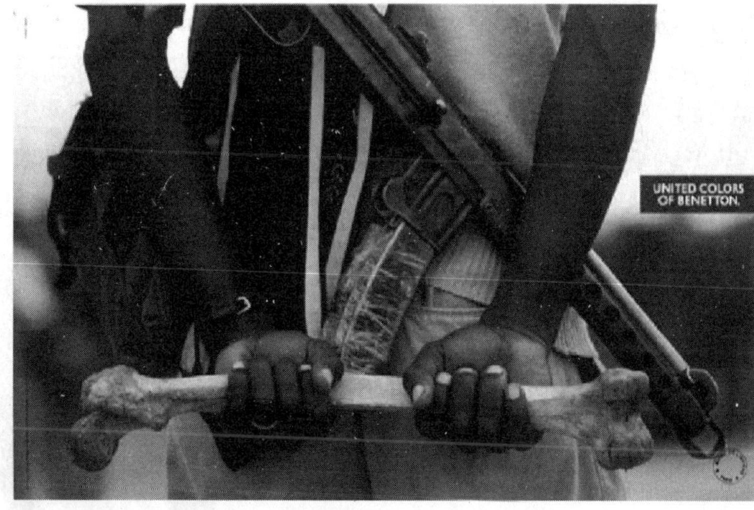

United Colors of Benetton: An African gorilla with Kalashnikov and a femur.

Sensory appeal

Some of the ads aim at one or more of five senses of touch, taste, vision, hearing and smell. For example, Tata Tea gold has banked on its aroma and those who refuse to take this tea, rue later on. Toyota has its signature line as the touch of perfection. The appeal in Apsara pencil is the well-crafted handwriting which is visual appeal. In fact, the advertisers use one of these appeals in advertisement either through words or pictures.

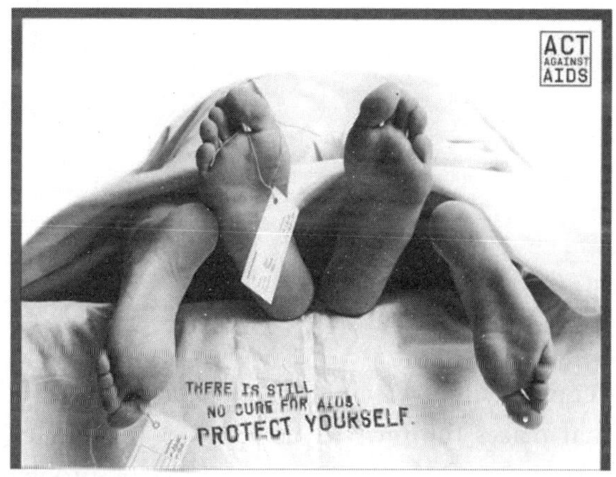

AIDS: Serious topic dealt in decent way.

Sex, love and social acceptance appeals

This is another very common appeal which is communicated explicitly or even implicitly. The wide gamut of feelings is revealed through personal interaction whether it is social acceptance, friendship, love and sex. In the advertisement for a crack cream, the lady is embarrassed because of her cracked heels. An *Itch Guard* ad shows a man tempted to itch his private parts because of the problem. So to avoid such situation of embarrassment, the *Itch Guard* is sure a solution. The advertisement of GenX undergarments, Calvin Klein's , Obsession perfume, Kamasutra condoms and Levis jeans has used sex and love to appeal the audiences. In some situations, sexy images are too suggestive to offend the readers and viewers.

Novelty appeal

When the advertisements are mushrooming at such a pace, to be different is challenging. Just to make an advertisement is not enough, but to make it really catchy and strange is the need of the time. "*Thanda matlab Coca cola*" was certainly different. The *Fevicol* advertisement in which the bus was moving in the terrain of dessert which is fully loaded with the wonderful music at the backdrop had its impact, for the campaign was novel. It is not necessary that you will buy the product but surely viewers will not forget the visual.

Fevicol: The adhesive can hold all.

TOO MUCH OF CREATIVITY

People say it is easier to create a memorable advertisement than it is to create an advertisement that makes the product memorable. A number of tests have proved that people often remember a commercial, but not a product. This problem is called **vampire creativity**. It occurs primarily with advertisements that are too entertaining, original, involving or provocative. The selling story of the advertisement can be so mesmerizing that it obscures the product quality. Using humour or celebrity in advertisement can cause this problem. But under one condition, vampire creativity could be effective. When people are exposed to that kind of commercials not just once but several times (higher frequency), the effectiveness could be relatively higher than the commonplace advertisements. However, it is crucial that the ads establish a strong link between the message and the product so that remembering the commercial means also remembering the product. See the ad of Smirnoff shown. Is this height of vagueness or creativity? At the most, one might be able to guess that it's a liquor ad and the rest is left to imagination.

Smirnoff: Heights of creativity.

CREATIVITY VERSUS PROFIT

In a commercial environment, within a business, the only judge of creativity is the fact how much money it eventually makes or saves. Of what use is a very beautiful ad if it doesn't sell? So creative artists should first make sure that the message is driven home and then add all the creative stuff they want without spoiling the prime purpose.

Some TV advertising campaigns are memorable works of art as they are glued to our imagination. They can brighten up our days or evenings. They give a common currency to pub and office talk. Adverts form a small but fond part of almost everybody's childhood memories. They reach our eyes and ears in the first place because a marketing manager inside a large company put together a proposal that his/her company should spend from a few hundred thousand to millions of rupees to create and buy the broadcast time for the advertisement. The company approved that expenditure.

The companies which advertise most are public companies and have shareholders to account for their expenditure, so their rationale has to be pretty tough—creative advertisements must usually pay dividends by improving product sales or the "brand value" of products. There are quite a few loopholes, which allow creative advertisements to get through unchecked. Sometimes the ad agencies do the work as showcase work, not as "commercial" or "profitable" work, only to win the awards. In the process, the essence of advertising is lost and a fortune of money is wasted just to show make beautiful art in the name of advertising.

Subaru and American Express: Campaigns that failed.

In 1991, Subaru and American Express rolled out major creative ad campaigns. However, none has revived lagging sales. Subaru sales remain flat. American Express has failed to reinvigorate its charge card with its new slogan, "The Card. The American Express Card." All the results are surprising because the campaigns come from agencies renowned for their creativity.

AWARD-WINNING ADVERTISING

Many people agree that creative awards are one of the best benchmarks of pure creative excellence. Creative awards are motivating and stimulating to creative people who operate for more than just money. They are the tools for an industry to set high standards. For the most part, however, advertisers are unconvinced of the value of creative awards. Some argue that it is not right to judge advertising without considering business results. Many people view creative awards with a great amount of scepticism. In the awards, ads are frequently judged on their artistic rather than selling merits. Some critics express negative opinions about creativity in advertising. They say that creativity is unpredictable and can upset the appearance of stability and predictability.

The creativity is judged by the jury on very simple criteria. They specify "impact" and "relevance" as two parameters to evaluate or judge creativity. Obviously, only creative people should be called upon to judge creativity. Shorn of its niceties, one school of thought lays out a case where creators of creativity are the best judges of it. The second school of thought advocates the inclusion of marketing people who, in any case, judge the creativity of agencies every day in the real world and decide what actually goes out to the ultimate consumer.

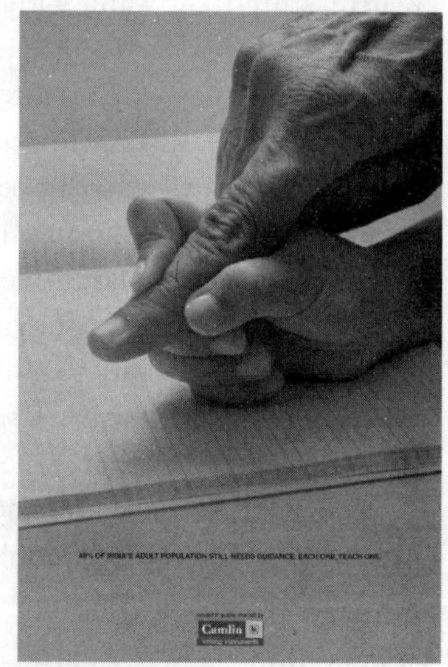

Camlin: A very different concept.

Firstly, when you have only eminent creative directors judging creative work, you tend to look for what the supposedly creative mind recognizes as truly creative. You end up with a view that almost none, or at least a very small proportion, of the work entered deserves to be awarded for creativity.

Well, judging from the Indian victories at Cannes, the overwhelming majority of the few pieces of work that have been hailed by the international creative community is work done for NGOs. Even if it is work done for a brand, it is probably some environmental message from the company, not its regular advertising.

So what does that mean? Why is it that there are a growing number of global majors increasing their advertising through a large number of global agency alliances and India could not get one single gold Lion at the Cannes advertising festival? Meanwhile, the bronzes India picked up are for everything other than "regular" advertising of large advertisers. At the risk of causing several others to quiver with indignation, we may say that Indian creativity was rewarded, as it richly deserved to be. Indian advertising was not.

What we have been winning is certainly not representative of Indian advertising. The 'Even second-hand smoke kills' hoarding with the Marlboro horse lying dead was a fantastic idea. The communication was seen in editorial space by Indians not as a solitary hoarding that came up at Worli, Mumbai. Why is it that all the big brands that are being advertised–*Ponds* or *Dettol* or *Surf* or *Pepsi* or *Asian Paints* or any of the other big-budget campaigns that advertisers choose to support on the wisdom of their experience and the evidence of their market research–are nowhere among the big awards?

It is predominantly the NGOs which are thrilled to bits to get free creatives and so do not 'interfere', that sweep the accolades. What does this mean? Does it mean that advertisers do not take the leap of faith that cutting-edge creative needs? Our spenders would do well to ponder upon this.

However, there was a fundamental problem which should not be ignored; no single set of criteria could be applied to judging effectiveness because each commercial had its own goal and standard, from raising sales to image and awareness.

In conclusion, an award-winning ad is more likely to sell the product than one that is not award-winning. This result seems to show a strong and positive relationship between creative commercials and sales, based on statistical figures, even if the objectives of the commercials are not just sales.

Now the questions remain: "Does creative advertising sell? Does 'effective' mean 'creative' ?" The success of ads doesn't seem to be directly influenced by creativity itself, even though, statistically, creative/award-winning advertising is about two-and-a-half times more likely to sell than uncreative advertising. Even if creative or award-winning advertising may sell more than uncreative or non-award-winning advertising, it is more valuable to note that creative advertising doesn't always sell. Creative commercials–the ads that are well liked by the ad industry and ordinary people, hailed in the press and recalled most frequently in surveys of television viewers–don't always work. They may provoke smile and laughter or warm memories of wonderful moments, but they frequently do not increase sales.

As mentioned above, we should not evaluate the creativity of the ads according to the universal definition of creativity. Applying it to the advertising business, we might get the above results. Therefore, it's time to redefine creativity to reflect new ways of reaching customers and building brands. Creativity has to include not only brand communication but also brand experiences which are collected over a period of time. It should embrace not only compelling words and visuals but also consumer-catching ideas that add value to the brand and generate action around it. Creativity needs to do more than please our sensibilities and win awards. It must reinforce the brand's image and materially augment the movement of the brand through its distribution channels and increase the information in the consumer's hands.

Based on this new definition, the creative advertising that doesn't sell is not creative advertising any more, regardless of its performance. Creative advertising must sell the products or brands. This should be the one condition of evaluating creativity in advertising. No doubt great creativity has the power to evoke purchases. The most profitable outfits and the most creative ones are one and the same. And if there is 'Creativity,' one-time exposure is enough to appeal to and convince customers.

SUMMARY

Creativity is always a fascinating and challenging area in advertising. The interpretation of an ad depends on the perception of the individual. While creating an ad, you should remember that the objective of advertising is just not to sell product but also to create images in the mind of prospective buyers so that they can transform experience of buying or using product or services. It is the creative strategy and creative tactics which will decide the advertising message. Sometimes the advertisement is creative but it doesn't have an impact on the sale of the product. Creativity is defined as doing something which is different from others. It is the old wine in the new bottle. Creativity is ability to generate novel and useful ideas and solutions to everyday problems and challenges. For advertising to stand distinct, creativity is must and should be blend with it. Advertising creativity depends on people, information and environment.

While working on creative strategy, one should not only try to make it memorable but communicate message very clearly. The job of the creative team is arduous as every market situation is different. Therefore, each campaign may require a different creative approach. Advertiser should be bold enough to take risk while developing a campaign. The creative process contains five steps—immersion, digestion, incubation, illumination and verification. Any ad message is developed around a big idea. Some marketers change their theme fast while others take a while.

There are different appeals in the advertising which can be to the head, heart or combination of both. The four best approaches for developing an effective advertising are using unique selling proposition, creating a brand Image, finding the inherent drama and positioning. Too much of creativity is bad as it makes the viewers remember the product but that doesn't necessarily make them buy it. This is called vampire advertising. Some advertisements are primarily made for winning awards.

QUESTIONS

1. What is more important in an advertising campaign–picture or the words?
2. What do you understand by creativity? Do you think advertising rules are antithesis to creativity?
3. What is the role of teamwork in developing an ad campaign?
4. Explain the five steps of creative process in advertising.
5. Differentiate between hard selling and soft selling in advertising. Give examples for each.
6. Discuss various types of appeals used in advertising. Which appeal according to you has the most recall value and why?
7. Vampire creativity is a problem faced by many advertisements. Give some examples of ads which you think were affected by vampire creativity. What were the steps taken to remedy this?
8. Take a marketing positioning statement, based on a situation analysis for a brand and product category that you may have worked on for some marketing project and attempt to come up with five different creative ideas that could be used in creative advertising for the selected brand.
9. Does the freedom of speech give the marketers full right to unleash ideas that may be termed obscene by the public and "creative" by the marketer?

10. Critically examine the ad given below and justify the reasons for finding it creative.

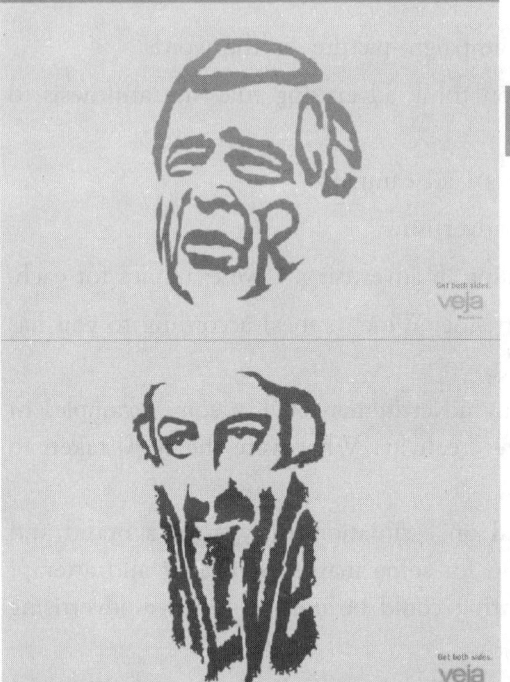

C H A P T E R 9

Creativity through Language

LEARNING OBJECTIVES:

After reading this chapter, you will be able to:

- Underscore the importance of language in advertising.
- Find out the role of copywriter in making of an advertisement.
- Discuss the devices used by a copywriter in making an ad creative.
- State all the deviations from the normal grammatical pattern.
- Study the role of fonts in the advertising layout.
- Compare the language and picture of an advertisement.

CASE STUDY: CULTURE SHOCK

The power of culture has a great influence in all decisions, and cultural creativity works the ultimate magic with consumers. Semiotic analysis is a form of focused desk research, which is done before touching base with consumers. One examines the communications of both the client and competitors—advertising, products, packaging, retail environments, promotions, historical and current. By analysing the data one can find out the cultural "body language" unconsciously coded into brand messages. This allows one to see how consumers (consciously and unconsciously) use contexts, codes, myths and metaphors to make those all important cultural connections with the brand and its spectrum of marketing messages.

Titoo Ahluwalia, Chairman, ORGMARG, while making a presentation in the Confederation of Indian Industry (CII) marketing summit held in Delhi recently, said, "The rational and psychological levels in communication can be probed using conventional research techniques but the cultural level is more difficult to access. That is because the culture is 'encoded' in everyday living and the average consumer cannot decode his own culture". When the hypotheses are developed by the semiotic analysis, one has an infinitely sharper and more focused set of questions when one does get to talk to people. It helps market researchers in analysing and understanding the data much better. Says Sonia Pal, Group Project Manager, MBL, RCG, "Semiotics is used frequently in interpretations of the research we do. Even if there is no formal semiotic research phase in the study, we use semiotics to help us understand data better".

Semiotics looks at things through the other end of the marketing telescope, the cultural end. It bases the interpretation of 'what it sees' firmly on the theory that consumers are not independent spirits, articulating their original opinions and making their own individual buying decisions. By and large, consumers are products of the popular culture in which they live. They are constructed by the communication of that culture.

Certain phrases stick firmly in our minds and we are not quite sure why. "Just do it", we may say as a way to motivate ourselves to take on a difficult task. "There is nothing official about it!" we may tell a friend during a heated debate.

But if we think for a moment where these phrases and catchwords actually originated, we may dimly recall that they were once slogans used in advertising campaigns for athletic shoes (Nike's "Just do it") or the cold drink(Coca Cola's "There is nothing official about it").

The purpose of such appealing messages in advertisements is to motivate people to buy the advertised goods and services. Copywriters who do this job dexterously create such messages. Advertising copywriters are the people who wrote these and other slogans, carefully crafting succinct and punchy phrases to cajole us into buying the deluge of products and services.

ROLE OF COPYWRITER

Advertising copywriters write the slogans for advertisements in newspapers, magazines and billboards, radio and television commercials and internet pop-up ads. Their catchy pitches (described by advertisers themselves as a mixture of flattery and threats) help companies gain exposure, publicity and prestige. In this era of consumerism, every day new products and services are making their way in the market. Competition is increasing and the outlook of customers is also changing. Since long business organizations have been depending on advertisements to lure customers in order to make their business and market share grow. But now the role of advertisements has become much more significant mainly because of the growing competition.

Not only we get to see more advertisements now but also the style of advertisements is changing very rapidly. In this environment, the requirement of copywriters has increased and their job has become more arduous. Even the simplest of well-timed campaigns can generate excitement and unprecedented sales for a company since millions of people watch, read and listen to these ads each day. Indeed, for most of us in this media age, advertisements of any kind are hard to escape. In addition to their work on ads, advertising copywriters also write press releases which are distributed to news-gathering organizations as well as promotional information and trade journal articles about products and services. Their goal is always to write interesting and original copy that will get people appreciating and buying. Depending on the needs, inputs like humour, family values, etc. are included in the advertisement copy.

Copywriters work in a creative partnership with an art director to conceive, develop and produce effective advertisements. While the art director deals mainly with the visual images, it is the copywriter who provides the verbal or written aspect. This involves writing 'copy', i.e. coming up with the original catch phrases, slogans and signatures lines. It also includes writing all the wording in any type of advertising such as:

- Posters
- Press
- Leaflets
- Brochures
- Radio or television scripts

Copywriters are often involved in the production process, which can include casting actors for voice-overs and dealing with production companies and directors or typographers, designers and printers.

A copywriter's work, depending upon the type of agency, may include:

- Meeting with the account management team to discuss client requirements and background to the product

- Working in a close-knit creative partnership with the art director to generate workable concepts and ideas
- Writing clear, persuasive and original copy
- Submitting ideas and discussing progress with the creative director
- Amending and revising campaigns according to feedback from the creative director or clients
- Working on several campaigns at once, under pressure and to tight deadlines
- Carefully proofreading copy to check spelling and grammar
- Overseeing campaigns through the production stage to final completion
- Casting actors for TV and radio work, listening to voice tapes
- Liaising with production companies, photographers, typographers, designers and printers
- Keeping up to date with popular culture and trends
- Advising 'would be' creatives and reviewing portfolios

In smaller firms, advertising copywriters often do more than just write. They find new clients and do market research. They often work for a diverse group of clients and must be versatile enough to adjust to each new product they work with and each new medium they write for.

Copywriting is a job that is often perceived as creative, stimulating and even glamorous. Copywriters help develop names for new products, often travel in the course of work and are offered free samples by companies whose products they pitch. Some even get to participate in the filming of television ads. Because their words can move people to buy products worth crores of rupees, it is a profession that can also be relatively lucrative. On the other hand, it is often stressful work, since being creative on a tight schedule isn't all that easy. The task of the copywriters include

- Writing ads for various media
- Analysing market data
- Consulting with clients
- Consulting with other members of the creative team
- Editing and rewriting copy

The skills, abilities and personal characteristics of a copywriter are as follows:

- Writing creatively and persuasively
- Working under pressure
- Meeting deadlines

- Working in team
- Working cohesively with clients
- Keeping abreast of market trends and research
- Translating clients' preferences into a finished product
- Presenting one's work to others for evaluation
- Working on several different projects simultaneously
- Having amazing sense of humour
- Being a wordsmith

Copywriters may also write publicity releases, promotional or informational booklets, sales promotion materials, or they may work on merchandising campaigns. They sometimes write radio and television commercials or trade journal articles about products or services. At times copywriters may be called upon to edit or rewrite existing copy. Copywriters may be assigned to a variety of accounts and must be versatile enough to adjust to each new product and medium and to vary the language and tone of each message.

Agency copywriters may also work on annual reports, sales brochures, point-of-purchase materials, instructional manuals and press releases. Some broadcasting stations employ copywriters to prepare advertising material and station announcements. Irrespective of the size of the operation, copywriters must be knowledgeable about copywriting, art and layout, space and time buying and selling copy.

IMPORTANCE OF LANGUAGE

Language has a powerful influence over people and their behaviour. This is especially true in the fields of marketing and advertising. The choice of language to convey specific messages with the intention of influencing people is vitally important.

Visual content and design in advertising have a very great impact on the consumer, but it is the language that helps people to identify a product and remember it.

First let us have a look at the various components of an advertisement. See Figure 9.1.

Parts of an advertisement:

(a) Headline: to grab attention
(b) Illustration: to retain interest
(c) Body copy: details and sales pitch
(d) Signature line: brand name, slogan, and trademark
(e) Standing details: address of firm

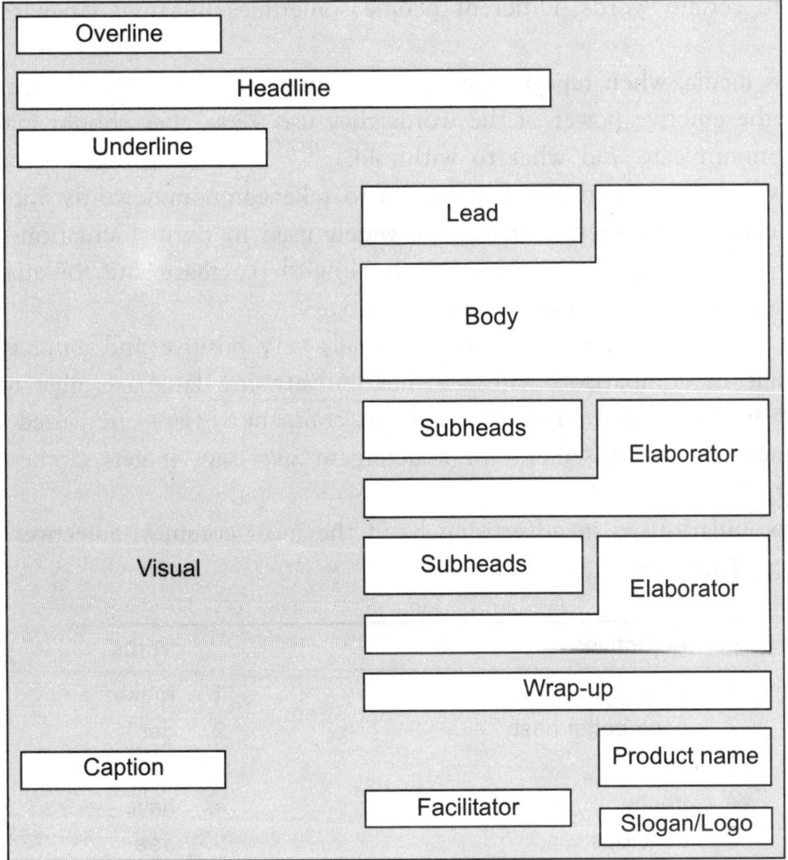

Fig. 9.1 Anatomy of an advertisement.

As you see, except for the 'illustration' part of it, rest of it is language in which you want to communicate. So the language we use in an advertisement has a major role to play.

Most of the ads we see today are in English language and English is known for its extensive vocabulary. Where many other languages have only one or two words, which carry a particular meaning, English may have innumerable.

Amul: Use of pun.

Moreover, the meanings of some words may differ very slightly and in a very subtle way. It is important to understand the connotation of a word. Connotation is the feeling or ideas that are suggested by a word, rather than the actual meaning of the word. Couch, for example, suggests comfort, whereas chair arouses no particular feelings. The target audience, of course, also puts its own meaning into certain words. Different people sometimes interpret language in different ways.

Both the mass media, when reporting news items, and marketing and advertising personnel have to consider the emotive power of the words they use. First, they should make a decision about what to communicate and what to withhold.

One way in which advertisers use language is to take compound words and use them as adjectives. These compounds often later become widely used in normal situations. Examples of these compounds, which have become part of the English language, are top-quality, king-size, chocolate-flavoured, feather-light and longer-lasting.

The language of advertising is, of course, normally very positive and emphasizes why one product stands out in comparison with another. Advertising language may not always be "correct" language in the normal sense. For example, comparatives are often used when no real comparison is made. An advertisement for a detergent may say "It gets clothes whiter", but whiter than what.

A study of vocabulary used in advertising listed the most common adjectives and verbs in order of frequency. They are:

	Adjectives		**Verbs**
1.	new	1.	make
2.	good/better/best	2.	get
3.	free	3.	give
4.	fresh	4.	have
5.	delicious	5.	see
6.	full	6.	buy
7.	sure	7.	come
8.	clean	8.	go
9.	wonderful	9.	know
10.	special	10.	keep
11.	crisp	11.	look
12.	fine	12.	need
13.	big	13.	love
14.	great	14.	use
15.	real	15.	feel
16.	easy	16.	like
17.	bright	17.	choose
18.	extra	18.	take
19.	safe	19.	start
20.	rich	20.	taste

The adjectives good and new were over twice as popular as any other adjective.

The common questions about the advertising language with which an individual grapples are:

- Is advertising language normal language?
- Does advertising language sometimes break the rules of normal language?

These questions relate to the place of advertising language in the context of the readers' general knowledge of language (we will presume that the language is English). In order to answer them, we must have some conception of what is meant by "normal language". The English language has evolved to have many different kinds of functionality, each of which corresponds to different situation and style of use. From an analytic point of view, it seems to make the most sense to understand "normal language" to include the variety of styles of English that mature speakers and readers control. This will form the backdrop of everyday language in its many functions, against which we can view advertising language.

Weasel Words

Advertisers often use special words or phrases. These words or phrases are often misleading. These words are called **weasel words**. Examples of weasel words are "helps", "virtual", "new and improved" and "like."

"Helps"

People often think "help" means stop. Advertisers use it so that they can say things that are not necessarily true. Legally, help means to aid or assist. For example, a product can "help" cure indigestion. In fact, the product does not cure indigestion.

Pimple-be-gone: Use of weasel word.

"Virtually"

To advertisers, "virtually" means "not really" or "not in fact." If you see an ad that says this cold medicine relieves virtually all symptoms, the ad could really mean it does not relieve any symptoms.

"New and improved"

A product can only be considered new for six months. Any small change in a product will make it new. Often, this change does not make a product better. Yet, the change often makes it more expensive. "New" is often used with "improved."

"Like"

"Like" can mean "not in fact". Some products claim they work "like magic". Like often takes the audience's attention off the product. Think of "like magic". If things are like magic, they are not magic.

"Presupposition"

An important aspect of any communication involves the presuppositions that are present. Presuppositions may be even more critical in television advertising (see Geis 1982) than in print advertising. However, even in print advertising, presuppositions are an important component of the overall message. As the name implies, a presupposition is a necessary precondition for the processing of any communication.

Presuppositions typically involve the existence of some object or idea.

The adjoining ad presupposes that there are leglines, curves and compliments, and thereby implicates that these things are related.

JEANS SHOULD
flatter the leg line.
Accentuate the curves.
INCREASE
the compliments.

A further example of presupposition, of a fact or proposition, is evident in this text from an ad of Apple Computer:

"I used to think it was my fault that Windows didn't work properly".

"I used to think it was my fault
that Windows didn't work properly."

Presuppositions are a crucial part of advertising as they can cause the reader to consider the existence of objects, propositions, and culturally-defined behavioural properties. For example, "Have you had your daily vitamins" presupposes that you take or need "daily vitamins", thereby creating and perpetuating the idea that the behaviour of taking vitamins daily is part of our culture.

RHETORIC OF ADVERTISING

According to Oxford Advanced Learner's Dictionary of Current English, 'rhetoric' is the art of persuasive or impressive, speaking or writing, language designed to persuade or to impress. Cuddon (1977) also gives a similar definition: "Rhetoric is the art of using language for persuasion, in speaking or writing". As the main aim of advertising is to persuade the customer to buy the product, the copywriter often uses different kinds of rhetorical devices to put forth an effective copy. Some such devices which use the figurative language of advertising and share it with poetry are rhyme, alliteration, simile, metaphor, parallelism, etc. These provide a foregrounding effect as they do in poetry. Most of these figures of speech involve repetition or recurrence of identical units, which need a well-defined context for their interpretation. Rhetoric thus plays a vital role in effective communication.

The effective language provides the copywriter multiple opportunities to be novel and original and the customer reads this language to derive aesthetic pleasure by going through figurative language. Finally, he is imperceptibly persuaded to examine and perhaps to buy the product which has been advertised. The copywriter disregards the literal meaning of words in order to show or imply a relationship between two or more things–the relationship may be direct or implied or may emphasize contrast. Certain figurative or rhetorical expressions used in advertisements have become a part of our daily vocabulary. We tend to forget that their usage is not normal. For example, in "Taste the Thunder", the signature line for Thums-up ad is not taken literally. We interpret it in the figurative meaning of a word. In the baseline "Taste the Thunder", the copywriter has used thunder inappropriately. Taste has been added to thunder, which is an abstract noun and not edible for a dramatic effect of adventure. It is, therefore, clear that poetic expression can be employed in advertising "solely for the purpose of communicating clearly, or making almost tangible the described product or situation, of transmitting the most reasonable facsimile possible of what is described" (Weir, 1960).

Advertising language is at times quite standard and unobtrusive, but more often it attracts attention to itself by being highly colourful and imaginative. Further, as pointed out earlier, it involves stretching or breaking the rules or conventions of 'normal' usage. The rhetorical figure is the mechanism which gives flexibility to move from normal usage to specialized usage. It is quite obvious that what has been said in figurative terms can always be expressed in more direct and simple language. The headline of Cathay Pacific ad says, "The best way to the Big Noodle". Big Noodle is used in figurative sense which can be easily substituted by Hong Kong or China. But to create better impact, it is stated in this manner.

Let us now turn our attention to the frequently used rhetorical devices that we discovered in our sample of advertisements. We shall take on each device and examine its impact on the potential buyer.

Metaphor

It is a figure of speech in which one thing is described in terms of another. This is a basic figure of speech in poetry. In metaphor, a comparison is usually implicit, whereas in Simile, it is explicit. "In a metaphor, a word, which in standard (or literal) usage denotes one kind of thing, quality or action, is applied to another, in the form of a statement of identity instead of comparison" (Abrams 1970). For example, the poem of Burns: 'O my love is a red, red rose' is a metaphor. It should be noted that metaphors can be analysed into two elements. I.A. Richards introduced the term 'tenor' for the subject to which the metaphoric word is applied and the term 'vehicle' for the metaphoric word itself.

A creative copywriter frequently uses metpahors. A metaphor, like a simile, declares an identity, but assimilates comparison. Metaphors are of real value to a copywriter as they can suggest those emotive associations for the product which is wished by the copywriter.

The signature line of Videocon reads "Bring home the leader, bring home the emotion". Leader and emotion are both equated to the television. Leader rightly points out that it is the top quality in the market and emotion gives it a sentimental value. Some more examples are:

MRF: *The tyre with muscles.*
Samsung: *Talk in colour.*
Goldflake: *It's Honeydew Smooth.*
Fiat Punto: *If your son drives like an animal, put him in this cage.*

Fiat Punto: If your son drives like an animal, put him in this cage.

Heineken: How Refreshing. How Heineken.

Heineken: How Refreshing. How Heinken.

Simile

In this figure of speech, one thing is linked to another, in such a way as to clarify and enhance an image. It is an explicit comparison recognizable by the use of words 'like' or 'as'. It is equally common in advertisements as it links two objects through a comparison. A copywriter tries to bring together his/her product and the would-be consumer with the use of a simile. Copywriters take care that in the simile the comparison is apt, fresh and meaningful to the reader. In a simile, as there is an overt comparison, it is more explicit than a metaphor. The use of a simile not only helps the copywriter to catch the immediate attention of the reader, but also keeps the attention captivated for some time.

Some examples of simile are given below:

Amul: Twice as creamy as any other condensed milk.

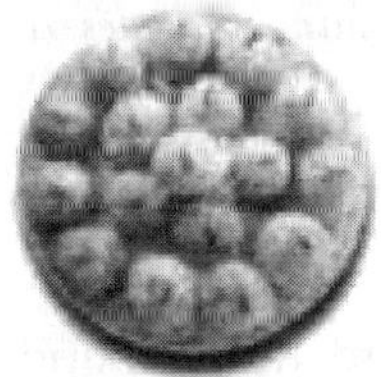

Honda Accord: As with most things in life, its true beauty lies within.

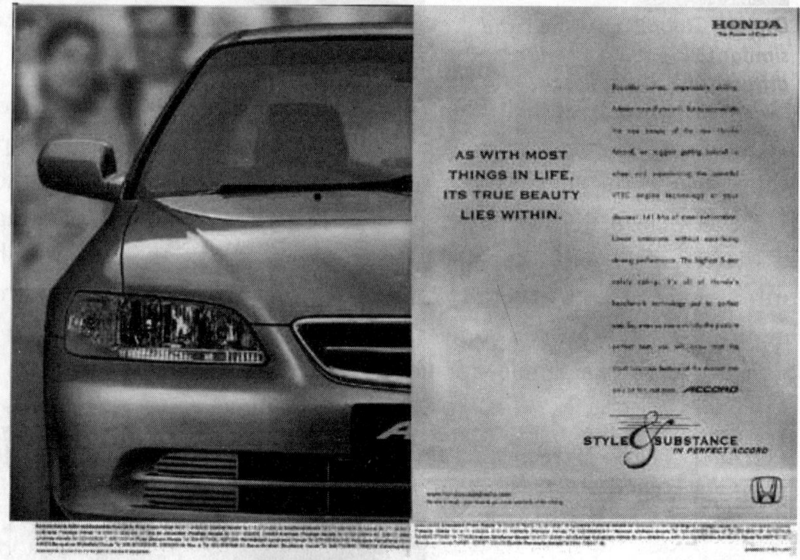

Personification

In this figure of speech, there is impersonation or embodiment of some quality or inanimate objects. Personification is inherent in many languages through use of gender, and it appears to be very frequent in ads. There are innumerable illustrations of personification in all types of ads but they are frequently used in the textile and cosmetic ads. A few illustrations of personification are given below against the product name.

Servo Kool Plus: *Let your car enjoy winter round the year.*

Fiat Sienna: *Power dressing just acquired a stylish new accessory.*

Oxymoron

It is a figure of speech which combines incongruous and apparently contradictory words and meanings for a special effect. In advertising, the use of this figure of speech is limited. There is juxtaposition of two expressions which are semantically incompatible.

Ford Ikon: *The josh machine provides a very welcome departure.*

DCM: *DCM textile has chaotic symmetries that screwball the eye.*

Onomatopoeia

It is the formation of a word using sounds that resemble or suggest the object or action to be named. It is capable of contributing to the magical effect of writing. See the examples below.

HYATT Regency: *Feel the HYATT touch.*

Digital Globalsoft: *Where the similarities end, the value differential begins.*

Digital GlobalSoft: When the similarities end, the value differential begins.

Alliteration

It is a figure of speech in which consonants, especially at the beginning of words or stress syllables, are repeated. Alliteration and rhyme are the most favourite figures of speech of the copywriter and he/she uses them lavishly to create an impression of his/her slogan on the reader's memory. By doing so, he/she draws the attention of the reader quite effectively to the product. Here's one of the oldest example: "Vini Vidi Vici" Julius Caeser (I came, I saw, I conquered).

Rhyme

There is an echo in a rhyme and so it is a source of aesthetic satisfaction. There is pleasure in the sound itself and in the coincidence of sounds, and this pleasure must be associated with the sense of music, of rhythmic and beat; the pulse sense which is common to all human beings. Rhyme is a rhythmical device for intensifying the meaning as well as for 'binding' the slogan together. Advertising men have discovered that rhyme, especially phrases tied together with rhyme, can be very effectively used in their slogans. The baseline for Park Avenue products, "A quest for the best," gives an example of a rhyme. It is a short and crisp slogan for an effective impact. Usually a copywriter makes use of a rhyme in the headline as it helps to catch the attention of the readers and thereby arouse their interest. As the first element of the ad, most of the readers do not fail to read it. It is also observed that the copywriter makes use of old songs to make them a basis of writing an ad. They create more impact and are easy to memorize.

Sansui: Good example of rhyme.

Allusion

It is usually an implicit reference, perhaps to another work of literature or art, to a person or an event. It is often a kind of appeal to the reader to share some experience with the writer. An allusion may enrich the work by association and give it depth. When using allusions, a writer tends to assure an established literary tradition, a tradition and an ability on the part of the audience to 'pick up' the reference. A copywriter makes use of an allusion with the point of view of expressiveness with economy. Sometimes the brand name itself is an allusion as in the case of Hotel Taj and Hotel Ashoka, where the name evokes all the splendour, grandeur and luxury of the royal courts.

McDonald ad: Use of allusion.

The above ad of **McDonald** uses the popular equation of energy from school science and relates it with the logo of the brand name. Topical allusions are also the copywriters' favourite. They exploit the latest interest of the reading public and use it as a theme in their ads.

Parallelism

This refers to a very common device consisting of phrases or sentences of similar constriction and meaning placed side by side, balancing each other. This is one of the figures of speech which a copywriter uses without hesitation. Parallelism is the opposite of deviation. In a deviation, there are aberrations from normal usage, while by use of parallelism, language is organized in a regular pattern. In rhyme and alliteration, there is a phonological parallelism where there is repetition of sound patterns. In syntactic parallelism, there is a repetition of sound structures which makes language neatly organized. To a copywriter, parallelism is a technique to enhance the memorability of his message. Parallelism may be either syntactic repetition of structure or verbal repetition. A syntactic parallelism may establish a relationship of similarity or of contrast (anti-thesis). Some examples of parallelism are given below:

Ford Ikon: *Go green, Go Ford.*

Coca-Cola: *Always the real thing, always Coca-Cola.*

Air India: *Take a big holiday on a small budget. (Contrasting Parallelism)*

Mercedes Benz: *Sometimes, the "other woman" is not a woman at all.*

Benz: Sometimes the "other woman" is not a woman at all.

We may point out that what was considered to be advertisers in full measure are now using the preserve of imaginative literature. The great diversity in the exploitation of the communication potential of language is really remarkable in the language of advertising.

LINGUISTIC DEVIATIONS

It is not very uncommon in our daily life to come across situations wherein we mean to say something and end up conveying something else. In advertising world also, it is the same story. The only difference is that here advertisers try to take advantage of this ambiguity in the name of creativity. But why would anyone try anything unless he/she has been appreciated for the same thing before? Linguistic deviations have been used very effectively in advertising and it is very important that we know about ins and outs of this aspect of advertising.

It is the copywriter who is assigned the task of composing the textual part of an advertisement in congruence with the professional involved with the illustration part. The copywriters are well known for playing with words and manipulating or distorting their everyday meaning. Catching the attention and imagination of the readers and aiding the memory are perhaps the primary functions of the advertising language. Advertising language, where creativity is of the utmost significance, gives the copywriter a license to deviate from the traditional rules and conventions just as a poet takes liberties with the language on in order to enrich his/her expression. An advertisement should not only given information about the product but also incite curiosity, create understanding, build conviction and develop the urge to investigate. The copywriters have come in for a certain amount of criticism from grammarians and others who want the rules of English grammar to be followed strictly in all writings intended for reading by the general public. Most copywriters are good writers and know the rules of grammar. Occasionally, however, writing and grammar rules are broken deliberately for better effect, in the same manner as poets break rules to achieve their effect.

The task of the copywriter is more challenging, as he/she knows nothing about the receiver's frame of mind. Also it is very difficult to code one message that suits the diverse needs and choices of different individuals. It is neither accurate nor representative of the actual overall effect. In his/her writings, the copywriter, therefore, adheres strictly to some of the rules of grammar. Other rules, which he/her implements, are especially adapted to the writing of advertising copy in order to achieve the first aim of an advertisement, that is, to catch the attention of his/her reader. The different kinds of deviations are phonological, graphological, grammatical, lexical, semantic and typographical. A system analysis and classification of these deviations in the language of advertising are discussed further.

Phonological Deviations

Advertising language does not give much scope for phonological deviations. It takes into consideration only those advertisements where the pronunciation of words is different from the accepted pronunciation. For example, in the advertisement for Lakme Mascara, the product promises **EYE-MANCIPATION for the today's girl**. Here the pronunciation of initial phoneme /i/ has been changed to the diphthong /ai/. The deviant spelling and pronunciation is for the purpose of highlighting the target of the product–the eye. See the ad of Mother Dairy on the next page which reads 'Very thundamental Funda!'

Mother Dairy: Phonological deviation.

See the ad below. The brandname **COINTREAU** is joined with 'versial' to be read as 'CONTROVERSIAL' just to catch attention. Similarly, *Hole of fame* (in place of 'hall of fame') is used in the ad of Polo.

Cointreau: Catching attention.

Polo: Playing with pronunciation.

The word "Fast" in **fast aid** (*Dettol*) is pronounced as 'first' and water relief (*Cello* water bottles) is pronounced as 'what a relief' (from heat). *Volvo*'s ReVOLVOlution is taken as revolution.

Graphological Deviations

These violations are more frequent in advertising than in any other register. The copywriter can make almost unlimited use of change in spelling keeping the pronunciation intact. For example, in *Cadbury's* KRISP brandname, the initial consonant of "CRISP", is phonologically and graphologically similar to that of the manufacturer's brandname, which has been changed for the sake of originality in spelling. Similarly, in the barndname 'electron', the consonant 'c' of the word 'electron' has been replaced by 'k'.

The use of lower case letters where upper case is normally used is another orthographic device to draw immediate attention of the reader.

Some examples of graphological deviations found in the advertising language are as follows:

Uncertain-tea to safe-tea. General Insurance Corp of India.

Just Fa-bulous! Fa-Soap.

Creating a new gold'smyth -Alapatt fashion jewellery.

Krack Foot Cream.

Tata Fone.

Kurl-on.

Servo Kool

Grammatical Deviations

It has been found that in most of the advertisements, there is deviation from the normal system of rules in using the language for writing the advertisement. This deviation can be explained in terms of rule omission or suspension, rule change or rule addition. Some examples of this deviation are given below:

VIP skybags: *It speaks the world of you.*

Maurya Sheraton Hotel: *The finest technologists put their heads together. So yours can rest easier.*

BPL TV and Video: *Unmatched picture quality.*

Nivea: Nivea Sun. For when there is'nt any.

Foursquare Cigarette: *Live life king-size. Foursquare kings–all the taste, all the way.*

Liberal use of disjunctive grammar is made where minor and non-finite clauses are independent. Geoffrey Leech says, "Disjunctive language is primarily associated with headlines, subheads and signature lines" (Leech 1966). Some of the examples of disjunctive grammar from advertisements are:

Philips sound system: *Because it speaks the language of excellence you understand.*

Promise tooth paste: *Tackling the germs that attack and cause bad breath.*

Amul Milk Powder: *With Amul Milk Powder, you have pure, rich, creamy milk mixed and ready in minutes.*

Moderana seating system: *Designed ergonomically for maximum comfort.*

In subheads, disjunctive grammar is much more infrequently employed. Sometimes subheads carry on disjunctive language the message of the headline. For example, Kissan's Tomato Chilly sauce's headline, *"a wicked chilly woos the luscious tomato" is continued in the subhead as "And irresistible things begin to happen."*

Likewise, the signature lines very often make use of disjunctive grammar as shown in the examples given below:

Today: A *woman's very personal contraceptive.*

Farex-veg: A *tastier way to grow.*

Nivea: *Soft, gentle skin care for every age.*

Yamaha: An *international favourite.*

In all the above-mentioned examples, the name of the product is followed by one of its most inviting qualities, the purpose apparently being to associate the name with a tag line which can be easily remembered.

Lexical Deviations

Copywriters take unlimited advantage of lexical deviations for their creative copy as this constitutes one of the richest sources of new expressions for them. The three types of lexical deviations, which are observed in advertisements are:

(a) Functional conversion
(b) Neologisms and nonce-formations
(c) Anomalous lexical collocation

Functional conversion

It is also known as 'zero affixation'. According to Geoffery Leech, "It consists in adapting an item to a new grammatical function" (1969). Since the order of words in a sentence is more or less fixed, functional shifts within the sentence do not endanger intelligibility greatly. When one part of speech operates as another part of speech, the language acquires fresh vitality and variety. A few examples of functional conversion as observed in a few advertisements are as follows:

Less oil is more health	(n-adj)
Queen-size	(n-adj)
In an international blister packing	(n-adj)
Perfectly partnered	(n-verb)
Have you gold spotted today	(n-verb)

Adjectives posses a dominant position in the vocabulary of advertising. So a copywriter formulates new epithets by his/her imagination. These are the multiple hyphenated adjectival groups which are placed before headwords. Some examples are given here:

Rallifan: *Built-in*

Optrex eye lotion: *Refreshed-in-a-minute*

Neologisms

Here the copywriters share with poets the prerogative to coin new words, most of which remain nonce words, made up for a few occasions, and unabsorbed by the standard language. So these neologisms widen the possibility of expression. These are formed by compounding, affixation, composition or derivation. A few examples are cited below under each category.

Compounding:	**Brandname**
Glycerin-rich	Pears
Once in a lifetime	LIC
Wholly owned	Thai
Skin care	Lakme
Tea times	Marie
Liril freshness	Liril
Fast-working	Anacin
Affixation:	
De-laminate	Bhutan board
Pre-lubricated	Yamaha
Non-stick	Khaitan Press
Adjectival derivatives:	
Munchy	Biscuits
Zing thing	Gold-spot
Lime n lemoni	Limca

Anomalous lexical collocation

When a copywriter is in search of a striking new adjective or a noun, anomalous lexical collocation comes to his/her aid. This deviation consists of an unrestricted choice of nouns where only a noun from a limited list of nouns is normally used. The deviation which occurs is in contrast to the expected occurrence. A few examples follow:

Limca: *Love appears at thirst site.*

Thirst appears in the place of first.

Cinkara: *Jo Peeta Wohi Sikandar.*

Peeta appears in place of *Jeeta.*

Semantic Deviations

Illogical, unqualified comparatives and role borrowing are few of the techniques of semantic deviation used by a copywriter. To quote Geoffery Leech, it is "a piece of language at odds with the immediate situation in which it occurs" (1966).

Some examples are given below:

Lipton: A *flavour that's pure Darjeeling.*

Brookebond: *Help yourself with some happiness.*

Halo shampoo: *Halo spells beauty all the world over.*

Unqualified comparatives

These are the comparative adjectives with nothing in the contact—either in the text or in the visual layout to compare them with. This is done in order to show the superiority of the product. A few examples are given below:

Promise toothpaste: *Healthier teeth and gums.*

Diamond super: *Longer life.*

Promise toothpaste: *Fresher breath.*

Role borrowing

In this deviation, the linguistic features of one role are employed in another. A few examples of role borrowing are as follows:

Hotshot: *Just aim and shoot.*

Bisleri: *Its slim neck provides truly admirable singing support by allowing for maneuverability in your mouth.*

Typographical Deviations

This discussion would not be complete without a reference to the departure from the usual way or using the fonts in print. To draw the attention of readers, the copywriters have devised a number of methods to present the printed matter. In this section, let us briefly look at this device.

The type of font used in advertisements plays a significant role. A study is made to know the calligraphic designs.

Calligraphic designs

It has been observed that font in advertisement plays a significant role. The dictionary meaning of calligraphy is "the art of beautiful handwriting/handwriting in general". We also presume that such a definition involves the intricacies which play a significant role.

Veja: Magic with varied fonts.

Font

With the advent of word-processing, many and varied fonts are available for use to the innovative copywriters. Ranging from the Anglo-Saxon period to the most modern computer age, these fonts come in quite unpredictable shapes and sizes. Their use and the resulting effect is interesting to observe and study.

The direction of slope of font attracts attention. For example, in general, a right sloping font is more comfortable with right hand people and the left sloping one is popular with the gauche. The kind of font used, in terms of the configuration of the letters and their protrusions, fluidity of motion, etc., are key factors that convey the user's attitude and value to the observer. Old fonts like the Gothic font and the old English font denote dainty, staid behaviour and faithfulness. Fonts without the frills denote a forthright intention and formality. Convoluted fonts denote complexity of thought and mystique iconoclasm. Modern fonts like the lettering in LCD displays hint at a taste not unlike distilled water-purely functional in nature but without much aesthetics.

See the ad below, for example, in two different fonts. One has its baseline in italics and the other one in regular font. Which one looks more emphatic?

Multiple font usage

The idea is to signify diversity and also to convey the view that the product/service is tailored to suit the needs of everyone. The technique is to combine the latest miscible fonts and format them by reducing or enlarging font size adding the magic touch of a generous splash of colour. *Softel* ice cream caused ripples when they put out their ADD FIZZ and cream to your corporate gifts advertisement using this concept. It boosted the image of the product and its use.

By using different fonts, it can be proved that a rather uninteresting and hard selling product could be turned into a chart topper. Tremendous potential lies in the deviations made use of here.

Softel: The same ad with different font styles.

Innerletter spacing

Though compromised with justifiable excuse of economy, and rarely paid serious attention to, the spacing between letters is of great subconscious importance. Well-spaced lettering shows generosity, abundance, surfeited ideas and sense of security and establishment. Cramped letters, on the other hand, display ill planning somewhere. A classic example of the complete exploitation of this concept is found in the **Wrangler Jeans** ad featuring a man with a horse. The spacing goes very well with the product advertised.

Word orientation

See the ad of Coca-Cola on the next page. The orientation of the words is such that it clearly depicts the mood of the person in the ad.

Coca-Cola: *It's not because of a woman. It's because of 11 men.*

Thus we see that the linguistic deviation at different levels is one of the most frequently used devices to meet the demands of a specific situation. There is a great deal of diversity and what we have touched upon in this Chapter simply provides a sample of the use of this important method of attracting the attention of the readers. Coupled with the linguistic deviation is typographical deviation, which we have referred to in the discussion above and also given a few examples for illustration.

Coca Cola: Creating impact with font style.

SUMMARY

In any advertisement, language plays a pivotal role. Though it is said that a picture is worth thousand words, it is not true in advertising as it fails to convey the meaning in isolation sans language. It is here that the role of copywriter becomes very important. A copywriter has the job of writing the advertisements in the newspaper, magazines, billboards, radio, television commercials and also for the Web. The role of a copywriter is very challenging because of the ever-increasing competition. To make the product superior than others he/she has to take full liberty with the language. He/she has to create excitement and unprecedented sales for the company.

After making the survey about the product and the psychology of the target audience, a copywriter he gets into copywriting. To lure the potential customer, copywriters use the rhetorical language. Rhetorical language is helpful in persuading the audience as it has several devices. Some such devices which the figurative language of advertising uses and shares with poetry are rhyme, alliteration, simile, metaphor, parallelism, etc. Of course, it has been observed that there is great diversity in the exploitation of the communication potential of language in advertising.

A copywriter also has license to deviate from the traditional rules and conventions of the language in order to enrich expression. He/she has the prerogative to be away from the criticism of grammarians. Occasionally, rules of writing and grammar are broken deliberately for better effect, in the same manner as the poets break rules to achieve their effect. The different kinds of deviations are phonological, graphological, grammatical, semantic and typographical. With the help of these deviations, copywriters make the text exciting and alluring.

QUESTIONS

1. Pick up ten advertisements at random. Study them carefully and analyse them in terms of the language and picture. Which one is the most important? Give reasons.
2. What is the job of a copywriter? What is the groundwork copywriters have to indulge in before they write an advertisement?
3. What are the skills and abilities possessed by a copywriter? Does a copywriter require formal training to acquire these abilities?
4. What are the weasel claims? Illustrate each one of them.
5. What do you understand by the term rhetorical devices? Why do copywriters use rhetorical devices in advertising? Give examples of metaphors in advertising.
6. Deviations are very common in advertising copy. Why does a copywriter take liberty to deviate from the normal pattern of language? Give examples of disjunctive grammar.
7. In an advertisement, which part is more important–headline or the signature line? What is the role of each in an advertisement?
8. Look at the advertisement given below. Interpret its meaning based on the font used.

CHAPTER 10

Layout of Advertising

LEARNING OBJECTIVES

After reading this chapter, you will be able to:

- Highlight the importance of print advertising.
- Know the prerequisite steps before making an ad campaign.
- Discuss in detail the various components of the print advertising.
- Compare different types of layout.
- Discuss the rule of thumb for the use of font, boxes and colours.

In advertising, the term *media* refers to communication vehicles such as newspapers, magazines, radio, television, billboards, direct mail, and the Internet. Advertisers use media to convey commercial messages to their target audience, and the media depend, to varying degrees, on advertising revenues to cover the cost of their operations. The media are usually classified into either **mass** or **niche** media. Newspapers, magazines, television and radio are considered mass media because they deliver messages to a widespread, anonymous audience. The wide coverage of the mass media makes them ideal vehicles for advertisers who need to reach a large audience. Advertising media such as cable television and direct mail are often viewed as "niche" media because they reach a narrowly defined audience with unique demographic characteristics or special interests.

Advertising in print media constitutes a major part of any advertising campaign. It is usually backed up by television ads and serves mainly as a reminder to the customers. While television ads are volatile and more expensive at the same time, print ads are relatively less expensive, and have a good reach. Moreover, ads in print media can be designed keeping in mind the kind of audience the magazine or newspaper is expected to be read by. Television ads, on the other hand, are universal and less plausible to be subjected to changes for different audiences. So a group of audiences watching an ad meant for a different group is bound to get bored. For example, ads meant for small kids are bound to bore the youth. So in more than one ways, print media has an upper hand in an advertising campaign and it is essential to know about all the technicalities involved in print advertising.

STEPS INVOLVED IN THE PREDESIGNING PHASE OF AN AD

1. *Decide on your communication objective.* The communication objective is the essence of a message. If you want to tell people not to drive fast because it is dangerous, then that is your communication objective. Though, perhaps, it is the most important step in the pre-design phase of an ad, it is also the one that most of the beginners tend to neglect. A precise and well-defined objective is crucial to a good ad. If your objective isn't right on, then everything that follows will be off as well.
2. *Decide on your target audience:* Who is your message intended for? If you are speaking to kids, then your language and arguments should have the lingo and mood of the kids. On the other hand, if you are speaking to high-income earners (for example, writing an ad to dissuade people from wearing fur coats), then your language should be sophisticated. So define who your target audience is because that will decide how your message is conveyed.
3. *Decide on your format:* Is it going to be a poster, a half-page magazine ad or a tiny box in the corner of a newspaper? Make this decision based on the target audience you're trying to reach and the amount of money you can afford to spend. If you're talking to

kids, posters in one high school wall will not only cost less but will actually reach more of your target audience than a full-page ad in the biggest paper in town. When it comes to deciding on the size of an ad, more the size, the more expensive it will be to produce and run. Don't let that discourage you. You can do a lot with a small ad as long as it is strong, clear and properly targeted.

4. *Develop your concept:* The concept is the underlying creative idea that drives your message. Even in a big ad campaign, the concept will typically remain the same from one ad to another, and from one medium to another. Only the execution of that concept will change. So, by developing a concept that is effective and powerful, you open the door to a number of very compelling ads. Therefore, take your time developing a concept that's strong.

   Now that we are done with the important steps in conceiving the idea of our ad, let us see the contents of an ad and learn how to develop them.

COMPONENTS OF A PRINT AD

The normal advertisement will have the following components but many a time, you will find slight variation. The reasons are obvious—to be different in the crowd, the advertisement is designed with anomalies.

1. Visual
2. Headline
3. Copy
4. Slogan
5. Logo

Visual

Though you don't absolutely require a visual, it will help draw attention to your ad. Research indicates that 70% of people will only look at the visual in an ad, whereas only 30% will read the headline. So if you use a visual, then you are already talking to twice as many people as you otherwise might. Another suggestion is to use photographs instead of illustrations whenever possible. People tend to relate to realistic photographs more easily than unrealistic ones. But whether you choose a photograph or an illustration, the most important criterion is that image should be as interesting as possible.

See the ad for Calvin Klein below. It uses a very attractive visual and that is all. The ad is for spectacles and the copy has only one line: 'eyewear'. But the visual itself is so impressive that the creator didn't feel the need for more text, lest it might dilute the effect of the visual.

Calvin Klein: Visual impact.

Headline

Headline is the first component of the advertisement. Let the name of the product be used in the headline for better recall value. The most important thing to remember here is that your headline must be short, snappy and must touch the people who read it. Your headline must influence the readers emotionally, by making them laugh, angry, curious or think. If you can't think of a headline that does one of these four things, then keep thinking. Here's a little tip that might help. Try to find an insight or inner truth to the message that you're trying to convey, something that readers will easily relate to and be touched by. "Will India's power needs be met by wind or water?" Ask IDFC. This is an example of a headline which makes an average reader curious to go further. From that inner truth, you might arrive at the headline– "Do unto others as you would have them do unto you". Of course, the headline doesn't have to be biblical, though that in itself will add meaning and power for many people. Finally, whenever possible, avoid a headline longer than fifteen words. People just don't read as much as they used to. It has been observed that the most commonly used words in the headlines are exceptionally, exorbitant, new improved, revolutionary, never before, introducing, at least, just arrived, etc.

Types of headlines

The headlines are used with variations depending on the advertising strategy. The basic aim of a headline is to present the big idea succinctly. These headlines can be classified according to the type of information they convey. They are *benefit, information, provocative, humour, question and command headlines.*

Benefit headline promises the audience that by using the product or service advertised, they will be certainly gaining experience. It need not have pun in it and should give a simple statement about product's benefit. For example, "Italian elegance and style–experience in our business class the 'made in Italy' lifestyle" promises the audience a new experience. Another example is a Clearsil ad which says, " If you do not get the pimple free skin in 5 days, take your money back". Both of these headlines highlight the benefits of using the product and not the features of the product.

Information headline informs the reader about the unknown fact or announces a news. The information must be credible, though. " For the Elevators. For the Escalators. For the Corporate. Ladder that suddenly seems to be child's play", the headline for Digjam Suitings and "This IT staff is armed and ready" for Microsoft are the appropriate examples of this category.

Copywriters use **provocative headline** mainly to provoke the readers' curiosity by roiling their thought process. For example, the headline for Philips TV "You'll never go back to ordinary TV" will make you curious to learn more about the product by reading the body copy. Sometimes the reader is lazy not to go further to read the body copy. In that case, let your visual be vivid and clear so that it can provide story appeal.

Number plate : Inscribed to evoke smile.

Humour headline is used in order to give the reader the light moments. "Penis mightier than sword" was written in this way to evoke humour. The *Amul* butter ad uses pun in the headline to sprinkle humour lavishly.

A **question headline** encourages the readers by asking question so that they can search for the answer in the body copy. This is a very good strategy to enthrall the reader. "Can you spot 14 servers in this picture?" the headline for IBM piques the curiosity of the readers. But if the headline asks a question, which readers can quickly answer in negative, it will not get attention. For example, in case of the headline "Are you looking for a better Kitchen," reader might say "No" and turn the page.

A **command headline** orders the reader in a way that might seem negative and impossible. This is a very good technique to have reader's attention. " Cut costs. Replace your inkjet printer (Xerox)" is an appropriate example of a command headline. Sometimes the headlines are combined to achieve a better impact. It is important how the headline is used and not which type has been used.

Copy

This is second major category which constitutes the text of an ad. Here's where you make the case. If you have compelling arguments, make them. If you have persuasive facts, state them. But don't overwhelm the ad with information. Two strong arguments will make more of an impression than a dozen weaker ones. Finally, be clear, precise and honest. Any hint of deception will instantly detract from your entire message.

The importance of body copy varies according to the nature of the advertisement. It states the sales message, develops argument, gives proof and provides explanation. Sometimes it is continuation of the headline while other time, it relates to the visual to get across the point. Some people think body copy is simply a waste as no one reads it but this is not necessarily true in all situations. The decision of the number of words to be used depends on the type of product advertised. For example, Nike shoes advertisement does not use long body copy while the advertisement for car will have a long body copy as it ought to have technical details for the serious buyers.

Styles

Like the headline, body copy also has different styles. **Straight-line copy** is continuation from the headline and is written in the words of an anonymous or unacknowledged source. **Narrative copy,** on the other hand, is used to tell a story in first or third person. It persuades the same selling point in different context. This is ideal for a copywriter as he/she creates a situation and then at the climax, resolves it by using the product or service being advertised. In most of the insurance company ads, this strategy is used. **Dialogue** lets the reader listen to the conversation of the characters that are in the ad. This makes the advertisement more believable as the characters portrayed in the print ad speak from their own experience. The copywriter though should be extra cautious for not making the dialogues dull and drab. Explanation gives the details how the things work and what are the precautions observed while using the product.

Picture and caption copy banks on the illustration and picture to communicate the message. It is particularly useful when the product has multifarious variety and varied uses.

Lakme: An effective body copy.

Bajaj Pulsar: Smooth blend of copy with illustration.

The *Lakme* and *Bajaj Pulsar* ads shown here use the 'copy' to drive the idea home. The visuals are smoothly blended with the pictures. So an effective and interesting copy is a must whether you have a good visual or not to support it.

Slogan

The other name for slogan is **theme line** or **tagline**. It sums up the advertisement. Slogans are equally important as the headline as it is not only used for advertising but for salespeople and the company employees. It is the component of the ad which has maximum recall value. Coca Cola kept its slogan 'Always Coca Cola' for several years but has changed it now. Can you recollect these slogans: 'The new sign of success', 'Think different', 'Everyone is invited', 'City never sleeps' and 'Don't leave home without it'.

Logos

Logo is symbolic representation of a company. It can be picture, letter or combination of both. Sometimes its significance is so much that the advertisers relies on the logo completely. The

Airtel logo can be recollected by anyone because of its colour and fonts. Before designing a logo, lot of research is done as it should be of profound significance. While designing the logos, the researchers take a decision if they have to use just the picture, fonts, human beings, colours or the combination of all. The logo of Pepsi given on the previous page has changed a great deal since 1898.

THE LAYOUT

There are many possible layouts and we will see the most prominent one among them. First let us highlight some general and basic tips while deciding on the layout. Your visual, headline and copy might be really good on their own when viewed or read separately, but what is the effect they are carrying when they are all put together. So enough hard work is to be done so that we have a very good overall effect.

Since many more people will look at your visual than read your copy, make your photograph or illustration at least half of your ad whenever possible. Keep your headline near the visual so that the reader's eye will flow to it naturally from the visual. If your headline is in an unusual place, it will probably never be read. Position your copy beneath the headline, laid out in two blocks two or three inches in length. Only about 5% of people will read your copy, whereas 30% will read your headline. By positioning your copy near your heading, you create a visual continuity, which will draw more people to the information you want to convey. Use a serif typeface for your copy whenever possible. Those little lines and swiggles on the letters make the reading easier and more pleasing to the eye.

Layout Stages

While designing an advertisement, the final development undergoes four stages. The designer uses thumbnails, roughs, dummies and comprehensives to establish the ad look and feel. In the next stage, he/she works in tandem with the artist to prepare mechanical, which is the final phase incorporating the visuals.

Thumbnail sketch

This is the first stage where the artist uses the rapidly produced sketches to visualize the very basic approach to position the various elements of ad. The objects are represented with boxes or squiggly lines to indicate the placement. From here, they are then developed to the next stage.

Rough layout

In this stage, the artist draws the actual size of the ad but ignores the details. It is used to make the decision. It is more like visualization which suggests the place of headline. Illustration and photographs are sketched and body copy place is finalized. Roughs are shown to the clients for cost estimation.

Comprehensive

The comprehensive layout or comp in short is the replica of the advertisement. It is quite elaborate with accuracy of the final ad, coloured photo and a glossy look. Comprehensive layouts are used for a formal presentation by the clients when they need a close-to-final version to show to persons who have to give the final approval. Art directors create a **dummy**, a mock-up for brochures, flyers and point-of-purchase displays serving the same functions as comp serves for print ads.

Mechanical

Once the ad is approved by the clients for the format and contents, the art director moves ahead with mechanical. This is the final stage of the ad where the ad is reproduced and colour keys, prints and films of the finished ad are created. The mechanical is referred to as paste-up as earlier in absence of computers, the ad was manually pasted indicating the hue and positioning of colour. Now this is done on computer.

At this time, the ad is ready for the production. Anytime during the designing process, before the final ink is put, the changes can be made. Some concepts of the print ad can be applied to television advertisement but with some modification.

Alignment

It refers to lining up the top, bottom, sides, middle of text or graphic elements on a page. Horizontal alignment includes flush-left (also called left-justified or ragged right), flush-right (also called right-justified or ragged left), centred and fully justified. With vertical alignment, elements can be aligned vertically–top, bottom or middle (centre).

Balance

It is a principle of design that places elements on the page so that the text and graphic elements are evenly distributed. In layouts with an even balance, the graphics don't overpower the text and the page doesn't seem to tilt to one side or the other.

Ragged alignment

Ragged alignment of text normally refers to lines of text that are allowed to end naturally, leaving varying amounts of white space at the end of lines rather than forcing it to line up flush with the margin. Ragged right is the most common ragged alignment.

Bleed

When an image or element on a page touches the edge of the page leaving no margin, that image or element is said to bleed off the page.

Park Avenue: an example of bleed.

Bleed allowance

To allow for any deviations in cutting the paper to the finished page size, an element that bleeds off the page is typically extended about 1/8" beyond the trim lines (corner or crop marks). The inset image (Park Avenue ad) shows the bleed allowance for this two page spread. Notice that the full page bleed extends beyond the corner marks at the top, bottom, and left but not the center. But the problem arises is that for the elements that bleed off the page can sometimes add to the cost of printing if the printer uses a larger size of paper to accommodate the bleed allowance.

Caption

It is a phrase, sentence or short paragraph describing the contents of an illustration such as a photograph or chart. The illustration on the next page shows a few ways that captions might appear.

Significance of captions

After headlines and graphics, captions are the third most looked at portion of most of the printed pages. Captions give you an opportunity not only to explain the illustration but to

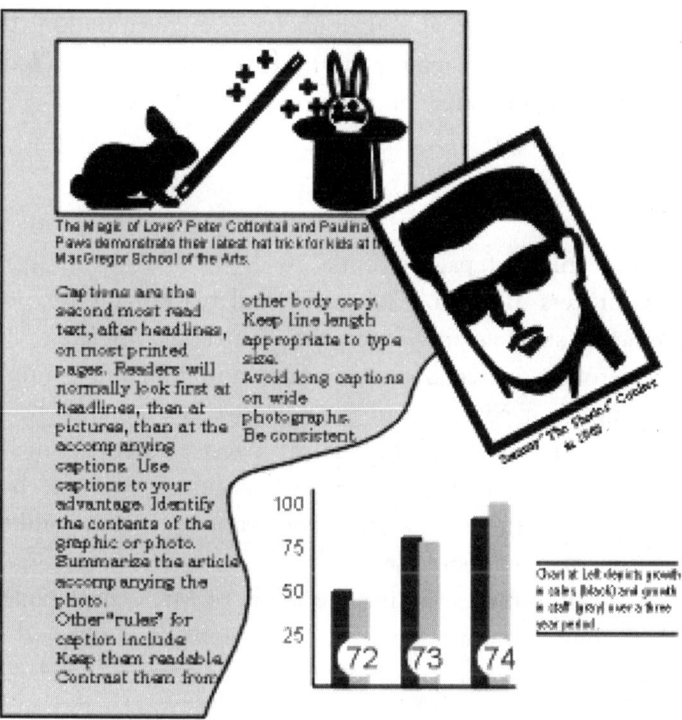

summarize the story or article they accompany. A well-written caption gives the editor/publisher one more opportunity to pull the reader into the publication.

A few ways to make captions more readable and to keep them from being mistaken for body copy are as follows:

- Use contrast (smaller typeface, sans serif captions with serif body copy, short centred captions, captions in colour)
- Set apart with spacing (keep separate from body copy but close to illustration, use rule lines to separate, place captions in margins)
- Group illustrations and captions (number the illustrations or provide a familiar pattern such as "left to right" or "clockwise from the top")
- Keep it short (edit carefully, avoid long captions under wide paragraphs, if very long captions with very wide photographs is necessary consider using two columns with a sufficiently wide gutter for the caption text)
- Be consistent (same type, colour, alignment, etc. throughout a publication)

If you have lots of copy, break it up with interesting subheads. This will make your ad more inviting, more organized and easier to read. This is where the name of the organization belongs, along with the address and phone number. If you don't have an organization, then think of a name that will help reinforce the message you're trying to convey. This isn't dishonest. Your organization doesn't have to be incorporated or registered for it to be real.

Types of Layouts

First, let us understand the meaning of page layout.

Page layout (*verb*) is the process of placing, arranging and rearranging text and graphics on the page to produce documents such as newsletters, brochures, books, etc.

Page layout (*noun*) refers to the actual document page and its composition.

One method of making sure your ad gets read is to arrange elements in the order from top to bottom. However, your ad should also lead with its strongest element. Sometimes the visual may be secondary to the headline. In that case, you may decide to put the headline first. A caption may not be necessary at all times and often you want to include additional elements such as secondary illustrations or a coupon box.

Perhaps, we just cannot do without mentioning the name of Mr. Ogilvy while talking of any aspect of advertising. He had come out with some basic variations of a standard layout. We will have a look at them with examples and then see other technical aspects of layout and design. While this isn't the only way to design an ad, it is an easy way to implement successful formula for many types of products or services.

Layout#1

This is the basic design that follows the same 5 elements outlined below. From this basic layout, other variations are derived.

1. **Visual** should at the top of the page. If you are using a photo, bleed it to the edge of the page or ad space.
2. For photos, place a descriptive **caption** below.
3. Put your **headline** next.
4. Follow with your **main ad copy**. Consider a drop cap as a lead-in.
5. Place your contact information (**signature**) in the lower right corner. That's generally the last place a reader's eye gravitates to when reading an ad.

Layout#2

This is the basic Ogilvy design but with copy in a three-column format and the addition of a coupon. Coupons attract attention and can increase response to your ad. It includes the following steps:

1. **Visual** should at the top of the page.
2. **Place the Caption** below the photo.
3. **Put the Headline** next.
4. Place **main ad copy** in first two columns of a three-column grid. Place your contact information **(signature)** at the bottom of the middle column.
5. In the third column put a **coupon**. Placing the coupon in the outside corner of your ad makes it easier to clip out.

Layout#3

This is the basic Ogilvy design but with copy in a two-column format and the headline moved above the visual. Use this variation when the headline is the most important element of the message. It has the following steps:

1. Put the **headline** first. When your headline packs a bigger punch or is more important than the photo, put it at the top to grab the reader's attention first.
2. Place the **visual** next.
3. Place the **caption** below photo.
4. Place the **main ad copy** in two columns.
5. Place your contact information **(signature)** at the bottom of the second column in the lower right corner

Layout#4

This is the basic Ogilvy design but with copy in a two-column format and the headline moved to the right side of the visual. This format equalizes the visual and headline as well as making more room for longer headlines or vertical images. It has the following steps:

Some visuals and headlines might benefit from a side-by-side treatment

Put your logo, business name, and contact information here.

1. Place the **Visual** first to the left. If the visual lends itself to a more vertical arrangement or if you want to equalize the importance of the visual and headline, try this.
2. Place the **headline** next to the right of the visual. When you break your headline up into several lines like this, you'll probably want to avoid headlines that are too long.
3. Put the **caption** below the photo.
4. Place the **main ad copy** in two columns. You might want to use a drop cap as a lead-in.
5. Place your contact information (**signature**) at the bottom of the second column in the lower right corner.

SOME MISTAKES TO AVOID

The most common mistake committed in designing an ad is visual clutter. Less is always better than more. So if you're not certain whether something is worth including, then leave it out. If your ad is chaotic, people will simply turn the page, and your message will never be read. The second most common mistake committed is to have an ad that's unclear or not easily understood (haven't you ever looked at an ad and wondered what it was for?). The best way to safeguard against this is to do some rough sketches of your visual with the headline and show it around. If people aren't clear about your message, then it's probably because your message is unclear. However tempting your ad looks, don't argue with them or assume that they're wrong and your ad is fine. You'll be in an unpleasant surprise. Proofread your ad, then give it to others to proofread, then proofread it again. Typographical errors diminish your credibility and have an uncanny habit of creeping into ads when you least expect it.

BE DIFFERENT

Use different fonts and sizes only to make it stand out in the crowd. Have a look at the ad below and then compare it with the advertisement that follows.

Custom Eyewear

by

Elegant Eyes

in Candel Centre
2540 Palm Dr.
Ste. 78-A
555-2368
by appointment only
featuring

Perilli Marsh Shades
CoolColorTM Contacts
Precious Metal Frames

Probably a reader would look twice at this ad. Sure we have a little contrast with that reversed headline, but other than this it says just, ignore me. Small space ads need to grab attention. Now look at the advertisement below.

Isn't it that nice script face a more *elegant* and appropriate choice? The two tone frame overlapped by the graphic lends a slightly 3D effect to the ad – helping it to grab attention on a crowded page.

While the vertical arrangement works for some ads, in our Elegant Eyes ad (above) we lose vital information in those monotonous lines of small centred text. Both size and placement help direct the reader to the most important information and organize the ad. Here are some ways we accomplish in our makeover ad:

- Placing the descriptions of the brand name sunglasses, coloured contacts and special frames directly below the 'custom eyewear' (and near the top of the ad) shows exactly what type of product is being offered.
- Emphasis on 'by appointment only' conveys an 'exclusive and uptown' image (as well as provides critical information to would-be-drop-in patrons).

The typeface choices and emphasis on elegance better conveys the upscale image of this business, attracting their target audience. The correct typeface choice can make or break an ad. In the yellow pages ad, the typefaces are not necessarily inappropriate for the business but the multiple styles and lack of clear contrast make the ad look disorganized and amateurish.

Following the Reader's Eye

Because of conditioning received during your early school years, you're used to see a printed page in a certain way. Typically, a reader views a page from the upper left to the lower right. Consider the ad of CompuBurger Software. The ad is well laid out, allowing the reader's eye to start where it would naturally fall on the page, and from there, provides a path to follow through to the bottom.

CompuBurger Software: Following the reader's eye.

This rule changes a bit, however, if an ad comprises more than just one page. When you see an ad that is a two-page spread, for instance, your eye will usually first see the information on the right-hand page. Check out the ad for DaVinci Coachworks, a two-page spread. These types of ads are best laid out using different rules from their one-page counterparts. Here, the tag line and the product (limousines) were deliberately placed on the right side of the ad and the reader's eye follows it off to the left. Similarly, as you flip through a magazine, note how your eye will generally first focus on the right side of any spread. Now you might look at the center-fold in India Today in a more matured way.

Maintaining Spread Consistency

The trick to maintain consistency over a two-page spread is to forget that there are two pages. Treat the spread as if it were a single full page. If you don't do this, you could end up with two single pages that might look fine on their own, but which work against each other when forming a spread. Again, avoid these problems by assuming that the spread is actually one complete page rather than "two single pages put together".

The Direction of Your Images

Which direction your image faces may play a role in how your reader sees your layout. Look at the layout below. Notice that the person in the picture is facing away from the rest of the layout, the reader's eye is drawn away from the main message–the eye follows the player's gaze upwards into the basketball and then off the page.

Correct this by simply flipping the picture around, and having the basketball player face the other direction–towards the page, as in the ad below . Now, the reader sees what the basketball player sees–the main article. A reader's eye, while tending to follow a fairly obvious trail from the upper left to lower right of a page, can be distracted and take a detour by the power of a graphic facing the wrong direction.

Boxes, Rules and Fonts

Shaping text boxes

It is easy to get carried away with all sorts of goofy-shaped text boxes. Use these box shapes at your discretion, but be careful not to get too "cute". Different shaped boxes can get old very quickly and make your page difficult to read. If you are going to use an odd-shaped box, consider whether or not you have sacrificed readability for creativity. The ad below shows that when the custom box is too constraining, it becomes a bit harder to read.

Try to use shaped boxes for copy when the shape serves a specific purpose. In the ad below, the shape of the box helps to mould the overall message of the page and becomes part of the design.

Using horizontal rules

Deciding on the best length for your rules can often be more of a creativity issue that can really enhance the look and feel of your layout. Although tastes will always differ, you'll probably find more success if your rule lengths are deliberately set to work with each other or with other parts of your page—not randomly or haphazardly sized.

For example, the ad on the left side below shows two places where horizontal rules are used under the headline and above the product name. In both the areas, the rules seem to be of random length and are not placed in conjunction with anything else on the page. They don't necessarily detract from the page, but they're not adding much, either. The ad on the right side

shows the same page with both the horizontal rules constrained to the body of text; this not only helps to separate off the central portion, but also adds a decorative addition to the layout.

Too many fonts

One of the detriments of having so many fonts on the market is that when they're in the hands of over-zealous designers, there can be an explosion of bad taste. As the newsletter cover below demonstrates, when too many fonts are added to the mix, attention can be drawn to different styles, detracting from the underlying message. As a general rule, try to avoid using more than three fonts on any page or spread. This will help keep the focus on the message and off the design.

The importance of white space

There is something to be said about the power of white space. White space is simply an area or areas on your piece in which there is no type or image–the page is left blank. White space can draw attention to an area or relieve tension from crowded area. Check out the original brochure page on the extreme left. It's very crowded and cramped. Not only is it tough to find the message, but also it's difficult to just look at it.

Adding white space to this image, however, can improve the overall appearance. The brochure page in the centre has kept the basic layout the same, but has added white space around many of the elements. This gives the headlines, body copy and images some breathing room, and a chance for the reader's eye to focus more clearly on the topic at hand.

The brouchure page on the extreme right uses significantly more white space to bring emphasized attention to each subhead that appears in the body copy. The bottom line: The entire page is now far more legible, all as a result of a little more white space.

Cancer campaign: Judicious use of white space.

SUMMARY

The print advertising constitutes major part of any advertising campaign. Before designing any advertisement, the advertisers identify the following steps:

- Decide on your communication objectives
- Decide on your target audience
- Decide on your format
- Develop your concept

An advertisement constitutes of the visual, headlines, body copy, slogan/signature line and logo. While selecting the visual, you have to choose the picture carefully. The size of picture should be in consonance with the complete layout. It has been found that 70% people just look at the visual and 30% will read the headline. You can communicate only with the visual if required. Headline is the first written component of an ad, therefore, should be succinct and catchy. There are various types of headlines like benefit, information, provocative, humour, question and command headlines. Choose the one according to the type of product and the audience to which the ad caters to. The copy is the next text of ad. Put the strong argument clearly, precisely and honestly. The importance of body copy varies according the nature of advertisement.

Like headlines, they also have different writing styles. Straight line copy, narrative copy, dialogue, picture and caption copy are some significant style of the copywriting. Slogans sum up the advertisement and the other name for slogan is theme line or tagline. Logo is the symbolic representation of the company which can be picture, words or combination of both. There are many possible layouts. One should be chosen which can create the maximum impact. The layout stages begin with thumbnail sketches, then the rough layout, comprehensive, dummy and mechanical. Alignment refers to the lining up from all the sides. It can be balance, ragged, bleed, bleed allowance, etc. Even for the layout, different options are available. Five types of outline are discussed in this chapter.

Avoid writing too much clutter in an advertisement. The power of white space is immense as white space can draw attention to an area or relieve tension from crowded area.

QUESTIONS

1. What are the prerequisite steps for making an ad campaign? Do you think that the audience for which the ad is targeted can make any impact on the decision?
2. How is visual important for an advertisement? Give two examples of the ads where there is no body copy.
3. What type of headline will best suit the baby food? Give reasons to support your argument.
4. Humour plays a vital role in advertising. Give some examples to corroborate your answer.
5. What are different styles of writing a body copy? Enumerate all the styles with suitable examples.
6. How does a different stage of layout lead to make an effective print advertisement? What are the first and last stages? What do you understand by roughs?
7. Design an advertisement for sunglasses with centre alignment. Choose the brand name also.
8. What is the importance of white space in an advertisement? If it is so important, then why do all advertisements not rely completely on white space?

9. What is appealing in the advertisement of *Ariel* below?

Part Four

Advertising Media

C H A P T E R 11

Print Media

LEARNING OBJECTIVES

After reading this chapter, you will be able to:

- Understand the concept of advertising media.
- Understand the characteristics of press.
- Know various categories of print media and understand how newspapers influence the masses.
- Understand and recognize the advantages and disadvantages of newspaper advertising.
- Know the impact of advertising in magazines and its pros and cons.
- Understand how Yellow Pages and direct mail advertising work.
- Know and understand outdoor and transit advertising.

CASE STUDY: BASS ATTACKS

Rusty Johnson has had a lifelong love for fishing of all types. He has been on the ocean, numerous lakes and streams, and occasionally, he has made trips to small ponds in the area just to catch small catfish. Having made a fairly significant amount of money in his real estate career, Rusty is looking for a new challenge. He decided to manufacture and sell bass fishing boats in the lake Ponchartrain area of Louisiana.

Fishing in southern Louisiana takes two forms. First, some anglers like going into the swamps and bayous to get near underwater foliage, where some kind of bass crappie hide. Others enjoy getting out on the larger lake, using radar equipment to identify bigger fish resting in the deeper and cooler areas of water in the summertime.

The swamp fisherman requires a maneuverable boat with a small hull, so it does not get hung or scratched in the shallow waters. The large lake fisherman wants more stability and a larger boat to negotiate waves in the deeper open areas. Both wanted a boat that made it easy to pull fish in, with a live well holding tank. Other accessories could then be added depending on the tastes of the fishermen.

Rusty created two kinds of boats in response to the marketplace. He designed the first, the Bass Attack Prowler, for smaller spaces. He named the larger boat the Bass Attack Mastercraft, figuring that Bass Attack sounded quite a bit like Bass Tracker, the leader in the field. He also believed that the name was unique enough for the seasoned fishermen who would know the difference.

As the company completed the development of a manufacturing site and production of the initial run of boats, it was time to advertise. Rusty knew the real estate advertising market quite well, but he did not feel confident about reaching the fishermen. He faced the problem of geographic dispersion. Beyond the locals in the area, bass fishermen were spread out through the entire state of Louisiana and across the country. They came from a wide variety of backgrounds—some wealthy, some quite poor. Rusty's goal was to get some of the locals to consider his boat instead of the higher-priced, better known model offered by Bass Tracker.

In the first year of operation, Rusty's company budgeted $200,000 for local advertising and more for "want ads" in some large outlets such as Internet sites, fishing magazines, and possibly, some travel magazines or newspapers. He also considered billboards and other low-cost possibilities. He knew he had a quality product. Now the goal was to get the word out and generate some sales.

1. Which media should Bass Attack use? Which media should the company eliminate and why?
2. For each of the following media, identify four specific outlets that Bass Attack could use for advertising. For instance, for magazines, a logical outlet would be *Field and Stream;* for television, *ESPN Fishing shows.*
   (a) Magazines
   (b) Radio
   (c) Television
   (d) Internet
3. What kind of ad do you think will be successful for this company? Defend your answer.

ADVERTISING MEDIA

Regardless of how well-designed and appropriate a particular advertisement is, its success is continuously dependent upon whether it is transmitted through the best media, given a particular target market. Selecting the appropriate media, or combination of media, is an extremely complex process. It involves the development of a comprehensive media plan that attempts to match the advertisement and the target consumer with the appropriate media mix and media schedule. Media planners must possess a great deal of knowledge in order to successfully develop the media plan. First, they must have a thorough understanding of the workings of all the media relevant to their particular situations. This includes the capabilities, limitations, trends, and terminology associated with each medium. Second, they must be familiar with the components that constitute a media plan. This involves the factors such as selecting media objectives, evaluating media in terms of target market characteristics and timing media, to name a few.

In this chapter, we will discuss various types of print media available for the media planners and how they can be effectively used. We will also deal with the hoarding and transit advertising.

CHARACTERISTICS OF THE PRESS

The power and dominance of the press is explained by the following special characteristics.

In-depth coverage and permanence

Both radio and television are ephemeral and usually brief, but newspapers and magazines can provide detailed reports that can be read, re-read and retained, if required. This is true even though the life of a city newspaper may be only a few hours, but many publications survive for some time, and items can be cut out and kept. Magazines have a large pass-on readership and are read almost everywhere.

Variety of subjects covered

Newspapers represent class-political, religious, ethnic and language groups. Magazines represent every sort of special interest. This is perhaps where the press best demonstrates its strength because by selecting the right journals, it is possible to reach particular and well-defined sections of the reading public. This cannot be done with mass media like radio and TV.

Mobility

Newspapers and magazines can be carried and read almost anywhere, for example in the house, while travelling, at the place of work, in a waiting room or a library.

Results assessable

By using coupons and by the traditional use of 'keys' or codes (which identify from which publication the coupon was clipped), it is possible to measure the pulling power and cost-effectiveness of different journals. Evaluation is possible by dividing the cost of space by the number of replies received.

Statistics available

In industrialized countries, and increasingly in others, net sales are audited and readerships are researched so that a wealth of statistical information about a large number of newspapers and magazines exists. The media planner can confront the media salesman with computer calculations to justify his/her media schedule of recommended space and airtime bookings.

Improved printing

The majority of newspapers and magazines are printed offset-litho. Picture quality, even in black and white, is nowadays very good since the dot screen used in offset-litho is usually nearly twice as fine as that formerly used for letterpress printing. Magazines printed in offset-litho are usually better printed than those produced by photogravure, halftones being produced more sharply and the paper being better finished.

CATEGORIES OF PRESS

Newspapers

During the past few decades, the newspaper industry has had to cope with an avalanche of change. The emergence of radio and television, restructuring of magazines as a result of the growth of special interest publications, dramatic growth of community newspapers, inserts, shoppers and total market coverage publications.

Despite the increasing changes that newspapers will have to go through in order to survive, they remain an important advertising vehicle. Daily and Sunday newspapers account for approximately 30 per cent of total advertising expenditure, four-fifths of which come directly or indirectly from the retailers.

Newspapers have a high level of credibility. Readers rely on newspapers for factual information in stories giving newspapers great credibility. Newspaper readers also hold high interest level in the articles they read. They tend to pay attention to advertisements as well as news stories. The increased audience's interest allows advertisers to provide a lot of copy detail in their ads. Newspaper readers take their own time to read a copy, unless simply too much information is jammed in a small space.

Newspaper advertisers receive volume discounts for buying large column inches of advertising space. Many newspapers grant these volume discounts, called *cumulative discounts*, over one-

month, three-month or even year-long time period. This potentially lowers the cost-per-exposure, because larger and repeated ads are more likely to garner the reader's attention.

Many local consumers rely heavily on newspaper advertising for information about grocery specials and other similar price discounts. Many local merchants use newspaper coupons. Newspapers also provide other special response features. For example, "Mention our ad in today's newspaper, and receive 10% off".

Kinds of newspaper advertising

One classification system based on the newspaper advertising rates separates advertising into the categories of classified, retail, national and reading notices.

Classified advertising

While classified advertising may be used by national or local advertisers, the bulk of the classified section of newspapers, referred to as **want ads,** is local in nature and placed by local firms or individuals. These ads are arranged by subject matter for the convenience of readers, and generally do not include headlines or illustrations. There is a form of classified advertising, known as **classified display,** which uses different type sizes, white space to attract attention and simple illustrations.

Retail advertising

As the name implies, retail advertising is placed by retail merchants and other local businessmen. Normally, it is of two types–**sales promotion advertising,** based on price features, sales or specials; and –**image advertising,** designed to position a retail store or business so that it appeals to a particular group of consumers. Retail advertising may be paid for entirely by the retailer or shared by a manufacturer. This latter form of advertising is also called **cooperative advertising.** It is run under the name of the local retailer in order to encourage retailer support and take advantage of local rates, which are lower than national advertising rates.

Nicholos sale: Sales promotion advertising.

National advertising

National advertising is used by manufacturers and producers to support their products. This advertising is part of the manufacturer's national advertising plan and is used to intensify coverage in a local area. National newspaper advertising is often used to introduce new products in test markets, assure widespread consumer recognition and aid in gaining retail distribution.

Reading notices

Reading notices are advertisements that are designed to resemble editorial material. They are charged at a higher rate than retail advertising. To prevent reading notices from being confused with news stories or editorial material, the word 'advertisement' must appear at the top of the notice.

Newspaper advertising rates

The major terms used to refer to newspaper advertising rates are flat, open, discount, short, combination, position charges, colour charges and split runs.

Flat rate

When the line rate is fixed, regardless of the volume of the advertising, it is designated as flat rate.

Open rate

If a newspaper offers discounts, the open rate is the price charged to advertisers who do not purchase a sufficient volume to qualify for a discount.

Discount

Many newspapers have established discount levels for advertisers who use an unusual amount of advertising space. While these discounts are initially negotiated, they become established, are published and are applied to any future advertisers offering a similar volume of linage. Discount practices vary significantly among newspapers. For example, while discounts on large purchases of advertising are commonplace, a number of newspapers offer no quantity discounts to national advertisers.

Short rate

When newspapers offer volume discounts, the advertisers estimate the amount of space that will be used during the next 12-month period and contracts for that amount at the discount earned, subject to the year-end adjustments.

Combination rate

Combination rates are discounts for advertising appearing in the morning and evening editions of the same newspaper, combining a weekday insertion with a Saturday or Sunday insertion, or advertising in more than one newspaper in a newspaper group. At one point, some newspaper policies forced advertisers to use the combination of insertions or newspapers. However, courts have ruled against this practice and such combinations are now optional.

Position charges

Advertisers may place their advertisements R.O.P. (Run of Paper). The R.O.P means that:

(a) The newspaper editor can place the advertisement anyplace; the advertiser has no control over where the advertisement will appear.

(b) The advertiser may specify a position on the page or within a particular section of the paper. Higher rates, depending on the newspaper involved and the nature of the preferred position, are generally charged for such preferred positions.

Colour charges

Normally, newspaper advertising appears in black and white. Colour advertising is available in many newspapers on a R.O.P. basis and can be used in any paper through the use of preprinted inserts. The R.O.P. colour does not provide dependable quality because of high-speed presses, porous paper stock, and problems of off-register reproduction. (Off-register is a term used to describe a situation in which colours overlap and demarcations between the colours are not clear). For this reason, the R.O.P. colour is used sparingly for making ads distinctive with bold backgrounds, designs or colour headlines. When the R.O.P. colour is used, there is an extra charge, and newspapers usually have the minimum space requirement.

Split runs

Many newspapers offer split runs at a slight extra charge. The simplest form of split run is when an advertiser prepares two ads of the same size differing in headline, illustration, coupon value or even product. The plate for one ad is put on one press and that for another ad is put on another press. Both presses feed alternatively into a common stacking of newspapers so that the two ads appear in the alternate copies of the newspaper.

Advantages of newspapers

1. Newspapers are flexible in the following ways:
   (i) Space for advertising ranging from one inch to multiple pages can be used.
   (ii) Advertisements can be scheduled on any day of the week.

(iii) The closing dates are short, so ads may be prepared on extremely short notice.
(iv) Provide geographical flexibility, allowing the advertisers to pinpoint their advertising pressure in terms of their advertising needs.

2. Advertising is relatively cheap as compared to other media on cost per thousand basis.
3. Newspapers are excellent vehicles for cooperative tie-ins.
4. They have high reader interest and broad coverage reaching 80 per cent of the adults.

Disadvantages of newspapers

1. Do not provide audience selectivity except on a geographical basis.
2. Their high waste circulation makes them too expensive to use on a national basis.
3. The life of a newspaper is short, i.e. unlikely to be put aside and read later like magazines.
4. They have poor colour reproduction and the inability to use fine artwork.
5. They have competition from retail advertising, which often distracts the readership of national ads.

Magazines

The glamour of television has overshadowed magazines for a long time. For many advertisers, magazines have always been a second choice. Recent research, however, indicates that in some cases, magazines are actually a better option than television. A study by the A.C. Neilson Company revealed that people who viewed ads in magazines were 2 per cent to 37 per cent more likely to purchase the product then the people who viewed the ads in TV.

Also, a study by Millward Brown, examining the cost effectiveness of magazine advertising, revealed promising information for magazines. The study suggested that magazine advertising is three times more effective than television advertising.

A major advantage of magazines is the high level of market segmentation available. Magazines are highly segmented by topic area. Specialized magazines are much more common than general magazines with broad readerships. Even within certain market segments such as automobiles, a number of magazines exist. Magazines are so highly differentiated that high audience interest becomes another advantage. People reading magazines also tend to view and pay attention to advertisements related to their needs and wants. Often, readers linger over an ad for a longer period of time, because they read magazines in waiting situations or during leisure time. This high level of interest, segmentation and differentiation are ideal for products with precisely defined target markets.

Carstar: An ad clipping from a magazine.

Magazines, both trade and business journals, are a major medium for business to business marketing. Businesses can target their advertisements. The copy provides a great level of detail about products. Readers, if interested, take time to read the information in an ad. Ads can provide toll-free telephone numbers and web addresses, so the interested parties can obtain further information.

Magazines offer high-quality colour and sophisticated production processes, providing the creative team with the opportunity to produce intriguing and exciting advertisements. Motion,

Benetton: Albanian refugees escaping from danger.

colour and unusual images can be used to attract attention. Magazines such as *Glamour, Elle and Cosmopolitan* use scratch and sniff ads to entice women to notice the fragrance of a perfume or cologne. Even car manufacturers have ventured into this type of advertising by producing a piece of leather in certain ads.

Magazines have a long advertising life, lasting beyond the immediate issue because subscribers read and reread them. This means that the same advertisement is often read by more than one person. It is not unusual for an avid magazine reader to examine a particular issue several times and spend considerable amount of time with each issue. This appeal is attractive to advertisers because they know the reader will be exposed more than once and likely will pay more attention to the ad. In addition, magazine ads last beyond the current issue. Weeks and even months later, other individuals may look at the magazine. In the business-to-business sector, trade journals are often passed around to several individuals or members of the buying centre. As long as the magazine lasts, the advertisement is still there to be viewed.

Advantages of magazines

1. Magazines can be selected to appeal to a variety of temperaments.
2. Have high quality reproduction on paper enabling the use of unusual space units so that interesting effects and high impact can be achieved.
3. Exposure life is long as they have pass-along readership.
4. Lend prestige to their products because of the education and relatively affluence of magazine readers.

Disadvantages of magazines

1. They have lack of penetration, thus selectivity of the medium is lost.
2. It is generally difficult to advertising pressure geographically with magazines.
3. Closing dates are often two or three months prior to the date of issue, thus precluding moving quickly to take advantage of market opportunities.
4. The production costs for magazines are relatively high because of high quality colour in production.

DIRECTORY ADVERTISING

Directories are a useful form of advertising for consumer product companies with limited distribution and industrial firms that market industrial supplies and equipment. Directory advertising may consist merely of the name of a firm or product, along with an address and/ or telephone number; or it may consist of display advertising. There are an infinite number of local, regional and national directories, ranging from industrial buying guides to the classified,

Yellow Pages of the telephone book. From the standpoint of consumer use, the best known directory is the Yellow Pages book.

Yellow Pages Advertising

The Yellow Pages book is the one constant in print advertising. If you need to find out who does what in a particular product or service category, the Yellow Pages book provides a listing and phone numbers of those companies that offer that product or service. But not too much information should be crammed into Yellow Pages as it won't attract people's attention.

Unlike other forms of print advertising, Yellow Pages advertising is sold on an annual basis. A basic one-line listing comes with your business telephone service. You can upgrade that listing and purchase a variety of ad sizes, ranging from just setting your listing in boldface type to a large full-page advertisement. You might add a second colour to emphasize a logo, graphic or line of type.

The cost for advertising in the Yellow Pages, obviously, depends upon the type of listing or advertising space you contract for as well as the circulation size of the book you will be listed in. A large metropolitan Yellow Pages book commands a much higher rate per ad than does a small-town book.

When considering Yellow Pages advertising and the type of listing or ad you want to have, remember that the competition will be brutal among some types of popular businesses–beauty salons, for instance.

You can support your Yellow Pages listing or ad with other types of advertising media. One small telecommunication firm, for example, supported its one-line Yellow Pages listing with image advertising. The basic premise to their strategy was that it was alright if people threw away their direct mail flyers without ordering a product or service. What counted was name recognition. When the time did come and the consumers were looking through the Yellow Pages for a telecommunication company, they would, at least, remember the name of the firm. The awareness factor would give the company an edge against the competition.

DIRECT MAIL ADVERTISING

Another major advertising medium is direct mail. Many companies send ads directly to target markets of consumers through mailing lists or blanket a region for more general products. Wal-Mart, Kmart, Target, Sears and other major retail chains often send advertisements to consumers through mail. Credit card companies are notorious for sending out enticements to apply for their cards, especially to lower-income families and college students. Major restaurant chains (Pizza hut, KFC, etc.) also mail directly to potential buyers. These firms mail free samples, coupons, and other special features to potential customers on a daily basis.

The major advantage of direct mail is that it normally lands in the hands of the person who opens the mail, who usually makes a significant amount of family purchasing decisions. Many mail offers include direct-response programmes, so results are quickly measured. Direct mail can also be targeted to geographic market segments.

The primary disadvantage of direct mail includes cost, clutter and the nuisance factor. To be noticed, direct mail advertising usually requires a colour brochure, making the mailing quite expensive to produce. As postage rates continue to rise, so do costs of direct mail. Mailings tend to clutter post office boxes and become more prevalent during key seasons such as Diwali, Christmas, Id, etc. Many people are genuinely annoyed by "junk mail" and actively seek to have their names taken off the mailing lists, especially for catalogue type operations.

Some people find direct mail to be the least "reputable" form of advertising, because many mail-fraud scams have arisen in the past few decades. Direct mail best suits well-known local or national firms seeking a more immediate response (e.g. coupon redemption) or when the company wants to reinforce ads presented in other media. Direct mail reaches some customers who do not buy newspapers. Record clubs, book clubs, and others have used direct mail effectively over the years. It is likely that many firms will continue to use the mail in the future.

Direct mail remains a favourite marketing tool for business-to-business marketers. It provides a method of bypassing gatekeepers when the names of actual members of the buying centre can be obtained. Direct mail can be one method of reaching businesses when they are in a rebuy situation and open to calls by salespeople. Even if the direct mail is ignored when it is received, many people often file it away for future use. Although the cost per contact is high for direct mail, so is the response rate as compared to other media. The key to success for businesses is to make sure that the direct-mail piece gets into the hands of the right person in the buying centre and is attractive enough to grab attention.

OUTDOOR ADVERTISING

Outdoor advertising is the oldest established form of advertising, and evidence of its use has been found on Greek and Roman remains. This is not surprising because even in those days public announcements had to be made, and a wall was as good a place as any on which to carve a message. One of the earliest forms of outdoor advertising was the inn sign which has remained in use to the present day. It is believed that the spread of the Great Fire of London in 1666 was assisted by the wooden signs which reached across the narrow streets of the City from one building to another.

In the 1930s, the well-designed posters on the hoardings were nicknamed the "poor man's art gallery". Among the wonderful "art gallery" posters of the 1930s were those of Pears Soap, especially the one of a filthy tramp writing a letter, the opening words being "Since using your soap, I have used no other". There was a man in blue pyjamas astride a large jar of *Bovril* which was floating on the sea, and the message was "*Bovril* prevents that sinking feeling". Cigarette posters often had beautiful sunset screens. Humour and artistry were characteristics of those posters sixty years ago. Today, they seem to depend on clever wordplay and the oblique attempts by one advertiser to avoid encouraging people to smoke!

Billboards along major roads are the most common form of outdoor advertising. Billboards, however, are only one form of outdoor advertising. Signs on cabs, buses, park benches and sports arenas are other types of outdoor advertising. Some would argue that even a blimp flying over a major sporting event is a form of outdoor advertising.

Outdoor advertising has changed its image from "booze and butts" advertising to a legitimate medium over the past few decades. Earlier outdoor advertising mainly constituted of tobacco and alcohol. However, it has changed over the period of time. Today outdoor advertising is for varied products, ranging from soap and shampoos to jewellery and mobile phones.

Currently, retailers account for approximately 10 per cent of outdoor advertising and media outlets for another 8 per cent. Other ads feature upcoming movies, video stores, broadcast television networks, newspapers and radio stations. Other fast growing outdoor programmes are from the fashion industry. The Gap, DKNY, Calvin Klein and Ralph Lauren regularly buy outdoor space.

One primary advantage of billboard advertising is its long life. For local companies, billboards are an excellent advertising medium because the message is seen only by local

Eton Thames: An attractive billboard.

audience. Local services like restaurants, universities, hotels, resorts, service stations, and amusement parks are heavy users of billboards. Billboards provide an effective way to communicate a firm's location to travellers. Individuals who want to eat at a particular restaurant while on the road can normally spot a billboard for that restaurant.

In terms of cost per impression, outdoor advertising is a low-cost media outlet. Outdoor advertising also offers a broad reach and a high level of frequency if multiple billboards are purchased. Every person who travels by a billboard has the potential of being exposed to the message. Many companies using billboards provide "rotation" packages in which an ad moves to different locations throughout a town during the course of the year, thereby increasing the reach of the ad.

Billboard ads can be large and spectacular, making them major attention-getting devices. A billboard's large size creates the impression that the product and the message are important. Movement and lighting can add to the attention-capturing qualities of a billboard.

A major drawback of outdoor advertising is the short exposure time. Drivers must pay attention to the traffic as they speed by an outdoor ad. Most either ignore billboards or give them a brief glance. Ironically, in large cities, along major arteries the cost of billboard spots is increasing. The reason: traffic jams. People stuck in slow moving traffic spend more time looking at billboards. If this space is not available, a firm can seek billboard locations where traffic stops for signals or at stop signs.

Billboards provide limited opportunities for creativity. The short exposure time means the message must be extremely brief. People usually ignore a complicated or detailed message. Further, billboards offer limited segmentation opportunities because a wide variety of people may not view the billboard's message. To help overcome this problem, some companies use geodemographic software technologies to identify the profile of individuals who will pass by a billboard in a specific neighbourhood. Such an approach works well on local streets of cities and towns but is not very effective along major highways, with local and long distance traffic.

In the past, outdoor advertising was seldom considered in a media plan. Now, it is an additional tool to reach consumers. To illustrate, Procter & Gamble in as late as 1994 spent virtually no money on outdoor advertising; today, this budget is magnanimously high. Billboard ads can be combined with other advertising media to repeat and reinforce messages for audience.

TRANSIT ADVERTISING

Transit advertising consists of paper posters placed inside or on transit vehicles and in transit stations. Transit advertising is a healthy and growing medium. Under the impact of the energy crisis and the apparent need for more public transportation, the industry will probably continue to grow.

Types of Transit Advertising

The most common types of transit advertising are **car cards, exterior displays** and **station posters.**

Car cards

Car cards are used as interior displays in overhead racks and other locations in subway trains, buses, commuter trains and other rapid transit systems. The standard car card size is 11 inches high, with width of 28, 42 and 56 inches. "Square" cards, measuring 21 by 22 inches, are also used at the ends of rail transit vehicles, and miscellaneous sizes are available for special positions such as over doors.

Exterior Displays

Exterior displays are waterproof posters appearing on the outside buses and other transit vehicles. There are a number of standard sizes specified by the transport departments but there is no limit to creativity in these as can be seen from the transit advertisements given below:

Transit ads: Quite catchy.

Station Posters

Although smaller in size, station posters are similar to outdoor posters and are displayed on and in stations of subways, rapid transit systems and suburban railroads. Although similar to outdoor posters, they are sold by the same firm selling car cards because of which they are located. Since waiting passengers have more time to read advertising copy than drivers of cars, station posters often carry more copy than the larger outdoor posters.

Other forms of Transit Advertising

In addition to these common forms of transit advertising, there are also floor exhibits, diorama displays and clock spectaculars located in train and airline terminals. Even when these are on a smaller scale, they are usually custom designed for advertisers and similar to advertising spectaculars.

Strengths and Weaknesses of Transit Advertising

Transit advertising is selective only in a geographic sense. Since large number vehicles carry transit advertising in densely populated areas, it has a potential for broad reach in these markets. Transit advertising also offers high frequency because transit riders repeat their trips frequently. Its cost-per-thousand is extremely low.

On the negative side, transit advertising is limited to urban areas, and there is little validated information on its effectiveness. Essentially, it is a supplementary medium for national advertisers, although it may be used as the primary medium for local firms.

SUMMARY

To place an advertisement in the appropriate media is extremely important task. A media planner must possess a great deal of knowledge in order to successfully develop the media plan. Media planning includes the factors like media objective evaluating media in terms of target market characteristics and timings to place it.

It has been observed that press is very powerful in terms of coverage and permanence, mobility, picture quality and availability. Newspapers are the oldest media for advertising which has undergone lot of changes. There are different kinds of newspaper advertising, which includes classified, retail, national and reading notices. Newspaper advertising rates depend on several factors and are flat rate, open rate, discount, short rate, combination rate, position rate, colour charges and split runs. There are many advantages of newspaper advertising like flexibility, broad coverage and cheapness but then there are disadvantages too. The life of a newspaper is short, the print is not refined and then there is lot of competition.

Magazines, on the other hand, have better quality of printing, although the glamour of TV has overshadowed magazines for long time. Magazines have their own advantages and disadvantages. They have long exposure life and cater to the better audience as compared to newspaper. However, they have lack of penetration and production cost is very high. Directories are also useful form of advertising for consumer product companies with limited distribution and industrial firms that market industrial supplies and equipment. The best known directory is the Yellow Pages. Another major advertising medium is direct mail. The advantage of direct mail is that it normally reaches the person who takes significant amount of family purchasing decision. The primary disadvantage includes cost, clutter and nuisance factor. The outdoor advertising is the oldest established form of advertising. Billboard ads in cities are large and spectacular. They not only catch attention but also create impression. The last form of the advertising is transit advertising which consists of paper posters placed inside or on transit vehicles and the transit stations. The most common types of transit ads are car cards, extension displays and station posters.

QUESTIONS

1. What is the oldest form of print advertising? What was the impact of Guttenberg's press on print media?
2. What are the advantages of newspaper advertising over magazine advertising. For the institutional advertising, which media will you prefer and why?
3. How is the rate decided for advertising space in a newspaper? Would you use white space in your advertisement when you pay so heavily for the small space? Support your answer with appropriate examples.
4. What factors let you decide to place your advertisement in a magazine? Do you think if your product is a tennis ball, the right magazine to place the ad is SportStar? If yes, why and if no, then why not?
5. Few years back, a gruesome accident took place at the crossing of busy Hyderabad road. The reason for that was the placement of an obscene hoarding at the crossing. Do you blame the planners for such decision or is it the masses to be blamed?
6. What do you understand by transit advertising? Make a transit advertisement to propagate the cultural festival which is going to be organized in your institute the next month.
7. In which category, will you put the advertising which is done indirectly when you move wearing a T-shirt embossed with the name and logo of your institute? Is this a form of advertising?

CHAPTER 12

Television and Radio

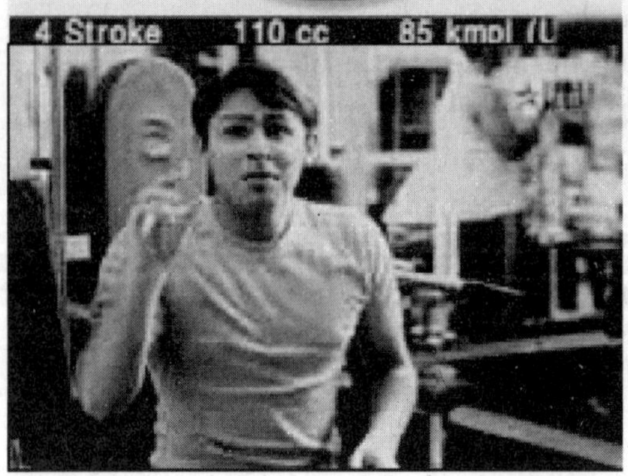

LEARNING OBJECTIVES

After reading this chapter, you will be able to:

- Understand the importance of television media over the other media for advertising.
- Understand the creative aspect in TV advertising because of sight and sound impact.
- Know the advantages and disadvantages of television advertising.
- Discuss different strategies to develop an effective advertising campaign for television.
- Know the growing importance of radio for advertising.
- Outline the pros and cons of radio advertising.

CASE STUDY: CAUTIONARY POSITION

What is mineral water all about? Well, about a germ-free, safe offering. And what happens when a brand that has become generic to mineral water in India wants to drive a subtle message? Well, it is bound to be noticed. In fact, *Bisleri's* latest 45-seconder (with an edited 30-second) gives the concept of safety a new, subtle, yet playful, twist.

The film opens with a couple sitting on a beach around a bonfire. The girl gives a 'come hither' look, suddenly gets up and runs off with the guy in hot pursuit. She then collapses on the sand, a la Hindi film song. The guy follows, trying to kiss her, panting excitedly. Very romantic, very passionate, very heated up. Just then she demurs and whispers something in his ear which sends him rushing back to the bonfire, to look through the bags and the car. Has he got the safe formula? Very progressive. But no, he hasn't got it. So, he zooms off to the nearest 24-hour chemist (where else?). The boy makes a desperate request to the chemist. The chemist's wife gives the boy a coy, knowing smile. The chemist returns with a huge carton (!) and hands it to the boy. Back at the beach, he rips open the carton to reveal... 500-ml *Bisleri* bottles. The girl glugs down the water, almost in ecstasy, as the boy watches her, comically. Then comes the caption: 'play safe'.

The commercial was specifically created by Ambience D'arcy for the 500-ml pack which Parle Bisleri Ltd claims is a hit with the younger generation. As Mohana Mogre, Brand Manager, Parle Bisleri Ltd, elaborates, "We wanted to communicate with the young audience of the MTV and Channel (V) kind. This category prefers to be daring, adventurous and sportive." The spot, which costs around Rs. 30 lakhs to make, has been conceived by Elsie Nanji and directed by White Light Productions. It is being aired on various channels like Sony, ETC, the Star channels, Channel [V], Zee News, Alpha Marathi, Sun TV and others.

Will the light-hearted approach compromise *Bisleri's* image of reliability? Mogre feels that the ad is in sync with the brand proposition of 'pure and safe'. Which is why it is being aired with *Bisleri's* other spots. In fact, *Bisleri* can probably talk about health issues, beyond just clean water. After all, health is not just about safe water, but also safe sex. So, however comical the setting, the ad is dead serious in its message. The ad does manage to do its bit for responsibility and for the cause of safe living. *Bisleri* being *Bisleri*, will still be taken seriously.

TELEVISION ADVERTISING

Television provides the ability to communicate sight, sound, motion and emotion. If a picture is worth a thousand words, a moving picture is worth ten thousand words. The viewer can instantly see the product, view it in a variety of situations, determine how it can be of benefit to their application and leave them with a lasting impression of the business.

Television gives a product a "larger than life" image and by virtue of being on television, it is sometimes enough to set a business apart from its competitors. Small businesses get benefitted from this immensely, and they can create an impression that they are a "big" company having their own television spot. This can be a great advantage for them when consumers are making their decisions about whom to do business with.

A dominant source of news is also, obviously, the best place for an ad-campaigner to place his/her ads for good *reach.* Despite a growing array of options, more people find out about what's happening in the world from television than from all other sources combined. Not only is TV the most dominant news source but also is considered to be the most credible news source. See Figure 12.1.

Advantages of Television Advertising

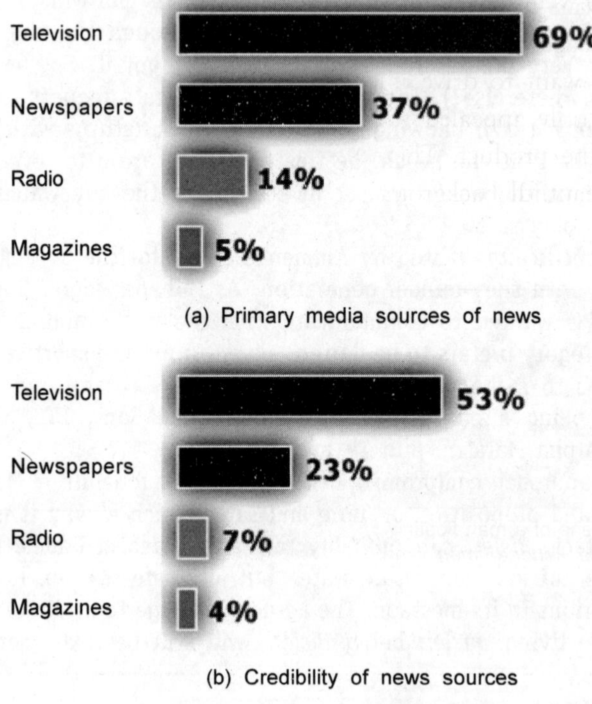

Figure 12.1

Television has numerous advantages over other media, which includes the following:

- creativity and impact
- coverage and cost-effectiveness
- captivity and attention
- selectivity and flexibility

Advertisers can generate trust, emotion and excitement that cannot be created as well through any other medium. This can help create a long lasting and memorable brand and corporate image.

Creativity and Impact

Perhaps the greatest advantage of TV is the opportunity it provides for presenting the advertising message. The interaction of sight and sound offers tremendous creative flexibility and makes possible dramatic, lifelike representations of production services. TV commercials can be used to convey a mood or image for a brand as well as to develop emotional or entertaining appeals that help make a dull product appear interesting.

Television is also an excellent medium for demonstrating a product or service. For example, print ads are effective for showing a car and communicating information regarding its features, but only TV commercial can put you in the driver's seat and give you the sense of actually driving the car. See the images of a TV ad of LML Freedom given below. The visuals are so impressive that one would want to drive it immediately. Had it been a print ad, on the other hand, the ad would have only appealed to the logical sense of the customer effectively about the advantages of buying the product. There would have been nothing like the video showing the vehicle in action in beautiful backgrounds, may be a beautiful girl could have been added for selling them.

LML Freedom Commercial.

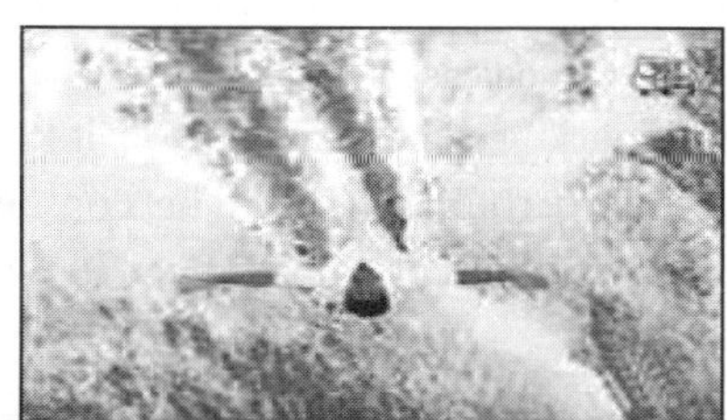

1. A scene of a man floating in the sea... *manzil se kehena, meri raha na...*

2. *... dekhe, mein na rukunga, mein azad hoon, plays in the background.*

3. Shots of a man riding a LML Freedom interspersed with ...

4 images of freedom. Birds flying away, kids jumping off a cliff...

5. MVO: LML Freedom...

6. *... azadi ka naya ahsas.*

Coverage and cost-effectiveness

Television advertising makes it possible to reach large audience. Nearly everyone, regardless of age, sex, income or educational level, watches TV at least for some time. Most people do so on a regular basis. Marketers selling products and services that appeal to broad target audience find that TV lets them reach mass markets, often very cost-effectively. Because of its ability to reach large audience in a cost-effective manner, TV is a popular medium among companies selling mass-consumption products. Companies with widespread distribution and availability of their products and services use TV to reach the mass market and deliver their advertising messages at a very low cost per thousand. Television has become indispensable to large consumer package-goods companies, carmakers and major retailers. Companies like Procter & Gamble and Coca-Cola spend more than 80% of their media-advertising budget on various forms of TV-network, spot, cable and syndicated programmes.

Captivity and attention

Television is basically intrusive in that commercials impose themselves on viewers as they watch their favourite programmes. Unless we make a special effort to avoid commercials, most of us are exposed to thousands of them each year. The increase in viewing options and the penetration of CD players, remote controls and other automatic devices have made it easier for TV viewers to avoid commercial messages. People learn through their senses. The combined power of sight, sound, motion and emotion creates a synergistic effect that is more effective than when individual senses are stimulated.

1. A driver walks up to a cleaner, as he starts his daily chore and asks, *"Yeh gaadi kaisi hai?"*

2. Pat comes the reply, *"Ae khajoor! Gaadi nahin* German *sher bol, haan! Kya* pick up. 0 to 60 in 4.89 seconds."

3. Other drivers crowd around and listen to his expert comments. *"Sadak par aati hai malai maar ke."*

4. The owner comes up from behind and listens to his cleaner singing his car's praises. Seeing him, our man grins sheepishly and steps back...

5. Super: 'Opel Corsa.' MVO adds, "Achtung Baby!" As the car smoothly glides out...

6. ...of the parking, one of the drivers muses to himself, *"Sahab ko bataana padega."*

Opel Corsa commercial.

1. A lady holds up a heart-shaped *jalebi* that she has just fried.

2. Her husband stares wide-eyed at the platter of heart-shaped *pakodas*.

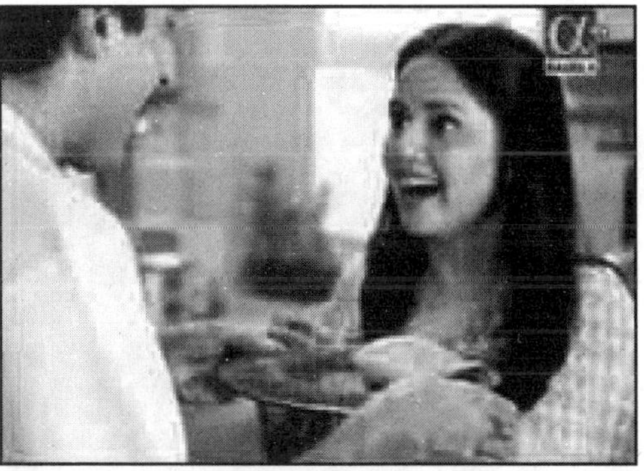

3. He then fries a heart-shaped *pakoda* and hands it over to her.

4 FVO: *Naya* Sundrop heart. *Isske rich* golden *tel main hai...*

5. ... nutrients *jo rakhe* cholesterol *ko kam aur hamare dilon ko swast...*

6. ... *hardam.* The healthyoil for healthy people.

Sundrop cooking oil commercial.

Above is a popular ad for cooking oil. The colours of the dishes, smiling faces, in short, the all-pervasive festive mood created in the house drives the ad home easily.

1. The shot of a deserted road seeped in darkness. A man negotiates his vehicle around the twists and rides along. The only illuminating beam...

2. ...is from the headlight. He comes to a screeching halt as he spots something in the middle of the road.

3. MVO: "Mr. Kumar has just discovered night vision on his new TVS Victor." The terrified rabbit scampers out of sight.

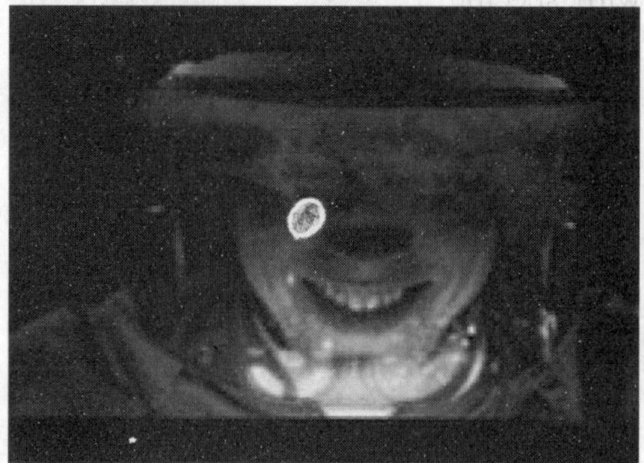

4. As a smile spreads across the young man's face, the MVO continues, "Mr. Rabbit just discovered its brakes."

5. Product window. Super: TVS Victor. Multi-reflector headlamp.

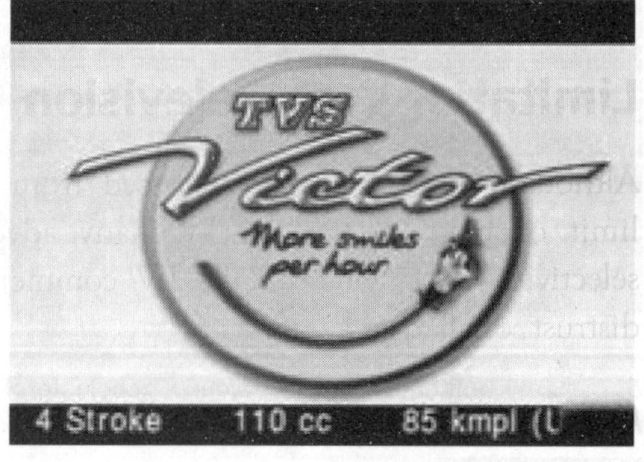

6. MVO: "New TVS Victor. More smiles per hour."

TVS Victor commercial.

What is more effective than actually showing the night-vision that the bike sports.

The low-involvement nature of consumer learning and response processes may mean TV ads have an impact on consumers simply through heavy repetition and exposure to catchy slogans and jingles.

Selectivity and flexibility

Television has often been criticized for being a non-selective medium, since it is difficult to reach a precisely-defined market segment through the use of TV advertising. But some selectivity is possible due to variations in the composition of audiences as a result of programme content, broadcast time and geographical coverage. For example, Sunday morning TV caters to children; Saturday and Sunday afternoon programmes are geared to sports-oriented male; and week-daytime shows appeal heavily to homemakers.

With the growth of cable TV, advertisers refine their coverage further by appealing to groups with specific interests such as sports, news, history, arts or music. Advertisers can also adjust their media strategies to take advantage of different geographic markets through local or spot ads in specific market areas. Ads can be scheduled to run repeatedly or to take advantage of special occasions. For example, companies such as Pepsi and LG are often major sponsors for cricket mega events, which allow advertising heavily. In short:

- Television has the highest daily and weekly reach among all the media.
- Television has an aura of importance. It is a prestigious medium, enhancing the advertisers' image by its use.
- Television appeals to the consumers' senses more than any other medium.
- Television can create a powerful and emotional impact.
- Television can create high impact with viewers by offering dynamic and visual messages.
- Television has power to create moods and images for brands.

Limitations of Television

Although television is unsurpassed from creative perspective, it has several disadvantages that limit or preclude its use by many advertisers. These problems include high cost, lack of selectivity, fleeting nature of TV commercial, commercial clutter, limited viewer attention and distrust of TV ads.

Costs

Despite the efficiency of TV in reaching large audience, it is an enormously expensive medium to advertise. The high cost of TV ads stems not only from the expense of buying airtime, but also from the cost of producing a quality commercial. More advertisers are using media-driven creative strategies that require production of a variety of commercials, which drive up their cost. Even local ads can be expensive to produce and often are not of high quality. The high cost of producing and airing commercials often price small- and medium-size advertisers out of the market.

Lack of selectivity

Some selectivity is available in television through variations in programmes and cable TV. But advertisers who are seeking a very specific, often small, target audience find the coverage of TV often extending beyond their market, thus reducing its cost-effectiveness. Geographic selectivity can be a problem for local advertisers such as retailers, since a station bases its rates on the total market area it reaches. Audience selectivity is improving as advertisers target certain groups of consumers through the type of programme or day and/or time they choose to advertise. However, TV still does not offer as much audience selectivity as radio, magazines, newspapers or direct mail for reaching precise segments of the market.

Fleeting message

Television commercials usually last only 30 seconds or less and leave nothing tangible for the viewer to examine or consider. Commercials have become considerably short as the demand for a limited amount of broadcast time has intensified and advertisers try to get more impressions from their media budgets.

The ad below comes hardly for 10 seconds. What effect can it have on a potential customer in that short period of time. At the most, it can inform the viewer that such a product exists. Is spending so much of money worth just this objective?

1. A shot of the Hindi movie *Rangeela*, where Aamir Khan creates a havoc in the theatre...

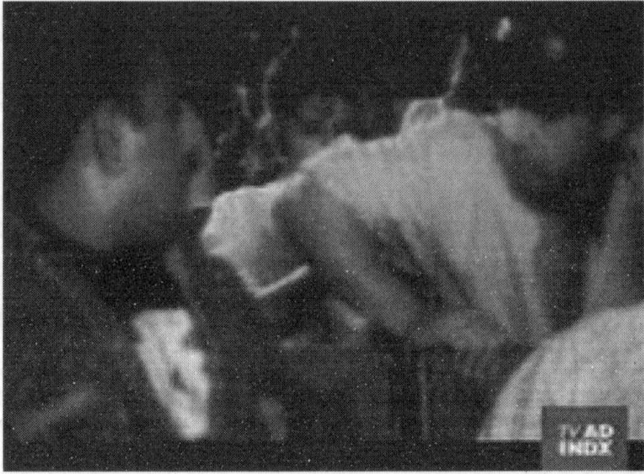

2. ...by getting into an argument with a man sitting in the front row.

3. Super: 'Why talk while watching movies?'

Nokia Mobile manners: A fleeting message.

4. Switch off your mobile phone at the movies. Nokia Mobile Manners.'

An important factor in the decline in the commercial length has been the spiralling inflation in media cost over the past decade. A 15-second spot typically sells for half the price of 30-second spot. By using 15- or even 10-second spots, advertisers think they can run additional spots to reinforce the message or reach a large audience. Many advertisers believe that short commercials can deliver a message just as effectively as long spots for much less money.

Clutter

The problems of fleeting messages and shorter commercials are compounded by the fact that since the advertiser's message is only one of many spots and other non-programming material seen during a commercial break, it may have trouble being noticed. One of the advertisers' greatest concerns with TV advertising is the potential decline in effectiveness because of such *clutter*.

Guy at gym gets all mushy and says, like a small bird tickles me and flies away.

This lady gushes she feels like bungee jumping into a river of chocolate.

This man mouths, like little bubblesof chocolate that burst and vanish.

MVO: Nayi Cadbury 5 Star. *Itni soft ki muh main ghul jaaye.*

Cadbury commercial: Creating clutter.

One cause of clutter is the use of short commercials and split-30s, 3-second spots, in which the advertiser promotes two different products with separate messages. The above ad is just a collection of three short scenes and such small ads, impressive nevertheless for products like chocolate, are primarily responsible for clutter. Clutter also results when the networks and individual stations run promotional announcements for their shows, make more time available for commercials and redistribute time to popular programmes.

Limited viewer attention

When advertisers buy time on a TV programme, they are not purchasing guaranteed exposure but rather the opportunity to communicate a message to large number of consumers. But there is increasing evidence that the size of the viewing audience shrinks during a commercial break. People leave the room to go to the bathroom or get something to eat or drink, or they are distracted in some way during commercials.

Getting consumers to pay attention to commercials has become a great challenge in recent years. The increased presence of remote controls has led to the problems of **zipping, zapping and grazing. Zipping** occurs when customers fast-forward through commercials as they play back a previously recorded programme. **Zapping** refers to changing channels to avoid commercials. **Grazing** is the use of remote control to scan number of channels in search of something interesting to watch. To tackle this problem, advertisers are using several new techniques like humour, suspense and excitement.

Deception in Television Advertising

When we examine television advertising, we once again find art and technology being used to create simulations that tell stories in an effort to evoke desired reaction from the audience. But in advertising, we see a strange new cultural creation—the 20-second "cinematic" production full of dancing, singing and joke-telling characters playing physicians, housewives and car salesmen, with ultra-abbreviated plots and quick resolutions of conflict in which the characters overcome obstacles and fulfil their desire in record time with the help of the product. Unlike movies, which will evoke the wrath of the audience if unfolding of the story is interrupted, in commercials, there is virtually no story to interrupt. The entire commercial is a dynamic and graphic field composed of images, music, theatrical performances, superimposed illustrations, narration and other elements, which reinforce each other to achieve their effect.

Like other complex simulations, these inventions of sound-bite television are typically made up of a great many individual forms of fakery and illusion. For example, they display products that are cosmetically altered to look more appealing to viewers. Raw turkeys are made to look baked and delicious with food colouring. Gelatin deserts are made denser than the real thing to look firm and symmetrical, while the sizzle of cooking food turns out to be a sound effect added during editing. These sensory deceptions are supplemented by exaggerated claims, to create a false identity for the product. Television commercials also include another kind of simulation in the form of digitally-manipulated images, which are used to portray another realm of fantasy in which the limits imposed by the physical world no longer seem to be in effect. As a result, they are full of talking dogs, children who grow to giant size, products that zoom into space, dancing credit cards and scenes that suddenly become two-dimensional screens, which spin out of existence, creating a virtual world that surpasses anything.

Television commercials take these three elements—visual fantasy, deceptive images of the products and false claims—and weave them into their various approaches. There are, perhaps, half a dozen kinds of approaches that they rely on and put together in different ways, just as the theme parks, video games, television and news fall into a few basic categories. Some present trivial product information as if it is of momentous importance. Others use glamour or sex, or try to evoke a sense of empathy and sincerity in an effort to melt the viewers emotionally into buying the product. A great many use humour to win over the viewers and reduce the pretentiousness of the message, since pretending to be absurd is the best camouflage for something that really is absurd.

Network Versus Spot

A basic decision for all advertisers to take is allocating their TV media budget to network versus local or spot announcements. Most national advertisers use network schedules to provide national coverage and supplement this with regional or local spot purchases to reach markets where additional coverage is desired.

Network advertising

Network advertising is a common way advertisers disseminate their messages by purchasing airtime from a television network. A network assembles a series of affiliated local TV stations, or affiliates, to which it supplies programmes and services. These affiliates, most of which are independently owned, contractually agree to preempt time during specified hours for programming provided by the networks and to carry the national advertising within the programme. The networks share the advertising revenue they receive during these time periods with the affiliates. The affiliates are also free to sell commercial time in non-network periods and during station breaks in the preempted periods to both national and local advertisers.

A major advantage of network advertising is the simplification of the purchase process. The advertiser has to deal with only one party or media representative to air a commercial nationwide. The networks also offer the most popular programmes and generally control prime-time programming.

Spot and local advertising

Spot advertising refers to commercials shown on local TV stations, with time negotiated and purchased directly from the individual stations. All non-network advertising done by a national advertiser is known as **national spot advertising**. Airtime sold to local firms such as retailers, restaurants, banks and auto dealers is known as **local advertising**. Local advertisers want media whose coverage is limited to the geographic markets in which they do business. This may be difficult to accomplish with TV, but many local businesses are large enough to make efficient use of TV advertising.

Spot advertising offers the national advertiser flexibility in adjusting to local market conditions. The advertiser can concentrate commercials in areas where market potential is greatest or where additional support is needed. This appeals to advertisers with uneven distribution or limited advertising budget as well as those interested in test marketing or introducing a product in limited market area. National advertisers often use spot television advertising through local retailers or dealers as part of their cooperative advertising programmes and to provide local dealer support.

The decision facing most of the national advertisers is how to combine network and spot advertising to make effective use of their TV advertising budget. Another factor that makes spot advertising attractive to national advertisers is the growth in **syndication** which is nothing but advertising on shows that are sold or distributed on a station-by-station, market-by-market basis.

Developing an Effective Campaign

Television is an influential medium for advertising. It gives a powerful opportunity to create a message bold enough to grab the viewers' attention, yet simplistic enough not to turn the viewers off. It's a 30 to 60 second "window of opportunity" to share a message with important target audience and create a lasting impression that ultimately leads the viewer to take action. The key to successfully executing a TV advertising campaign begins and ends with research, with a whole lot of strategy and creativity sandwiched in between.

For any new TV advertising campaign, the creative process begins with our knowledge of what works best for television campaigns. Consumers respond best to television commercials that employ one of the following elements:

1. Celebrities
2. Humour, especially a surprise or twist
3. A storyline
4. A simple concept
5. Many layers, especially visually, so they notice different elements every time they see the commercial

These elements have been consistently favoured across demographic factors such as age and race, so it is a safe starting point for a consumer-oriented campaign. The challenge is to communicate one message that would embrace a diverse group, without alienating any of them.

The research process continues throughout the creative phase of ad campaign development, as the messages and various elements of the ads are tested to ensure their optimal effectiveness. This is a critical step that should not be overlooked or eliminated to save money, as some organizations are inclined to do.

Another major consideration in a television campaign is media placement. The importance of the media buying function is sometimes underestimated, until your ad runs multiple times during a show that no one is watching because your target audience is tuned in to a cricket match on a competing network. The initial research phase of TV campaign development includes analysis of the media and determination of the best opportunities to reach your target audience.

It is better to spend more to make a high-quality, good-looking commercial, if you are selling an expensive product or service and you are offering quality and prestige. But if you are selling a bargain-priced local service, an expensive commercial may actually work against you, by making your service look expensive. But daytime and late-night spots in local markets can be surprisingly inexpensive. Therefore, we have to explore all the avenues before taking the final leap in order to reach a good number of right audience for the money being spent.

After the campaign runs for its first season, research is again conducted to determine the results of the programme and to assess the need for any adjustments to our approach. Television is a powerful tool that has the ability to legitimize a product or service. The fundamental approach is to remember that television is an intrusion in people's lives, and therefore, each layer of the story being told must be carefully analysed so that the finished product makes a memorable statement for the viewer.

Effective TV commercials merge *video* and *audio* into a powerful sales tool. But never think that one is more important than the other. Audio and video must synchronize to create a right impact. For example, turn down the volume on any commercial. The benefits of purchasing a product just from the video can be identified. The same holds true for audio. Close your eyes and listen to the announcer. If the audio doesn't explain the product in detail, then the commercial isn't effective. Potential customers should be able to hear the message even if they're not in the room to see it. So usage of a strong audio and video combination is strongly advised.

The video must match audio to drive home the selling points. For instance, one wouldn't want to see video of a woman struggling with a large vacuum cleaner while the audio claims, "Our handheld vacuum cleaner is great for cleaning the inside of your home!". The message gets distorted. The viewer gets confused and you lose the sale.

Television should be thought of as an intimate medium. Combining sight and sound should spark the viewers' emotions and help them identify themselves with the product. If they can identify themselves with the product, the job is done!

RADIO ADVERTISING

Radio may not be considered as glamorous as television. This makes it difficult to attract talented creatives to prepare ads. At the same time, a well-placed, clever ad appeals as being a one-on-one message (announcer to driver in a car stuck in traffic). Many smaller local companies still heavily rely on radio advertising, and most radio ads are produced locally and with small budgets.

Radio offers several advantages to advertisers. Skilful radio advertisers help the listener remember the message by creating a powerful image to visualize or through repetition. It is important to help the consumer move the ad from short-term to long-term memory. Various sound effects and lively memorable tunes assist in this process. Through repetition, a person hears an advertisement often enough to assist in recall, just like by repeating a phone number or an e-mail address, you remember the numbers or letters.

Radio stations tend to have a definable target markets based on their formats. Certain formats attract similar audience. This means a firm that wants to advertise on pop stations in a particular region can find similar stations across the country.

Radio stations offer considerable flexibility and a short lead time. Commercials can be recorded and placed on air within a few days and sometimes within hours. Ads can be changed quickly. This is especially in volatile markets or in the retail sector wherein companies want to change the items featured on sale. Radio also helps a national company that wants to modify each advertisement to local conditions. In other words, a manufacturer can develop one national advertisement and change it for each dealer or retailer that carries the manufacturer's merchandise. The modification can be as simple as providing an address, phone number or web address for each local outlet.

One major advantage of radio is intimacy. Introduction of radio *Mirchi*, FM, etc. have really given boost to radio advertising. Listeners can develop a proximity to the DJs and other radio personalities. This closeness grows over time. Listening to the same individual becomes somewhat personalized, especially if the listener has a conversation with the DJ during a contest or when requesting for a song. The bond or the intimacy level gives a radio personality a higher level of credibility and an edge to products and services the radio celebrity endorses. No other medium offers this advantage.

Besides intimacy, radio is mobile. People carry radio to the beach, park, workplace and picnic. They listen to radio at home, at work and on the road in-between. No other medium stays with the audience quite like the radio.

Radio also has some disadvantages. One is the short exposure time of an ad. Like television advertisements, most radio advertisements last only 15 or 30 seconds. Listeners involved in other activities, such as driving or working on a computer, may not pay attention to the radio. Further, people often use radio as a background to fade out other distractions, especially at work.

For national advertisers, covering a large area with radio advertisements is challenging. To place a national advertisement requires contacting a large number of companies. Few large radio conglomerates means contacts must be made with multiple stations. Because of this independence, negotiating lower rates with individual stations based on volume or because it will be a national advertisement does not occur. In fact, local advertiser can negotiate better rates than a national advertiser because of the relationship the local radio stations develop with the local firms over time.

In large metropolitan areas, another problem is target duplication. Several radio stations may try to reach the same target market. For instances, in any city, there are many radio stations and advertising on all of them is not financially feasible, yet reaching everyone in that target market is not possible unless all the stations are used. The radio stations have loyal listeners who do not prefer to listen to other stations.

Finally, because many ads are locally produced, a common problem with radio ads is putting too much information into one ad. It overloads the consumer and very little is retained.

Radio advertising is a low-cost option for a local firm. Ads can be placed at ideal times and adapted to local conditions. The key to radio is the careful selection of station and time and construction of the ad. Tests can be carried out to see if ads effectively reach customers. Immediate response techniques, contest entries and other devices provide information about whether customers heard and responded to ads. Radio *remotes* occur when the firm broadcasts from a business location. Remotes are a popular method of attracting attention to a new business (restaurants, small retail shops, etc.) or to a company trying to make a major push for immediate customers. Effective radio promotions can be combined with other media (local television, newspapers, etc.) to send out an integrated message.

For business-to-business advertisers, radio provides the opportunity to reach businesses during working hours, because many employees listen to the radio during office hours. More importantly, radio can reach businesspeople while in transit to or from the work. Both radio and television usage has increased for business to business marketing.

SUMMARY

Television has tremendous impact on the viewers as it provides the ability to communicate sight, sound, motion and emotion. The inclusion of so many channels has further fuelled the scope of television advertising. Television has got innumerable advantages over other media such as creativity and impact, coverage and effectiveness, captivity and attention and selectivity and flexibility. Despite its unsurpassed advantages from creative perspective, this medium has some disadvantages also. These problems include high cost, lack of selectivity, fleeting nature of commercial clutter, limited viewers' attention and distrust of TV advertisements. Deception in television advertising is another drawback as the elements of visual fantasy, deceptive images, and false claims are blended in various approaches. Some very measly information is projected as if it is of momentous importance.

A basic decision for all advertisers to take is allocating their TV media budget to network versus local or spot announcements. Television is an influential medium and provides an opportunity to create a bold message to grab the attention of viewers. The advertisement employs celebrities, humour, storyline, simple concept or visual attention. The sound and picture must synchronize to create a good impact.

Radio advertising might not be considered glamorous but has picked its importance with the introduction of new stations like Radio FM, Radio Mirchi, etc. Before the advent of television in 60s and late 70s, radio was quite popular. The listeners mitigated in 80s, but since the turn of the century, radio has regained its lost listeners. One major advantage of radio is intimacy, which no other medium offers. It is mobile and handy too. The major disadvantage, on the other hand, is the short exposure of an ad.

QUESTIONS

1. How is television advertising different from print advertising? How does the strategy for developing advertisements vary in TV and print media and why?
2. Compare and contrast the advantages and disadvantages of television advertising. Have you ever felt that TV advertising is more of a nuisance than entertainment? Exemplify.

3. What are the factors that have led to the encroachment of deception in television advertising? How can you weed them out? Is deception permissible?
4. Define zipping, zapping and grazing. How can you stop the viewers from indulging in these three activities? What is the main factor responsible for these problems?
5. Design an ad campaign for an energy drink for children to be run on television. What strategy will you adopt to captivate the maximum number of viewers?
6. Which advertisement has greater recall value—television or print? Give adequate reasons to support your answer.
7. What is the major advantages of radio advertising? Write a script for a radio advertisement for *Tina* talcum powder.

CHAPTER 13

Web Advertising

AD CONTENT

Ad Type	FOR SALE
Price	$16,995.00
Ad Text	1996 HARLEY Hartiage Nostalgia, super cln, very low mi, all the right original Nostalgia parts, #051096, $16,995 - Lifestyle Cycles

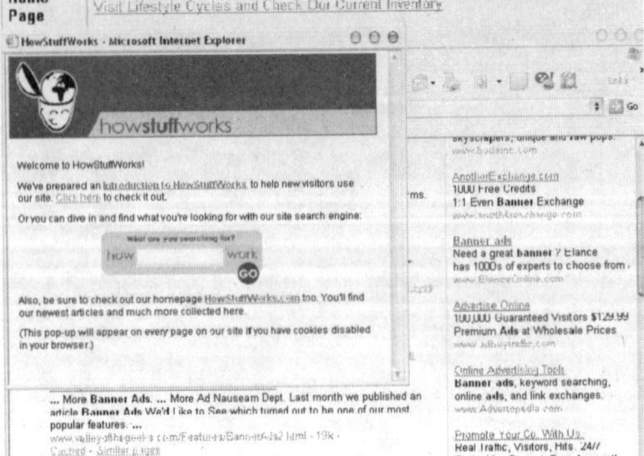

LEARNING OBJECTIVES

After reading this chapter, you will be able to:

- Gain an insight into web advertising and its various types.
- Know the main advantages of e-advertising over traditional media.
- Deal with the problems arising due to the implementation of web advertising.
- Know the challenges faced by the users of web advertising.
- Explain the tools that aid e-advertising.
- Know the new developments in web advertising arena.

CASE STUDY: IBM COMBS THE GLOBE FOR E-BUSINESS

When is a computer just not a computer? Well, in IBM's way of thinking about things, that would be when a computer is an e-business tool. Faced with potent competitors such as Compaq, Hewlett-Packard and Dell, IBM needed a way to reposition its laptops and PCs to accelerate its sales. Building on its own much-mimicked e-business concept, it was logical for IBM to pursue a repositioning of these products as e-business tools. The marketing strategy was to launch a revamped product line designed specifically to help companies get on the Internet and other networks to boost their business. A carefully orchestrated ad campaign could help consumers see IBM computers in this light.

The e-business campaign was launched with extravagant eight-page insert in various national newspapers. This was followed by giant IBM posters plastered on construction sites, in airports and in subway stations in major metropolitan markets, along with magazine and TV ads and the ever-present website promotion. To add a touch of style and grace to its campaign, IBM employed a photographer who previously specialized in glamour shots for Clinique cosmetics. These stylish black-and-white photos of products such as the IBM ThinkPad were common throughout the various media used in this repositioning campaign.

How much to spend on a campaign to promote e-business tools around the world? In the year 1998 global campaign was funded at the $ 100 million level. Gee, $ 100 million here and $ 100 million there, and all of a sudden, you are talking about some real money. IBM spends in the order of $ 750 million each year on advertising.

Source: Raju Narisetti, "IBM Blitz to introduce e-business tools", Wall Street Journal, April 15, 1998, B4.

While a 30-second commercial on TV or radio can only begin to tell a company's story, the Internet serves as an integrated tool to help tell the rest of the story. Most of the traditional paper ads are printing web addresses of advertisers for finding lot of information the prospective consumers require. In fact, every ad has a website address posted to it. **Online** or **web advertising** can be defined as the promotion of products or services by advertising through the Internet media.

IMPORTANCE OF ONLINE ADVERTISING

With the advent of technology, the Internet has positioned itself as one of the very few media alternatives that can be used for almost all advertising purposes across all possible market segments.

The growing popularity of the Internet and the mass media hype surrounding its commercial potential has triggered an avalanche of interest in using this new tool for marketing and advertising. In fact, the Internet has taken only few years to achieve a critical mass of almost 50 million users. The radio, television and cable have taken a lot more years to achieve this number than the Internet took. This suggests the rapid acceptance of the Internet as a medium of connectivity and commerce. As the Internet gained popularity, marketers began to explore if this medium was lucrative to advertise on and found that it gave them more than what the other media could offer. The Internet provided their customers with interactivity–consumers could now interact with their product and build their own experience with it. The marketers believed that this form of brand conditioning would enhance the consumer's brand experience. The rate of technological change in the marketing environment is an important factor that influences the marketing success. The growth of the Internet as a provider of standard global access to systems and networks all over the world is an area of huge interest currently and will very soon become a major consideration for the marketing departments of most Indian organizations marketing to consumers and businesses.

In the initial stages, Internet advertising was essentially done through news groups, e-mail, insertions in newsletters and e-zincs, and distributed via list servers. Classified ads have long been a part of the Internet scene but it was only in 1994 that the advertisements for the Internet, as we know it today, started.

Comparison of online advertising with traditional advertising

Online advertising is very interactive compared to the other forms of traditional advertising. The consumers can pick and choose the information, sales message and buying modes that fit their individual needs.

Online advertising offers the best of push and pull advertising in that merchants can pull consumers in based on their advertising and push material out to them once they have created a relationship. Because users select the sites they visit, advertisers are almost guaranteed highly qualified prospects.

Impact of interactive ads

Interactive ads have a great impact on brand awareness and a single exposure to a web banner generates greater awareness than a television or a print ad. It is estimated that the number of new web advertisers will grow at a faster rate than the number of web viewers.

It is possible to target specific consumer segments based on geographical location, while they are online, etc., with relevant ads. In addition, the Net has the capability to compile statistics regarding how many people viewed each advertisement on an hourly, daily and monthly basis (reach), and for how long each viewer actually looked at an advertisement (exposure time), which helps companies track down the effectiveness of their advertisements in terms of the number of purchases. This mechanism is more effective than advertising in magazines or on television.

OBJECTIVES OF ONLINE ADVERTISING

Online advertising can be used to achieve the following four basic objectives:

Build brand

Many Fortune 500 companies, from Kodak to IBM, use the Internet to tell the world about their products, support their deal channels and educate the public about their companies or products.

Drive traffic to the website

Online advertisements offer a proven way to steer interested buyers to the website, where one can know more about the products and services.

Develop qualified leads

While at the website, the best copywriting and photographs can convince the prospects and provide good business. How best one follows each qualified prospect determines the business.

Conduct sales

As the prospects become warm, one can close sales either online or direct the buyers to their dealer channel, if that is the seller's sales strategy.

CASE STUDY: HOTEL DISCOUNTS

Hotel Discounts, **www.hoteldiscounts.com** sells hotel rooms via the Internet. To stimulate traffic to its site, it created a contest in which business travelers were asked to write about their "Trip from Hell". The prize was a weekend vacation in Boca Raton, Florida.

More than 13,000 people either entered the contest or read the entries. All entries were posted online. The site was so popular that 50 people a day still visit the site even though the contest ended months ago.

The contest helped the company create a brand name and increased traffic, which resulted in sales.

"It was so successful, we will do it again"!, said Larry Chase, President of Chase Online Marketing Strategies.

They intend to run banner ads on the search engines with the head line: "Just when you thought it was safe: Trip from Hell 2".

TYPES OF ONLINE ADVERTISING

Web advertising comes in many types with the ultimate objective of attracting the attention of the browser. Some of the forms are discussed further.

Banner Ads

Banner ads are rectangular boxes of a pre-specified size by the Internet Advertising Bureau that appear on websites communicating the marketer's message. These ads generally provide a link to another website where the marketers provide further information of their products or services.

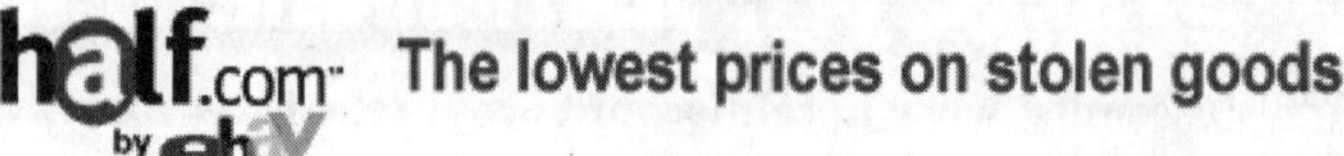

Banner ads: Some examples.

Logos

Company logos are very famous these days. A logo which is placed at the top of the website ads credibility to the site. A well known company can be easily identified with the help of its logo. Logo really have recognition and are part of advertising campaign of the companies. A logo of a company generally depicts the motto or operations of the company. A few logos of very famous companies are shown below:

Logos: Some examples.

Logos can be changed depending on the period of the year. Several companies like Google, Yahoo, etc. release their special logos depending on the eve.

Given below are some of the special logos of the Google site:

Happy Father's Day, June 20, 2004

Mother's Day, May 9, 2004

Leap Year, February 29, 2004

Happy Valentine's Day, February 14, 2004

Google 2004 Summer Olympics Doodle

Google: Some special logos.

E-mail Ads

E-mail advertising belongs to the first generation of interactive advertisements. By creating compelling e-mail experiences, marketers hope to convey their messages in a better way.

A sample e-mail copy is given below:

An e-mail ad.

Packing Tips – Everything You Need with Room to Spare

There are two kinds of travelers in the world: those who packed light and those who wish they had. To include everything needed in as little space as possible, follow these helpful guidelines compiled by the American Society of Travel Agents (ASTA). Some of the most travel-wise people in the world, ASTA members know the techniques of efficient packing for all types of travel. More

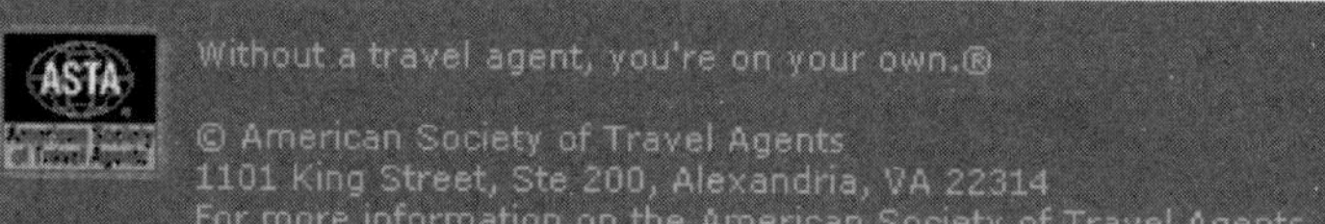

Keywords on Search Engines

Advertisers can buy keywords on search engines to increase their exposure. When a consumer types in a keyword like computers, airplanes or hotels, he/she sees a banner ad paid for by a company that sells the respective products, along with the related sites available in the library.

This proved to be a great concept as the users identify themselves as being in the market for those products at that time.

There are two parts of this strategy. The first is that the consumer sees the banner advertisement and the second part occurs when the user clicks the banner, thereby linking to the specific page of the site.

A search engine claims of getting more click-through rates than the banner ads. Search engine ads work because search engine is the website that people visit with the explicit goal of finding someplace else to go. Thus, if users see an ad for what they are looking for, there is a high probability that they'll click that ad. Advertisers can satisfy a user's immediate needs because they target ads based on the user's query terms. (This also explains why ads on search engine homepages do not work: it is impossible to target the ad to the user's current quest until the server knows what that quest is.)

Classified Ads

Classified ads work because as far as users are concerned, they are **content**, not advertising: people actively seek out the classifieds when they are looking to buy. This explains the success of eBay, Monster/Hot Jobs and many such sites. The superiority of Web classifieds portends dire times ahead for traditional printed newspapers, as their most lucrative income source continues to migrate online.

The picture below shows a classified ad for Harley bikes and a subsequent click through the link gives the next picture with all the details of the bike including its cost (see the picture on the next page). The photo aids the customer to know even the condition of the bike.

A classified ad.

DATE	AD TEXT	OTHER	CONTACT	TYPE	PRICE
	Add a Photo!! A Picture is Worth a Thousand Words...and We Only Allow 150!!! CLICK HERE!				
09/02 new!	1999 HARLEY SPORTSTER beautiful red/white, w bags, dual seat, sissy bar, windshield and more, 4600 miles from new, #UNUSA, $5995 IRV Seaver Motorcycles		(click)	B	$6995
09/02 new!	2000 HARLEY FATBOY, chrm H.D. mag, high flow filter, V/H pipes, C.V. carb, #002420, $17,499, Lifestyle Cycles	link	(click)	B	$17499
09/02 new!	1987 HARLEY Softail, rare model, fac matching frm /pnt, apes chrm frnt end, S&S carb, low miles, #020050, $11,995 - Lifestyle Cycles	link	(click)	B	$11995
09/02 new!	1996 HARLEY Hertiage Nostalgia, super cln, very low mi, all the right original Nostalgia parts, #051096, $16,995 - Lifestyle Cycles	link	(click)	B	$16995
09/02 new!	99 HARLEY SOFTAIL, CHROME LOWR PEGS, DRAG PIPES, LUGGAGE RACK, #041773, $14,995	link	(click)	B	$14995

AD CONTENT	
Ad Type	FOR SALE
Price	$16,995.00
Ad Text	1996 HARLEY Hertiage Nostalgia, super cln, very low mi, all the right original Nostalgia parts, #051096, $16,995 - Lifestyle Cycles
AD FEATURES	
Photo 1	
Home Page	Visit Lifestyle Cycles and Check Our Current Inventory

Picture with all details.

Interstitials

An interstitial ad is one that **pops up** when the user loads a new page. In other words, when the user hits a button to link to a new page, the interstitial is displayed. It disappears and the new page is loaded. This type of ad begins to follow the format used in television advertising in that you see content that you want to see and then they throw in an ad before letting you see more of what you want to see.

Interstitial began showing its ugly head in early 1997 and is not widely used yet. People see these ads as annoying and even leave sites that have them at times. They hate the slowness of the Internet and attribute it to these interstitial ads.

But interstitials can be twice as effective than the traditional online banners if they are presented properly to the consumers. See the following ad:

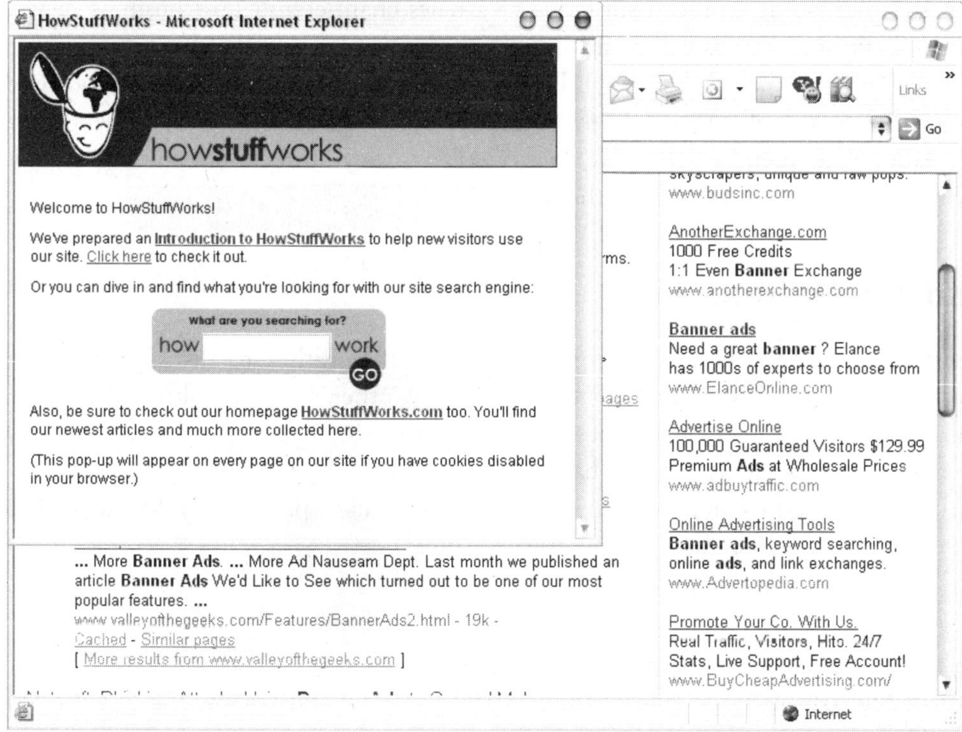

An example of interstitial.

Websites

Websites can be viewed as anchors to all types of online ads discussed earlier. In the end, each of these ads is linked to its home page or specific links on the company's website. So it is important to have an effective and impressive website that urges the user to buy that specific product or service. Many giants like Nike, Adidas, etc. are having websites that are full of dynamic effects, flash animations and creativity, of course. These websites contain all the information about the company. We can even see the web addresses coming up in the company's advertisements in the traditional media, hinting the users that they can always visit the website for more information.

Push Technologies or Web Casting

The biggest headlines these days seem to be reserved for push technologies or web casting. This model tries to mimic television in that consumers subscribe to "channels" published by advertisers, who send information and ads to the consumer on a schedule determined by the consumer. In other words, one can subscribe to a news channel and read business news updates every half an hour and the ads will come along with the news. The consumer can receive targeted ads also which means the ads are published according to the interests of the consumer.

This technology will allow almost any website to become a channel that delivers information to the desktop. Web users will be able to subscribe to any site and specify when they would like the information to be sent over the web.

Sponsored Mailing Lists

Mailing lists offer advertisers highly targeted audience that gather to discuss specific interests. Even the rates tend to be very low when compared to other ways of online advertising. These give it a bit of advantage over other types of online advertising but many of them are left unread by the receivers. This is a major drawback for these lists.

Sponsored mailing lists may lead to several problems like spam or unwanted mail, Internet frauds due to innocence on the part of the consumers, etc.

Spam

To begin with, your e-mail is just that–yours. In most cases, it is a resource that you must pay for as part of the cost of connecting to the Internet. Reading and responding to your e-mail also represents an investment of your time and as such, has a value attached to it.

If someone sends a junk mail through one's e-mail account, he/she is wasting the time and money. If we are busy on the Net for some personal work, we will never like to pay attention to any number of advertisements which pops up in different ways. Our daily snail mail is buried in flyers for supermarkets we will never shop at and health clubs we will never sweat in. We have just as much right to feel abused when we receive e-mails which we did not request, never gave anyone permission to send and do not want.

Receiving one or two such messages a day is annoying. Receiving hundreds of them is a large drain on one's time and resources, and one should not put up with it. Unlike traditional junk snail mail, it is not even good for use as kindling.

Some types of commercial spams are discussed further.

Spam from suits

One of the most prevalent sorts of junk e-mail is commercial advertising. A few years ago, most of it originated from spammers who were essentially ignorant of the prerogatives of users of the Internet. Judging by the content of most of these messages, their perpetrators had all just signed up with an Internet access provider and were given complimentary copies of one of the many "How to Make Lots of Money on the Internet" books. Some of them were genuinely inconsiderate of the rights of other users of the Net. The bulk of them, however, were merely confused, deluded and ignorant.

Spam from grunts

It must be said that the foregoing marginal - if misguided - businesspeople have largely been supplanted in the hearts, minds and spam filters of the Net by spammers several levels lower in the food chain. A huge volume of spam is generated by stupid people hoping against hope to find "customers" with fewer working brain cells than they have. The odds against this happening make even state-run lotteries look promising by comparison, but spam is essentially free to send, and it is a safe bet that none of these guys can deal with large numbers.

Spam from viruses

The third common manifestation of unsolicited e-mail is generated by viruses attempting to propagate themselves across the Internet. Depending upon the intent of the author of a virus, having your computer infected with one might entail it becoming the source of a great deal of virus-laden e-mail, sent to every e-mail address stored on your system. This is not likely to endear you to your friends, colleagues and business contacts. Viruses can also attempt to compromise your personal information to third parties—several of them have appeared of late to steal credit card information. There have been a number of viruses which have been designed to turn the systems they infect into "zombies", to be controlled by the virus authors, typically to send out more spam. A few viruses have been the work of malicious vandals who just want to nuke the machines they infect.

Remedies for spam

Despite the relatively unpoliced nature of the Internet, there are steps you can take to reduce the amount of unsolicited e-mail you receive. They are by no means completely effective. However, if you undertake them, you will probably keep your junk e-mail down to a reasonable level of hugeness. If you do not, you will eventually get swamped by it. These steps are discussed briefly below:

- When you receive unsolicited commercial e-mail, reply to it with a message which states unequivocally that you are not amused.
- Never open an attachment to e-mail unless you are really certain you know where it has come from. Attachments with the extension .EXE, .COM, .PIF, .BAT and .SCR are especially nasty. Use a virus checker to scan your hard drive at frequent intervals and keep its virus database up to date.
- Here is another bit of interaction with spammers you will want to avoid. Some spam messages include ostensible opt-out functions—links you can click on to remove yourself from the list that sent you the spam in question. Do not use these removal functions. In most cases, what they are really there for is to verify that your e-mail address is valid and its mail is being read by a live human being. Using a spam removal function will typically guarantee that you will receive a lot more spam.

- Use a Filter. Regrettably, some spam just will not go away voluntarily. There are spam generators who feel that flooding the inboxes of the known universe with advertisements for the unthinkable, unnamable and unwanted is an inalienable right, or something they are just entitled to get away with. Perhaps, more to the point, there are spammers who take a long, long time to appreciate that no one is buying their stuff, even though they blast out tens of millions of e-mail messages a week. Finally, there are spam advertisers who have gone to considerable lengths to defend themselves from the outrage of their victims, and as such rarely appreciate that they are making few friends in cyberspace.

A mail filter will watch your incoming mail, search it for indications of unsolicited content and act as a gatekeeper. Properly thought-out and maintained, a mail filter can substantially reduce the volume of spam you have to address. Your best defence against unwanted e-mail is an understanding of the people who send it, and of the nature of the parties who run the servers which make up the Internet.

THE FIVE MUTABLE LAWS OF WEB MARKETING

The following five laws form the backbone of present-day web marketing lore.

- The law of the dead-end street
- The law of giving and selling
- The law of trust
- The law of pull and push
- The law of the niche

The Law of the Dead-End Street

The first law goes like this: Setting up a website is like building a storefront on a dead-end street. If you want any shoppers, you must give them a reason to come.

The most wonderful site in the world is wasted unless people stop by to admire and purchase. It is because of the same reason that most great craftsmen are not millionaires. They have learned to make a great product, but do not have a clue about marketing. Give visitors good reason to visit you and they will never disappoint you.

The Law of Giving and Selling

An important element of web culture is "free stuff". The law of giving and selling says: Attract visitors to your site by giving away something free, and then try to sell something additional to those who visit. "Give them something free, then try to sell them something".

CASE STUDY: WILSON INTERNET SERVICES

In mid-1995, Wilson Internet Services launched their website design business with a goal of attracting business nationally via the Web. At that time, even local website designers were considered oddities. How could they succeed at a national level? First, they identified the most likely customers: small-to medium-size businesses. Second, they asked, "What do the customers want to know?" Of course, the people wondered how to construct a website. But that was what they wanted to sell them. The customers also wanted to know how to market their business on the Web, as the Wilson people reasoned.

So they scoured for the rather sparse offering of articles on web marketing available at that time and made a link list of about 20 articles and resources. Then every month, without fail, these people would scour the Web again for more materials. The Web Marketing Info Center (http://www.wilsonweb.com/webmarket/) grew into a resource containing links to 2000+ articles and resources, the largest collection of information of its kind on the Web. In addition, they began to write articles explaining to small businesspeople how to market their site. Some of those articles were linked to by major sites and brought many visitors. This became a destination Site—a portal site to the literature on web marketing—and their business prospered.

Here is the simple strategy. Attract people to your site by giving away lots of free information. Then let people know about your products and services. Learn this rhythm of giving something away and selling something. The strategy works. But to sell, you need to master a third law.

The Law of Trust

When the products or services are priced competitively and are of good quality, the most significant sales barrier is trust. Trust is the essential lubricant of Web business; without trust, business grinds to a halt.

In case of small business, one can not afford such trust-building advertising campaigns. Alternatively, one can build trust by selling well-known brand name products, by displaying clear shipping and return policies, joining nationally-respected organizations and offering guarantees. Gain credibility by having a professionally-designed site.

The Law of Pull and Push

The fourth mutable law of web marketing is: Pull people to your site by your attractive content, and then push quality information to them regularly via e-mail.

Getting an invitation to send e-mail to your visitors is the key to this strategy. Include a form that will collect their e-mail address. To convince your visitors to give you their e-mail addresses, however, you need to promise two things—you will e-mail them something of value and that you will not sell or rent their addresses to another company, hence the need for a clear privacy policy. But once the visitor has given you permission to e-mail additional information, you have wonderful marketing leverage.

A way to use this strategy is sending a newsletter to the customer in regular intervals, thereby building trust among them. But a regular newsletter will give a tremendous boost to your business and will build your trust level with customers as well as bring them back to your site again and again.

This law, too, has its own rhythm. Pull the customer to your website by attractive power, and then push good content and offers to the customer via e-mail to draw them back to your site.

The Law of the Niche

This last law is the most important as it can not be ignored. Big businesses like Amazon.com and Wal-Mart have the money and clout to own whole segments of the marketplace. Small businesses succeed by finding niches that are either unfilled or only partially filled and filling them with excellence.

The key to this kind of savvy niche marketing is to carefully write a business plan that defines the Unique Selling Proposition (USP). This is best stated in a sentence or two. It defines what makes the business unique from every other competitor in your field. It spells out the precise niche you seek to fill, and how you aim to fill it. The law of the niche is not any more or less important than the other immutable laws of Web marketing. They are all important. Together, they offer you a path towards creating a successful business on the Web.

INTEGRATING ONLINE ADVERTISING WITH TRADITIONAL MEDIA

Major corporations as well as small businesses and home offices should consider using the Internet as a part of their integrated marketing programme. Because paid advertisements on TV and radio and in the newspaper can tell only so much about the product, the best they can hope is create interest. Traditionally, that interest is intended to stimulate a consumer to call the company or visit a store to find out more about the product and buy it. Online marketers know that they can save time and money by using their traditional ads to steer traffic to their websites, where consumers can read and hear about the products when it is convenient for them. If the website is designed and written properly, it can do an admirable job of playing the role of salesperson. When the consumers are ready to buy, they can order in the manner they are most comfortable with–online, by phone or by visiting the merchant's store.

Examples of this tight integration can be seen daily on TV and radio and in newspaper displays and classified ads placed by nearly every type of company. Movie studios run ads on TV and always include the web address for that movie. Business-to-business companies place the web address and e-mail address in print ads in trade publications. Consumer companies do the same with their newspaper advertising. Even smaller consultants, tax consultants and home-based businesses use their classified ads to draw people to their websites.

INCREASING EFFICIENCY OF BANNER ADS

Banner ads work best when the advertising brand can be closely associated with the information available on that site. The real goal of an ad is to entice a potential customer to seek out more information. There is a general belief that banner ads are too small to create any brand recognition, brand awareness and brand equity. In addition, there is a notion that click-through of a banner ad is the only way to measure its effectiveness. Mere exposure to banner ads may not push the message irrespective of the audience interest. Good click-through rates can be obtained through creative thinking. If the advertiser knows the background colour of the main site the company ad runs on, he/she can use this information to make an effective banner ad. The reason for using a news banner on a news site is that the viewers are looking for new stories. As we know that the speed of viewing the Web changes dynamically with load factors, even if we are using the fastest technology at the server end, ads have to be cleverly and compactly designed. The economics of banner ads is based on the lifetime value of the customer.

MORE RELEVANT ADS

Relevance, or the ability to target ads to the most interested consumers, was a big selling point for advertisers when they began to flock online in the late 1990s. But it turns out that although many advertisers have been collecting data about consumer behaviour and purchasing patterns, they have not been making good use of it. According to Forrester Research, 74% of marketers placed ads based on audience demographics. Despite the fact that when asked for the most effective way to reach their target audience, almost three times as many marketers preferred sites where consumers research purchases over sites with a demographic profile that suits the brand. It is not easy to put together complex "action profiles", which analyse when a consumer is motivated or ready to buy. Moreover, advertisers are used to design a one-size-fits-all plan, not a series of ads that must be tested and retested to target consumers at each stage of the purchasing process. Still, those who take the time will reap the rewards. A particular Agency Avenue reports that one of its clients achieved a 162% improvement in sales when it targeted based on actual purchases instead of solely on demographics and click behaviour.

TEXT-ONLY ADS

Text-only advertisements work far better than banners. Search engine text ads will retain their superiority over time, but text ads on other sites will work only if they focus on directly meeting users' needs. Text-only ads on search engines have become particularly successful in recent years, and non-search sites are now experimenting with this format in hope of replicating that success. However, it is doubtful that their efforts will work because non-search sites lack the equation's crucial element–users' single-minded goal to leave the site as quickly as possible. Text-only ads might continue to work better than traditional graphics-based ads for some time to come. Web users have long exhibited strong **banner blindness** and avoid anything that looks like an advertisement. Text-only ads do not resemble the designs that people have trained themselves to screen out, and the resulting visibility surely contributes to the success of text-only ads.

Also, text-only ads are benefitted from a temporary **novelty effect**, as does any new advertising format that people have not yet learned to ignore.

LINK EXCHANGES

An effective and low-cost (or free!) way of driving traffic to your site is to get other websites to link to you. Not only will you get the traffic that results from people clicking on those links, but having a number of high-quality related sites linked to you will also help your site rank higher in Google's search listings. Link exchange programs make it easy for advertisers to find others ready to share the respective links with them.

Tips for Link Exchange

- Send the other website the exact text you would like them to use–this is a form of marketing and you should treat it like one.
- Use the keywords you think people will type in search in your link exchange text.
- Links are most effective when they are from high-quality or established related sites.

Tools

Macromedia Flash MX

Macromedia Flash MX is the professional standard authoring tool for producing high-impact Web experiences. Whether you are creating animated logos, website navigation controls, long-form animations, entire Flash websites, or web applications, you will find the power and flexibility of Flash ideal for your own creativity. There are many ways you can create interactive motion with Macromedia Flash.

Flash MX enhances creativity by providing designers with a high-level of control and expanded integration capabilities with a rich set of design tools. Macromedia Flash MX movies are graphics, text, animation and applications for websites. They consist primarily of vector graphics, but they can also contain imported video, bitmap graphics and sounds. Flash movies can incorporate interactivity to permit input from viewers.

Adobe Photoshop

Photoshop 7.0 rounds off its comprehensive toolset with new capabilities that help you meet every creative challenge, master every production demand and handle any image-editing task efficiently. It delivers new and enhanced tools to help you achieve your creative best. Experiment with sophisticated painting effects and patterns to turn your ideas into images that stand out. It provides new controls and security settings for superior images, precise output and worry-free file sharing. With its comprehensive set of retouching, painting, drawing, and web tools, Photoshop helps you complete any image-editing task efficiently. With features like the history palette and editable layer effects, you can experiment freely without sacrificing efficiency.

Java

Java is being extensively used in the Internet media these days. We can see the presence of Java applets in most of the major websites. These applets are ready-made packages mostly used for graphics and other interactive applications. The cookies concept in Java is also being exploited by the advertisers to give a personal touch to the site. The example which follows corroborates how the sale of the company can be boosted by use of these packages.

Example

James is a prospective dealer for a major electronic goods company. With the expansion in his business, he was badly in need of an extra computer for maintaining his accounts. He visited the site of Dell Computers and gave an order for a PC of his choice. He was also asked his details like name, location, etc. along with the credit card number and the delivery point. Later, when he again visited the site to learn about the maintenance of the PC, he was greeted by a message, "Welcome James!! You have bought a PC for $ 2000 with this configuration. In case of any complaint, follow the red link, for learning about and in case of a fresh purchase, follow the green link. You will be given a discount of 10% for any fresh purchase you make". James was taken aback to see the message and was a bit thrilled to be greeted personally. He was also amused to be offered a discount. He even referred this site to many of his friends that ultimately enhanced the sales of the company.

Here the cookies actually performed the magic and it resulted in augmenting the sales. They are small capsules of information stored in the browser memory of computer that accesses that particular web page so that when the site is visited again, the data is retrieved from them and used accordingly. Here in this case, the information that James filled while purchasing was stored in the form of cookies in his computer itself so that when he opens the page again his details were extracted and a greeting message was displayed.

HTML

Hyper Text Markup Language is very useful in creating web pages. It is very simple to use and very easy to learn, which makes it one of the most popular tools for web advertising.

DHTML

It is the dynamic form of the pre-existing HTML. With its extensive features, it is being more widely used than the HTML, which is static in nature to some extent. It allows changes in the existing patterns as per the need.

ASP and JSP

Active Server Pages and Java Server Pages are the latest technologies being used in making interactive web pages, with the former being the more recent and extensively used these days. They are more advanced than the HTML and DHTML, which are simple with limited flexibility.

CHALLENGES OF ONLINE ADVERTISING

Online advertising has its own challenges apart from the vast number of advantages it enjoys with the other types of media.

Marketing Challenges

Online advertising faces a number of marketing challenges. One of these is the need for simpler language and where it is practical, we should use the same language. There is also the need for selling the Internet in a simpler way. The third challenge is to obtain and distribute accurate figures about the size of the online audience. This involves collating research about online penetration and attentiveness.

Educational Challenges

The infancy of the online media brand remains a challenge. Advertisers are less familiar with the Internet brands and Internet media properties than the media properties of traditional channels. This situation can be changed through a range of education initiatives, such as showing advertisers the boost that online advertising can provide to their brands and also stressing the major impact that Internet advertising can have when used in a cross-media campaign with TV, radio and press. What is required is the education of the client when they first encounter the Internet in order to counteract lack of understanding of cross-media optimization. There is a need to focus on the way agencies present the option of online advertising. There is also a lack of awareness and visibility of great online creativity in most of the ads that are uploaded in the sites.

Structural Challenges

At present, the planning process presents a particular challenge. Budgets remain small and the planning and agency costs are often a relatively higher proportion of total budget than they are in other media channels. The Interactive Advertising Bureau (IAB) standards and best practice would reduce these costs.

Filler Available

Personal filters

People might not want to see ads, or act on them. Just as another media, only a small percentage of people will ever buy the product. The solution is to target the message so that people who are interested in the product will buy it.

Technology filters

Software programs like Internet Fast Forward, www.privnet.com, are being created to filter out advertisements such as banner ads. Because of all these, that particular ad might never reach its target.

Lack of Good Writing or Marketing Techniques

Many websites do not use the tried-and-true methods of selling off the page. Merely presenting features and benefits is not enough to sell in the online world. You must make a compelling offer that is irresistible to the prospective consumers.

Holding the Internet to a Higher Standard than Other Advertising Media

To expect the Internet to be the all-in-one answer is almost impossible. Its efficiency can be measured with different yardsticks like response rates for cold calls, walk-in traffic. Subsequent remedies have to be taken to gain upper hand over other media.

NEW DEVELOPMENTS IN ONLINE ADVERTISING

Better Metrics

Now that the advertising industry is starting to break free of the ubiquitous number-of-unique-visitors and click-through metrics, it expects to see many other measures of success. Online advertisers are beginning to use traditional testing to gauge the effectiveness of their ads, including brand-awareness and intent-to-purchase studies. The new metrics already are bringing optimism to the business.

Greater use of sound in advertising and customer support

With so many computers sold as multimedia systems with high-speed modems and stereo sound speakers, the market is ripe for advertisers to put audio on their web pages. Audio can be used in the sales cycle to create the right frame of mind for a person entering the page, thus setting a convenient atmosphere for effective presentation. Audio technology will help customer support operations as people will be able to hear responses to their questions, record them, and play them back when needed. Combined with video, it can do miracles to the field of interactive online advertising.

A new wave of measurement techniques and standards

Publishing sites must offer verifiable demographics of their viewers for marketers to become truly comfortable spending large dollars on the Web. Because publishers want to make that day come sooner than later, they will be creating measurement tools and devising ways of identifying consumers and their demographics.

Initiatives

Manufacturers will begin to see the value in advertising on the Internet and will open cooperative advertising programmes to include funding of websites, banner ad advertising links back to the manufacturer's home page and new techniques that will evolve.

Customized websites

Creating individual websites on the fly for customers based on their registration numbers will become increasingly important for companies and is even expected by the customers. Greeting a customer personally like "Hi Sanjay! Welcome to your shopping site" on loading the page and asking him to visit the page again or thanking him for visiting the page on logging out makes the customer feel at shop.

Integration of help desks and information centres with the Internet

Companies that use software to distribute their products or services will tie the consumer's computer into an online service for support services such as help systems, programme updates and announcements. This process will help cut the delivery cost of new products and information and give consumers access to the latest help files available. This application would work well for any company that publishes information that quickly goes out of date. The field of online marketing is new and constantly changing. As new tools develop and evolve so will the strategies marketers use to win new customers and build long-lasting relationships with existing consumers.

It is creativity and efficient usage of all available tools and means that matters a lot, for making good ads in the online media. Internet advertising has marked its own boundary in the advertising industry and is even competing with the traditional media.

SUMMARY

Web advertising is another name for e-advertising or online advertising, which has changed the face of advertising tremendously. Web advertising is defined as the promotion of product or services by advertising through the Internet media. As the importance of the Net grew, the scope of e-advertising triggered. The extra feature of e-advertising is providing the customer with interactivity. It offers the best of push and pull advertising. Interactive advertising has a greater impact on brand awareness than a television or print advertisement. The main objective of online advertising is build brand, drive traffic to the website, develop qualified lead and conduct sales. There are different types of web advertising possible. They are banner ads, logos, e-mail ads, interstitials, websites, push technologies or web casting and sponsored mailing lists. The main drawback of e-advertising is spam mails which are of different nature. To combat this problem, the users are advised to use filters.

Major corporations as well as small businesses should consider using the Internet as part of their integrated marketing programme. There are several tools available for developing advertisements for the Web. You require special skill for making these ads. The several tools for making web ads are Macromedia Flash MX, Adobe Photoshop, Java, HTML DHTML, ASP and JSP. Online advertising has its own challenges apart from the vast number of advantages it enjoys with the other type of media. These challenges are marketing challenges, educational challenges, structural challenges, filters available and lack of marketing techniques. But the new metrics, greater use of sound and customer support and initiatives already are bringing optimism to the business.

QUESTIONS

1. Google.com has released the following logo on the occasion of Einstein's birthday. Google celebrates Einstein's birthday–March 14, 2003

   Prepare a logo for Google.com for the occasion of 2007 Cricket World Cup.

2. The Travelex Company offers tour packages across Europe and America. It has recently introduced a package of 40 days across Africa. The trip costs $7999 and it includes most of the important places in the African continent. Prepare a sample e-mail to be sent to the company's previous customers, describing the package.

3. Read the following case study carefully and answer the questions that follow it:

   CASE STUDY

   1800 FLOWERS is one of the most successful direct sales businesses on the Internet. The site also supports the company's integrated marketing programme. The website URL is www.1800flowers.com. The consumers are greeted by the message "welcome to our world" and an equally cheery image of an entrance to a nursery when they open the company Web page. They can select shop the company's store. In that section, they can choose from four main categories.

   1. Season's best, an assortment of bouquets, with enticing names like "Fields of Europe", "Fresh Noble Fir Wreath" and "Dried Floral Winter Centerpiece".

2. Shop by occasion, including birthday, anniversary, congratulations, best wishes, thank you, new baby, get well and sympathy.
3. Shop by product category such as flowers, roses, plants, gift baskets, gourmet items, balloons and decorative keepsakes.
4. Shop by price range, from under $25 to $65 and over.

Each product is accompanied by a photo and enticing descriptive catalogue copy. Each arrangement can be ordered in small, medium and large sizes. Prices and shipping charges are clearly visible.

To purchase, customers select the product and quantity. They then click the Ad button. After each selection, an invoice pops up showing the products ordered, total price and service charge. When they have finished selecting, consumers click the Go to the Checkout lane button to pay for their purchases by filling in their home, address, phone number and credit card information. If they make mistakes, they can reset the form to empty their shopping basket.

The company allows purchases through Netscape's commerce server and a standard protocol for people who do not use Netscape. It has a joint marketing arrangement with United Airlines, so members can get 300 miles for purchases over $29.95.

Based on the above case study, answer the following questions:

1. What was the mission of 1-800-FLOWERS in going online?
2. What role does the site play in promoting the sales of the company?
3. Why do you think the company made a marketing arrangement with United Airlines and is offering 300 miles for purchases over $29.95?
4. What additional steps can the company take for promoting its sales using the online media?

4. The Rajasthan BSNL management wants to launch extensive publicity drive for its Excel prepaid service. Prepare suitable ads for both print and online media and compare the elements of interactivity in them. Discuss the merits and demerits of implementing these strategies in Rajasthan (for example, Rajasthan shows less literacy rate and hence e-advertising may not be successful). Suggest any other better medium for publicity and brand awareness.

5.

The world's networking company℠

The above figure shows the logo of the networking giant, AT&T. Discuss the prominence of the globe and the caption in the logo. Suggest any other suitable caption for the company.

6. List 5–10 action call statements that are apt for web advertising. (For example, "Hurry up!! Available only for this spring", etc.)
7. Give the rough sketch of the website of Nike sports and suggest some improvements in the existing site stating the reasons why you think they are required.

Part Five

Integrated Marketing Communications

CHAPTER 14

Advertising and Integrated Marketing Communications

LEARNING OBJECTIVES

After reading this chapter, you will be able to:

- Know the role of integrated marketing communications (IMC).
- Know and understand various tools used in IMC.
- Understand how various IMC tools work.
- Develop various elements of IMC into an effective communication programme.
- Describe and explain consumer and trade promotions.
- Explain above-the-line and below-the-line media.

For many years companies have heavily relied on advertising agencies for promotion of their products and services. However, most marketers did use additional promotional tools but all such tools like sales promotion, direct marketing, packaging and personal selling, etc. were used only as auxiliary tools. Marketers planned and managed those tools separately and independently with different budgets, views and objectives. The problem with such separate approach is that the company fails to project a unified and consistent image to the consumer. In this case, each promotional tool communicates separate identity and image.

During the 1980s, many companies realized the need for integrating their promotional tools. The companies started moving towards the process of integrated marketing communications (IMC), which involves coordinating the various promotional elements and other marketing activities that communicate with the firm's customers. Many advertising agencies realized the need of bringing various promotional tools under their folds to comprehensively offer all types of specialist services to their clients.

American Association of Advertising Agencies (4As) developed the first definition of integrated marketing communications (IMC) as follows:

"Integrated marketing communications is a concept of marketing communication planning that recognizes the added value of a comprehensive plan that evaluate the strategic roles of a variety of communication discipline–for example, general advertising, direct response, sales promotion and public relations–and combines these disciplines to provide clarity, consistency and maximum communication impact".

The 4As definition focuses on the process of using all forms of promotion to achieve maximum communication impact. However, another advocate of the IMC concept, Don Shultz of Northwestern University, argue for an even broader perspective that considers all sources of brand or company contact that a customer or prospective customer has with a product or service.

Shultz and others note that the process of integrated marketing communications calls for a "big-picture" approach to plan marketing and promotion programmes and coordinate the various communication functions. It requires that firms develop a total marketing communication strategy that recognizes how all of a firm's marketing activities, not just promotion, communicate with its customers.

Consumers' perceptions of a company and/or its various brands are synthesis of the bundle of messages they receive or contacts they have, such as media advertisements, price, package design, direct marketing efforts, publicity, sales promotion website, point-of-purchase displays and even the type of store where a product or service is sold.

The integrated marketing communications approach seeks to have all of a company's marketing and promotional activities project a consistent and unified image to the marketplace. It calls for a centralized messaging function so that everything a company says and does communicates a common theme and positioning. A large number of companies have adopted this broad perspective of IMC. They see it as a way to coordinate and manage their marketing communication programmes to ensure that they give customers a consistent message about the company and/or its brand.

The IMC approach helps companies identify the most appropriate and effective methods for communicating and building relationships with their customers as well as other stakeholders such as employees, suppliers, investors, interest groups and the general public.

Tom Duncan and Sandra Moriarty observe that IMC is a new-generation marketing approach being used by companies to focus their efforts in acquiring, retaining and developing relationships with customers and other stakeholders. They have developed a communication-based marketing model that emphasizes the importance of managing all corporate or brand communications, as they collectively create, maintain or weaken the companies' relationships with the customers and stakeholders that drive brand value. Message can originate at three levels—corporate, marketing and marketing communications—since all of a company's corporate activities, marketing-mix activities and marketing communication efforts have communication dimensions and play a role in attracting and keeping customers.

At the corporate level, various aspects of a firm's business practices and philosophies—such as its mission, hiring practices, philanthropies, corporate culture and ways of responding to inquires—all have dimensions that communicate with customers and stakeholders and influence relationships

At the marketing level, companies send messages to customers and other stakeholders through all aspects of their marketing mix, not just promotion. Consumers make inferences about a product on the basis of elements such as its design, appearance, performance, pricing, service support and where and how it is distributed. For example, a high price of a product may symbolize quality to customers, as may be its shape or design its packaging, brand name or the image of the stores in which it is sold.

At the marketing communication level, Duncan and Moriarty observe that all messages should be delivered and received on a platform of exceptional and strategic consistency in order to create coherent perceptions among the customers and stakeholders. This requires the interaction of various marketing communication messages and the functions of various promotional facilitators such as ad agencies, public relation firms, direct-response specialists and interactive agencies. The goal is to communicate with one voice, look and image across all the marketing communication functions and to identify and position the company and/or the brand in a consistent manner.

Many companies are realizing that communicating effectively with customers and stakeholders involves more than traditional marketing communication tools. Many marketers, as well as advertising agencies, are embracing the IMC approach and adopting total communication solution to create and sustain relationships between companies or brands and their customers.

The IMC approach is proving to be a permanent change that offers significant value to marketers in the rapidly changing communication environment they are facing in the new millennium.

WHY IMC IS GAINING IMPORTANCE

The IMC approach in marketing planning and strategy has been gaining popularity since 1990s and is being adopted by both large and small companies. It has gained immense popularity for companies engaged in consumer durable as well consumer non-durable goods. By coordinating their marketing communication efforts, companies can avoid duplication, take advantage of synergy among various promotional tools, and develop efficient and effective marketing communication programmes. Proponents of IMC argue that it is one of the easiest ways for a company to maximize the return on its investment in marketing and promotion.

Marketers' shift towards integrated marketing communications indicates an adaptation by marketers to a dynamic environment, especially with respect to consumers, technology and media. Significant changes that have occurred among consumers are with respect to demographics, lifestyle, media use and buying and shopping patterns.

The advancements in technology is creating new ways to reach to customers but these are affecting the traditional media. Television, radio, newspapers and magazines are now getting fragmented and reaching less number of and more selective audience than in the past. Other problems faced by marketers are poor response by consumers to the traditional advertising, new and interactive media availability, cluttering of advertisements and high advertising pitch from the competitors.

Some of the reasons for growing importance of IMC include the following:

- Marketing budget is being shifted from advertising to other forms of promotion, particularly consumer and trade promotions.
- Retailers are becoming more powerful and dominating than the manufacturers.
- New tools of marketing communication are emerging that are economical and target specific rather than the mass media.
- The Internet and e-commerce have emerged which have redefined the way business is done and the way companies interact and communicate with consumers.
- Companies are giving emphasis on communication with the consumers.
- Advertisers are emphasizing more accountability on the part of the ad agencies and the change is taking place in the way ad agencies are compensated.
- There is rapid growth and development of database marketing.

THE PROMOTIONAL MIX: THE TOOL FOR IMC

Every aspect and interaction of a business organization with the consumer and stakeholder communicates and every element of marketing mix implicitly communicates about the company and its brand. But most of an organization's communication with marketplace happens through carefully planned and controlled promotional programme. The tools used to accomplish an organization's communication objectives are referred to as **promotional mix**. The **promotion** has been defined as the coordination of all seller-initiated efforts to set up channels of information and persuasion to sell goods and services or promote an idea.

Promotional mix has various elements that need to be appropriately chosen to design an integrated marketing communication campaign. The elements that comprise IMC are advertising, direct marketing, public relations, sales promotions, publicity, personal selling interactive/Internet marketing. Each of the elements has certain advantage over the other. The elements are indicated in Figure 14.1

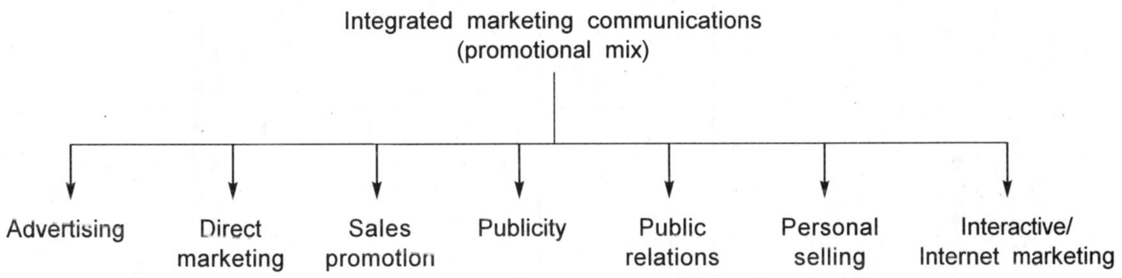

Fig. 14.1 Elements of IMC.

Each of the elements of IMC is a tool in the integrated marketing communications and plays a specific and distinctive role in an IMC programme. All elements may not be suitable for achieving a given communication objective. It is also required to understand that a given communication objective may require more than one or more element.

THE PROMOTIONAL PLANNING PROCESS

A promotional plan provides the framework for developing, implementing, and controlling the organization's integrated marketing communication programmes and activities. It must be remembered that promotion is only one part of marketing plan. Therefore, the promotion plan must be integrated to the overall marketing plan. The individuals responsible for planning promotional strategy must specify the role and function of each element of the promotional mix. They need to develop strategies and implementation tactics for each of the element.

A graphical representation of IMC planning process is indicated in Figure 14.2.

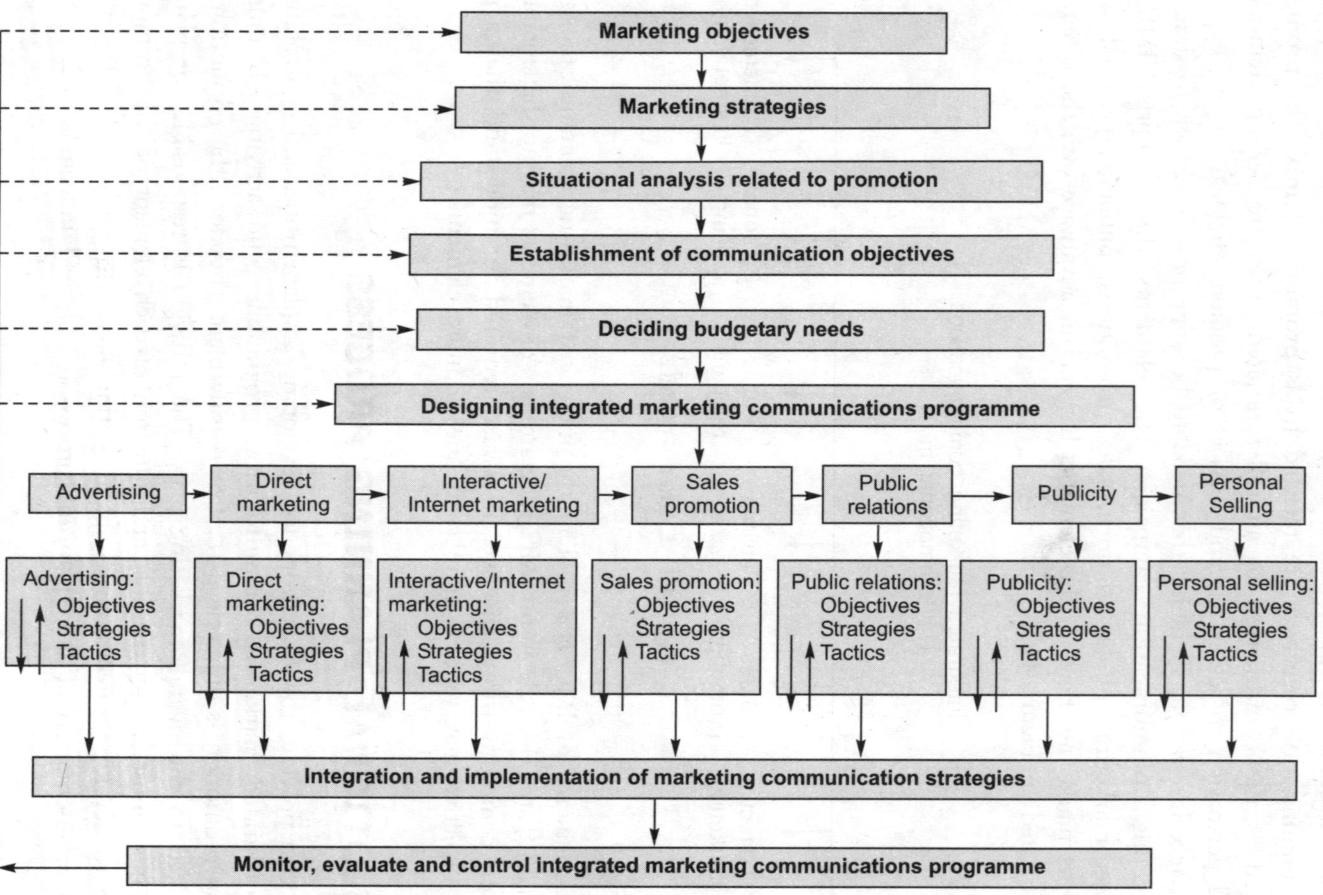

Fig. 14.2 The IMC planning process.

The process of integrated marketing communication begins with the review of marketing plan. The promotional manager/marketing manager must understand where the brand has been, its current position in the market, where it intends to go and finally, how it plans to get there. The review of marketing plan shall update the marketer about all these issues.

Thus, a marketing plan is a written document that describes the marketing strategy and programmes developed for a brand or product line. Basically, a marketing plan contains the following information:

Market situational analysis based on internal and external factors

Internal analysis covers assessment of company's promotional capabilities, review of company's previous promotional programmes and results, assessment of brand image and assessment of brand's or product line's relative strengths and weaknesses. External analysis covers customer analysis, competitor analysis and any trends and developments in the environment that might affect the promotional programme.

Specific marketing objectives

These objectives provide direction and a time frame for marketing activities and mechanism for measuring performance.

Marketing strategy

It includes the selection of target market(s) and the decisions related to marketing mix.

An action programme (tactics)

It is required for implementing the marketing strategies, including determining specific tasks and responsibilities.

Evaluation and control mechanism

It involves evaluating performance and providing feedback so that necessary control activities can be introduced and necessary changes can be made at the required places to assure that the objectives are met.

In reality, a promotional plan, in majority of the firms, is an integral part of the marketing strategy. The promotional manager must know the specific roles being played by advertising and other promotional mix elements in the overall marketing strategy. Promotional plan is developed based on the marketing plan and using detailed information contained in marketing strategy.

Promotional Programme's Situation Analysis

Situational analysis, here, focuses on those factors that influence or are relevant to development of a promotional plan. It includes both internal and external factors. Internal factors analysis assesses product/service offered, the relative strengths and weaknesses of the product/services, strength and weakness of the firm, capabilities and abilities of the firm to develop and implement promotional programme. External factor analysis focuses on factors such as characteristics of firm's existing and potential customers, impact of positioning strategy, competitors and other relevant environment, socio-eco-legal factors, etc.

Establishing Communications Objectives

Communications objectives are derived from marketing objectives. Communications objectives are what the firm seeks to accomplish with its promotional programme. These are generally stated in terms of nature of the message to be communicated or what specific communication effects are to be achieved. Communications objectives should become a guiding force for development of the objectives for each promotional mix.

Budget Determination

Determining how much to be spent for achieving what needs to be achieved is the next big question to be answered by a promotional manager. In practicality, promotional budgets are often determined on the basis of how much money is available for the purpose or percentage of company's or brand's sales revenue or what must be done to accomplish communications objectives. The next question is how this money is to be allotted among various elements of promotion mix. This decision is based on the role and function of each of the element of the promotion mix or how much contribution each element makes for achieving communications objectives.

Developing the Integrated Marketing Communications Programme

As discussed earlier, each element of promotional mix has certain advantages and limitations. Each of these elements is suitable and effective for a specific product category and situation. At this stage of the process, the promotional manager must review marketing objectives and strategy to understand what has to be accomplished and how it must be accomplished so that decisions can be made regarding the roles and functions of elements and their coordination with one another.

As indicated in Figure 14.2, each element is now specified in terms of objectives, strategies and action plan based on the role and function assigned to it by the promotional manager. While doing so, it must be ensured that there is no over lapping of objectives and programmes and necessary synergy is established for getting maximum efficiency and effectiveness.

Monitoring, Evaluation and Control

Once the implementation of various elements of promotional mix starts, a flurry of activities begins to take place and results start rolling. At this stage, it is important to determine how well the promotional programme is meeting communication objectives and helping the firm accomplish its overall marketing objectives. The manager needs to decide what to measure, where to measure, when to measure and who will measure the results or performance. The actual measured performance is then compared with the standard performance (communications objectives). Any deviation observed in actual performance needs to be immediately corrected with required programmes and activities.

ELEMENTS OF INTEGRATED MARKETING COMMUNICATIONS

Promotion is the coordination of all seller-initiated efforts to set up channels of information and persuasion to sell goods and services or promote an idea. These efforts may be in various forms and are to be carefully planned and controlled. All the tools and techniques used to promote the goods or services of an organization are referred to as elements or components of promotion or also known as promotional mix. These are as follows:

- Advertising
- Direct marketing
- Sales promotion
- Publicity
- Public relations
- Personal selling
- Interactive/Internet marketing

Each of these components is discussed further in detail.

ADVERTISING

Advertising is defined as any paid form of non-personal communication about an organization, product, service or idea by an identified sponsor. The paid aspect in this definition reflects the fact that the space or time for an advertising message generally must be bought. The non-personal component means advertising involves mass media (e.g. TV, radio, magazines, newspapers) that can transmit a message to large groups and an individual, often at the same time. Also, there is no opportunity for immediate feedback from the message recipient. Advertising is the most used and practised form of promotion for companies manufacturing mass consumption goods.

Ariel: Catching attention.

The advertisements of Ariel and Coca-Cola shown here indicate the power of advertising to catch attention and influence the consumers as desired by the companies.

There are valid reasons why advertising is so important for marketers. These are as follows:

- A cost-effective medium to reach vast audience.
- Very effective medium for generating awareness, providing knowledge and changing attitude.
- A highly used tool for creating brand images.
- Extensively used as a tool for creating differentiation among various brands.

Coca-cola: The power of advertising.

Advertising as a component of promotional tool has been discussed in depth throughout this book in many chapters.

DIRECT MARKETING

Direct marketing is the use of consumer direct channels to reach and deliver goods and services to customers without using marketing middlemen. It is a fast growing method in modern economy in which marketers communicate directly with target customers to generate a response and/or a transaction.

Direct marketing not only includes direct mail and mail order Catalogues but includes a number of activities like database management, direct selling, telemarketing, direct-response ads, websites, kiosks, interactive TV and radio, mobile phone devices. Direct marketing is becoming one of the fastest means of serving customers and growing in demand. Today, the direct-marketers use it for building long-term relationship with customer (customer-relationship marketing). Airlines, hotels and other businesses build strong customer relationships through frequency award programmes and club programmes. They send birthday cards, information materials or small premiums to select customers.

The companies like Amway and Tupperware, etc. do not use any other distribution channels and rely heavily on independent contractors to sell their products directly to consumers. Companies like Dell Computers and Gateway have been very successful by selling products through direct selling.

A typical sales letter, an important tool for direct marketing, is shown below.

Dear Sir,

We have honour to introduce ourselves as very old manufacture & supplier of Scientific Laboratory Glasswares (fabricated from borosilicate glass). Our factory was established in the year 1858, then we used to supply the Scientific Laboratory glassware all over the Indian including your establishment too in the brand name of 'ASGI'. In continuation of it with the same management, factory & skilled staff, in the year 1987, due to unavoidable circumstances we had to change our brand names as '*AGARWAL*'

We have been regularly supplying our 'AGARWAL' brand Scientific Laboratory Glassware to the Govt., Semi Govt. bodies & Defence research laboratories, Educational institutions for the last three decades. We are patronized with Annual rate contract with most of the establishments throughout India and the supplies are being make in bulk quantity to their entire satisfaction.

We M/s AGARWAL SCIENTIFIC GLASS INDUSTRIES used to supply you the Scientific laboratory Glassware in the brand name of 'AGARWAL'. And you have also been accepting the 'AGARWAL' brand name for the last three decade. But it is seen that some of our valuable dealer/customer are still placing the order to us in written or on phone for brand name of 'ASGI' (in short name). Hence it is requested please ask for 'AGARWAL' brand name in place of 'ASGI'.

It is a matter of proud for us to inform you that we have got. ISO 9001 : 2000 certificate specially in manufacturing and supply of Scientific Laboratory Glassware. SO we have proved ourselves the superfine manufacture of these items. Hence our company is a hub of Scientific Laboratory Glassware.

We would also like to mention that we have extended the validity of our Price List date 01.04.2005 up to 31.03.2007, with the same terms and conditions.

We hope we will get your same affection and cooperation as we got earlier.

Thanking you and assuming you of our best services and cooperation at all time

Yours faithfully.

A typical sales letter.

One of the major tools of direct marketing is **direct response advertising**, whereby a product is promoted through an ad that encourages the consumer to purchase directly from the manufacturer.

Factors Causing Growth of Direct Marketing

Direct marketing has been around for the past many centuries. This medium was in use since eighteenth century. Introduction of Catalogue marketing provided the impetus to the direct marketing. However, there are many other reasons that led to increased interest in direct marketing. These factors made direct marketing a highly attractive medium for both buyer and seller. These are discussed further.

Consumer credit cards

Huge amount of credit and debit cards is in circulation in India. A large amount of shopping centres, hotels, petrol pumps, retail shops are accepting payment through cards. This makes it feasible for consumers to purchase both low and high value items through direct-response channels and assure the sellers that they will be paid.

Direct-marketing syndicates

Companies specializing in list development, statement inserts, Catalogues and sweepstakes have opened many new opportunities to marketers. The number of these companies continues to expand, creating even more new users.

A salesman interacting with the consumer and explaining various attributes of the product.

Changing structure of the society and the market

The people world over have become economically well off and time poor. The salaries have grown rapidly, new jobs have emerged and families with dual income are growing. People now less prefer shopping because of paucity of time and this increased the attractiveness of direct purchases.

Technological advances

The rapid technological advancements in media and computers has made it easier for consumers to shop and for marketers to successfully reach the desired target market.

Telemarketing is an important tool of direct marketing in modern times.

Other factors

Various other factors have contributed to the increased effectiveness of direct marketing. These factors are sophisticated marketing techniques, changing values, industry's improved image, etc.. These factors will continue to ensure the success of direct marketing in the future.

Many companies rely solely on direct marketing to generate consumer response, whereas in case of many others, direct marketing is an integral part of IMC programme. In this case, direct marketing may have different role to play than sales objectives.

Direct Marketing Process

Direct marketing has number of elements that are required to be used appropriately. The various elements and their relationship is shown in Figure 15.3.

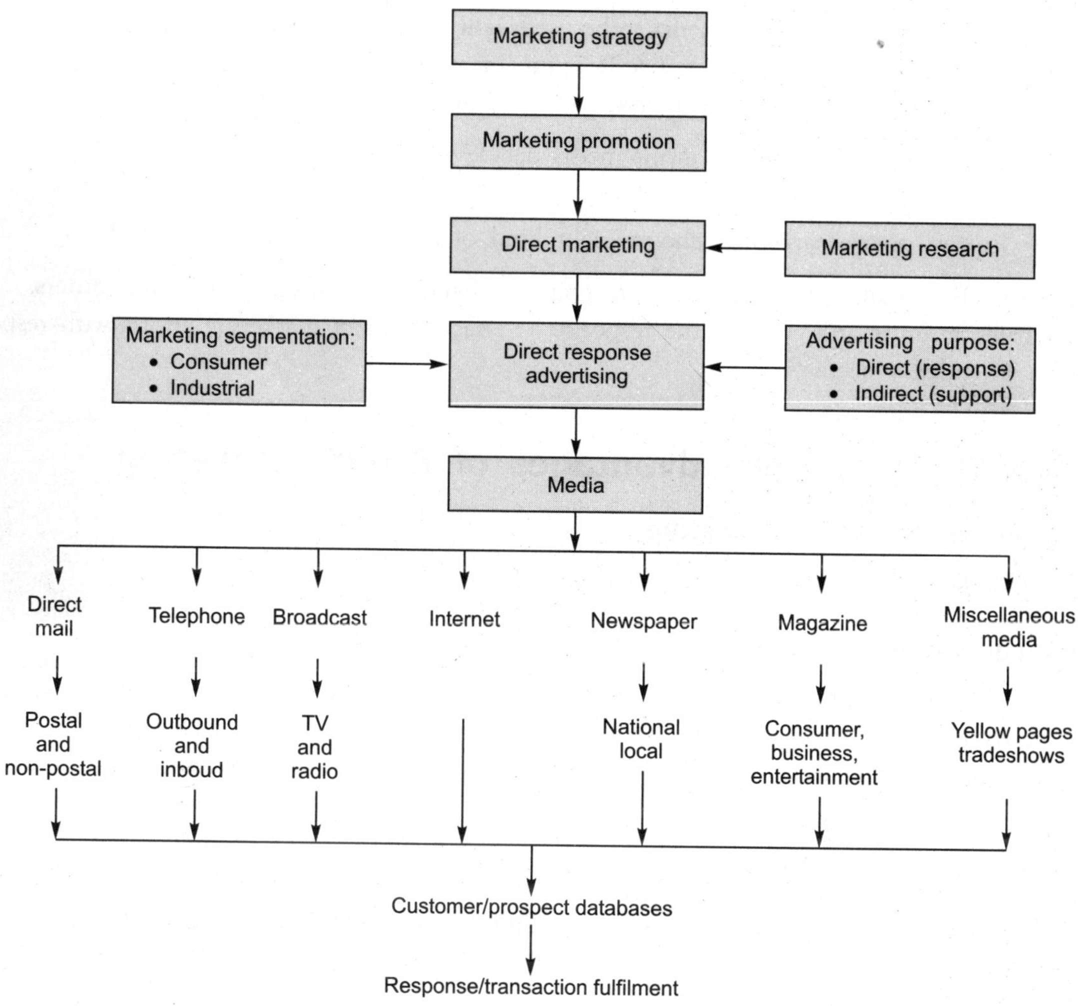

Fig. 14.3 Various elements of direct marketing process.

Operationalizing Direct Marketing

The first step in operationalizing direct marketing is to establish objectives for direct marketing. Decide what is the role of the direct marketing in an overall promotional planning of the brand.

The second step is to collect database of the target audience.

- The database source must be identified.
- Decide what information related to the customers is needed.
- Assure that the information obtained is complete, correct and current.

In the third step, decide the media to be used. Is it going to be direct mail, broadcast media, catalogues, telemarketing, electronic teleshopping or print media.

In the fourth step, decide the message to be sent to the customers.

- In case of direct mail and print media decide what do you want to say– the quality of paper, envelop, words and message, etc.
- In case of telemarketing, choose right kind of people and train them well.

In the fifth step, decide how you are going to handle responses, queries and orders.

Finally, measure and evaluate the response or effect of direct marketing efforts with respect to the intended objectives.

Advantages and Disadvantages of Direct Marketing

Advantages of direct marketing

Direct Marketing has the following advantages:

Personalization

It is the biggest advantage of direct marketing as this medium has the capability to personalize the message to the target audience. No other medium can do it so well. The message can be adapted for use depending upon the age, sex, education, purchase habits and lifestyle, etc.

Cost

Though the cost per thousand (CPT) may be high in absolute terms and a relative basis, its ability to specifically target the audience and eliminate waste coverage reduces the actual CPT. Also, the cost per sale is much lower than in other media. It is because, the cost of media being low, each sale costs less.

Measures of effectiveness

Since the feedback is immediate, direct and accurate, the measurement of effectiveness is far better than any other advertising medium.

Selective reach

Direct marketing makes possible to pinpoint the target audience and send message to them, thereby eliminating waste coverage. It is possible to target the audience that has a very high potential.

Segmentation capabilities

The marketers today can purchase the data such as a list of students who have appeared in CBSE class 12 examination in 2005, people who have purchased car, credit card holders club members, etc. The list so obtained allows a marketer to segment on the basis of geographic location, age, income level, educational qualification and occupation, etc. This can help the marketer to develop effective segmentation strategies.

Frequency

Depending upon the medium used, it may be possible to build frequency levels. Since direct-response TV advertising is very economical to use, a marketer can afford to purchase repeat times. But direct mail may not offer frequency, as consumers may be annoyed to receive the same mail repeatedly.

Flexibility

Direct marketing can use a variety of forms—a simple letter, videotape, brochure or any other creative promotional material.

Timing

Direct-response advertising takes less time to conceptualize and execute. It can quickly be assembled and sent to the audience.

Disadvantages of direct marketing

Some of the disadvantages of direct marketing are as follows:

(1) **Image factor:** Direct mail is generally considered as junk mail. Many people consider unsolicited mail promotes poor quality products. Some people do not like being solicited.

(2) **Accuracy:** The accuracy of database is doubtful. Lot of people move away, change occupation or change telephones.

If the list were not kept current, the response rate would be poor.

(3) **Rising Costs:** The postal and stationery cost is increasing day by day which directly impacts the profit.

(4) **Content Support:** The effectiveness of communication depends upon the contents. Creating the content that is attention grabbing and interest generating is a difficult task as far as direct mail and online is concerned.

SALES PROMOTION

In modern times, marketers have realized that advertising alone is not always enough to move their products off the store shelves into the hands of the ultimate buyer. Therefore, companies use sales promotion activities targeted both at consumers and trade partners. In addition, most companies also include in their integrated marketing communications programmes, the activities like direct marketing, advertising, publicity, public relations and personal selling.

A typical sales promotion ad.

An ad showing discounts or extra item.

Sales promotion is defined as "a direct inducement that offers an extra value or incentive for the product to the sales force, distributors or the ultimate consumer with the primary objective of creating an immediate sale.

Important Features of Sales Promotion

1. Sales promotion involves some type of inducement that provides an extra incentive to buy.
2. The incentive is the key element in a promotional programme. It may be coupon or price reduction, the opportunity to enter a contest or sweepstakes, refund or rebate, an extra amount of product or a free sample, etc.
3. It attempts to add value to the product or service while advertising appeals to the mind and emotions to give the consumer a reason to buy. Sales promotion appeals to the "value" (pocket) and provides an incentive for purchasing a brand.
4. It provides an inducement to marketing intermediaries. A trade allowance or discount gives retailers a financial incentive to stock and promote the company's product.
5. It acts as an acceleration tool. It is designed to speed up the selling process and maximize sales volume. It gives an inducement to the consumer to speed up his/her buying decision.
6. Sales promotion activities can be targeted at different parties with different types and levels of incentives.

Types of Sales Promotion Activities

There exists a plethora of activities that are practised by marketers to attract both consumers and retailers to maximize its marketing effectiveness. All sales activities can be divided broadly into two categories:

Consumer-oriented promotion: Activities like, samples, coupons, premiums, refunds/rebates, contests/sweepstakes, bonus packs, price off, frequency programmes, event marketing.

Trade-oriented promotion: Activities like contests and dealer incentives, trade allowances, point of purchase displays, training programmes, trade shows, cooperative advertising.

Consumer-oriented sales promotion: Consumer-oriented sales promotion programmes are directed at consumers to induce them to purchase the marketer's brand. It is also called **pull strategy.** It includes all the promotions and activities done by the marketers to attract the buyers to stores or dealers' place. Consumer-oriented sales promotion includes coupons, price off, extra quantity, bonus packs, frequency programmes, refunds, contests and sweepstakes, premiums, free samples, etc. This strategy works along with advertising to encourage consumers to purchase a particular brand. Consumer promotion is used by retailers to encourage consumers to buy in their showrooms. Many stores/retailers use their own coupons or sponsor contests and other promotions to increase store patronage.

An ad showing some advantage to consumers to attract them.

Trade-oriented sales promotion

Trade-oriented sales promotion programmes are directed at dealer network of the company to motivate it to sell more of the company's brand than other brands. The company designs programmes to motivate the dealer network to push the company's brand to the consumer. The assumption is that if the dealer network is provided greater incentives, it is likely to push company's brand on priority in comparison to competitor's brand. It is also known as **push strategy**, which is directed at dealer network so that they push the brand to the consumers by giving priority over other competitor brands because the brand offers greater pay back or more return on their money and efforts invested.

Trade-oriented sales promotion includes deal contests and incentives, trade allowances, point-of-purchase displays, sales training programmes, trade shows, cooperative advertising, etc. It is designed to motivate distributors and retailers to carry the additional stocks of the brand and make an extra effort to push it to their customers.

Many marketing programmes include both trade and consumer-oriented promotions since motivating both the groups maximizes the effectiveness of the promotional programme.

Why Sales Promotion is Gaining Importance

Though sales promotion has been part of the marketing process for a long time, its role and significance in integrated marketing communication programme has gained immense popularity during the 1990s. The total money on sales promotion has since then increased manifold, and also percentage of marketer's budget allocated to promotion has grown as well.

However, the allocation of marketing budget by an industry or company among consumer promotions, trade promotions and media advertising varies. It is also worth noting that a significant amount of the money that marketers allocate to media advertising is spent on ads that deliver promotion messages regarding contest, games, sweepstakes and rebate offers.

Some of the reasons for sales promotion gaining importance are discussed further.

Growing power of retailers

There is a shift at the marketplace from manufacturers to retailers. In the past, manufacturers of all major brands had great power and influence; retailers were just passive distributors of the brand. The retailer relied heavily on the manufacturers for everything. With the advent of new technology, intense competition, information explosion and consolidation of store, the retailers have now started dictating terms.

A supermarket showing myriad of products.

Declining brand loyalty

Over the last few years, the brand differentiation on functional and quality parameters has vanished. Thus, the brand loyalty is on the decline and the customers are purchasing more on the basis of price, value and convenience. However, some consumers always buy their preferred brand irrespective of promotional offers. But, there are many consumers who always look for coupons and deals when they make a purchase. When they view all brands equal, they may shift from one brand to another. The brands are essentially viewed as satisfactory and interchangeable.

A consumer choosing among many brands.

Brand proliferation

The market has become saturated with new brands across all product categories. Often new brands lack any significant advantages that can be used as the basis of an advertising campaign. Thus companies increasingly depend upon sales promotion activities to encourage consumers to try these brands. Sales promotion techniques can be used as part of shaping process to lead the consumer from initial trial to repeat purchase at full price. Marketers are relying more on samples, coupons, rebates, premiums and various other promotional tools to achieve trial usage of their new brands and encourage repeat purchase.

Competition

To maintain competitive advantage, manufacturers are increasingly using sales promotion. The markets for many products are stagnant and mature and it is becoming very difficult to boost sales through advertising. Thus, companies have started reworking their promotional budgets.

Rather than spending money on running off repeated dull advertising campaigns, the companies have started diverting a good portion of their budget to sales promotion.

Coke vs. Pepsi— The great competition.

Battle of the beverages
A breakdown of Coke and Pepsi's financials and products

	Coca-Cola	Pepsi
Stock Price*	$56.50	$52.06
52-Week High	$57.91	$53.50
Price change YTD	20.3%	7.2%
P/E	31.6	26.7
2002 Est Earnings Gr.	13.3%	13.4%
2003 Est Earnings Gr.	11.2%	12.3%
Market Value	$140.4 billion	$92.0 billion
2002 Est Revenue	$19.8 billion	$26.2 billion
New product	Vanilla Coke	Pepsi Blue
Top soft drink brands	Coke, Sprite, Fanta	Pepsi, Slice, Mountain Dew

*All stock price data as of May 9
Sources: First Call, CNN/Money, company reports

Many companies are using co-marketing (account specific marketing), a recent development whereby a manufacturer collaborates with an individual retailer to create a customized promotion that accomplishes mutual objectives.

Increased accountability

The companies have started asking their brand managers the returns they get for their promotional expenditures. Results from sales promotion are easier to measure than those from advertising. A large number of companies are demanding measurable, accountable ways to relate promotional expenditures to sales and profitability. It is a tendency of the product/brand manager, who is being held responsible for results, to often use price discounts or coupons, since these produce quick and easily-measured increase in sales. Also, at the same time, marketers are facing pressure from powerful retailers who demand sales performance from their brands.

Short-term focus

A good number of managers view consumer and trade promotions as the most dependable way to generate short-term sales, particularly when they are price-related. The dependence on sales promotion is high in mature and slow-growing markets, where it is difficult to stimulate consumer demand through advertising. The brand managers receive requests from sales force, retailers and wholesellers for sales promotion activities to meet short-term targets.

Fragmentation of the consumer market

Marketers are turning towards more segmented and highly-targeted approaches as the consumer markets are getting fragmented and mass media advertising is becoming less effective. The companies are trying to tailor their offerings and promotional efforts to the specific needs of the market. A large number of marketers are also using sales promotion techniques to target ethnic markets. The marketers try to host grassroot events at stores and have tie-ins with local festivals.

PUBLIC RELATIONS

Public relations is an important element of the overall communication programme of a business corporation. However, it may not have any specific objectives of product and service promotion. These activities are designed more to change attitude towards an organization or an issue than to promote specific products or influence behaviour directly.

Public relations is defined as "the management function which evaluates public attitudes, identifies the policies and procedures of an organization with the public interest and executes a programme of action (and communication) to earn public understanding and acceptance". Public relations involves the following steps:

- Determination and understanding of public attitudes
- Identification of policies and procedures of the organization that are offending the public interest and attitudes
- Designing and implementing the communication programme to bring about necessary changes in public understanding and attitudes

Role of Public Relations

Public relations (PR) must be viewed as a continuum because of the way companies use it in modern times. Public relations has two types of function—marketing and non-marketing.

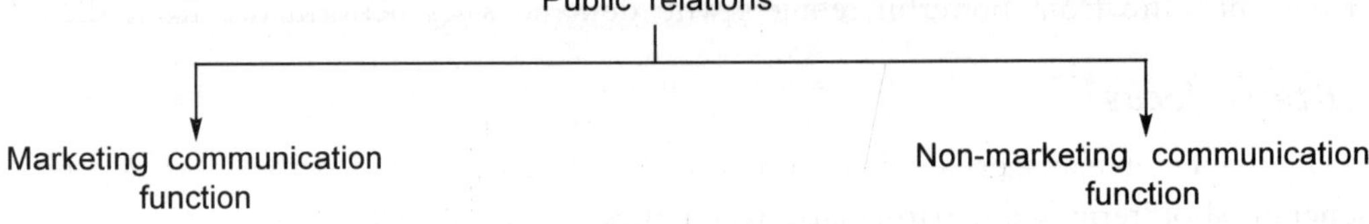

Marketing Functions

According to Thomas L. Harris, marketing public relations (MPR) functions are the PR activities designed to support marketing objectives. Some of the marketing objectives that may be aided by PR activities include raising awareness, informing and educating, gaining understanding, building trust, giving consumers a reason to buy and motivating consumer acceptance.

MPR plays the following roles in integrated marketing communication:

- Building marketplace excitement before media advertising breaks
- Creating advertising news where there is no product news
- Introducing a product with little or no advertising
- Providing a value-added customer service
- Building brand-to-customer bonds
- Influencing the influential
- Defending products at risk and giving consumers a reason to buy

Non-marketing PR functions

As a non-marketing function, the primary responsibility of a PR executive is to maintain mutually beneficial relationship between the organization and the publics, employees, community, investors, government, customers and other interest groups. At the other end of the continuum, PR is primarily considered to have marketing communication functions. In this, all non-customer relationships are perceived as necessary only in a marketing context.

Pictures showing PR executives on their work.

Cutlip, Centre and Broom have noted that marketing and public relations are complementary functions, "with each making unique and complementary contributions to build and maintain many relationships essential for organizational survival and growth." To ignore one is to risk failure in the other. This relationship is consistent with our thinking that PR is an important part of integrated marketing communication process, contributing in its own way but also in a way consistent with marketing goals.

Integrating PR into the promotional mix

Since PR has broader responsibilities, the issue is how to integrate it into the promotional mix. As discussed earlier, PR plays multiple roles at each of the extreme of the continuum. Marketing or PR can be the dominant function or both can be equal but have separate functions, or two can perform the separate roles.

Whether public relations takes on traditional role or a marketing-oriented one, PR activities are still tied to specific communication objectives. Assessing public attitudes and creating a favourable corporate image are as important roles as promoting products or services directly.

The Process of Public Relations

The PR process comprises of numerous series of steps in which PR is integrated with promotional mix and implemented. These are discussed below.

Determining and evaluating public attitudes

Because attitude may affect sales of a firm's product and no company wants to be perceived as a bad entity determining and evaluating public attitudes becomes a necessary part of a PR process. It has the following advantages:

- Provides input into the planning process
- Serves as an early warning system
- Secures support internally
- Increases the effectiveness of the communication

Establishing a PR plan

It involves the following steps:

- Define public relation problems
- Plan the programme
- Take action and communicate
- Evaluate the programme

Developing and executing the PR programme

It involves determining the relevant target audience–internal and external.

Internal audience includes employees, shareholders and investors, members of the local community, suppliers and current customers. External audience includes the people who are not closely connected with the organization–media, educators, civic and business organizations, governments and financial groups.

Implementing the PR programme

Once the research has been conducted and the target audience identified, the PR programme must be developed and delivered to the receivers. The tools used may be:

- Press releases
- Press conferences
- Exclusives
- Interviews
- Community involvement
- Internet

Advantages of PR

- Credibility of the corporation increases as PR is not perceived as paid communication.
- Cost of PR is very low when effects are considered.
- It avoids clutter. Since PR communication is perceived as news item, PR messages are not subject to the clutter of ads.
- Public relations facilitates lead generation. Information about technological innovations, medical breakthroughs and others results into large number of inquiries. These inquires may give the firm some good leads.
- Public relations has the ability to reach specific groups.
- It facilitates image building. Effective public relation helps to develop a positive image for the organization. A strong image helps a lot against later misfortunes.

Disadvantages of PR

- Public relations has the potential for not completing the communication process.
- Though PR messages can break through the clutter of commercials, the receiver may not make the connection to the course. Many a time, PR efforts are never connected with their sponsors in the public mind.

- It may also misfire as a result of mismanagement and lack of co-ordination with the marketing department.
- When marketing and PR departments operate independently, there is a danger of inconsistent communication, redundancies in efforts, etc.

PUBLICITY

Publicity refers to the creation of news about a person, product or service that appears in broadcast or print media. To many, publicity and PR are synonymous. In fact, publicity, in reality, is a part of public relation. However, publicity is different from public relations on issues like being a short-term strategy. While PR is designed to provide positive information about the firm and is usually controlled by the firm or its agent, publicity is not always positive and is not under control of, or paid for by the organization. Publicity, both positive and negative, often originates from sources other than the firm. Generally, publicity is controlled and disseminated by the PR department.

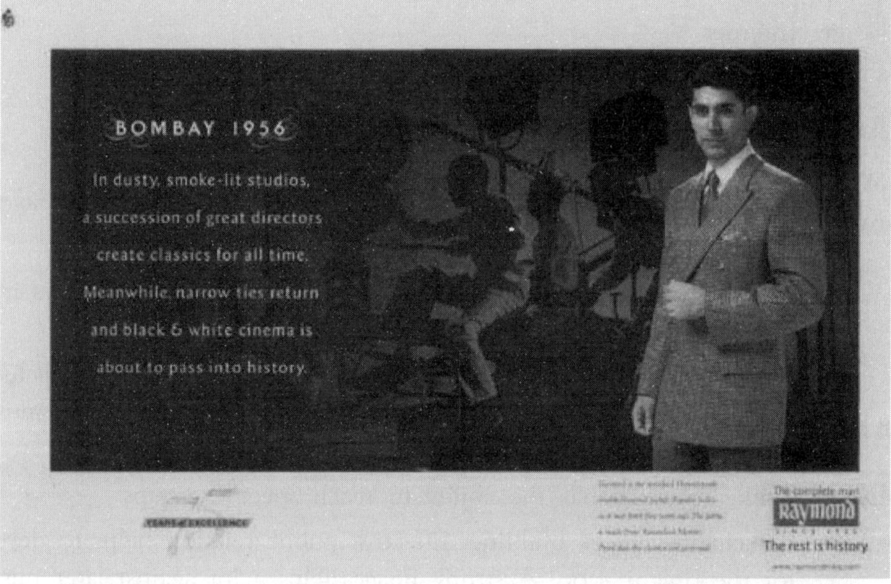

A news item about a company describing its achievements.

The Power of Publicity

The power which publicity wields is the important factor that separates it from other elements of IMC programme. Unfortunately, for the marketers, this power is not always realized in the way they would like it to be. Publicity can make or break a product or even a company.

Why Publicity is So Powerful

The following factors make publicity a powerful element of IMC programme:

- Publicity is highly credible, as it is not usually perceived as being sponsored by the company. Therefore, consumers perceive publicity information as more objective and place more confidence in it than information given by other elements of IMC programme.
- Publicity information may be perceived as endorsed by the medium in which it appears.
- Its news values and the frequency of exposure it generates also makes it powerful.
- Finally, publicity is news, and people like to pass on information that has news value. Publicity, thus, results in a significant amount of free, credible, word-of-mouth information regarding the firm and its products.

The Control Over Publicity

Unfortunately, the control of publicity is not in the hands of the company. Companies can not do much to stop media from releasing negative information. When publicity becomes news, it is reported by the media, sometimes, despite the efforts of the firm. However, publicity must be managed like any other promotional tool. Marketers must have control as much as possible over the time and place where the information is released. One of the ways is to have video news release, the video produced by the concerned organization, so that stations can air it as a news story.

There are courses offered and books written on how to manage publicity. The coverage includes: how to make a presentation, whom to contact, how to issue a press release and what to know about each medium addressed.

Advantages and Disadvantages of Publicity

Advantages of publicity

Publicity provides numerous advantages including:

- Credibility
- News value
- Significant word-of-mouth communication
- A perception of being endorsed by the media

Disadvantages of publicity

Publicity has the following disadvantages:

- It has potential for negative publicity.
- Timing is not always completely under the control of the marketer. Unless the press thinks the information has very high news value, the timing of the press release is entirely up to the media. Thus, the information may be released earlier than desired or too late to make an impact.
- Press release is the major source of publicity. Unfortunately, information sometimes gets lost in translation, i.e. it is not always reported the way the provider wishes it to be. As a result, inaccurate information, omissions or other errors may result.

Personal Selling

Personal selling is face-to-face selling and it involves direct person-to-person communication. In this the manufacturers directly sell their products to the customers. Personal selling establishes direct contact between the seller and the buyer, thereby reducing the need for intermediaries such as distributors, dealers and retailers. The functions of the intermediaries are now performed by the members of the sales team.

Salesmen negotiating deals across the table with their clients by exhibiting the products.

To get results from an effective promotional plan, the roles and responsibilities of the sales force must be integrated with overall communication programme. In most of the organizations, personal selling falls under the authority sales manager's and plays very important role in overall promotions effort. The importance varies from company to company depending upon the following factors:

- The nature of the product or service being sold
- Size of the organization
- Type of the product
- Belief of the corporation in personal selling

A salesman on the street to meet potential customers.

The responsibilities and specific tasks assigned to sales team may vary depending upon the objectives decided by the company for personal selling. Therefore, we can say that personal selling is an integral part of IMC as a partner, not a substitute for any other promotional mix element.

Generally, the companies involved in producing low-priced consumer non-durables do not emphasize on personal selling. However, small firms producing such goods do use personal selling heavily to sell their product at the initial stage by employing salespersons on commission basis.

Differences between Personal Selling and Other Forms of Promotional Elements

1. In personal selling, the message flows from the sender (salesperson) to the receiver (customer) directly.
2. The direct and interpersonal communication in personal selling process allows the sender to immediately receive and evaluate the feedback.
3. It permits the sender to modify and change its communication and market offer immediately based on the results of feedback evaluation to cater to the specific needs and wants of the receiver.
4. Personal selling offers greater opportunity for tailoring the message and more personalized communication than any other type of promotional element.
5. It has the ability to focus on identification and solution of specific problems, whereas a standard communication sent using any other promotional element does not measure up to the consumer's expectations.
6. Personal selling is important not only in industrial goods market but also in consumer non-durables and durables market as it helps in motivating intermediaries to stock and promote the product.
7. It reduces the distance between the company and the customer substantially and the salesperson is the face of the company who is believed to offer all solutions to the problems of consumer and the intermediaries.

Assigning the Role to Personal Selling

How do you determine what you want to accomplish through your sales team? What specific tasks these members of the sales team must attain for the company?

A head of the marketing function in a corporation must raise a few questions and find answers before identifying the role and responsibility for the personal selling in a promotional programme of the company.

A manager may be guided by the following questions before the role and responsibility is assigned to personal selling:

What communication objectives should be accomplished?

A salesperson may have variety of communication objectives to accomplish such as creating awareness of the product or service, demonstration of product benefits for attitudinal change, initiating trial use and/or closing the sale. He/she may also have to answer numerous questions, counter preconceived notions and identify unmet needs of the consumer.

What are various alternative ways to accomplish communication objectives?

Various promotional mix elements offer specific advantages over the others depending upon the category and nature of the product. While developing promotional mix, advantages and disadvantages of each element or promotional mix may be considered. Personal selling offers certain specific advantages in some situations and less appropriate in others.

How effective is each of the element in accomplishing communication objectives?

The effectiveness of each alternative must be evaluated based on criteria selected. It may be evident that personal selling is highly effective in many situations but other elements may be found more attractive in many other situations. Some of the major criteria that may be used for evaluating the alternatives are:

- The cost
- Benefits/returns
- The reach
- Uniqueness and consistency of message

How cost effective is each element?

Personal selling is a costly affair as it involves people who directly reach out to the customers. The overall cost per sale is much higher in consumer goods but it may turn out to be cost effective for industrial products. The cost of communicating the message is high in personal selling than in any other media.

Role and Responsibility of Personal Selling

The role and responsibility assigned to a salesperson varies from company to company and it also depends, to some extent, on the product category. For example, the role played by a salesperson selling industrial goods will vary from that of selling consumer non-durable goods.

Some of the roles or responsibilities of a salesperson are described below. However, it is not an exhaustive list.

Prospecting

It is the process of locating new customers. It involves the search for and qualification of prospective customers. A salesperson should generate leads and follow them. Leads may be generated from friends, existing customers, referrals, Yellow Pages or cold calls. Through leads, the salesperson identifies prospects (those who needs the product or service) and checks if those prospects are qualified, that is whether they have ability and willing to buy the product.

Identifying customer needs and wants

A salesperson gathers more information on the prospects and decides how to reach the potential customer. Through well-planned communication, salesperson identifies the exact need of the customers and assists them in determining their needs.

Providing solution to the customer's problem or need

Here the salesperson acts as an advisor who offers the potential customers various alternatives to solve their problems. The salesperson may provide the customers with information, which they may be unaware of or educate them on various aspects of a problem and its solution.

Attitude change

At this stage, a salesperson tries to influence the customers/prospectives favourably by showing them the capability of the firm and the product. He/she assures the customers that the company's product will satisfy their needs better than others. His/her task becomes easier in case the company has good corporate image (created through advertising and other promotional tools).

Closing the sale

Getting the sales order from the customer is one of the most difficult roles of a salesperson. Many salespersons make excellent presentation but hesitate in asking the customer to order for the product. The salesperson must be trained for closing the sale because after having done all the hard work, he/she must not stumble at this crucial stage.

Follow-up

Responsibilities of a salesperson do not end with sale. He/she must monitor the satisfaction level of the customer. Follow-up calls are important for maintaining good customer relationship, generating repeat sales and getting the opportunity to cross sell. Also, keeping the existing customer is more economical than finding a new customer.

The biggest advantage of a salesperson is the direct access he/she has with the customer. He/she can assess the situation first-hand and adapt the message accordingly. No other promotional tool provides this opportunity. A smart salesperson continuously analyses the situation, interprets the feedback from the customer and design the message to specifically meet the customer's needs.

Advantages and Disadvantages of Personal Selling

The nature of personal selling provides certain advantages over other promotional tools. Some of these advantages are given below:

(a) Possibility of two-way interaction
(b) Tailoring the message
(c) Lack of distraction
(d) Involvement in decision process
(e) Adaptability to the situation

Some of the disadvantages associated with personal selling are as follows:

(a) Inconsistent message
(b) Sales force/management conflict
(c) High cost
(d) Poor reach

INTERNET MARKETING

An incredible media got developed across the world in 1990s. It has become so popular that the entire global youth is hooked to it. It is growing at an astounding rate. The Internet is a worldwide means of exchanging information and communicating through a series of interconnected computers. The main component of the Internet is World Wide Web (WWW) but there are other features as well like e-mail, telnet, file transfer protocol, client server, hypertext transfer protocol (http) and gopher, etc.

The Web (Internet) has both users (customers) and the marketers (who want to reach out to users like sponsors, people engaged in e-commerce and advertisers, etc.). Over a period of time, the Web has widened a lot and there are sites developed that are targeted to consumers and sites for business to business (B to B) and business to customers (B-to-C).

The phenomenal growth of the Internet has been due to numerous reasons like continued economic prosperity, Internet innovations, heavy investment by corporations and the changing lifestyle of the people (between the age group of 15–40 years). The demographic profile of the Internet users is also changing.

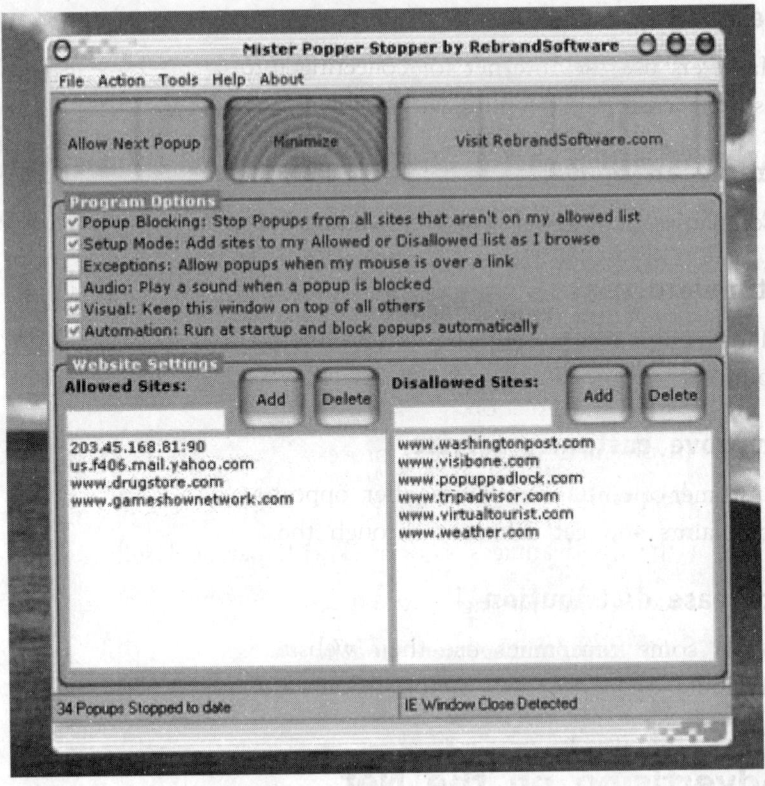

A typical Internet page for advertisement.

Why Companies Use the Internet

The Internet is a mixed media. It is a communication medium for companies to create awareness, provide information and influence attitudes and also pursue other communication objectives. It is also a direct-response medium, allowing the user to both purchase and sell products through e-commerce.

Basically, companies use the Internet for various communication objectives described briefly below.

Disseminate information

The Web is primarily used for providing in-depth information about a company's products and services. The customers, nowadays, expect a company to have a website which can provide them with detailed information about its products or services.

Create awareness

Advertising on the Web can be useful in creating awareness of an organization as well as product or service offerings.

Research

Marketers use the Internet for collecting information on the competitors and marketplace and also the customer profiling is possible.

Create an image

Companies design websites for building their image.

Stimulate trial

Many companies encourage visits to their sites through advertising and also offer electronic coupons.

Improve customer service

Customer-oriented companies offer opportunities to their customers to seek information, file complaints and get solutions through the Internet.

Increase distribution

While some companies use their websites to sell theirs products and others use them to distribute e-coupons and samples. Some companies even cross sell each other's products.

Advertising on the Net

The advocates of the Internet predicted death for the traditional media and closure of large outlet chains because the companies will move their advertising budget to the Internet and the customers will use e-commerce extensively. But fortunately, the traditional media as well as retail chains are alive and kicking. In fact, the Internet has come to be yet another media to be used by the corporate world. Now companies have started using it as an integrated part of IMC programme.

It is important to note that the Internet supports advertising and also relies on advertising for its own success. The Internet companies have been a boon to the traditional media as it spends huge amount of money to promote their sites. Like any other media, the Internet has become an important media for advertising products and services.

Advertising on the Internet may take a variety of forms such as banners, sponsorship, pop-ups, interstitials and push technologies.

Banners

Banner ads are the common form of advertising, which accounts for almost more than half the total budget for the Internet advertising. Banner ads are mainly used for creating awareness or recognition or for direct marketing purpose.

Banner ad on the Internet screen.

Sponsorship

Mainly, two types of advertising–regular and sponsorships–occur when a company pays to sponsor a section of a site. In content sponsorship, the advertiser not only provides money but also participates in providing the content itself.

Sponsorship ads on the Internet screen.

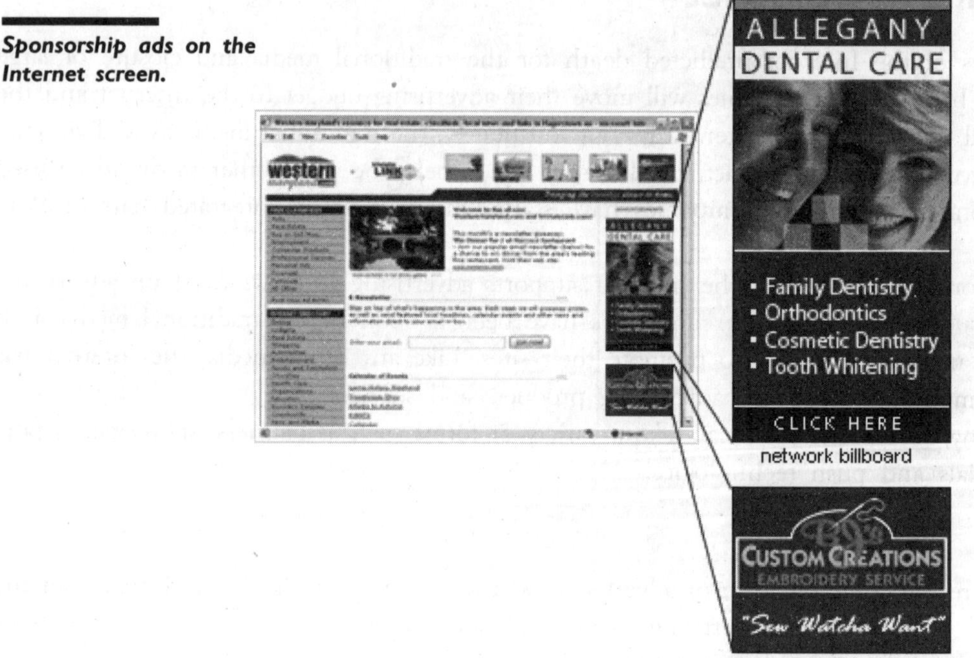

Pop-ups

Whenever a net surfer accesses the Internet, a small window appears which is known as pop-up. Pop-ups contain the advertisers' message. These are usually larger than a banner but smaller than a full screen.

Pop-up ads on the Internet screen.

Interstitials

Interstitials are those ads that appear on the screen while the surfer waits for a site's content to appear on the screen.

Push Technologies

This technology allows the companies to push a "message" to consumers rather than waiting for them to find it. It dispatches web pages and news updates and may have sound and video created to specific audience.

Sales Promotion on the Internet

Sales promotion is the most often used tools on the sites. The sites encourage the surfers to revisit again and again because it is the measure most sites use to charge money from the advertisers and sponsors.

Websites offer everything as sales promotion from the client. The offers such as free e-mail, sweepstakes, discounts, gifts, coupons, etc. are available. All kinds of companies use the Internet for sales promotion activities. If you visit sites of airlines, automobile companies, telecommunication, etc., you could find the same.

Direct Marketing on the Net

Direct marketing on the Internet can be seen from two perspectives–one as a tool for communication objectives and other as e-commerce. Many direct marketing tools like direct mail, database marketing, infomercials have been adopted on the Internet. This method is found to be very cost effective and prompt. E-commerce or as it is called direct sales, has really taken off well. The use of e-commerce is expanding in India not only in volume but also on varieties of products offered. Consumers buy more and more items online. Most of the products purchased on the Internet are CDs, books, travel packages, air tickets and stocks, etc. Many other products like clothing, automobiles and computers, etc. are finding their way to the Internet purchase.

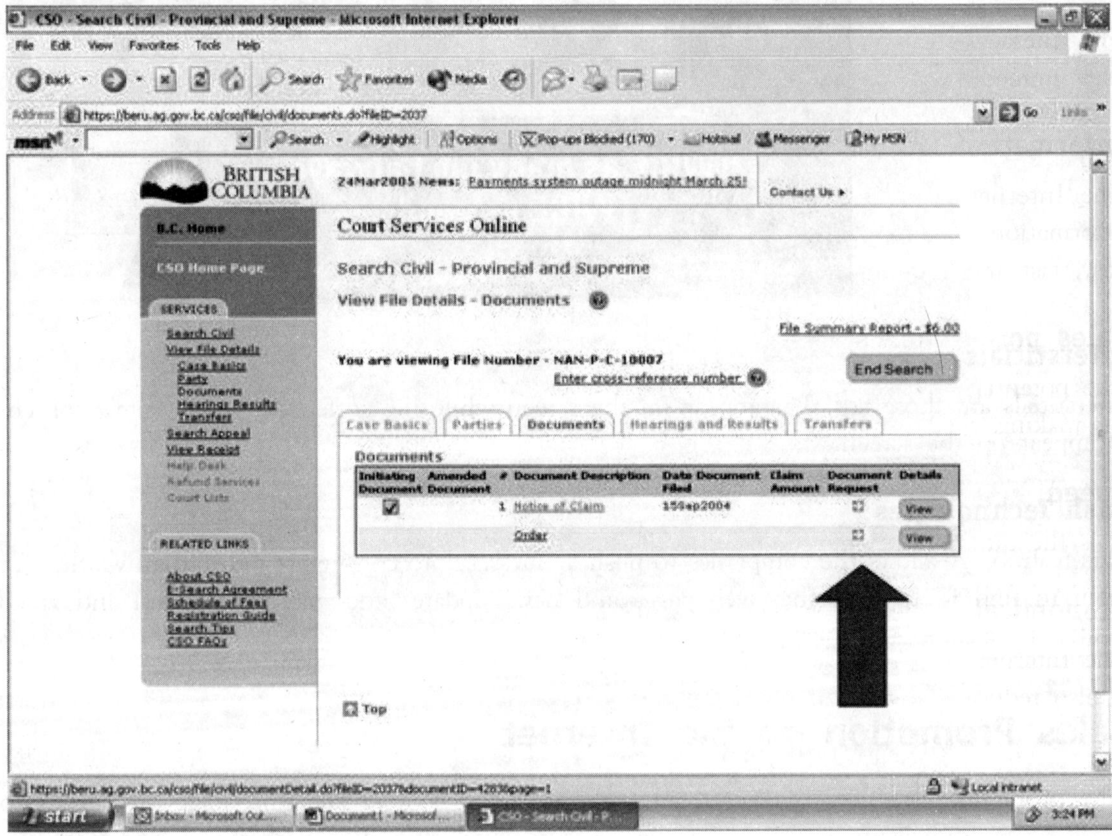

A typical online purchase screen on the Net.

Advantages and Disadvantages of the Internet

Advantages

The Internet provides a number of advantages over other traditional media used for marketing communication. Some of them are as follows:

Target audience

The Internet has the greatest ability to target the specific individuals or groups with a minimum cost and time. The companies are making their sites more tailored to meet the customer's needs and wants.

Message factoring

Ability to target the customers helps design the message as per the specific needs of the target audience.

Interactive capability

The interactive capability of the Internet enhances the consumer involvement and satisfaction as it immediately provides the feedback.

Information access

The Internet is a big information house. The Internet users can find a large amount of information on a particular topic or issue of interest. Getting relevant information is made very easy, fast and economical.

Sales potential

The potential for sales is very big in the Internet marketing. It provides sufficient information for making sales decision. The consumer needs to visit the seller's place for buying.

Speed

It is the quickest means of acquiring information and also making a transaction.

Economical

The Internet is great medium to economize expenses for small companies selling their goods. It also reduces the cost of operation of the buyer.

Disadvantages

The Internet though have many advantages, it also has certain disadvantages. Some of the disadvantages of the Internet are as follows:

Chances of fraud

Hacking is creating lot of problems for the Internet. Many sellers attempt to dupe the buyers through false promises and delivery.

Internet snarls

Increasing number of users is causing slowdown in the speed of the Internet. Downloading of information takes a long time. At times, many sites become inaccessible due to large number of visitors or technical snags.

Clutter

There are chances that an advertisement may not be noticed due to excessive proliferation of ads.

Costs

Though use of the Internet is cheap, it is getting costlier with its increasing demand.

Other major problems related to the Internet are measurement of effectiveness and audience characteristics.

The Internet as a medium is emerging as a powerful tool which often marketing managers overlook. But what is important here is how to fit the Internet into an IMC programme. A marketing manager should have to decide what exactly are the objectives that the Internet can meet. This medium will become an integral part of IMC in the near future and may garner a great share of total IMC budget.

SUMMARY

Integrated marketing communications (IMC) uses all forms of promotion to achieve maximum communication impact. The IMC would require a firm to develop a total marketing communication strategy that emphasizes not just the promotion but also how all of a firm's marketing activities communicate with its customers. It seeks to have all of a company's marketing and promotional activities project a consistent and unified image to the marketplace.

The growing importance of IMC is because of the growing power of retailers, emerging communications tools which are economical and target specific, growing database marketing and greater accountability demanded by advertisers from the ad agencies. The process of integrated marketing communications starts with marketing situation analysis, review of marketing plan, establishing communication objectives and choosing elements of promotional mix.

The IMC has a mix of elements such as advertising, direct marketing, public relations, sales promotions, publicity, personal selling and Internet marketing.

Advertising is any paid form of non-personal communication about an organization, product, service or idea by an identified sponsor. Direct marketing is the use of consumer direct channels to reach and deliver goods and services to customers without using marketing middlemen. Sales promotion is a direct inducement that offers an extra value or incentive for the product to the sales force, distributors or the ultimate consumers with the primary objective of creating an immediate sale. Public relations is a management function, which evaluates public attitudes, identifies the policies and procedures of an organization with the public interest and executes a programme of action to earn public understanding and acceptance. Publicity is the creation of news about a person, product or service that appears in broadcast or print media. Personal selling is face-to-face selling and it involves direct person-to-person communication. Internet marketing is a mixed medium. It is a communication medium for companies to create awareness, provide information and influence attitudes and also a direct-response medium, allowing the user to both purchase and sell products through e-commerce.

QUESTIONS

1. Discuss various reasons why IMC has become so popular among marketers over the last one decade?
2. Do you think the growth of IMC will continue in the future? If yes, why? If no, why not?
3. Analyse the role of integrated marketing communications in the marketing airline services and health care products in India?
4. Why has direct marketing become so significant at the marketplace for the last few years?
5. Discuss how the following companies might employ database marketing: A hotel company, an industrial goods company and a finance company.
6. Why is the Internet gaining popularity in media planning of marketing managers? What kind of product category is the Internet best suited for?
7. Identify some advantages and disadvantages that an automobile company might have while using the Internet for its brand promotions.

8. How consumer-oriented and trade-oriented sales promotions differ from each other? How these can fit into IMC of a consumer goods company?
9. Identify the reasons that have led to the shift of marketing budget from traditional advertising media to sales promotion. Discuss the impact of this shift.
10. Why public relations should be a part of IMC? Describe advantages and disadvantages of use of public relations in IMC.
11. Explain how personal selling is a cost-effective and high result-oriented activity. What advantages it might provide to an automobile company?
12. Identify role of a salesperson. How can a salesperson become more effective in his/her role?

CHAPTER 15

Advertising in a Multicultural Environment

LEARNING OBJECTIVES

After reading this chapter, you will be able to:

- Examine the basic principles of advertising and how they are applied globally.
- Review the evolution of international advertising.
- Understand intercultural effects on international advertising.
- Know the various factors in the international environment which influence advertising and promotion decisions.
- Examine the pros and cons of global versus localized advertising.
- Understand the new media of international advertising, i.e. the Internet and e-mail advertising
- Examine laws and regulations pertaining to international advertising.

CASE STUDY: RELEVANCE OF KISS RULE IN GLOBAL ADVERTISING

Years ago, a management guru said, "Keep It Simple, Stupid", giving birth to the KISS rule in American management philosophy. Well, it turns out that KISS has a place in global advertising as well.

Over the last decade, advertisers have been getting better and better at creating advertising campaigns that succeed on a global level. The International Advertising Festival at Cannes demonstrates this fact annually. Every year, more and more of the winning campaigns are found to the global campaigns, not just domestic market campaigns. They work as well in Boston as they do in Brussels. Another demonstrated fact annually is that these winning campaigns are actually quite simple in terms of message theme and visual structure. Certainly, some product categories lend themselves more readily to a global stage than do others. Lifestyle products such as soft drinks, jeans, sneakers and candy translate well across cultures. The brands like Nike, Pepsi and Levi's speak to the world and each has been the subject of memorable award-winning campaigns. But what makes these brands as well suited to a global audience—even beyond the natural fit of lifestyle product category?

The campaigns that work best on a global scale are those where the brand and its imagery are inextricably one and the same. Innovative product demonstrations or images where the pictures tell the story are the foundation of effective global advertising. Advertising that succeeds in the global arena draws on four constants—simplicity, clarity, humour and clever demonstration. Simplicity, clarity, humour and clever demonstration (SCHC) does not exactly spell KISS, but the reason that global ads that highlight these qualities can bridge the complexities and distinctiveness of one culture to other is simple. Granted, what is funny to a Brit may be lost on a Brazilian, but the key is to find not the culturally-bound humour in a demonstration, but the culturally-shared humour. When it comes to copy, simplicity and clarity rule. Apart from their inherent value, their ability to communicate across the cultures is quite, clear. In short, actually trying to bridge cultures may be just the thing that complicates the situation. Reducing a brand and its message to the simplest and most common human values has a great chance of succeeding. (***Source***: Jay Schulberg, "Successful Global Ads Need Smplicity Clarity", *Advertising Age*, June 30, 1997, 17)

In this chapter, we will look at international advertising and the various issues advertisers must consider while communicating with consumers around the globe. We will examine the cultural environment of international advertising and how companies often must adapt their messages to conditions in each country. We will review the debate over whether a company should use a global advertising approach or tailor it specifically for various countries. We will also consider the new medium of global adverting, i.e. the Internet.

EVOLUTION OF INTERNATIONAL ADVERTISING

For most companies, industrialized nations represent the greatest marketing and advertising opportunities. But most of these countries have stable population bases, and their markets for many products and services are already saturated. Many marketers are turning their attention to parts of the world whose economies and consumer markets are growing. In the early to mid-1990s, many marketers began turning their attention to the "four tigers" of Asia—South Korea, Singapore, Honk Kong and Taiwan—which were among the fastest growing markets in the world. However, in 1997, the Asian economy crisis hit, and these countries, as well as other parts of Asia, experienced a serious recession, which resulted in major decline in consumer spending. Latin America also has been experiencing a severe economic crisis over the past several years. The global economic slowdown that began in 2001 has created problems for most multinational companies and has led to reductions in advertising spending in most countries. The economies in many countries are stagnant, making it difficult for companies to meet their growth objectives. However, a number of multinational companies are focusing on markets experiencing stronger economic growth, such as those in China. Many companies are also turning their attention towards third-world countries where consumer markets are slowly emerging.

Coca-Cola : Reflects Style 1907.

INTERNATIONAL PERSPECTIVE

Companies are focusing on international markets for a number of reasons which are discussed further.

1. Many companies recognize that their domestic markets offer them limited opportunities for expansion because of slow population growth, saturated markets, intense

competition and/or an unfavourable marketing environment. The rates of annual population and household growth for North America, Western Europe and Japan have slowed down to 2 or 3 per cent per year.

2. Many companies must focus on foreign companies to survive. Most European nations, which are relatively small in size and without foreign markets, would not have the economies of scale to compete against large US and Japanese companies.
3. The mature markets of developed countries in America and Europe are becoming even more price-competitive (and less profitable) for major brands, with an increasing number of consumers preferring to buy cheaper private label brands. On the other hand, consumers in the rapidly-developing markets of Asia (and elsewhere) are showing a voracious appetite for branded goods, which often serve a need to reflect rapidly-changing social aspirations.
4. The crumbling of political, economic and customs barriers in the last few years has made it much easier for companies to operate in a truly global manner, instead of merely multinationally or in a multidomestic manner. For instance, the increasing integration of western European economies and formation of the European Union and the opening up of the eastern European markets to the West, means that companies can now more easily consolidate their production facilities for Europe in one country instead of producing locally in every European country, thus realizing economies of scale. This has led to the increased attention to the need to create truly global brands that can take advantage of such economies.
5. The growth of global media has led both to the increasing homogenization of consumer tastes across the world and the increasing use of standardized or global advertising campaigns which can be seen simultaneously in many different countries.
6. Since international advertising sells essentially the same product in multiple countries, a global company can invest far more resources in research and development than smaller local competitors. The R&D expenses of a global company can be amortized over its much larger sales volume. Also, it can exploit good ideas on a worldwide basis and introduce products quickly into various world markets.
7. International advertising also ensures a consistent international brand and/or company image.
8. It also leads to simplification of coordination and control of marketing and promotional programs.

The argument for global commonality of tastes was made very strongly by Harvard Marketing professor Ted Levitt, who wrote in 1983 that nothing confirmed such globalization more than "the success of McDonald's from the Champs Elysees to the Ginza, of Coca-Cola in Bahrain and Pepsi-Cola in Moscow and of rock music, Greek salad, Hollywood movies, Revlon cosmetics, Sony televisions and Levi jeans everywhere." Levitt argued that such homogenization of tastes allowed perceptive global marketers to market very similar products worldwide at lower cost than small-scale local producers.

Gillette used global advertising in the early 90s to launch its sensor shaving system, which became one of the most successful products in the company's history. The advertising theme for the global campaign was "The Best a Man Can Get." At the end of the decade, Gillette launched the Mach3, its new triple-bladed shaving system, and once again used a global campaign built around the high-tech theme of the product and retaining the same tagline. Prior to the introduction of the new product, Gillette launched the Mach3.com website, which was supported by online advertising to educate prospective customers about the intricacies of the triple-bladed razor. The Web campaign was followed by a $200 million global media blitz that helped make the Mach3 the number one selling shaving system after less than a year on the market.

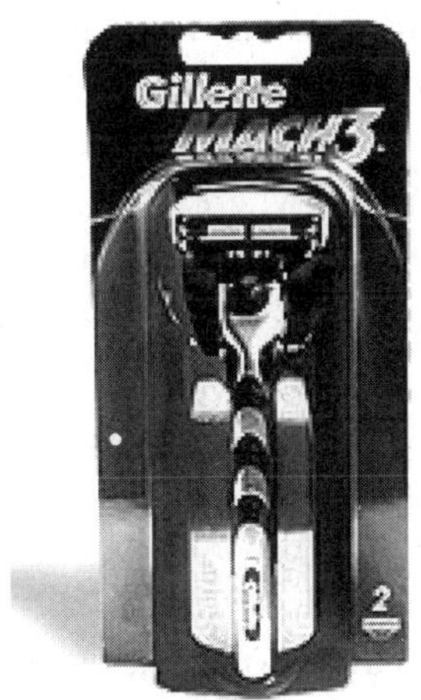

Gillette: Quite successful.

INTERCULTURAL ADVERTISING

There is the reality, of course, that consumers in every country are still somewhat different from each other, with different habits, tastes and preferences. Therefore, the product or brand that works in one market may not work in other. For example, while Americans like to drink orange juice for breakfast, French consumers do not. Generally, people living in different countries often belong to different cultures and cultures may even vary widely within a large and multiethnic country (such as India). Every culture is a complex web of social relations, religious beliefs, languages and consumption attitudes and habits, all of which will obviously impact on how communications are delivered and received. It is a basic principle in communication theory that, for any communication to be successful, the sender of the message must understand the frame of reference of the receiver of the message. Obviously, therefore, a multinational advertiser must understand the cultural nuances of a local market in order to be successful, because it may vary substantially from the culture of the "home" market.

There are many ways to contrast cultures, such as their degree of *traditionalism* versus *secularization*, the degree to which they rely on explicit and verbal information (so-called *low-context cultures*) versus implicit and nonverbal information (called *high-context cultures*), and the degree to which they are *individual-oriented* versus *interdependent* or *relational*. For instance, researchers classify North America and West European cultures as relatively more secular, low-context and individual-oriented, compared to Asian cultures, with Hispanic cultures falling somewhere in between. Given the demonstrated differences across cultures on these and other dimensions–including level of economic development–it seems entirely logical that consumers in different countries may have different ways of deciding which brands to buy, different levels of involvement towards the same product categories, different attitudes towards advertising and so on.

Certain product categories such as food and beverages, have a high degree of *cultural grounding*, where such cultural differences make global standardization more difficult than in other categories. Media availability and distribution arrangements are often very different and government regulations also vary. Consumers have different expectations and preferences concerning colours (purple is a death colour in Brazil, whereas white is the colour of funerals in Hong Kong). And the competitive environment for a particular brand may vary dramatically; it may be the leader in one market, but a minor brand in another. It may face brands that follow very different positioning strategies across these many markets. It may even be at different stages of the life cycle in different markets–new in one, mature in another–so that having a standardization advertising approach makes little sense.

Finally, advertising campaigns that are standardized and so can be used in multiple markets, if not the whole world, have the obvious disadvantage that they may be aimed at the lowest common denominator and may end up not appealing strongly enough to any particular market. As Laurence Hagan, the London-based Director of Marketing Development for J. Walter Thompson, put it, "The greater the audience for any message, the more bland and general, the less specific and compelling, that message will be."

We will now discuss in detail the various factors in international environment which influence international advertising.

ECONOMIC ENVIRONMENT

A country's economic conditions indicate its present and future potential for consuming, since products and services can be sold only to countries where there is enough income to buy them. Developed countries have the economic infrastructure in terms of the communications, transportation, financial and distribution networks needed to conduct business in these markets effectively. By contrast, many developing countries lack purchasing power and have limited communication networks available to firms that want to promote their products or services in these markets.

Advertising also can be, and often is, a tool of the "phenomenon of consumerism," as Pope John Paul II delineated it when he said, "It is not wrong to want to live better; what is wrong is a style of life which is presumed to be better when it is directed towards 'having' rather than 'being', and which wants to have more, not in order to be more but in order to spend life in enjoyment as an end in itself." Sometimes, advertisers speak of it as part of their task to "create" needs for products and services, -that is, to cause people to feel and act upon cravings for items and services they do not need. "If a direct appeal is made to his instincts—while ignoring in various ways the reality of the person as intelligent and free—then consumer attitudes and life-styles can be created which are objectively improper and often damaging to his physical and spiritual health."

This is a serious abuse, an affront to human dignity and the common good when it occurs in affluent societies. But the abuse is still more grave when consumerist attitudes and values are transmitted by communication media and advertising to developing countries, where they exacerbate socio-economic problems and harm the poor. It is true that a judicious use of advertising can stimulate developing countries to improve their standard of living. But serious harm can be done to them if advertising and commercial pressure become so irresponsible that communities seeking to rise from poverty to a reasonable standard of living are persuaded to seek this progress by satisfying wants that have been artificially created. The result of this is that they waste their resources and neglect their real needs, and genuine development falls behind.

De Beers and Nirvana: Extremely alluring.

Similarly, the task of countries attempting to develop types of market economies that serve human needs and interests after decades under centralized, state-controlled systems is made more difficult by advertising that promotes consumerist attitudes and values offensive to human dignity and the common good. The problem is particularly acute when, as often happens, the dignity and welfare of society's poor and weak members are at stake. It is necessary always to bear in mind that there are "goods which by their very nature cannot and must not be bought or sold" and to avoid "an 'idolatry' of the market" that, aided and abetted by advertising, ignores this crucial fact.

DEMOGRAPHIC ENVIRONMENT

Major demographic differences exist among countries as well as within them. Marketers must consider income levels and distribution, age and occupation, distributions of the population, household size, education and employment rates. Demographic data provides an insight into the living standards and lifestyles in a particular country to help companies plan ad campaigns. It also reveals the market potential of various foreign markets.

Tendencies towards globalization of tastes and of trends, are especially apparent when one looks at particular demographic subcategories. Teenagers the world over, for example, are more exposed than adults to cultural influences from other countries, through fashions, music, clothing, food, personal appearance, and sports. While regional and national differences still persist, teenagers the world over increasingly watch the same TV channels and movies, listen to the same music, idolize the same music and sports stars, and play the same videogames. Their lives and aspirations are shaped worldwide by the same global trends of increasing divorce among parents, a fear of AIDS and environmental concerns. Teens typically travel abroad more than their parents and are more likely to know a foreign language, especially English. Not surprisingly, teenagers are less likely to be parochial and nationalistic, and more likely to identify with pan-national organizations (such as a feeling of being an "European" and not simply "German" or "French").

Malbora: Appeal to teenagers around the globe.

It should be noted, by way of warning, that it is entirely possible that the trend towards more homogeneous brand preferences we are seeing is not one of true globalization but rather simply one of the increasing popularity in the rapidly-developing parts of the world (such as China, India, South America and Eastern Europe) of the brands and cultural symbols that imply a larger-than-life "western" or even "American" lifestyle—such as Coca-Cola, Marlboro cigarettes (with its Marlboro man cowboy imagery), Levi jeans, Nike shoes and so on. Thus, it is possible that the apparent increase in demand for certain well-known brands is largely because they are seen by consumers in many newly-opened markets as symbols of the freedom and affluent lifestyles of the West, and not because they are seen as global brands per se.

Much advertising directed at children apparently tries to exploit their credulity and suggestibility, in the hope that they will put pressure on their parents to buy products of no real benefit to them. Advertising like this offends against the dignity and rights of both the children and the parents. It intrudes upon the parent-child relationship and seeks to manipulate it to its own base ends. Also, some of the comparatively little advertising directed specifically at the elderly or culturally-disadvantaged seems designed to play upon their fears so as to persuade them to allocate some of their limited resources to goods or services of dubious value.

Communicators also can find themselves tempted to ignore the educational and social needs of certain segments of the audience—the very young, the very old, the poor—who do not match the demographic patterns (age, education, income, habits of buying and consuming, etc.) of the kinds of audience advertisers want to reach. In this way, the tone and indeed the level of moral responsibility of the communication media in general Calvin Klein: Universal appeal are lowered.

Calvin Klein: Universal appeal.

All too often, advertising contributes to the invidious stereotyping of particular groups that places them at a disadvantage in relation to others. This often is true of the way advertising treats women; and the exploitation of women, both in and by advertising, is a frequent deplorable abuse. They are often treated not as persons with an inviolable dignity but as objects whose purpose is to satisfy others' appetite for pleasure or power.

How often is the role of woman as wife and mother undervalued or even ridiculed? How often is the role of women in business or professional life depicted as a musculine caricature, a denial of the specific gifts of feminine insight, compassion, and understanding, which so greatly contribute to the 'civilization of love'?" Women world over are seeking to actively participate in workplace success and identify less closely than before with the traditional female roles of mother/nurturer and wife/homemaker.

CULTURAL ENVIRONMENT

Advertising also can have a corrupting influence upon culture and cultural values. We have spoken of the economic harm that can be done to developing nations by advertising that fosters consumerism and destructive patterns of consumption. Consider also the cultural injury done to these nations and their people by advertising whose content and methods, reflecting those prevalent in the first world, are at war with sound traditional values in indigenous cultures. Today this kind of "domination and manipulation" via media rightly is "a concern of developing nations in relation to developed ones," as well as a "concern of minorities within particular nations."

Cultural variables which the marketers must consider include language, customs, tastes, attitudes, lifestyles, values and ethical/moral standards. Marketers must be sensitive not only in determining what products and services they can sell to foreign cultures but also in communicating with them.

International advertisers often have problems with language. The advertiser must know not only the native tongue of the country, but also its nuances, idioms and subtleties. They must be aware of the connotations of words and symbols used in their messages and understanding how advertising copy and slogans are translated. For example, *Pepsodent* toothpaste was unsuccessful in Southeast Asia because it promised white teeth to a culture where black and yellow teeth are symbols of prestige. An American ad using various shades of green was a disaster in Malaysia, where the colour symbolizes death and disease.

Tastes, traditions, values and customs are also important parts of cultural considerations. The customs of a society influence what products and services its people will buy and how they must be marketed. Cultural values are beliefs and goals shared by members of a society regarding ideal end states of life and modes of conduct. Society shapes consumers' basic values, which influence their behaviour and determine how they respond to various situations. Values such as *ethnocentrism,* which refers to the tendency for the individuals to view their own group or society as the centre of the universe, or *nationalism* often influence the way consumers in various countries respond to foreign brands or even advertising messages.

Religion is another aspect of culture that influences norms, values and behaviours. For example, in many Arab countries, advertisers must be aware of various taboos resulting from conservative applications of the Islamic religion. Alcohol and pork cannot be advertised. Human nudity is forbidden, as are pictures of anything sacred such as images of a cross or photographs of Mecca. The faces of women may not be shown in photos, so cosmetics use drawings of women's faces in ads. In conservative Islamic countries, many religious authorities are opposed to advertising on the grounds that it promotes Western icons and culture and the associated non-Islamic consumerism.

POLITICAL AND LEGAL ENVIRONMENT

The political and legal environment in a country is one of the most important factors influencing the advertising and promotional programmes of international marketers. Regulations differ owing to economic and national sovereignty considerations, nationalistic and cultural factors and the goal of protecting consumers not only from false or misleading advertising but, in some cases, from advertising in general. Government regulations and restrictions can affect various aspects of a company's advertising programme, including the types of products, content or creative approach, media, amount of advertising a single advertiser may use in total or in a specific medium, use of foreign languages, use of local versus international advertising agencies, specific taxes levied against advertising and so on.

A number of countries ban or restrict the advertising of various products. Cigarette advertising is banned in some or all media in the United States, Argentina, Canada, France, Italy, Norway, Sweden, Switzerland and now in India. The Australian government has restricted tobacco advertising to point of purchase and excludes tobacco companies from sponsoring sporting events.

In Europe, there has been a long-standing ban on advertising for prescription-drug products, which is designed to keep government-subsidized health care costs under control. The European Union has argued that advertising increases the marketing budgets of drug companies and results in higher prices. Also, margarine cannot be advertised in France, nor can restaurant chains. Earlier, the French government restricted travel advertising because it encourages the French to spend their francs outside the country.

Many countries restrict the media advertisers can use. Greece has banned toy adverting on day-time television, so advertisers can advertise toys on TV only during the evening hours. Commercial TV advertising did not begin in Sweden until 1992, and both Sweden and Denmark limit the amount of time available for commercials. Advertising aimed at children is not legal in Sweden. In Saudi Arabia, commercial advertising is allowed on its national TV, but not on the state-run radio system. Advertising in magazines and newspapers is subject to government and religious restrictions.

There are also rules and regulations that affect the advertising message. For example, **comparative advertising** is legal and widely used in the United States and Canada, but is illegal in some countries like Korea and Belgium. Many Asian and South American countries have started accepting comparative ads. However, Brazil's self-regulatory advertising codes are so strict that few advertisers have been able to create a comparative message that has been approved. Many countries restrict the type of claims advertisers can make, the words they can use and the way products can be represented in ads. In Greece, specific claims for a product, such as "20 per cent less calories" are not permitted in an advertising message. Copyright and other legal restrictions make it difficult to maintain the same name from market to market. For example, Diet Coke is known as Coca-Cola Light in Germany, France and many other countries, because of legal restrictions prohibiting the word *diet*.

Most countries allow the use of foreign languages in print ads and direct mail. However, some do not allow foreign language commercials on TV or radio or in cinema ads, and some restrict foreign ads to media directed at foreigners in their country. Some countries also restrict the use of foreign-produced ads and foreign talent.

Diet coke: Known as Coca-Cola light in some countries.

These restrictions are motivated primarily by economic considerations. Many countries require local production of at least a portion of commercials to build local film industries and to create more jobs for local producers of print and audiovisual materials. Nationalistic and cultural factors also contribute to these restrictions, along with a desire to prevent large foreign ad agencies form dominating the advertising business in a country and thus hampering its development.

In some countries, steps are being taken to ease some of the legal restrictions and other barriers facing international advertisers. For example, the Maastricht Treaty was designed to create a single European market and remove many of the barriers to trade among the 12 member nations of the European community.

INTERNATIONAL ADVERTISING

The global versus local debate is really pointless, because, in reality, the issue is not one of whether an ad campaign for a brand can be completely *globalized*, but rather of the extent or degree to which a global brand's campaign can be *standardized* across the world.

Such advertising standardization can vary on a continuum, if one breaks up an ad into its *message strategy* and *tactical execution* components. At one extreme, an advertiser could totally standardize both the advertising message strategy and the tactical message executions. Next on the continuum would be a standardized strategy with *translated executions*, followed by standardized strategy with *modified executions*, to *totally localized* strategy and executions on the other extreme. The extreme of having the same strategy and identical execution in every country implies a nonverbal presentation (to get around language barriers).

UCB campaign: Catering to larger audience.

Standardization appears to be more common for television advertisements than for print advertisements, among business-to-business and high-tech product categories (like computers, audio and video equipments, cars) and among emotion-, image- and fashion-oriented (so-called high-touch) product categories. Standardization strategies and campaigns appear more appropriate and effective when the product is utilitarian and the message is informational, or when the brand's identity and desirability are integrally linked to a specific national character (e.g. Coca-Cola and McDonald's). Ad campaigns for food and beverage products are often the hardest to standardize, since eating and drinking habits and beliefs are often very culture-bound. It is easier to standardize advertising for a new brand than for an old and established brand, which may multiple hard-to reconcile images in different local regions of the world and may be at different life-cycle stages in different markets, thus facing incompatible marketing challenges.

Table 15.1 Ten well-known international advertisers

S. No.	Advertiser (parent company)	Headquarters	Primary business	Countries in which spending was reported
1	Procter & Gamble	Cincinnati	Soaps	Australia, Austria, Britain, Canada, France, Germany, Greece, India, Italy, Japan, Malaysia, Mexico, Netherlands, Pan Arabia, Puerto Rico, Taiwan, Thailand, Turkey, USA.
2	Unliever	Rotterdam/London	Soaps	Argentina, Australia, Brazil, Britain, Canada, Denmark, France, Germany, Greece, India, Italy, Japan, Malaysia, Mexico, Netherlands, Pan Arabia, Portugal, Puerto Rico, South Africa, Spain, Switzerland, Taiwan, Thailand, Turkey, USA.
3	Nestle SA	Vevey, Switzerland	Food	Argentina, Australia, Austria, Brazil, Britain, France, Germany, India, Japan, Malaysia, Mexico, Netherlands, Pan Arabia, Portugal, Puerto Rico, Spain, Switzerland, Taiwan, Thailand, Turkey, USA.
4	Toyota Motor Corp.	Toyota City, Japan	Automotive	Canada, Finland, Japan, Norway, Taiwan, Thailand, USA.
5	PSA Peugeot Citroen SA	Paris	Automotive	Argentina, Austria, Britain, Denmark, France, Germany, Netherlands, Pan Arabia, Portugal, Spain, Switzerland, Thailand, USA.
6	Volkswagen AG	Wolfsburg, Germany	Automotive	Brazil, Britain, France, Germany, Mexico, South Africa, Spain, Sweden, Switzerland, Thailand, USA.
7	Nissan Motor Co.	Tokyo, Japan	Automotive	Austria, Britain, Germany, Japan, Mexico, Pan Arabia, Switzerland, Thailand, USA.
8	Coca Cola Co.	Atlanta	Soft drinks	Argentina, Belgium, Brazil, Canada, Chile, Czech Republic, Greece, Hungary, Mexico, Peru, Romania, Slovak Republic, Turkey, USA, Vietnam.
9	Philip Mortis Cos.	New York	Food	Argentina, Australia, Austria, Brazil, Britain, Canada, Denmark, France, Germany, Hong Kong, Japan, Malaysia, Mexico, Netherlands, Pan Arabia, Spain, Taiwan, Thailand, USA.
10	General Motors	Detroit	Automotive	Brazil, Canada, Switzerland, UK, USA.

The advancement of international advertising is an immediate outcome of economic liberalization in South Asia—the advent or resurgence of some truly global brands such as IBM, McDonald's, Sony, Ray Ban, Coke, Pepsi, Arrow, Lacoste, Marlboro, Ariel. And this we are assured is just the beginning. There is something in these very names to fuel the fires of populist political debate. However, the days of "either - or" choices between local and international brands are mercifully behind us. The customers will become more discerning and demanding as they realize what they have been missing in terms of world-class quality. Manufacturers must stop thinking that there is something patriotic in accepting the second best! They ought, instead, to get on with the more serious business of delivering to the consumer—a housewife, the working man or even a company—competitive value and something approaching world class.

Appropriateness of Globalization

While globalization of advertising is viewed by many in the advertising industry as a difficult task, some progress has been made in learning what products and services are best suited to worldwide appeals. These are as follows:

1. Brands or messages that can be adapted for a visual appeal, avoiding the problems of trying to translate words into dozens of languages.
2. Brands that are promoted with image campaigns that play to universal appeals such as sex or wealth.
3. Hi-tech products and new products coming to the world for the first time not steeped in the cultural heritage of the country.
4. Products with nationalistic flavour, if the country has a reputation in the field.
5. Products that appeal to a market segment with universally similar tastes, interests, needs and values.

Good Year: Advertisement for many countries.

Global companies must advertise not only in their home country but also overseas to cover the distribution element of their marketing strategies. To promote its snow tires, Goodyear (www.goodyear.com) targets German consumers in their native language by suggesting that its tires offer protection "against risks and side effects."

Brands are not built in a day. Some have evolved over centuries, as can be seen in Table 15.2.

Table 15.2 Historic brands

	Brand	Country of origin	Product category	year
1.	Schweppes	UK	Soft drinks	1798
2.	Colgate	UK	Toothpaste	1806
3.	Levi's	USA	Jeans	1850
4.	Nestle	Switzerland	Beverages	1866
5.	Coca-Cola	USA	Soft drinks	1886
6.	Omega	Switzerland	Watches	1894
7.	Martini	Italy	Liquor	1896
8.	Fiat	Italy	Automobiles	1899
9.	Gillette	UK	Razor blades	1902
10.	Max Factor	USA	Cosmetics	1909
11.	Hitachi	Japan	Domestic goods	1910
12.	Marlboro	USA	Cigarettes	1924

It is, of course, possible to compress the time it takes to establish a new brand, by investing heavily in promotions in a short burst. This may accelerate the attainment of a peak level of trial and market share, but sustained repurchase, which reflects loyalty, can only be gained over time. Great spending power does not automatically ensure success–a lesson which both Procter & Gamble and Pepsi have learnt at great cost recently in India.

INTERNET ADVERTISING

The Internet is revolutionizing the way companies and individuals interact. Some people view it as another form of publishing marketing material. Others think that the potential of the Internet goes way beyond this. It revolutionizes the company-customer relationship by offering a new way to make transactions and access information. Company websites have a number of roles, only one of which is advertising. However, websites are the new customer interface. Advertising on the Internet can be carried out externally from the company website. The most popular method is advertising banners on other sites. Other methods include sponsorship of sites, classified ads and sending e-mails to potential customers. The Internet penetration in India and other developing countries is increasing at a very fast rate. Currently many Indian households have access to the Internet. The Internet penetration in the majority of countries all over the world has dramatically increased in the past few years due to the introduction of free access. Previously, Internet Service Providers (ISPs) charged a monthly subscription fee. However, the market has become increasingly competitive and there are now around 200 free ISPs in operation. Their revenue is gained from advertising, telephony revenue sharing and transaction revenues based on sales over the Internet. The introduction of the free access model emphasizes the importance of advertising revenue to ISPs. The Internet advertising market has so far been dominated by computing and financial advertisers. Indeed, the primary

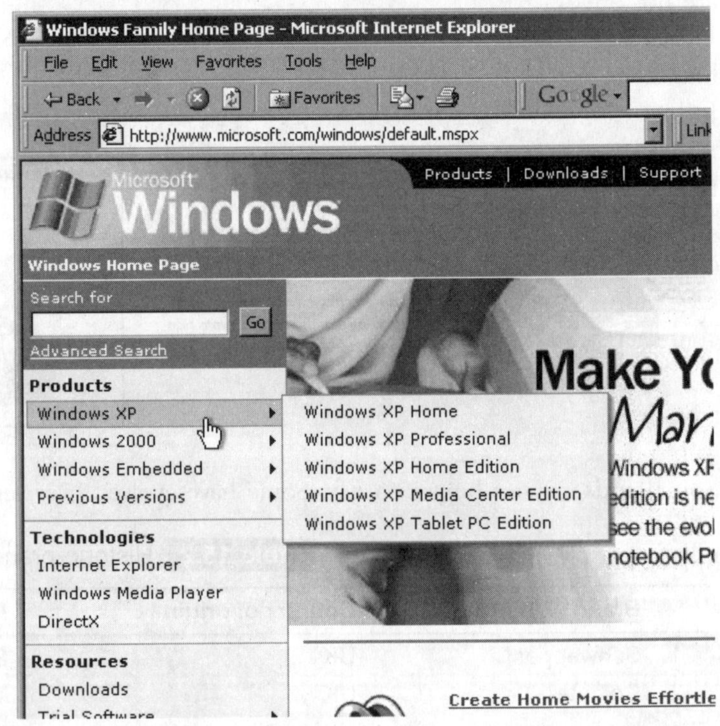

advertising spenders on the Internet are still IT corporations such as Microsoft and IBM and financial service organizations (FSOs) such as Prudential. However, consumer brand advertising is increasing on the Internet. Many customer brands experimented with Internet advertising in 1998, notably during the football World Cup as many brands used campaigns linked to this event. This experimentation is now developing into use of the Internet as an ongoing integrated part of marketing activity. Online advertising largely generates traffic to websites and then offers consumers the opportunity to make purchases online. The development of secure electronic transaction (SET) protocols has enabled payment for goods and services by credit card over the Internet (electronic commerce). The development of electronic commerce has not simply been a matter of technological advances. It has also been influenced by the acceptance of the new media by a wider audience. Online demographics are changing and the frequent Internet users are not only the young single early adopters but also older professional ABs with a young family.

Currently the most active e-commerce markets are those of computer hardware and software, books, music and entertainment products. However, clothing, sports and leisurewear are set to follow.

In the US, high Internet penetration and a greater willingness to adopt the Internet as a regular part of the marketing mix has led to rapid growth in the Internet advertising market. This growth is slowing down now compared to growth rates in the UK and other European countries, although this reflects the greater maturity of the US market. The expenditure on the US online ad is very concentrated amongst the top ten Web properties and this is a characteristic likely to develop in Europe in the future.

The main sites on which advertising banners are placed are web portals which are the starting point for users on the Internet. These are high traffic sites, although one criticism of their value as ad space is that users do not necessarily spend much time looking at the content of these sites. Development of portal site content has been one of the main Internet phenomena for the past few years. Early portal sites were search engines such as *Yahoo!* and *Excite*. Realizing their transitory usage, these sites developed content and charged for ad space. Some portal sites developed e-commerce operations.

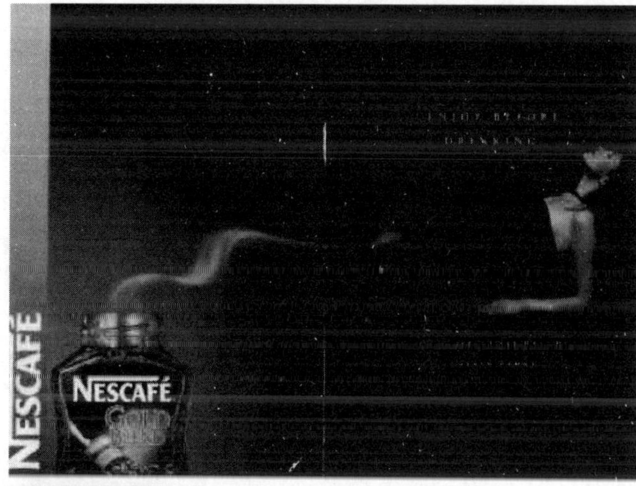

Nescafe: An ad placed on web portals.

Advantages of Web Advertising

The three categories that we see dominating the Internet advertising going forward are considered purchases, highly varied items and services and electronic delivery services.

Considered purchases

These are goods or services that require research before a purchase is made. Automobiles and travel are two such areas, as consumers are apt to do extensive research before purchasing these high-cost items.

Highly varied items and services

Items for which many different variations exist are likely to be advertised heavily on the Internet. Jobs fit this category, as consumers can use the Internet's search abilities to dig deeply into databases to find what they are looking for.

Electronic delivery services

Services that can be conducted electronically will also be big advertisers on the Internet. Financial services, insurance and credit card issuers fit this category.

LAWS AND REGULATIONS

The Federal Trade Commission Act allows the FTC to act in the interest of all consumers to prevent deceptive and unfair acts or practices. In interpreting Section 5 of the Act, the Commission has determined that a representation, omission or practice is *deceptive* if it is likely to:

- mislead consumers and
- affect consumers' behaviour or decisions about the product or service.

In addition, an act or practice is *unfair* if the injury it causes, or is likely to cause, is:

- substantial,
- not outweighed by other benefits and
- not reasonably avoidable.

The FTC Act prohibits unfair or deceptive advertising in any medium. That is, advertising must tell the truth and not mislead consumers. A claim can be misleading if relevant information is left out or if the claim implies something that is not true. For example, a lease advertisement for an automobile that promotes "$0 Down" may be misleading if significant and undisclosed charges are due at lease signing.

In addition, claims must be **substantiated**, especially when they concern health, safety or performance. The type of evidence may depend on the product, the claims and what experts think necessary. If your ad specifies a certain level of support for a claim–"*tests show X*"–you must have at least that level of support.

Sellers are responsible for claims they make about their products and services. Third parties, such as advertising agencies or website designers and catalogue marketers, also may be liable for making or disseminating deceptive representations if they participate in the preparation or distribution of the advertising or know about the deceptive claims.

Advertising agencies or **website designers** are responsible for reviewing the information used to substantiate ad claims. They may not simply rely on an advertiser's assurance that the claims are substantiated. In determining whether an ad agency should be held liable, the FTC looks at the extent of the agency's participation in the preparation of the challenged ad, and whether the agency knew or should have known that the ad included false or deceptive claims.

To protect themselves, **catalogue marketers** should ask for material to back up the claims rather than repeat what the manufacturer says about the product. If the manufacturer does not come forward with proof or turns over proof that looks questionable, the catalogue marketer should see a yellow "caution light" and proceed appropriately, especially when it comes to extravagant performance claims, health or weight loss promises or earnings guarantees. In writing on ad copy, catalogue marketers should stick to the claims that can be supported. Most importantly, catalogue marketers should trust their instincts when a product sounds too good to be true.

Apart from this, there are other factors for which the advertisers should be careful. These are as follows:

- **Disclaimers** and **disclosures** must be clear and conspicuous. That is, consumers must be able to notice, read or hear, and understand the information. Still, a disclaimer or disclosure alone usually is not enough to remedy a false or deceptive claim.
- **Demonstrations** must show how the product will perform under normal use.
- **Refunds** must be made to dissatisfied consumers–if you promised to make them.
- **Advertising directed at children** raises special issues. Children may have greater difficulty evaluating advertising claims and understanding the nature of the information you provide than adults. Sellers should take special care not to misrepresent a product or its performance while advertising to children. The Children's Advertising Review Unit (CARU) of the Council of Better Business Bureaus has published specific guidelines for children's advertising that you may find helpful.

Laws Related to E-mail Marketing

E-mail marketing provides companies with an efficient low-cost channel to reach consumers. An unfortunate side-result of e-mail marketing is the abuse of the channel. Very often, the most offensive marketers are those that transmit bulk e-mail messages to recipients with whom they do not have a prior relationship and whose messages are often of a prurient nature. While consumers and consumer groups have attempted to stop these marketers from engaging in such practices, the most vocal group has been the ISPs, those entities that bear the cost of carrying these messages. E-mails sent in bulk quantities and without the permission of the intended recipient occupy valuable storage space of these third-party facilities, which have been suing bulk e-mailers on a variety of legal theories.

Governing laws

State regulation

Several states have enacted anti-spam legislation. State requirements vary, but generally marketers are required to include "ADV:" or, in the case of adult-related material, "ADV: ADLT", in the subject line. In addition, the laws prohibit falsification of the sender's contact information and require certain disclosures and opt-out notices. Other states prohibit using a third party's Internet address or domain name without permission, or using false or missing routing information or a third party's name for the return address without permission. Some states permit ISPs to block unsolicited commercial e-mail or otherwise, prohibit a marketer from violating an ISP's posted policy.

Central/Federal regulation

There is no existing federal regulation expressly relating to e-mail marketing. Over the past few years, several bills are considered, but no legislation has been enacted.

General list considerations

Mailing a third-party list

Third-party lists can be obtained directly from another company, a list broker or a marketing partner. There are many types of lists to choose from, with varying degrees of specificity to a marketer's particular target audience. Lists created with an opt-in model are typically expensive. Mailing a third-party list carries certain regulatory and reputational risks, as the intended messages may very well be considered by the recipients to be unsolicited.

Third-party opt-in lists

Before renting or purchasing a third-party opt-in list, try to determine how and when the list was compiled and what type of notice, if any, was provided to the consumers on the list at the time they provided their information. For example, what were consumers told when they provided their personal contact information, such as "May we share your information with our partners?" or the more specific "May we provide your contact information to a partner that may offer you special deals on exercise products"

e-mail transmission

After you have determined to whom you will send your e-mails, consider whether any of the state laws described above apply to your campaign. If you intend to mail to a house list, you may qualify for a "pre-existing relationship" exemption under many state's laws. If you have bought or rented a third-party opt-in list, you will not enjoy the pre-existing relationship exception and it is questionable whether you have the consent of the intended recipients. A question that often arises in these situations is whether the consent purportedly granted to the list developer extends to subsequent purchasers of the list. Consider whether a header notice ("ADV:" or "ADV: ADLT") or any other additional information is required by statute, and whether there are any further policies of the Internet service provider that must be followed. Do not use false headers, subject lines, originating addresses or misleading routing information. E-mail solicitations should clearly identify the purpose of the message and the sender. Include a notice at the beginning of the message informing recipients why they are receiving the message. Include a notice in the e-mail informing recipients of their right to opt-out or unsubscribe from future messages and the method for doing so. Honour all opt-out requests.

FUTURE OF GLOBAL ADVERTISING

Though it is always difficult to predict the future of such a drastically changing phase of advertising, certain trends can be predicted. What was observed in the last decade is an implication of the following observations:

1. The rapid advancement in technology and full satellite deployment will open new media options for global advertisers.
2. Large nations like India and China will make lot of difference to the advertising by providing viable markets as their buying powers increase steadily.
3. After getting expertise in global advertising, advertising professional will succeed better in foreign countries than in their native country.
4. New technologies like computer interfacing, electronic mail and radio frequency identification technology (RFID) will offer lot of creative challenges.
5. Relaxation in trade barriers will increase the competition among the nations.
6. Advertising expenditure is likely to increase manifolds worldwide and the face of web advertising too will change.

It might happen with such fierce competition that satiating point reaches fast and advertising is completely obliterated from the society.

SUMMARY

The most significant reason for the emergence of international advertising is the cut-throat competition amongst the multinational companies. For most of the companies, industrialized nations represent the greatest marketing and advertising opportunities. As the trade laws become less stringent, the boundaries for the world get seamless and the scope for international market increases, thereby increasing the advertising. There are a number of reasons for the companies to focus on international market. Many companies emerged because of their global campaigns.

While designing an ad campaign for any country, it is must to study the social, cultural, political and educational norms. It is observed that these parameters vary a lot and therefore, are to be put into consideration. To take economic environment into consideration is important as a country's economic conditions indicate its present and future potential for consuming. Demographic differences exist among countries as well as within them.

Tendencies towards globalization of tastes and trends are apparent when one looks at particular demographic subcategories. The advertisements directed at children and women are different in different nations as the sentiments and the laws vary. The cultural environment is an important parameter for consideration, which includes language, customs, tastes, attitudes, values, ethics and moral standards. The political and legal environment in a country is one of the most important factors influencing the advertising and promotional programmes of international marketers.

For international advertising campaign, the advertisers have to think globally and act locally. They can have standardized strategy with modified execution, to totally localized strategy and execution at the other end. The globalization is appropriate because of the several benefits. Today, we do not even realize which Internet advertising has revolutionized the way in which companies and individuals are doing marketing. Internet advertising is instrumental is bringing the world together. There are laws and regulations, which monitor the advertising which is likely to be deceptive and misleading. We can predict the future of global advertising after the observation in the trend since the last decade. New technology has opened new vistas for advertising to mushroom in ever increasing pace.

With the growing importance of the Internet, this, however, is not required, as we can have a truly global brand and ad campaign, as the world is becoming a common marketplace, where people have the same basic needs, wants, desires and tastes, no matter where they live.

QUESTIONS

1. Discuss the challenges companies face in marketing their products to the world's poorest consumers. How do they have to adapt their advertising programmes in selling to these consumers?
2. What is meant by the "think global, act local" approach to global advertising? Discuss some of the ways marketers can adapt their advertising to local markets.
3. Do you agree that North American and western European cultures are relatively more "secular", "low-context" and "individual-oriented" as compared to Asian cultures? Why or why not?
4. From a strictly moral point of view, is it right to enforce a foreign culture on another culture by implying that the foreign culture is more open-minded, rich and aesthetic? Is it right to knowingly lead large masses away from their culture, towards an unwritten path, where they will be caught in a trap between their indigenous culture and the foreign culture, as in the case of MTV?
5. Why do you think the advertisement below is globally suitable?

Bibliography

Ailloni, Dan, *Promotion: A Guide to Effective Promotion Planning, Strategies and Executions*, John Wiley, 1984.

Arens, William F., *Contemporary Advertising*, 6th ed., Irwin, Chicago, 1996.

Arthur, Lance, "Clear Cut Lessons for Effective E-mail", *Direct Marketing*, Vol. 64, No. 6: 62-63, May 2001.

Baker, Stephen, *A Systematic Approach to Advertising Creativity*, McGraw-Hill, New York, 1979.

Batra, R., J.G. Myers and Aaker A. David, *Advertising Management*, 5th ed., Pearson Education, 2002.

Berkowitz, Eric N., Roger A. Kerin and William Rudelius, *Marketing* 6th ed., Irwin/ McGraw-Hill, 2000.

Betsy, Cummings, *Star Power, Sales and Marketing Management*, pp. 52–59, April 2001.

Bogart, Leo, *Strategy in Advertising*, 2nd ed., NTC Business Books, 1990.

Bovee, Courtland L., John V. Thill and George P. Dovel, *Advertising Excellence*, McGraw-Hill, New York, 1995.

Burton, George, *An Outline of Advertising*, Macmillan, 1950,

Caples, John, "A Dozen Ways to Develop Advertising Ideas", *Advertising Age*, pp M-4ff, November 14, 1983.

——, *How to Make Your Advertising Make Money*, Prentice Hall, Englewood Cliffs, New Jersey, 1983.

Clark, Darral G., "Econometric Measurement of the Duration of Advertising Effect on Sales", *Journal of Marketing Research*, November, 1976.

Clow, Kenneth E. and Donald Baack, *Integrated Advertising, Promotion, and Marketing Communications*, Pearson Education, New Delhi, 2003.

Curry, William N., "PR Isn't Marketing", *Advertising Age*, p. 18, December 18, 1991.

David, Aaker, *Managing Brand Equity*, Free Press, 1991.

David, Martin, *Romancing the Brand*, Amacon, New York, 1989.

David, Stewart W. and Furse F. David, *Effective Television Advertising: A Study of 1000 commericals*, Lexiton Books, 1986.

Davis, Aaker A., Asker A. and Myers G. John, *Advertising Management*, 3rd ed., Prentice Hall, Englewood Cliffs, New Jersey, 1987.

Ditcher, Ernest, *Handbook of Consumer Motivations*, McGraw-Hill.

Dom, Rossi, "Rethink 'Prime Time", *Advertising Age*, p. 1, April 29, 2002.

Durchslag, Stephen P., "Agency Liability Extends to False Advertising Claims", *Promo*, 17, October 1992, 17.

Erwin, Ephron, "Direct Response or Banding?" *Advertising Age*, p. 14, November 5, 2001.

Everett, Rogers M., *Diffusion of Innovation*, Free Press, New York, 1962.

Feuev, Jack, "What Clients Think about Media", *Adweek*, pp. 38–42, June 4, 2001.

George, Belch E. and Belch A. Michael, *Advertising and Promotion: An Integrated Marketing Communications Perspective*, Tata McGraw-Hill.

Gullew, Phil and Hugh Johnson, "Relating Product Purchasing and TV Viewing", *Journal of Advertising Research*, pp. 9–19, December 1986/January 1987.

Henry, Assael, *Consumer Behaviour and Marketing Action*, 3rd ed., Kent, Boston, 1987.

Herbert, Kanzenstein and Sachs S. William, *Direct Marketing*, 2nd ed., Macmillan, New York, 1992.

Jagdish, Sheth N., "Marketing Mega-trends", *Journal of Consumer Marketing*, **1**(1), pp. 5–13, June 1983.

James, Engle F. and Blackwell D. Roger, *Consumer Behaviour*, 4th ed., Dryden, 1982.

James, Young Webb, *A Technique for Producing Ideas*, 3rd ed., Crain Books, p. 42, 1975.

Jaue, Niefeld S., "Corporate Advertising", *Industrial Marketing*, pp. 64–74, July 1980.

Jewel, A. Jerome and Bonnie L. Drewniany, *Creative Strategy in Advertising*, 8th ed., Wadsworth/ Thomson Learning, 2004.

John, Howard A. and Jagdish, Sheth N., *The Theory of Consumer Behaviour*, 4th ed., Prentice-Hall, 1991.

John, Martson E., *Modern Public Relations*, McGraw-Hill, New York, 1979.

John, O'Toole, *The Trouble with Advertising*, 2nd ed., Random House, New York, 1985.

John, Quelch A., *Sales Promotion Management*, Prentice-Hall, 1989.

John, Steel, *Truth, Lies* and *Advertising: The Art of Account Planning,* Wiley, New York, 1998.

Kazmi, S.H.H. and Batra S.K., *Advertsing and Sales Promotion*, 2nd ed., Excel Books, 2004.

Keith, Hafer W. and White E. Gordon, *Advertising Writing*, 3rd ed., West Publishing, 1989.

Kneal, Dennis, "Zapping of TV Ads Appears Pervasive", *The Wall Street Journal*, p. 27, April 25, 1998.

Krugman, Dean M, S. Watson Dunn, Arnold M. Barbon and Leonard N. Reid, *Advertising: Its Role in Modern Marketing*, 8th ed., The Dryden Press, Fort Worth, 1990.

Lavidge, Robert C. and Gary A. Steiner, "A Model for Predictive Measurements of Advertising Effectiveness", *Journal of Marketing*, pp. 59–62, October 1961.

Lavidge, Robert J., "Mass Customization is not an Oxy-Moron", *Journal of Advertising Research*, pp. 70-72, July-August 1999.

London, David L. and Albert Della Bitta, *Consumer Behaviour*, 4th ed., McGraw-Hill, 1993.

Mandese, Joe, "Media Buying and Planning", *Advertising Age*, S1, S18, August 3, 1998.

Marshall, McLuhan, *Understanding Media: The Extensions of Man,* McGraw-Hill, New York, 1966.

Michael, Ray L. and Wilkie L. William, "Fear: The Potential of an Appeal Neglected by Marketing", *Journal of Marketing,* 34, pp. 54–62, January 1970.

Michael, Solomon, *Consumer Behaviour*, 5th ed., Prentice Hall, 2001.

Mick, David G., "Levels of Subjective Comprehensions in Advertising Processing and Their Relations to Ad Perceptions, Attitudes, and Memory", *Journal of Consumer Research*, March, 1992.

Moriarty, Sandra and Brett Robbs, "Advertising", in the *Encyclopedia of Creativity*, pp. 23–29, Vol. 1, Academic Press, San Deigo, California, 1999.

Myers, Jack, "More is Indeed Better", *Media Week*, pp. 14–18, September 6, 1993.

Ogilvy, David, "*Ogilvy On Advertising*", Crown, 1985.

———, *Confessions of an Advertising Man*, Alheneum, 1964.

Parameswaran, M.G., *Brand Building Advertising: Concept and Cases*, Tata McGraw-Hill, New Delhi, 2001.

Patricia, Sellers, "Do You Need Your Ad Agency?" *Fortune*, pp. 47–61, November, 15, 1993.

Paul, Peter J. and Olson C. Jerry, *Consumer Behaviour*, 2nd ed., McGraw-Hill, 1990.

Philip, Kolter, *Marketing Management: Analysis, Planning, Implementation and Control*, 9th ed., Prentice-Hall, Upper Saddle River, New Jersey, 1997.

Pine II, B. Joseph, Don Peppers and Martha Rogers, "Do You Want to Keep Your Customers Forever?", *Harvard Business Review*, 73(2).

Raghubir, Priya and Kim Korfman, "When Do Price Promotions Affect Pretrial Brand Evaluation?" *Journal of Marketing Research*, 36, pp. 211–22, May 1999.

Ralph, Anderson E., Hair F. Joseph and Bish J. Alan, *Professional Sales Management*, McGraw-Hill, New York, 1988.

Ray, Michael L., *Advertising and Communication Management*, Prentice-Hall, Englewood Cliffs, New Jersey, 1982.

Rice, Faye, "A Cure for What Ails Advertising?", *Fortune*, pp. 199–122, December 16, 1991.

Richard, Vaughn, "How Advertising Works: A Planning Model Revisited", *Journal of Advertising Research*, 26, No. 1, pp. 57–66, February/March 1986.

Ries, Al and Jack Trout, "Positioning Cuts through Chaos in the Marketplace", *Advertising Age*, pp. 51–53, May 1, 1972.

———, *Positioning: The Battle of Your Mind*, McGraw-Hill, New York, 1985.

Robert, Kriegel A., "How to Choose the Right Communications Objectives", *Business Marketing*, pp. 94–106, April 1986.

Rogers, Everett M., *Diffusion of Innovation*, Fress Press, 1962.

Rosenspan, Alan, "Participation Marketing", *Direct Marketing*, 54–55, June 2001.

Sally, Beatty Goll, "Global Needs Challenge Midsize Agencies", *The Wall Street Journal*, p. 89, December 14, 1995.

Sandra, Moriarty E., *Creative Advertising: Theory and Practice*, Prentice-Hall, 1986.

Schultz, Don E., *Strategic Advertising Campaigns*, 3rd ed., NTC Business Books, Lincoln, IL, 1990.

———, "Integrated Marketing Communications: May be Definition is in the Point of View", *Marketing News*, p. 17, January 18, 1993.

———, Tannenbaum I. Stanley and Lauterborn F. Robert, *Integrated Marketing Communications*, NTC Publishing Group, p. 72, Lincolnwood, Illinois, 1993.

Scott, Cutlip M., Centre H. Allen and Broom M. Gleen, *Effective Public Relations*, 8th ed., Prentice Hall, 2000.

Simon, Raymond, *Public Relations: Concepts and Practices*, 3rd ed., Macmillan, New York, 1986.

Stan, Rapp and Collins I. Thomas, *Maximarketing*, McGraw-Hill, New York, 1987.

Stephen, Baker, *Advertising Layout and Art Direction*, McGraw-Hill, New York, 1959.

Thomas, Duncon R., "To Fathom Integrated Marketing, Dive!" *Advertising Age*, p. 18, October 11, 1993.

Thomas, Harris L., "How MPR Adds Value to Integrated Marketing Communications", *Public Relations* Quarterly, pp. 13–18, Summer 1993.

Thomas, Madden J. and Weinberger G. Marc, "Humor in Advertising: A Practitioner View", *Journal of Advertising Research 24*, No. 4, pp. 23–26, August/September 1984.

Triandis, H.C., *Attitudes and Attitude Change,* Wiley, New York, 1971.

Vaughn, Richard, "How Advertising Works: A Planning Model", *Journal of Advertising Research,* pp. 27–33, October 1980.

Vranica, Suzanne, "Volvo Campaign Tests New-Media Waters", *Wall Street Journal,* B5, March 16, 2001.

Wells, William, Burneff Joun and Moriarty Sandra, *Advertising: Principles and Practice,* 6th ed., Prentice-Hall of India, 2005.

Wentz, Laurel and Juliana Koranteng, "Global Media," *Ad. Age International,* pp 15–17, February 9, 1998.

William, Walkie L. and Paul W. Farris, "Comparative Advertising: Problems and Potential", *Journal of Marketing,* 39, pp. 7–15, 1975.

William, Weilbacher M., *Advertising,* 2nd ed., Macmillan, New York, 1984.

Wunderman, Lester, "Going Strong: The Father of Direct Marketing Sees the Future in Cyberspace," *Advertising Age,* pp. 25, April 17, 2000.

Index